India's Foreign Policy in the Post-Covid World

Through the Eyes of Indian Diplomats

Editor

Amb Surendra Kumar (Retd)

wisdom tree

First published 2022

ISBN 978-81-8328-579-7 (HB)
ISBN 978-81-8328-581-0 (PB)

Published by
Wisdom Tree
4779/23, Ansari Road
Darya Ganj, New Delhi-110 002
Ph.: 011-23247966/67/68
wisdomtreebooks@gmail.com

Printed in India

CONTENTS

ACKNOWLEDGEMENTS

In Corona pandemic times, attempting an ambitious book of this nature is a risky business. So, first of all, I would like to applaud and thank the publishers, Wisdom Tree for showing courage to go along with my idea and reposing confidence in my ability to persuade such a large number of contributors for the book.

I can't thank enough the contributors. They include some of the brightest minds and most experienced and respected diplomats of India, who have become iconic in many ways, have books to their credit and who contribute op-eds to national dailies and appear on TV channels every day.

I will be failing in my duty if I don't thank the publisher's team that has done an excellent job in putting together this book in such a short time.

EDITOR'S NOTE

Sometime in the middle of September 2020, amidst the anxiety and concern-filled Covid-19 days, I got an email from Shobit Arya, the publisher of the book, *India and the World through the Eyes of Indian Diplomats*, edited by me inquiring if I could assist in updating the book for its new edition. My instant reaction was: no way! It was too much of a hassle to contact thirty-four contributors after five years and cajole them to take the trouble of updating their respective pieces in the changed world.

So, I sent him a counter query: what about bringing out a new book on India's foreign policy in the backdrop of the devastation and disruption caused by Covid-19, following the format of the earlier book but introducing thirty new contributors? After mulling over for a few days and calculating production cost and payment of honorarium etc, he agreed.

Keeping in mind the success of the Bollywood film, *Dhoom II*, my endeavour was that this book should turn out to be a notch higher than *India and the World* in terms of content, long-term relevance and its overall appeal. In *Dhoom II*, the hero, heroine and other characters were all new but the police inspector remained the same. In this volume, all contributors are new but the Editor, yours sincerely, stays put.

We have expanded the scope of the book; unlike the earlier volume, there are articles about India's foreign relations with all immediate neighbours: Afghanistan, Bangladesh, Bhutan, China, Iran, Nepal, Pakistan and Sri Lanka, and major powers: USA, the UK, Russia, Japan, Brazil and Mexico. The book also includes articles about major regions: Africa, ASEAN, Central Asian Republics, the EU, the Middle East, the Gulf, Latin America and the Caribbean.

We haven't forgotten international organisations that matter and have a bearing on India's foreign policy: the UN, the World Bank, the IMF and the WTO. We also have an article about the Indo-Pacific and the Quad, which continue to remain the hot topics in any strategic discussion. Climate Change, effects of which are staring in our face has also been analysed and assessed. Arguably, for the first time, in a foreign policy book, we have addressed a sensitive but extremely relevant subject: India's foreign policy and the North East.

The significance of India's soft power which has expanded from music, dance, fine arts, Bollywood and cricket to yoga and vaccines has been discussed objectively. The article on India's diaspora acknowledges the enviable rise in its political, economic and social clout in different countries, especially in the US and the UK. And we have two articles that don't fall in any of these categories but are hugely significant: India's internal and external security challenges and the world order in which we live.

My determined attempt was to try to persuade some of the most distinguished and respected diplomats who have professionally handled India's relations with and preferably served in countries/regions/organisations they were writing about. Their personal experiences have introduced an element of authenticity, honesty and realism in their essays.

While inviting contribution through personal letters, I had advised the potential contributors not to delve too much in history and put the self on the shelf (no references like when I met Donald Trump or Xi Jinping) but have a close and dispassionate look at India's relations with the world in Covid-19 times and focus on how we have faced the unprecedented challenges and how we move forward with optimism and imaginative, innovative ideas and smart strategies.

The book has several unique features: the contributors include a former NSA, a former envoy of the Prime Minister, three former foreign secretaries, five former secretaries of the MEA, the current chief information commissioner, the current secretary (ER) and the current chairman of the National Security Advisory Board. The decision of such eminent and busy individuals to contribute to this book underlines their recognition of its value and its potential to initiate a serious public discourse and conversation on numerous issues that impinge on India's foreign policy. In a way, it's a small effort to educate public opinion about India's foreign policy in the post-Covid-19 world.

This book is a fragrant bouquet of different ideas and perspectives on India's foreign policy expressed in numerous distinct styles by a galaxy of contributors, such as Shivshankar Menon, Shyam Saran, Deb Mukharji, Surendra Kumar, KC Singh, Ranjan Mathai, Neelam Sabharwal, Rahul Chhabra, Anil Wadhwa, Ruchi Ghanashyam, Amarendra Khatua, Tsewang Topden, Jayant Prasad, Deepa Wadhwa, Vishnu Prakash, PS Raghavan, TCA Raghavan, YK Sinha, Dilip Sinha, Arun Singh, Asoke Mukerji, Ranjit Rae, Anil Trigunayat, Manjeev Puri, Sujan Chinoy, VP Haran, Ajit Kumar, Sunil Lal, Gurjit Singh, Anjali Prasad and Vinod Kumar. It should interest practitioners of diplomacy, both serving and retired, academics, scholars and students of international relations, think tanks, strategic analysts and informed citizens.

Surendra Kumar

NARENDRA MODI'S FOREIGN POLICY: ROBUST AND IMAGINATIVE, STRONGLY WEDDED TO INDIA'S DEVELOPMENTAL AGENDA

SURENDRA KUMAR

While dealing with his counterparts from different countries and participating in global summits, Narendra Damodardas Modi exudes supreme confidence and seems perfectly at home, even though he had visited only China and Japan as the chief minister of Gujarat. Many analysts wonder if this could be attributed to the strict discipline and discourses of the RSS.

His thirteen-year-long stint as the chief minister of Gujarat, where economic development witnessed a huge transformation, must have given him hands-on administrative experience and confidence and a sense of achievement. The Vibrant Gujarat Summit, a biennial event showcasing the progress of the state and flagging numerous government incentives for investors, was launched in 2003, attracting the who's who of India Inc. and representatives from around 100 countries. On 11 January 2015, addressing the seventh summit, the then US Secretary of State John Kerry (now President Joe Biden's Envoy for Climate Change), said that 'the PM [prime minister] has brought a particular energy and made Gujarat synonymous with possibilities, change and energy' and felt that Modi's Make in India initiative was a 'win-win' opportunity for the world.

Known as a business-friendly chief minister, he boldly attacked bureaucratic delays, red tape, outdated rules and regulations and excessive paperwork, and created an investor-friendly ecosystem.

Modi's self-confidence and pride flow from the fact that, notwithstanding his humble beginnings, he has risen to represent 1.3 billion Indians as the PM. His tireless campaigning led the BJP to gain absolute majority in the Parliament in 2014 and take its tally to 307 in 2019. Evidently, he is not constrained by the Coalition Dharma.

His characteristic Modi phenomenon was on mega display on his first visit to the US as India's PM. Free from any rancour and bitterness for having been denied an American visa for ten years, he arrived at the White House for the private dinner in his honour on 30 September 2014 in a spotlessly white *kurta* and *choorida*r, black Indian sandals and a black Nehru Jacket, his white beard and white eminence immaculately in place, after attending a rapturous rock star-like reception from the jostling Indian-American community at Madison Square Garden, New York attended by roughly 20,000 guests, including thirty US congressmen/senators; making a passionate appeal for the Comprehensive Convention against International Terrorism at the United Nations General Assembly (UNGA); rubbing shoulders with Hollywood icon Hugh Jackman at the Global Youth Festival at Central Park, New York, and talking about the Swachh Bharat Abhiyaan; cautioning the US government against withdrawing from Iraq in haste at the Council of Foreign Relations, and sat through the entire dinner sipping warm water with honey, observing his Navaratri fast! The White House had never seen anything like this. Barack Obama, who received him with a '*kem cho*', was clean bowled; he accompanied the Indian PM on his visit to the Lincoln Memorial the next morning.

Today, despite serious differences on a number of issues—climate change included—Indo-US relations are witnessing their best phase yet: bilateral trade has ballooned, defence trade and cooperation in security-related matters has increased exponentially, dozens of government-to-government missions are in operation and the leaders of the two countries have interacted with unprecedented frequency—bilaterally, at regional/international summits and over the hot line. There is greater geostrategic convergence on regional and global commons.

It's a tribute to his enviable ability of generating positive vibes that Modi was able to develop a personal chemistry with two such contrasting personalities as Barack Obama and Donald Trump. He invited Obama to be the chief guest at the Republic Day parade on 26 January 2015, the first US president to be honoured so. Modi called Obama by his first name many times at his *Man Ki*

Baat radio broadcast at Hyderabad House (27 January 2015). He held the hand of President Trump and introduced him to 50,000 Indian-Americans at the Howdy Modi Community reception in Houston on 22 September 2019 and received him at the Namaste Trump public reception at the Motera Stadium in Ahmedabad on 24 February 2020 with 125,000 guests!

Under PM Modi, India has overcome the hesitation of history; it is not shy of being perceived as close to the US, short of an alliance. Three foundational agreements—the Logistics Exchange Memorandum of Agreement (LEMOA), the Communications Compatibility and Security Agreement (COMCASA) and the Basic Exchange and Cooperation Agreement for Geo-Spatial Cooperation (BECA)—signed by the US and India; over 300 joint military exercises, including the tri-service Tiger Triumph and Malabar exercises, and USA according India Major Defence Partner and STA-1 status (on par with America's closest allies) have brought the two countries very close in terms of military cooperation. The annual 2+2 dialogues, India–US Business Council and CEO Forum meetings, etc. have broadened the scope and level of bilateral consultations. Not surprisingly, the US criticised China for its aggression on the LAC in May/ June 2020, more strongly and unambiguously than ever before.

Modi and Joe Biden, who had spoken over the phone, met virtually at the 'historic' Quad summit called by Biden on 12 March 2021. The Quad Leaders' Joint Statement lay emphasis on working towards a 'free, open, inclusive, healthy' Indo-Pacific, 'anchored by democratic values and unconstrained by coercion'. The Quad leaders are committed to address the challenges to the rule-based maritime order in the East and South China Sea. Covid-19, climate change, cyber space, critical technologies, counterterrorism, maritime security, investment in infrastructure, humanitarian assistance and disaster relief were identified as areas for cooperation. The US International Development Finance Corporation (DFC) will finance Indian firm Biological E Ltd's production of one billion doses of the Covid-19 vaccine by the end of 2022 for countries in the Indo-Pacific region and the ASEAN.

The US extended all possible help to India during its second wave of the Covid-19 pandemic on a mission mode. The Covid-19-related assistance from the US, including from Indian-Americans, was worth over US$ 500 million.

During his visit, US Climate Envoy John Kerry met PM Modi and several ministers (7 April 2021) and discussed targets for net zero emissions and renewable energy prospects. During his second visit in September, Kerry launched the Climate Action and Finance Mobilization (CAFM) with India that will focus on finance mobilisation, clean energy and climate adaptation measures.

Biden met Modi at the virtual summit of Leaders on Climate hosted by the former on 22 and 23 April 2021. They might meet again in person at the United Nations Climate Change Conference (COP26) in Glasgow in November. US Defense Secretary Lloyd Austin and US Secretary of State Antony Blinken have visited India; China, Pakistan and Afghanistan reportedly figured in their talks. PM Modi's meetings with President Biden and Vice President Kamala Harris in September showed that the magic of his *jadoo ki jhappi* that worked on Obama and Trump was working on them too.

Narendra Modi will go down in the history of independent India as, arguably, the most imaginative, innovative and experimental PM. Modi's handling of India's relationship with Pakistan and China bear the hallmark of a statesman. Inviting all the heads of state of the SAARC countries, including Pakistan and Afghanistan, to his swearing-in ceremony on 26 May 2014 was a diplomatic masterstroke. This out-of-the-box gesture underlined Modi's Neighbours First Policy, signalled to Pakistan that he wanted peaceful relations and projected him as a moderate and visionary leader.

Even his decision to stop by Nawaz Sharif's ancestral home at Jati Umera near Lahore on his way back from Kabul to wish Sharif on his sixty-sixth birthday on 25 December 2015 was an example of Modi's audacious, out-of-the-box diplomacy. What could have been a stronger confidence-building measure by an Indian PM than to hug his Pakistani counterpart, hop in his helicopter unchecked by Indian security agencies, meet his family members, publicly touch the feet of Sharif's mother, Shamim Akhtar, break bread with the Sharifs and walk out with him hand-in-hand?

This stopover, barely four hours long, created positive buzz about India and Modi in Pakistan. The Indian PM appeared a simple, cultured, respectful, peace-loving man, so different from his tough-talking, RSS *pracharak* and a Muslim-hater image.

The deep state of Pakistan has always been against normal relations with India and resorted to violence: Modi's Lahore stopover was responded to with an attack on the IAF base in Pathankot on 1 January 2016! Modi's gesture wasn't wooly-eyed romanticism cut off from ground realities; it was a bold act of statesmanship. It's better to have tried and failed than never to have tried at all!

Except for a Pakistani antiterrorism court (ATC) handing out a prison sentence against Lashkar-e-Taiba Commander Zaki-ur-Rehman Lakhvi, Pakistan hasn't taken action against other masterminds of the 26/11 Mumbai attacks. Terrorists are still trained in Pakistan and roam around freely. A convoy of forty CRPF personnel was killed by its terrorists on 14 February 2019 at Pulwama. The Pakistani claims that the Pakistani government has nothing to do with the terrorist attacks against India was proven to be totally false when, while speaking in the National Assembly on 29 October 2020, Pakistani Science and Technology Minister Fawad Chaudhry claimed: 'Our success in Pulwama is a success of this nation under the leadership of Imran Khan.'

The Pulwama tragedy was the tipping point. Modi ordered an air strike (code name Bander) in which 20 Mirage 2000 aircrafts participated—16 of them crossed over 15 km into PoK and dropped Israeli made Spices 2000 bombs at the JeM training camp at Balakot in Pakhtunkhwa, killing 130-170 terrorists.

The Balakot air strike was a strong message to Pakistani terrorists: they weren't safe in their hideouts. India's concerted diplomatic efforts led to the listing of Masood Azhar as a designated terrorist by the UN, Pakistan remaining on the grey list of the Financial Action Task Force (FATF) and the Jammu and Kashmir issue not being discussed by the United Nations Security Council (UNSC). There are no takers of Pakistani allegations of Indian terrorist attacks in Pakistan.

The abrogation of Article 370 and creation of the union territories of Jammu and Kashmir and Ladakh on 31 October 2019 are believed to have weakened Pakistan-dependent Kashmiri leaders' ability to spur the radicalisation of Kashmiri youth. Panchayat elections were conducted in December 2020 with high participation notwithstanding terrorists' threats augured well for stabilising the internal situation.

Pakistan, like a leopard, won't change its spots so long as the army and the Inter-Services Intelligence (ISI) call the shots. Solutions often emerge from dialogues. Engaging with Pakistan in imaginative ways does not mean acquiescing to its wrong-doings nor showing weakness. The ceasefire agreement along the LOC, signed on 24 February 2021, believed to have been facilitated by the United Arab Emirates (UAE), suggests that international pressure does work on Pakistan. But in the wake of the installation of the Taliban government in Kabul, which has given Pakistan its much-aspired strategic depth in Afghanistan, India should be prepared to address a sharp spike in terrorist attacks in Jammu and Kashmir.

India should try to nudge the US, China, Saudi Arabia, UAE, Iran, Turkey and Malaysia to reason with Pakistan that the developmental and welfare needs of its people are not served by permanent hostility towards India, but by being a part of India's economic strides. But first, Pakistan will have to drop its pathological hatred for India, say good-bye to terrorism and clasp the hand of friendship. If the US and Vietnam, and Egypt and Israel can be friends after all the wounds they have inflicted on each other, why can't India and Pakistan be peaceful neighbours?

The stroll with Chinese President Xi Jinping in Nehru jacket and his wife, Peng Liyuan, on the Sabarmati river front, Ahmedabad, on 17 September 2014, their visit to Mahatma Gandhi's Sabarmati Ashram where Xi sat bare feet and spun on the *charkha* while 1000 PLA soldiers had intruded in Chumar Sector of Eastern Ladakh, an informal summit in Wuhan (27/28 April 2018) and Mamallapuram (11 October 2019) were Modi's initiatives to develop mutual trust, understanding and personal rapport with the core leader of China with which India shares 3488 km of border. Since the time of Jawaharlal Nehru, all Indian prime ministers have tried to have peaceful and mutually beneficial relations with China in their distinct styles. But these efforts have never been at the cost of India's security, territorial integrity and national interests. PM Modi has tried a three-pronged policy towards China: cooperation, competition and engagement but no bullying or intimidation.

Notwithstanding China's border dispute with India, its blind support of Pakistan and its attempts to raise Jammu and Kashmir-related issues in the UNSC at the behest of Pakistan, India has cooperated with China as part of the Russia–India–China (RIC), Brazil–Russia–India–China–South Africa (BRICS), Group of 20 (G20) and Shanghai Cooperation Organisation (SCO) alliances and on the subject of climate change. But India insists on respect for each other's sovereignty, territorial integrity and non-interference in each other's internal matters and no intimidation or aggression.

India competes with China in Africa, ASEAN/South East Asia and Latin

America for trade, business, investment, energy resources, minerals, raw material and influence. China's increasing influence in Nepal, Sri Lanka, Maldives, Myanmar and Bangladesh has been a serious cause of concern to India. Besides, India can't ignore the string of pearls that China has created around it and the Belt and Road Initiative (BRI) that has roped in all the countries of South Asia except Bhutan.

When China tried to change the status quo at the India–Bhutan–China tri-junction in Doklam (2017), India stood firm. China was taken aback and eventually withdrew to status quo after an impasse of seventy-two days (from 16 June 2017 to 28 August 2017).

Similarly, when the People's Liberation Army (PLA) soldiers breached a 43-year-long period of peace and tranquillity on the border and brutally killed twenty army personnel in the Galwan valley on 15 June 2020, the 16 Bihar Regiment caused as many deaths on the Chinese side. As a result of twelve rounds of commander-level talks and two face-to-face meetings between Indian Minister of External Affairs S Jaishankar and Chinese Foreign Minister Wang Yi (10 September 2020, Moscow, and 14 July 2021, Dushanbe), the two countries agreed to a mutual disengagement on the North and South bank of Pangong Tso Lake and Gogra heights. Yet, the stalemate at the other flash points on the LAC continues. The infrastructure—roads, link roads, helipads, bunkers built in the last six years along the LAC; weaponry—tanks, artillery, fighter planes loaded with missiles; and troops deployed by India along with its unmistakable resolve to stay for the long haul even in harsh winter might have changed China's perception of India as an enemy. India's occupation of the high ground overlooking the Chinese Army position at Finger 4 along the Pangong Tso Lake (given up later) and China's inability to lower tensions with the US might encourage China to rethinks its tactic and disengage further over a period. However, a return to status quo (April 2020) looks unlikely. At the India Today Conclave–South (14 March 2021), Minister of External Affairs S Jaishankar made it clear that progress in our relations with China is linked to peace and tranquillity on the LAC. If China extends a hand of friendship, India will extend one as well. However, if China chooses to point a gun at India, the latter will do the same. Under the present PM, India's message to China is simple: India of 2021 is not India of 1962 and Modi is not Nehru!

We must never lower our guard against China nor trust it fully. Unless we attain economic and military parity with China, it will not treat India as an equal. Besides, our growing closeness with the US will remain an issue for Beijing. It's an open secret that the US keenness to deepen relations with India is directly proportionate to the level of tension in its relation with China.

Modi's visit to Nepal (3 and 4 August 2014), the first bilateral visit by an Indian PM in seventeen years, left a very positive impact and received praise from PM Sushil Koirala and Pushpa Kamal Dahal, chairman of the UCPN (M). However, in spite of 'shared heritage of nature, history, culture, spiritualism and religion' stressed by PM Modi and '*roti beti ka rishta*' that other Indian leaders never cease to underline, the relations with the northern land-locked neighbour have soured. While internal power tussle between two Nepali Communist leaders—Prachand and KP Sharma Oli—is an important factor for this, China's inroads and increasing influence in Nepali politics (Nepal has joined the BRI bandwagon) creates complications. We, somehow, took the eye off the ball while the new constitution was being framed and upset both the Madheshis and the central government in Nepal. The former felt let down and the latter thought we were interfering in their internal matters.

Lockdowns imposed by a big country upon a small country, irrespective of the legitimate grounds, are seen as the big brother squeezing the smaller one. Lockdowns against Nepal tried by Indira Gandhi, Rajiv Gandhi and the present dispensation resulted in negative publicity and caused serious inconvenience to thousands of people. They were ill-advised.

Our aid in the aftermath of the Nepal earthquake, completion of the cross-border petroleum pipeline (inaugurated by Oli and Modi in September 2019) and progress on the railway line and Terai roads have been appreciated by Nepal. However, the delay in implementation of hydropower projects has been a sore point in the bilateral relationship.

Issues like the revision of the Treaty of Friendship and Cooperation of 1950 and the dispute about Kalapani and Lipulekh are not new; they shouldn't have been allowed to fester for decades. Had they been addressed in a timely manner, delicately and maturely, with understanding and accommodation, we wouldn't be flinging our respective maps at each other to prove our territorial claims.

Reflecting changed times, presently, the Chinese ambassador acts as a peacemaker to avert the vertical split of the Communist Party of Nepal whose leaders have lived in India for years. KP Sharma Oli often exploited Nepal's long-held narrative of big brother squeezing the small brother and played the China card brazenly. While fighting judicial battles, he had turned amenable but he is not trustworthy. Following the Supreme Court judgment, the Nepali Congress's Sher Bahadur Deuba has returned as the PM for the fifth time. This might reduce the turbulence in bilateral relations. With sensitive and persuasive diplomacy, we can make Nepal realise that its national interests are best served by strengthening its historically close ties with India and not by antagonising its neighbour.

PM Modi has tried to develop close relations with Sri Lanka. India's nuclear energy deal, agreement for a US$ 400 million currency swap, investment of US$ 100 million for three solar projects, supply of essential medicines to fight Covid-19, provision of help by the Indian Navy to douse the fire on the MT New Diamond ship are part of this strategy. Sri Lanka's decision to treat the revocation of Article 370 as India's internal matter was appreciated by the Indian government.

Modi paid his first visit to Sri Lanka in March 2015. He was also the first foreign head of state to visit Sri Lanka in 2019 after the ghastly terror attack at St Anthony's Shrine in Kochchikade. The visits to India by President Gotabaya Rajapaksa in November 2019 and PM Mahinda Rajapaksa in February 2020 and the virtual summit between Modi and Rajapaksa on 26 September 2020 underline the significance India attaches to its relation with Sri Lanka.

However, India can't wish away China's shadows in Sri Lanka. The Sri Lankan president, PM and foreign secretary have made it clear that while it maintains a cordial relationship with India, it will do so with both China and Pakistan as well. On the issues of India's security, Sri Lanka will stand with India, but it will continue availing of the trade, business and investment opportunities offered by China.

Sri Lanka, a part of China's BRI, is facing the effects of a debt trap. It has ejected India and Japan from the East Corridor Terminal project because of alleged Chinese pressure. However, according to press reports, the Sri Lankan government wants private companies in India and Japan to develop the West Corridor Terminal. Any pressure on Sri Lanka to shed economic cooperation with China will not work. We may not match China's deep pockets but our softer, more nuanced and focused assistance in areas crucial to Sri Lanka might earn us their goodwill.

India's emphasis on the implementation of the thirteenth amendment to the constitution, which envisages the devolution of power to the Tamil community, is not liked by the current Sri Lankan leadership. India has a delicate task of not abandoning the Tamil cause as it reverberates in Tamil Nadu and also ensuring that Sri Lanka does not see India as interfering in its internal affairs. Modi has been doing this deft balancing act with considerable success.

Despite China's deep inroads, the growing radicalisation of some sections of Bangladeshi youth and negative reaction to certain domestic decisions and utterances of Indian politicians, PM Modi has succeeded in cementing relations with Bangladesh through mutually beneficial projects. On his visit in 2015, the land and maritime boundary agreements stood out for their historic context and impact. Both countries have inked many instruments in high-tech areas, which should boost the bilateral economic ties and trade (US$ 10.46 billion in 2018-19).

The current supply of 1,200 MW of electricity from India to Bangladesh is likely to rise to 2,500 MW if the Bangladesh–India Friendship Power Company and the Adani group's plant in Jharkhand begins supply, as expected, by December 2021. Both countries are cooperating in the nuclear and renewable energy sectors too. Once the US$ 1 billion Reliance LNG-based 3,000 MW power plant near Dhaka is completed, Bangladesh's power supply situation will improve significantly.

Bangladesh's willingness to hand over insurgents wanted in India, let it use Chittagong and Mangla ports and allow it to take electric transmission lines to the North East through its territory are commendable gestures of good neighbourly cooperation.

Though seven agreements were signed at Modi's virtual summit with Bangladesh PM Sheikh Hasina on 17 October 2020, Bangladesh's long-pending demand for releasing 50 per cent of the water in the Teesta river has remained a sore point. Like Manmohan Singh, Modi has been bogged down by the opposition of West Bengal CM Mamata Banerjee.

Certain remarks about Bangladesh's illegal immigrants by Indian ministers and members of parliament did not go down well with the Bangladeshi government. These should have been avoided in view of larger national interests.

With Bangladesh's GDP growing at a higher rate than India's, its garment export surpassing India's and China being ready to pump in billions of dollars, we must deal with Bangladesh with foresight, maturity and sensitivity.

Sheikh Hasina's invitation to Modi to be the chief guest at Bangladesh's fiftieth anniversary of independence and centenary of Bangabandhu's birthday was a warm gesture. MoUs regarding trade, railway connectivity, start-ups and border development that were signed on 27 March 2021 underline both the countries' resolve to nurture close relations.

Arresting the clear pro-China tilt of the former Maldivian president, Abdulla Yameen, stopping increasing radicalisation of local youth and countering Pakistan's influence in the tiny yet strategically located island state has been a top priority for Modi. Maldives is in the vicinity of many major SLOCs (sea lanes of communication) through which 50 per cent of India's oil imports and 80 per cent of its trade flows. Modi had invited the Maldivian president to his swearing-in ceremony in May 2014 and chose Maldives as the first foreign country to visit after getting sworn in for the second time in 2019. Helping during Male drinking water crises (2014 Operation Neer); providing currency swap of US$ 150 million to mitigate impact of Covid-19; airlifting tons of essential medicine and sending medical team under Operation Sanjeevani; offering US$ 1.4 billion in developmental assistance and attending the swearing-in ceremony of Ibrahim Mohamed Solih are concrete steps for bringing the relations back on an even keel.

In his interview with the *Print* (18 January 2021), Foreign Minister Abdulla Shahid said, 'The previous government tried to play India and China against each other, which is a childish policy. In international relations, you don't play your friends against each other. You establish principled relationships.' While calling Male's relationship with India as 'outstanding', Shahid acknowledged China's help in social developmental projects as 'generous'. He stressed, 'When we deal with India we don't look at the size. Our relationship is based on principles. Our policy is based on mutual respect.' His comments have an unstated message for India. Though very small in size, Maldives expects respect; bullying won't work.

Bhutan was the first country that Modi visited (15-16 June 2014) after getting sworn in as the PM in May 2014. His swearing-in ceremony was attended by the PM of Bhutan. The revision of the India–Bhutan trade and transit agreement in 2015 was a way forward. Since the revision of the Treaty of Peace and

Friendship in 2007, India does not advise Bhutan on foreign affairs. During the 72-day-long stalemate between India and China in Doklam (Zhoglam), Bhutan stood by India in spite of pressure from China, which keeps on laying claims on the Bhutanese territory in Chumbi Valley and Doklam. Though Bhutan is not a part of the BRI, China is keen to expand its diplomatic and economic relations with Bhutan. India has to remain vigilant about China's overtures towards Bhutan without being perceived as interfering in their internal affairs.

The use of the dense Bhutanese forests by militants is a security concern for India. Bhutan's cooperation is must for addressing the militant problem.

India ought to counter the lingering misleading perception that hydropower projects built by India benefit India more than Bhutan. Setting up an ISRO ground station in Bhutan to offer weather forecasts that can benefit remote areas in Bhutan was a wise decision.

Myanmar and India are intertwined by history, culture and religion, and share a 1,624 km land and maritime border. Myanmar is a significant part of India's Act East and South East Asia policy and is crucial for its national security and economic development of its North East. The last coup d'état in Myanmar disrupted India's carefully crafted relationship with Burmese military generals and leader of the National League for Democracy Aung San Su Kyi. India has joined the USA and other Western countries in demanding of the military junta an end to the mounting violence, the release of Aung San Su Kyi who is facing fresh corruption charges and restoration of normalcy.

Modi's Act East Policy has upscaled relations with the ASEAN countries and the South East Asia. Hosting ten heads of state of the ASEAN countries as chief guests at the Republic Day parade (26 January 2018) was an imaginative initiative. The ASEAN nations are crucial for the success of the Indo-Pacific region. But to expect them to stand up against China openly is unrealistic; China is their largest trading partner.

The then Afghan President Hamid Karzai, attended Modi's swearing-in on 26 May 2014. On 25 December 2015, PM Modi inaugurated Afghanistan's parliament building built by India and, on 4 June 2016, jointly opened the Salma Dam or the Afghan-India Friendship Dam with the then Afghan President Ashraf Ghani.

Developments in Afghanistan in August 2021 shocked India. President Ghani, whom it supported, fled. The Taliban has captured the entire country;

it has crushed, at least for the time being, the last resistance in the Panjshir Valley by the former Vice President Amrullah Saleh and Ahmad Masoud, son of the former leader of the Northern Alliance, Ahmad Shah Massoud. Having invested over US$ 3 billion and created the much-needed infrastructure—highways, roads, schools, health care, education—and trained Afghan security personnel, bureaucrats and diplomats, India has suffered a setback. The US, keen to exit, cut a deal with the Taliban and left the country in utter chaos. The US helicopters taking off from the rooftop of its embassy in Kabul were reminiscent of the moment of its Saigon evacuation in 1975. Pakistan feels excited that, at last, the Taliban is offering it the strategic depth in Afghanistan it has longed for. Both China and Russia might be the earliest to recognise the Taliban regime. Many EU members are likely to follow the US. Iran has been interacting with the Taliban for a few years. India was understandably in a dilemma. Millions of Indians loath the Taliban for their role in the hijacking of the IC-814 in 1999, their violent and undemocratic methods, support to terrorists and repressive treatment of women. At present, India has evacuated most of the Indians and has no option but to wait and watch, which is dubbed in the media as 'strategic patience'.

Taliban's return to power in Kabul with fourteen internationally wanted terrorists in the interim Cabinet poses serious security challenges to India. From the prevailing political and humanitarian crises in Afghanistan, India should draw two valuable lessons: never put all your eggs in one basket and never put too much trust in the friendship with the US.

Modi has nurtured a 'special and privileged strategic partnership' with Russia. His numerous summits with Russian President Vladimir Putin and his decision not to drop the purchase of the Russian S-400 surface-to-air defence system despite American pressure have helped. Putin has honoured Modi by bestowing upon him Russia's highest honour (Order of Saint Andrew the Apostle).

In June 2021, Russia began construction of the fifth nuclear power plant at Kundankulam, Tamil Nadu, which was hailed by the Russian Ambassador Nikolay Kudashev as a 'a significant milestone in bilateral nuclear cooperation'. (*Mint* 29 June 2021).

As for the cooperation in defence field, according to the Indian embassy in Moscow, over the years, 'cooperation in the military technical sphere has evolved from a purely buyer–seller relationship to joint research, design development and production of state-of-the-art military platforms. Production of the Brahmos cruise missile is an example of this trend. The two countries are also engaged in joint design and development of the fifth generation fighter aircraft and multi-role transport aircraft. Bilateral projects currently underway include indigenous production of T-90 tanks and Su-30-MKI aircraft, supply of MiG-29-K aircraft and Kamov-31 and Mi-17 helicopters, upgrade of MiG-29 aircraft and supply of multi-barrel rocket launcher, Smerch.'

Putin invited Modi to attend the fifth Eastern Economic Forum (EEC) in September 2019 in Vladivostok as the chief guest. He supports Modi's Make in India and Smart City initiatives and hopes to boost bilateral trade to US$ 30 billion by 2025 through the India–Russia Inter-Governmental Commission (IRIGC). Russia supports India's membership to the UNSC and Nuclear Suppliers Group (NSG), cooperates in fighting international terrorism and maintains a neutral position on the India–China LAC stalemate.

The burgeoning India–US defence trade causes Russia some concern, though it still accounts for roughly 62 per cent of India's defence imports. Russia's growing closeness to China is a strategic hedging of bets against the US. But Russia's warming up to Pakistan and its stand on the Taliban in Afghanistan warrant a close watch. In the changed world, unlike in 1971, Russia shouldn't be expected to stand by India openly; not against China.

While China views closer relations between the US and India with suspicion, the US and Western sanctions against Russia are pushing economically vulnerable Russia closer to China. Maintaining fruitful relations with the US, Russia and China, in spite of their mutual rivalry and competition, is a constant challenge, which Modi's diplomacy has addressed with adroit pragmatism.

Modi and Japanese Prime Minister Shinzo Abe's personal rapport facilitated the convergence of the economic, defence, security, regional and international interests of India and Japan. They met twelve times, which includes five annual summits, all marked by personal warmth. The Mumbai–Ahmedabad high speed rail, a dedicated freight corridor, a nuclear deal for the supply of reactors, the setting up of a 2+2 dialogue, the Japan–India Coordination Forum, increasing trade and investment and cooperation in the Quad, Indo-Pacific and G20 alliances underline that the India–Japan Special Strategic and

Global Partnership is working. On the other hand, India's withdrawal from the Regional Comprehensive Economic Partnership (RCEP) disappointed Japan.

Modi who has met Abe's successor Yoshihide Suga at Quad's virtual summit in March 2021 and at the summit in person in Washington in September 2021 maintains that Japan has contributed a lot to India's economic and technological modernisation.

African countries still remember Mahatma Gandhi, Jawaharlal Nehru and Indira Gandhi for their contribution to the anti-colonial movement and Africa's struggle for independence. Thanks to PM Modi's personal initiative and push, a number of visits to African countries till early 2020 at the president, vice president and PM (30) and cabinet minister (54) levels have taken place. Similarly, a number of visits have been made by multiple African heads of state to India (32). The number of visits that have taken place in the last six years between India and the African continent are the highest they have been in the last fifty years! The decision to open eighteen new diplomatic missions, which will take the number of India's resident missions in Africa from twenty-nine to forty-seven, is farsighted. This new proactive approach to Africa will pay huge dividends.

Modi pointed out his ten-point guideline for India's policy towards the African continent while addressing the parliament in Uganda in July 2018. The main thrust of India's African policy is building trust and reliability as a friend, developing a partnership through capacity building and training, offering credit lines and enhancing trade and business. The countries that have been selected for opening new diplomatic missions are strategically significant, offer valuable raw material and show potential for India's trade and investment.

Modi has tried to develop relations with countries in the Persian Gulf with strategic objectives. In 2015, he became the first Indian PM to visit the UAE in thirty years. Since then, he has visited thrice. He has developed a personal rapport with Saudi Crown Prince Mohammed bin Salman (MBS) and visited Bahrain, Qatar and Oman. Modi's intense interaction with the Gulf Region is boosting India's energy security, enhancing the inflow of investment, helping in its anti-terrorist campaigns, blunting support for Pakistan and protecting the interests of nearly 9 million Indian workers in the region. India's defence agreement with Oman allows the Indian Air Force and Indian Navy the use of Al Duqm port and other ports for anti-piracy actions. Honouring Sultan

Qaboos bin Said of Oman posthumously with the Gandhi Peace Prize (2019) is an example of Modi's strategic soft power diplomacy.

The invitation to Minister of External Affairs Sushma Swaraj to attend the OIC Summit (March 2019) in spite of Pakistan's objection, was a historic shift. The Gulf region's reaction to the abrogation of Article 370 and reorganisation of Jammu and Kashmir has been muted.

The decision of Saudi Arabia, UAE, Bahrain and the Palestinian authorities to confer their respective highest civilian awards on PM Modi is an acknowledgement of his enormous efforts to strengthen relations with them.

While the UAE supposedly helped in the ceasefire agreement between India and Pakistan (February 2021), Qatar is believed to have assisted India in communicating with the Taliban.

Though cooperation on the strategic Chabahar Port and International North–South Transport Corridor (INSC) continues, relations with Iran are experiencing some chill on account of our succumbing to US pressure and not buying their oil. India and Iran are not entirely on the same page regarding the Taliban government in Afghanistan. If Iran's relations with the US witness some thaw under Biden, apparent wrinkles in India–Iran relations might also ease.

Close relations with Israel serve India's interests significantly in the defence, security and agricultural sectors and help fight terrorism. However, we must continue supporting the legitimate rights and aspirations of the people of Palestine.

Due to its population of 620 million, per capita income of US$ 8000, abundance of minerals like iron, copper, lithium, gold and silver, having 20 per cent of the world's crude oil reserves and considerable production of fruits and food grains, Latin America and the Caribbean Islands warrant more attention from India. PM Modi visited Brazil in 2014 to attend the BRICS summit, Argentina in November 2018 to attend the G20 summit and Mexico in 2016 for a bilateral meeting. President Kovind has visited Suriname and Cuba and Vice President Venkaiah Naidu visited Panama, Peru and Guatemala. Brazilian President Jair Bolsonaro was the chief guest at India's Republic Day parade in January 2020. While India and Latin America's annual bilateral trade totals a meagre US$ 42 billion, 15 per cent of India's oil import comes from Latin America. Besides offering energy security, Latin America can be an asset for fulfilling India's global ambitions: a permanent seat in the UNSC and membership in the NSG.

Though India and the EU are strategic partners and democracies with multidimensional relations, a bilateral trade investment agreement (BTIA) has remained elusive. Through his visits to France, Germany, the UK, Switzerland, Sweden, Spain, the Netherlands, Belgium and Ireland, Modi has tried to improve relations. Though the Rafale deal was criticised by government's detractors, the delivery of five Rafale jet fighters during the 2020 standoff with China at the LAC was widely welcomed.

India and the EU are committed to implementing the Paris Climate Agreement. They cooperate under the Clean Energy and Climate Partnership and International Solar Alliance and in fighting international terrorism, cyber-crime and piracy. Both support digital economy and fair competition based on globally accepted standards for 5G, artificial intelligence (AI) and the Internet of Things.

The fifteenth India–EU Summit, co-chaired by PM Modi, Charles Michel, president of the European Council and Ursula von der Leyen, president of the European Commission, was held virtually on 15 July 2020. It 'affirmed their determination to promote effective multilateralism and a rules-based multilateral order with the United Nations (UN) and the World Trade Organization (WTO) at its core'.

Covid-19 prevented UK PM Boris Johnson from becoming the chief guest at the Indian Republic Day parade in 2021. Embracing post-Brexit UK and entering into bilateral agreements that boost trade, business and investment and further strengthen ongoing cooperation on the issues of climate change, fighting terrorism, cyber-crime and money laundering will be mutually beneficial. Johnson and Modi might meet at the COP26 Summit in Glasgow in November 2021.

Kanwal Sibal, a former foreign secretary of India feels, 'Modi has projected India internationally more confidently and defended India's interests more robustly. Special importance has been accorded to maritime security to consolidate the country's dominance in the Indian Ocean area. No other leader has galvanised the Indian diaspora as much as he has done.'

Lord Meghnad Desai believes, 'Modi has made serious friendships with

Arab states in the Middle East. This is a shrewd move both to confuse Pakistan and to thwart criticisms at home and in the West that he is anti-Muslim.'

'Modi's ascent to power constitutes a historic confluence of interests and opportunities. After the end of the cold war, various models such as the Washington Consensus, the Beijing Consensus, and the Arab Spring have been attempted without much success. Now India's attempt to develop as a major power under a liberal democratic set-up might carry great historic significance.'[1]

'Perhaps the most salient aspect of India's foreign policy during Modi's first term was its explicit reorientation toward a vision of India as a major world power. This reorientation has all but negated the meaning of "non-alignment" as a pillar of Indian diplomacy.'[2]

India's new aspiration is 'to be a leading power, rather than just a balancing power', underlines Minister of External Affairs Dr S Jaishankar.

Endnotes

1. Takenori, Horimoto. 'Explaining India's Foreign Policy', *International Relations of the Asia Pacific*, volume 17, Issue 3, September 2017.
2. Takenori, Horimoto. '"Modi Diplomacy" and the Future of Japan–India Relations', Available at: https://www.bilaterals.org/?modi-diplomacy-and-the-future-of.

CHAPTER 1

THE WORLD AROUND THE CORNER: INDIA'S CHALLENGES IN THE POST-COVID-19 ERA

SHYAM SARAN

It may be premature to pronounce the end of the Covid-19 pandemic but it appears to be receding in most parts of the world. India had a catastrophic second wave over March and April 2021 with horrific images of funeral pyres burning on the roadside and dead bodies floating in our rivers. In cities like New Delhi, the urban middle class came face-to-face with the inadequacies of India's healthcare system and the apathy of elected governments. Fortunately, that traumatic phase is over and there is hope that India's mass vaccination drive, which is picking up after a slow start, will spare its people a replay of the tragedy which left virtually no family untouched. This may be a good occasion as any to refocus our attention on what the world will look like in a post-pandemic era. What are some of the key trends to look out for?

One, there are likely to be several 'black swan' or unexpected events which will have the potential to overwhelm even the most carefully drawn-up plans. We need to prepare our societies, our businesses and our governance systems to deal with these contingencies even as we remain committed to realising our developmental objectives. Coping with large-scale emergencies takes away resources from other pressing needs. So it is wiser to focus on prevention and amelioration of risks than wait for crises to unfold. Dealing with consequences is usually more costly than money spent on prevention.

Two, these black swan events may arise outside our borders, as, indeed, did the Covid-19 pandemic. In fact, most of the potential threats in the coming decade and beyond are likely to arise from global and cross-cutting issues, such as climate change or another pandemic. Our rapid embrace of the digital economy has made us more vulnerable to hostile cyberattacks. The globalised nature of our financial markets makes our interconnected economies subject to acute disruptions by any perturbation half a world away. The only effective way to deal with them is through global, collaborative responses. One of the significant challenges for our foreign policy would be initiating, when necessary and participating, when possible, in multilateral approaches to deal with such issues with a global salience. We can no longer treat national security or national interests as defined exclusively by political boundaries of a sovereign state.

In preparing India for the new world that lurks around the corner, two things, therefore, are indispensable.

One, anticipating risks and developing both societal and state capacities to deal with them. The emphasis must be on prevention and minimisation of risks so as to avoid much larger need for resources to deal with the consequences of a crisis that could not be prevented.

Two, since the salience of most of the challenges we are confronting and will continue to confront in the future, will be cross-national and global, only multilateral approaches through empowered international institutions of governance will be up to the task of dealing with them. We only have to witness the ugly consequences of 'vaccine nationalism' and the sidelining of the World Health Organization to appreciate the importance of multilateralism. In this pandemic, nobody is safe unless everyone living on this planet is safe. National or regional boundaries are irrelevant and yet countries behave as if they have national agency in tackling the pandemic.

It follows from the above propositions that countries which are good at anticipating emerging risks are, by the same token, adept at identifying emerging opportunities. They profit by staying ahead of the curve. In embracing a spirit of internationalism and promoting multilateralism, they can position themselves in a leadership role. The world is crying out for statesmanship that has the ability to mobilise the intellectual and material resources of the world—which are considerable—to identify emerging risks, formulate collaborative responses and make the world safer and more prosperous in this unfolding millennium.

How should India prepare its large and diverse population to deal with the twenty-first century challenges?

First and foremost, India needs a national strategy that goes beyond the narrower definition of national security, but will include national security as commonly understood. A strategy implies making informed choices from among a range of possible alternatives. It should provide a broad template on the basis of which decisions may be taken on specific, day-to-day and topical issues. It should serve as a guide, a road map and a well-considered benchmark for both the organs and agencies of the state and society as a whole. It should enable not only a whole of government approach but also a whole of society approach. It would acknowledge that we are faced with challenges that are increasingly cross-domain in nature and where the line dividing the domestic from the external has become increasingly blurred. Above all, it must reflect the temperament and aspirations of the people and also seek to mould them in the direction of overall social and economic advancement. It should be subject to constant review and revision as the situation changes. In a rapidly changing environment in multiple dimensions, a national strategy may serve as an anchor for both society and state. It stands to reason that if such a strategy is to be a guide for the society as much as for the state, then ways must be found to seek the active participation of different constituencies of society in drawing up a national strategy. It cannot be the result of a top-down approach.

The awareness of the interrelated nature of the challenges that a modern state confronts and the feedback loops that bind different domains together, require the agencies of the state to break down the silos through which they operate and learn to collaborate rather than merely coordinate. For example, water, energy and food security are integrally linked together and interventions in one domain may enhance or neutralise an intervention in the other. The use of chemical fertilisers and toxic pesticides may appear necessary to enhance food security by raising crop yields. But they also create health related issues for farmers who use them—sometimes without protective gear. Also, much of the existing energy generation is water-intensive. Increasing electric power may be deemed necessary for supporting industrialisation, but this may also undermine water security, especially when the country is already facing acute water stress.

This points to the need for designing interventions which recognise these feedback loops. This awareness is necessary not only for the agencies of the state, but also for citizens so that there is a buy-in from the latter in interventions that become necessary. A strategy that is unable to mobilise a broad political and social consensus in a democratic state has little chance of succeeding. What is important to understand here is that just as the state must be prepared to inform and educate the citizenry on the need for various policy interventions, it must also be open to orienting its policymaking in response to innovative thinking and ground-level experience of the citizenry.

India confronts a series of paradoxes which further underline the need for a national strategy that leverages the country's assets and overcomes its liabilities. The country has a young and growing population, but this demographic advantage will last for a decade and a half before India heads towards an ageing society. This turning point is likely to occur around 2035 when India's population is expected to stabilise at 1.6 billion. We speak of India's demographic dividend, but this will be realised only if there are expanding opportunities for employment. This demands investment in education and in the acquisition of skills. If we are unable to provide jobs for the ten million or so youth who are joining the job market each year as is currently the case, we will end up with an unemployment overhang which could spell perilous consequences for India's social and political fabric. The productivity of a population is also linked to its health, to whether in childhood proper nutrition was available. Gender equity is critical in ensuring that women have equal opportunities in employment as men do. The situation in India today is that female participation in the labour force has been declining. This constitutes an underutilisation, if not enormous loss, of a most valuable human resource. What a national strategy would do is take this demographic dividend as a key asset and then go about formulating an economic strategy built around its fuller utilisation. This would include a high priority to education, both at the elementary and higher levels, and vocational training. Since this demographic dividend is available only for the next fifteen years, we need to ensure that this asset is not wasted.

India possesses a wealth of natural resources. It enjoys a market scale that few countries have. Its entrepreneurs and managers are world class. In niche areas, like space sciences, atomic energy and information technology, it has attained standards comparable to the best in the world. Though some people consider India's noisy democracy a constraint on its development, the opposite is true. Democracy fosters open debate and dissent, the free interchange of ideas and innovative thinking. It is the failure of the institutions of governance and a politics focused on winning elections that have failed to create a citizen-centred polity. This is why the best and the brightest from a handful of our top universities prefer to seek opportunities in distant climes. Successful societies of the future will be knowledge societies, and unless India invests in its people and enable their acquisition of knowledge, it will fall behind.

India is on track to becoming the world's third largest economy in the world by mid-century, behind only China and the US. But this, and other projections, are based on assumptions that may not materialise. One must also ask the question whether the current glaring income inequalities will persist, worsen or improve. The present income pyramid has over 860 million in the poor and relatively poor category, a middle class of 280 million and a top-income category of 70 million. This income distribution is incompatible with democracy.

India cannot be another China, replicating the fossil energy- and resource-intensive growth strategy that it pursued in its high-growth years from 1978 onwards. China itself is discovering that such a growth strategy is ecologically unsustainable. Nor does India have as favourable an international economic environment as China enjoyed from 1978 right up to the global financial and economic crisis of 2007-08, with easy access to the world's largest markets of the US, Europe and Japan and modern technologies. An export-driven growth strategy has become more difficult, as protectionist trends take hold in major economies. It is crystal clear that India cannot aspire to the levels and nature of affluence enjoyed by Western economies and increasingly by China. Our pursuit of affluence must be compatible with a resource-efficient and an energy-frugal strategy of development which is ecologically sustainable. For example, India cannot aspire to have a private car population that is even a fraction of what it is in the US (nearly 900 per thousand) or in Europe (700-800 per thousand). Not all the oil in the world and not all the land area available in India could sustain such a large private vehicle population. The answer lies in massive investment in efficient and affordable public transportation and progressively heavy taxation of private vehicles. If the current focus on developing the passenger car industry continues, then we shall end up by having a small elite owning cars while the vast majority must fend for itself. We see no reflection of this reality in our policymaking. If we do not rethink our economic strategy, ecological stress in multiple dimensions may overwhelm the country. Water stress has already assumed crisis proportions in several parts of the country. The degradation of forests and spoliation of our river systems and increasing desertification are leading to irreparable loss of biodiversity and this will limit our future prospects of development.

India is still at an early stage of its development. Much of its infrastructure remains to be built. It is not yet locked into a resource-intensive and pollution-generating pattern of economic activities. There is still an opportunity to pioneer and pursue a different and more equitable strategy of growth which delivers affluence with frugality and higher standards of living, balancing material well-being with ecological sustainability. There is no trade-off between development and the preservation of the country's fragile ecology. In fact, the latter has become the indispensable condition for achieving the former.

Here, again, the ongoing pandemic holds lessons for us. The Covid-19 virus may have jumped from wild species of bats, which came in contact with domesticated animals being sold in the market, where large number of humans also gather. Wild species come into contact with domesticated animals and humans when their habitat in the forests is destroyed. The more such wild habitats are encroached upon by expanding human settlement, the chances of 'virus-hopping' become more frequent. There is a link between pandemics and loss of biodiversity. The 'precaution principle' enjoins upon us to heed this growing threat and stop and reverse biodiversity loss. Otherwise, whatever development occurs in the short run by over-exploitation of biodiversity may be wiped out subsequently in an instant. This is also the lesson of the recent avalanche in the fragile mountains of Uttarakhand which led to the destruction downstream of a hydroelectric dam in a matter of minutes.

As pointed out earlier, in tackling the many challenges India confronts, there are several which are cross-national in nature and require international collaboration. We are living in a globalised world and the advance of digital technologies is making globalisation even more salient than before. National interests must be redefined to take into account the international dimensions of tackling the challenges which India will increasingly confront as the current millennium advances.

One of the other paradoxes of our time is the resurgence of narrow nationalism even as we need an international spirit, a sense of international solidarity to be able to resolve cross-cutting issues that have a global dimension, such as climate change, the melting of ice in the poles and in the Himalayas, the ravaging of the oceans and marine life from dumping of plastic waste, prevention of public healthcare crises such as pandemics, the proliferation of weapons of mass destruction, international crime, cybersecurity and regulating the use of space which is now crowded with several thousand satellites. These are challenges which are not amenable to national or even regional solutions. What is more, they are inherent in the process of globalisation. There may be some stalling, even reversal of globalisation in some areas, but globalisation is here to stay because it is inherent in the process of rapid technological change. People have perhaps failed to notice that, thanks to the pandemic our use of digital communications has accelerated beyond our most optimistic expectations. One could say that there is 'galloping globalisation' taking place in the digital economy since the pandemic began and this is unlikely to be reversed even when the pandemic ends. Therefore, countries which recognise this trend and stay ahead of the globalisation curve will be the winners in the future. This must be the guiding star of India's external policies, both political and economic. We should seek to benefit from globalisation rather than resist it or fall back on more defensive and protectionist policies. Maintaining an open economy, easing the flow of foreign capital and technology and absorbing advanced knowledge and capabilities from wherever they could be sourced, that is what will put India back on a high growth path. Some contradictory policies need to be revised. Currently, foreign portfolio investment in India enjoys a very favourable regulatory regime. This brings in a lot of funds, but also volatility. In comparison, the regulatory regime for fixed asset investment is relatively more difficult even though the ease of doing business has recorded encouraging improvements. Our strategy should be to facilitate fixed investment over portfolio investment.

India has an interest in the global regimes that will emerge to regulate as yet ungoverned spaces such as cybersecurity. We will need to ensure that any global climate change regime enhances rather than constrains our development prospects. This will demand a major focus on multilateral diplomacy and in building coalitions of like-minded countries to pursue equitable solutions. Despite deploying limited economic power in the initial years after gaining independence, India was able to mobilise a large constituency of newly emerging and developing countries in advancing its own political and economic interests. While a revival of the Non-Aligned Movement is unrealistic, there is no reason why India cannot aspire to a leadership role of developing countries that are facing similar challenges. This will require a certain reorientation of our foreign policy which, in recent years, has emphasised much more our relations with the major powers than with the developing countries' constituency. As part of this reorientation, India would also attach priority to its relations with its South Asian neighbours, positioning itself as an engine of growth for the entire region and a net security provider in areas that are not contentious, such as cybersecurity and data privacy. In any event, regional cooperation is necessary to tackle the melting of the Himalayan glaciers or to manage river basins in the subcontinent that straddle national borders. The economic integration of South Asia, led by India, will become the platform for seeking integration with the larger Asian and global economy.

China is a major preoccupation for India and its impact on India's security will expand rather than diminish in the coming decade. At the heart of India's China dilemma is the growing asymmetry in economic, military and, increasingly, technological capabilities, between the two countries, which are the major powers in Asia and are also civilisational states. Addressing this asymmetry is indispensable to meeting the China challenge, but this will not be possible by striving to replicate the China development experience or seeking to become another China. India will need to chart out a different economic trajectory as spelt out in this article which is resource-frugal and ecologically sustainable. If India succeeds in this endeavour, it will also become a model for sustainable growth in developing countries. A new equilibrium in India–China relations will then become feasible. If the asymmetry continues to expand, as is currently the trend, then we would have to increasingly seek external balancing, such as through the Quadrilateral (of India, the US, Japan and Australia). This will, inevitably, constrain our strategic autonomy which has been a defining feature of our foreign policy since independence in 1947. China has already passed the stage of its demographic dividend and entered a stage of declining growth. India will still enjoy this dividend for another fifteen years. Our aim should be to achieve double-digit growth in this period by fully mobilising our young population, creating much more expanded opportunities for its productive employment. If we are able to do this successfully, then Chinese domination of Asia will be prevented. I continue to believe that if there is one country which, in terms of its size, population, scientific and technological capabilities and a sense of itself as a civilisation rather than a mere state, can match China, it is India.

India's encounter with the new world around the corner need not be fraught with anxiety. We have the instruments to shape that world in the service of a bright future for India.

CHAPTER 2

INDIA'S SECURITY CHALLENGES

SHIVSHANKAR MENON

How should one think of India's security today, when the world is more uncertain than ever, and when global geopolitics and great power contention have heated up? On the other side of the ledger, India's security capabilities have grown considerably over the last few decades. Unlike the early years of the republic, there are no external existential threats to India. And yet, polls show that Indian citizens do not necessarily feel more secure than their forefathers.

Why is this so? Most analyses of India's security concentrate on the security of the state and, therefore, list traditional threats to the state—other adversarial states, boundary and territorial disputes, political rivals and so on. In doing so, they conflate the security of the state with the security and safety of its citizens, assuming, mistakenly, that they are one.[1] We, today, have a situation in India where all the indices of violence and indicators of state security show steady improvement over the last two decades, but our cities have seen a mushrooming of private security guards, walls and gated communities, and rural violence is rising.

It is, therefore, time that we took a holistic view of India's security challenges. India's security calculus, today, needs to go beyond the state to include the security and safety of its citizens, and this paper will suggest some ways in which we might do so.

Let us first consider the security of the Indian state. As a result of its transformation over the last seven decades, the Indian republic, which had to fight four wars in its first twenty-five years of existence, built sufficient deterrence and an effective balance of power on the border that kept an uneasy peace with potential adversaries since 1971.

Attempts to change the territorial status quo since then have been beaten back, and, by and large, the borders remained as they were. This changed in spring 2020 when, for the first time since 1962, the Chinese People's Liberation Army (PLA) simultaneously changed the status quo in several places along the line of actual control (LAC), seeking both local tactical gains—preventing the Indian Army from patrolling in areas it had visited for years—and acting in ways which called into question the agreements, protocols and confidence-building measures which had kept the peace. The effect has been to create a crisis in India–China relations that is still being worked through by both sides. While negotiations have shown some success in de-escalating the situation in one area, Chinese actions have now made the entire border live. India has taken a series of steps in response. The Chinese actions come at a time when India is beginning a far-reaching set of military reforms, which will hasten India's self-strengthening efforts. It is clear that India–China relations will not go back to their earlier state, and a higher risk of conflict must now be factored into Indian security planning. With troops in proximity, trust absent and overlapping claims of control, incidents such as that in the Galwan Valley in June 2020 cannot yet be ruled out and have the potential of leading to wider clashes, unless both sides negotiate and implement disengagement and a restoration of the status quo ante. For the present, that appears a difficult prospect.

India's other security preoccupation has been Pakistan. Once the three wars in twenty-four years made it clear that Pakistan could not take Jammu and Kashmir (J&K) from India by force and it turned to asymmetric means, such as cross-border terrorism and nuclear threats to achieve revenge for 1971 and weaken India, India had to learn and develop new means of dealing with this daily tactical challenge. That India did, so is clear from the fact that the years when Pakistan most attempted to foment trouble using terrorism in Punjab and J&K, were the years when India was most successful in transforming itself and pulling an unprecedented 160 million people out of poverty.

Today, however, both the regional and global situation is no longer what it was during India's high-growth years until the second decade of this century. Today, the centre of gravity of world geopolitics is in the Asia-Pacific, China–US strategic contention is the central fault line in international politics and the Indian subcontinent is no longer geographically peripheral to a Euro-centric Cold War world. The world is between orders, not binary as in the Cold War, or unipolar as it was until the global financial crisis in 2008, but in a confused transition, yet to find equilibrium with China and other rising powers.

The consequence is that external powers are now much more interested in the subcontinent, particularly China, which sees it as a secondary theatre of contention with the US, a periphery abutting restive minority areas in Tibet and Xinjiang, and the littoral of the Indian Ocean through which its energy and essential supplies pass. China has doubled down on its investment in Pakistan's defence forces and increased its military presence there; it is now an active participant in the internal politics of Myanmar, Nepal, Sri Lanka and the Maldives, and has promised over US$ 100 billion in the Belt and Road Initiative projects in the subcontinent to countries other than India.

While pulling out of Afghanistan, the US is countering China through a maritime strategy, focused on the Indo-Pacific, and India is a participant in that strategy through bilateral defence and security links and the Quad (of India, Japan, the USA and Australia). At the same time, given the fluctuations in US policy over the last decade, all the states on China's southern periphery have been both balancing and hedging against China and, often, the US as well. Their cooperation in defence, security and intelligence has increased manifold in the last twenty years.

All in all, none of these external preoccupations represents an existential threat to the Indian state, and India now has the means and experience to deal with them. While they could distract, delay or divert India from its primarily internal goals, they can and should be managed successfully. The goal of Indian security policy since 1947 has been to provide sufficient security for the transformation of India into a prosperous, safe and modern country, creating, where possible, an enabling environment. It has done so for most of the life of the republic. India has been more radically and rapidly transformed in the last seventy years than at any other time in history, particularly in the high-growth years before 2012. While state-to-state violence has continued—as evident in ceasefire violations along the line of control (LoC) with Pakistan, cross-border terrorism sponsored by Pakistan and escalating incidents along the line of actual control with China—it has so far not been allowed to impede India's own progress.

Today, it is internal security concerns that most challenge the Indian state. Since the beginning of this century, indices of terrorist or separatist violence and counts of their victims in India have declined steadily. Instead, it is communal violence and crimes against a person, such as rape, that have increased, not just from a more complete recording of these crimes. We are a society in churn, with rapid urbanisation taking people from familiar family and village to urban anonymity. Within a decade, most Indians will probably be living and working in cities. At the same time, technology is bringing new ideas and sights into the palms of every person with a smartphone, and social media and the Internet are feeding the politics of emotion and mass mobilisation on a scale unprecedented in human history. These pose a new set of security issues for the Indian state.

The Indian state has been relatively quick to adapt and change its practices in response to external, traditional threats. The 1962 war saw the first of several rounds of military reform, some of which are still going on now. Lessons learned from 1962 and 1965 led to the creation of a separate external intelligence agency, and the Kargil experience led to the creation of national technical means and work on cyber and other forms of security. India responded to changes in the external environment by becoming an overt nuclear weapon state in 1998, and set up a National Security Council soon thereafter to take an integrated view of state security issues.

Unfortunately, there has not been a similar evolution in either the apparatus, the doctrines or practices relating to internal security. One has only to think of the lack of police reform, despite clear directives from the Supreme Court in 1996, or the use of colonial era laws on sedition, etc. abandoned by democracies, or punitive and arbitrary detention laws and practices, to see how little policing and security practices have evolved in independent India. While India has learned how to counter terrorism tactically, continuing Naxalite violence and communal polarisation suggest that much more remains to be done to address the social and other factors which enable the radicalisation and recruitment of terrorists, many of whom are now, unlike the eighties and nineties, home-grown.

It, therefore, seems to me that the primary security challenge to the Indian state today is internal security. External criticism and even attempts by hostile powers to destabilise India will only be effective and work if they find local resonance, support and recruits. The administrative reorganisation of J&K will be judged a success or failure by its ability to carry the people of J&K with it, for, as we have seen through the nineties and noughts, it is only in the absence of a local political process and when they are able to arouse local support that the ISI and Pakistan are able to trouble the Indian state.

This is what makes the safety and security of the Indian citizen so important. Unless the overwhelming majority of Indian citizens feel safe and see the state as their protector, not just against imaginary or foreign enemies but also in their daily lives, we will not have a stable and secure internal environment and the strong India that we seek. The real question to ask is, would you turn to an Indian policeman for help if you needed it? Sadly, the answer is less and less likely to be 'yes'.

What makes this quest more complicated today, apart from the use of polarisation and lawlessness as a political instrument by some in our polity, is the fact that the distinction between internal and external security threats is being steadily eroded in our time. We live in a globalised world where our economic security is tied to and dependent on external factors to a greater degree than ever before. More than half our gross domestic product (GDP) is today accounted for by the external sector. We depend on the world for essentials like energy, technology and capital.

At the same time, technology, too, has obliterated boundaries and weakened sovereignties. The Internet and communications technology have empowered small groups, weakened the state's monopoly of violence and made possible new modes of social and other mobilisation for good or bad purposes. The new domain of cyberspace operates to its own rules, different from other domains. For instance, unlike the nuclear domain, deterrence is ineffective in cyberspace, given the speed of attack and the difficulty of ascription.

Nor does our geography permit us to take a view of our security that is limited to the boundaries of the republic of India. Climate change and its potentially devastating effects are a good example of new security threats that not only transcend boundaries, but also threaten the daily lives of citizens as much as the state, and which require action not just by several states but also by society and citizens across borders.

We are, therefore, in a world where our security calculus itself has to evolve and change in multiple ways. It must expand to put the citizen at its centre. It must think beyond boundaries. And it must use, as its criterion to build a hierarchy, or to prioritise among threats and opportunities, the transformation of the lives of Indians. In other words, a threat becomes more or less important depending on its effect on the transformation of our lives.

By this standard, clearly, territorial integrity is the first and overriding priority. But once that is assured, the development imperative leads us to list threats according to how they affect our ability to transform Indian lives. Climate change, energy security and other non-traditional security threats would come much higher in this calculus than they did traditionally. Maritime security, for its effect on Indian lives, would also be relatively high. Terrorism, which relies less on its actual kinetic effects than on its psychological impact and the reaction of the victim, would come lower on this list.

Now that the significance of national political boundaries in the security calculus has significantly lessened, and the new transnational security agenda is what will determine our future, it would be logical to think of the subcontinent and Asia as one. In terms of security, the Indian subcontinent is a single unit—history, geography, culture and circumstance make us so. Common security and common prosperity are, therefore, a logical imperative. And yet, ours is one of the least integrated subregions of the world and we seem to prove our nationalisms against each other. Yet, we have tremendous advantages in our affinities and in the daily lived experience of our peoples, not states, of living together over the centuries and across political boundaries. It is probably time that we began a real conversation about security and stability in the subcontinent.

Our own recent experience suggests the utility of thinking in these broader terms. We not only survived but also overcame civil wars in Nepal and Sri Lanka, and progressed in reducing poverty in the last two decades, not due to any external balancers that were brought in, but due to our own efforts within the subcontinent and because of our integration.

A security dialogue in the subcontinent becomes even more important when it is now central to global geopolitics. Unlike the Cold War, when the central fault line of global politics was in Europe between the USA and the Soviet Union, today's geopolitics centre on Eurasia and the Asia-Pacific. The rise of China has produced a predictable reaction from the established powers. It is the strategic contention between the established superpower, the USA, and a rising China that forms the driver of global geopolitics and geoeconomics. And the subcontinent and the Indian Ocean are surrounded by the hotspots and flashpoints of today—the Senkaku/Diaoyu islands in the East China Sea, Taiwan, the South China Sea, Afghanistan, Yemen, Syria and so on which ring us.

One final thought. Our fates are now interlinked across domains, issues and borders. We are at a moment when what we do about these security issues will have long-term effects across expanses of time and space, well beyond our lifetimes. This is our generation's real test.

Endnotes

1. China has two separate ministries of state security and public security. The former protects the state from other states, and the latter seems designed to protect the state from the public.

CHAPTER 3

INDIA'S ECONOMIC DIPLOMACY IN THE POST-COVID-19 WORLD

Rahul Chhabra

Introduction

It is more than a year since the Covid-19 pandemic—a black swan event—pushed the world into the realm of massive socio-economic uncertainties. Initially, nobody knew how this pandemic would play out for economies, societies and countries, at large. What the world has endured with Covid-19, through 2020, is unique. However, more than a year into the pandemic, India has set global benchmarks in the tackling of an outbreak of such intense proportions. India has been proactive in assessing and dealing with the challenges caused by the Covid-19 crisis. Saving lives has been the government's foremost priority during the pandemic. On this count, India has fared comparatively better than many other countries, displaying remarkable resilience in the face of trying times, with one of the lowest death rates of 115 per million population and one of the lowest active cases of about 242 per million. This noteworthy control over the progression of the disease has laid the foundation for the much anticipated economic revival. Today, India has two vaccines available, and has begun vaccinating not only its own population, but also those of over seventy countries.

India's Global Engagement during and after the Pandemic

India was among the first few countries to have recognised the need for global engagement on the Covid-19 crisis. It took the lead in engaging world leaders for evolving a coordinated response to the pandemic.

Even before India responded to the pandemic with its national lockdown, Prime Minister Narendra Modi took the initiative to hold a meeting of South Asian Association for Regional Cooperation (SAARC) heads of governments to fashion a regional response. As a result of this meeting, the SAARC Covid-19 Fund was created; this fund was instrumental in providing crucial early-stage scientific and policy exchanges on the evolving coronavirus epidemic within the region. The fund also supported workshops and capacity-building training courses in the field of public health and Covid-19 management, including handling of vaccination logistics and programmes. It was this early initiative of the prime minister that enabled effective policy responses at later stages of the epidemic.

The prime minister also encouraged an early convening of the virtual G20 summit. He subsequently attended the online Non-Aligned Movement (NAM) summit, and the virtual Global Vaccine Summit, where India pledged US$ 15 million to Gavi, the international vaccine alliance. India is massively contributing to the global efforts to develop vaccines and other treatments with its large capacities to produce quality medicines and vaccines at low cost, as well as its scientific talent.

India has remained responsible and dependable in living up to its international commitments even in these difficult times. Rapid response teams were promptly deployed to Maldives, Kuwait, Mauritius and Comoros to deal with the pandemic. The Government of India also worked to ensure supply of drugs like hydroxychloroquine, paracetamol and essential antibiotics and life-saving drugs to friendly countries, while also meeting its domestic demand. Despite the global lockdown and the severe restrictions on cross-border travel and logistics, India supplied more than 300 tonnes of essential drugs, life-saving antibiotics and personal protective equipment (PPE) kits to more than fifty countries in Africa and Latin America. As these medicines arrived in the ports of our partner countries, India reinforced its reputation as a 'pharmacy to the world' for cost-effective manufacturing of quality generic drugs. These medicines were crucial inputs to the healthcare systems whose supply chains had been impacted by the lockdown restrictions and complemented the national efforts of various countries to combat the pandemic. With the development and imminent availability of vaccines, in December 2020, the Ministry of External Affairs (MEA) took foreign envoys from more than sixty countries to leading biotech companies in Hyderabad to allow them to see first-hand the world-class vaccine-manufacturing capacities. Such vaccine diplomacy was a part of the larger reach-out efforts to ensure future cooperation on the Covid-19 front.

In the wake of the global outbreak of Covid-19 pandemic in early 2020, a majority of nations, across the world, imposed lockdowns/border closure, which severely restricted international travel. Anticipating the severity of the situation, and to contain the contagion, the Indian Technical and Economic Cooperation (ITEC) programme—our flagship capacity-building programme—was suspended in the first week of March 2020. The MEA commenced evacuation of ITEC participants before the imposition of the lockdown on 24 March through special relief/evacuation flights arranged by native countries for which passage was booked by Indian missions abroad. Around 1,200 ITEC trainees were evacuated during the lockdown period to their home stations. Moreover, more than five million people returned to India under the Vande Bharat Mission by March 2021.

Responding to the prime minister's outreach to SAARC countries at the onset of the outbreak of Covid-19 pandemic, the MEA nimbly strengthened its newly rolled out 'e-ITEC' platform for capacity building. Fourteen e-ITEC courses, focusing on public health and Covid-19 management, were promptly organised in the early days of the pandemic, which benefitted nearly 1,200 professionals from forty-seven countries. These courses were delivered in partnership with premier institutions like the All India Institute of Medical Sciences (AIIMS), New Delhi, and Post Graduate Institute of Medical Education & Research (PGIMER), Chandigarh. AIIMS-Bhubaneswar conducted an e-ITEC programme exclusively in Bangla language for Bangladeshi healthcare professionals. These courses were helpful in developing a robust approach in fighting the pandemic and enhanced capacity building for healthcare professionals. Apart from public health, e-ITEC courses were also organised on a wide range of subjects like traditional medicine/Ayurveda and Vipassana meditation to give a holistic approach to healthcare and well-being. The first ever defence e-ITEC course was conducted with the help of Armed Forces

Medical Services for medical officers of Cambodia, Myanmar, Lao PDR and Vietnam on the subject of management and prevention of Covid-19.

Continuing with our engagement with partner countries despite the ongoing pandemic, up to March 2021, eighty-four e-ITEC courses on diverse subjects, including big data, good governance, law, audit, finance, online teaching tools, Buddhism, sustainable housing and policing, have been conducted, in which more than 3,000 participants from nearly eighty countries have received training.

Adding to India's overall capacity building and focus on cooperation in the field of education, the MEA is also currently implementing a flagship project in tele-education and telemedicine for Africa called e-VidyaBharti and e-ArogyaBharti Project (e-VBAB). So far, seventeen African countries have signed agreements, including from the Central and West Africa region.

India has always stood in solidarity with the countries and people in the developing world, and has partnered in undertaking development, capacity-building and humanitarian assistance programmes. As part of the various phases of Mission Sagar, India is providing assistance to countries in the Indian Ocean Rim Association (IORA) and African countries to overcome natural calamities. During 2020, India provided more than 3,300 tonnes of foodgrain aid to drought and famine-affected countries like Sudan, South Sudan, Djibouti, Eritrea, Madagascar and Comoros. Human assistance and disaster relief exercises were also undertaken by the Indian Navy to provide supplies to countries like Maldives, Mauritius and Seychelles. India also responded to countries affected by other forms of natural disasters, like hurricanes (Fiji, Cambodia) and locust attacks (Iran), by prompt supply of life-support material and pesticides, respectively.

Since the outbreak of the Covid-19 pandemic, India has worked closely with the governments of more than 118 countries for evacuation/repatriation of more than 110,000 foreign nationals through special flights; assistance for medical aid has been given to more than 150 countries in the form of grants-in-aid worth Rs 100 crore to eighty-two countries and grant of clearance to commercial consignments of about 56 crore hydroxychloroquine tablets and about 154.4 crore tablets of paracetamol, when these items were restricted for export.

As the world progressed towards development of effective vaccines, Prime Minister Modi, in his virtual address to the UN General Assembly in September 2020, declared that India's vaccine production and delivery capacity will be used to help all humanity. In keeping with this commitment, India started assisting our immediate neighbours soon after commencing its own domestic vaccination programme. With the availability of emergency use authorisation (EUA) by several countries around the world, India undertook the mammoth 'Vaccine Maitri' initiative of providing made-in-India vaccines across the globe. As on March 2021, India had provided more than sixty-four million doses of indigenously produced vaccines to eighty-two countries, out of this, more than ten million doses have been provided as grants to over fifty countries.

AatmaNirbhar Bharat Initiative: Repositioning India as the 'Nerve Centre' of Global Supply Chains

In May 2020, the Government of India announced the AatmaNirbhar Bharat package—ANB 1.0). To sustain the recovery, further into the year, two more AatmaNirbhar Bharat packages—ANB 2.0 and ANB 3.0—were also rolled out. The total financial impact of all AatmaNirbhar Bharat packages, including measures taken by the Reserve Bank of India (RBI), was estimated to about Rs 27.1 lakh crore, which amounts to more than 13 per cent of the gross domestic product (GDP). There are five key pillars of this initiative—economy, infrastructure, demography, democracy and supply chains. Achieving rapid growth and development will depend on successful integration and assimilation of all these factors.

The idea of self-reliance or *Aatmanirbharta* does not mean seeking self-centred arrangements or turning the country inwards. What it aims to achieve is ensuring India's positioning as the nerve centre of the global supply chains. Through building self-sufficiency, we intend to contribute towards mitigating disruptions in global supply chains by enhancing availability of products where we have the capacity and build capacities where we have the potential to do so. The AatmaNirbhar Bharat packages have also accelerated our pace of structural reforms. Redefinition of micro, small and medium enterprises (MSMEs); commercialisation of the mineral sector; agriculture and labour reforms; privatisation of public sector undertakings (PSUs); and One Nation One Ration

Card and production-linked incentive (PLI) schemes are some of the notable reforms carried out during this period. Faceless income tax assessment, Direct Benefit Transfer (DBT) and financial inclusion are the others.

The Indian manufacturing sector, especially, has been opened up to investments in the form of finance and technology. Given the rebound in domestic demand and the promise it holds, the manufacturing sector of India is expected to fetch high returns in the future. To promote investments in the MSME sector, the Government of India has brought in several ground-breaking policy changes. Production-linked incentive (PLI) schemes, announced by the government to create manufacturing global champions for an AatmaNirbhar Bharat, have been announced for *thirteen sectors*. For this, the government has committed nearly Rs 1.97 lakh crore, over five years starting FY 2021-22. This initiative will help bring scale and size in key sectors, create and nurture global champions and provide jobs to the youth.

Besides, private sector participation has been given a big push in eight areas, including coal, minerals, defence production, civil aviation, power distribution, social infrastructure, space and atomic energy. The new public sector enterprises policy will also be a significant step in enabling private participation in a greater number of sectors. The government has also announced plans to invite private players to run trains on certain routes and modernise railway stations. These are just a few examples of opening previously restricted sectors to private participation. The government has also made access to affordable capital easier for small businesses, which are important economic engines and job creators. These reforms aim to level the field for the Indian industry, the growth of which has been hampered by complicated laws and regulations.

In order to strengthen its position as the global supplier of low-cost generic medicines and further develop the country's healthcare sector in the post-pandemic times, the Government of India has undertaken several key initiatives, which include the channelling of government resources to the healthcare sector for the development of hospitals and emergency rooms; provision of equipment and supplies (PPEs, ventilators, etc); and training of healthcare professionals. Healthcare products will be customised and standardised as per the global standards and requirements.

India will also move to strengthen its position in the pharma sector for generics, application programming interfaces (APIs), biologics, clinical research and equipment and ensure that our products meet USFDA/CE standards, just as its pharma has done with more than 125 FDA/EU certified manufacturing facilities. The Government of India is also working to facilitate a focused and concerted effort for collaborations in digital innovations in healthcare—research, diagnostics, monitoring, epidemiology and insurance—in partnership with the country's industry, MSMEs and start-ups.

The Government of India is also committed to easing the 'doing of business' ecosystem in India. To this end, the numerous labour laws have been simplified and codified into four codes; project development cells have been set up in ministries to prepare investible projects and coordinate with investors and central/state governments; incoming investments are being fast-tracked for investment clearance through the Empowered Group of Secretaries; and streamlining processes, such as granting of permits and clearance, self-certification and third party certification, have been undertaken, among others. The government is working on a mission mode on the next phase of 'ease of doing business' reforms relating to easy registration of property, fast disposal of commercial disputes and simpler tax regime for making India one of the easiest places to do business.

Sustained measures taken by the Government of India have resulted in steadily improving India's position in the World Bank's Doing Business Report rank from 142 in 2014 to 63 in 2019.

Budget 2021, announced by the finance minister in February, lays emphasis on six key pillars, including:

- Health and well-being
- Physical and financial capital and infrastructure
- Inclusive development for aspirational India
- Reinvigorating human capital
- Innovation and R&D
- Minimum government and maximum governance

A new, centrally sponsored scheme—Prime Minister Atmanirbhar Swasth Bharat Yojana (PMASBY)—is to be launched with an outlay of about Rs 64,180 crore over six years. This will develop capacities of primary, secondary and tertiary care health systems; strengthen existing national institutions; and create new institutions to cater to detection and cure of new and emerging diseases. The budget has provided Rs 35,000 crore for Covid-19 vaccine in 2021-22.

MEA's Efforts for Investment and Trade Promotion in Post-Covid-19 World

The MEA has also worked to ensure that India's development is shared with the countries in our near and extended neighbourhood. To this end, the MEA's development partnership initiatives have been strengthened and significantly expanded. Development assistance in the form of lines of credit (LOCs) is extended by the Government of India to developing countries around the world under the Indian Development and Economic Assistance Scheme (IDEAS). More than 300 LOCs worth more than US$ 30 billion have been extended to sixty-four countries in various sectors of socio-economic development. The projects under the LOCs cover critical infrastructure sectors, such as transport connectivity through railways, roads and ports; power generation and distribution; agriculture and irrigation; manufacturing industries; healthcare; education; and capacity building.

Since all such LOC projects are to be executed by Indian companies with at least 75 per cent mandatory Indian content, all these LOC funds flow back into the Indian economy and contribute towards boosting of exports of Indian goods and services, providing crucial market access to our business and industry to hitherto untapped markets and regions. These LOC projects help to successfully showcase India's expertise in project planning, design and execution, and assist the Indian industry in projecting itself as a viable and technologically sound partner of developing countries in diverse sectors. In this way, the LOCs have helped to promote 'Make in India' initiatives and also helped to promote new sectors of the Indian industry.

Continuing support to developing and least developed countries (LDCs), India pledged US$ 10 billion under LOCs, US$ 600 million as grant and 50,000 capacity-building slots for the period 2015-20 during the Third India–Africa Forum Summit. More than US$ 6.4 billion under LOCs have been committed; more than US$ 700 million have been committed as grant assistance; and 43,000 slots for training, scholarship and capacity building have been utilised.

The MEA is also working in collaboration with Indian missions abroad to chalk out a detailed strategy to increase exports of goods and services. The ministry is working to identify the areas and countries where Indian manufacturers have the potential to emerge as the low-cost preferred alternative for imports. Missions have been working to promote India's image as a safe and reliable destination where all investment related requirements can be facilitated for the manufacturing units planning to shift their base to India in the post-Covid-19 situation.

Missions are providing detailed inputs on the non-tariff barriers being faced by Indian exporters in their respective countries of accreditation. The MEA, in collaboration with the missions, is also working to identify newer lines of goods and services, as well as new destinations where India's exports can be enhanced. Since the Covid-19 pandemic has brought the possibilities of a physical conduct of trade fairs and buyer-seller meets to a halt, missions are working to devise effective marketing and promotion strategies which can be carried out digitally. Online B2B and B2C meetings between Indian trade chambers and local trade bodies is a part of the agenda.

In order to identify and plug in the immediate gaps in the global supply chains, missions, in collaboration with the MEA and the Department for Promotion of Industry and Internal Trade (DPIIT), are already in the process of exploring sourcing and export opportunities in various countries and guiding our exporters by putting potential suppliers and buyers in touch with our engineering, procurement and construction companies (EPCs) and industry and facilitate B2B meetings for them. The EPCs/industry bodies are being put in touch with the missions directly, seeking B2B meetings to hedge the risks of supplies disruptions and, wherever possible, fill in the supply gaps. Support of industry is also being sought as the administrative department for certain product groups, in expeditiously reaching out to their industry stakeholders and ramp up production in areas where India needed to fill in supply gaps both in new markets and the existing ones. To this end, India has also been instrumental in the post-pandemic economic recovery, by moving quickly to restore supply chain connectivity and resilience, especially for medical supplies, food and essential commodities.

Additionally, the MEA is working in close collaboration with the concerned line ministries for expanding India's agri-exports to countries. For this, the Government of India has developed 'country-specific export strategies'. Enhancing agri-exports and food processing will be one the government's primary areas of focus in the near future. The MEA is collaborating extensively with regional groupings, such as Brazil, Russia, India, China, and South Africa (BRICS); G20; and the European Union (EU) in areas such as space, digital/cyber cooperation, mobility and migration, renewable energy, fintech, science and technology, among other issues.

The MEA has been working in collaboration with the missions to promote the 3Ts—Trade, Tourism and Technology—into India. Missions are being encouraged to focus on the various aspects of India's commercial and economic priorities in their outreach efforts.

Conclusion

The global fight against Covid-19 continues well into 2021. However, with the Government of India's timely and well-executed initiatives, India is on a path to recovery, which promises to position it as the future nerve centre of global supply and value chains. The changing contours of political, economic and strategic relations in the post-Covid-19 world offer India with a plethora of opportunities to contribute to global revival through its knowledge, expertise and, most importantly, resilience.

CHAPTER 4

INDIA–SRI LANKA RELATIONS IN THE POST-COVID-19 ERA

RANJAN MATHAI

Analysts tell us that we live in an era of populist identity politics and nationalism that gathered pace in the post-Cold War period, when ideological competition gave way to the 'clash of civilisations'. Sri Lanka has actually experienced polarising identity politics and civilisational discord since at least 1956, though it was the most advanced country in South Asia in human development rankings. India, as a giant neighbour, has, since the 1980s, loomed larger than earlier as a factor in the identity politics of the island, as civil discord descended into civil war. That adds to the complexity of managing relations with this neighbour, whose location off our southern coast, and placed centrally along sea lanes in the Indian Ocean, gives it great strategic importance.

The relationship between Sri Lanka and India is one of the most ancient of any two nations in the world. The stories of the migration of the Sinhala people from India's eastern seaboard, and the missionary activity by which Mahinda and Sanghamitta—Emperor Ashoka's son and daughter—carried the Buddha dhamma to Sri Lanka have been extensively written about. The ancient history of the Sri Lanka Tamils is also reasonably documented. Less known in India is the way the Sinhala people's sense of distinctiveness from the rest of the subcontinent developed, as also their unbroken civilisational consciousness over the centuries. In 1837, when George Turnour of the Ceylon Civil Service provided James Prinsep a clue to the identity of Ashoka, he was reading from the *Dipavamsa*, which was in Pali and quite accessible to scholars on the island; whereas the latter was cracking the code of the Brahmi script—long forgotten in India—and with it, much knowledge of our ancient history.

Indian understanding of Sri Lanka's historical evolution also misses out on the extent to which the decline in Buddhism in India added to the distinctiveness of the Sinhala identity, as the external orientation of traditional religious leadership on the island veered towards the wider Buddhist world. In the eighteenth century, when the Buddhist clergy began the process of revival and reform, some turned to Thailand and others to Burma for guidance, and then set up the dominant schools—the Siama and Amarapura Nikayas, respectively—whose members were drawn from dominant castes which are unique to the island. 'Sinhala Buddhism', as it has come to be known, underpins the deep-rooted sense of identity among the Sinhala people, despite four centuries of adaptation to Western rule—including adoption of European names on a scale unimaginable in India—which drives the politics of majoritarianism seen over the last six decades. In 1978, while a very junior representative of India in Colombo, I was cautioned by an older and wiser Sri Lankan friend (whose family was linked to the lay custodian of the sacred Dalada Maligawa temple) to see through the superficiality of the manifestations of blended culture and way of life in the capital—'like in a West Indian island', he muttered.

The pioneering work of Anagarika Dharmapala, who built the Mahabodhi Society in India at the end of the nineteenth century did not quite renew the Buddhist connection between our countries. Rebuilding India's civilisational linkages with Sri Lanka has been a work in progress since the independence of both countries, despite Prime Minister Jawaharlal Nehru's profound attachment to the insights of Buddhist teachings, and every government's patronage of cultural exchanges. Prime Minister Narendra Modi's meetings with members of the Sangha in Colombo in 2015 and 2017, and his attendance at the International Vesak Day celebrations are initiatives we must build on. The Mulagandha Kuti Vihara in Sanchi and other heritage sites can be used to build institutional ties with the Sinhala Buddhist clergy. Studies of Sri Lankan culture and civilisation (rather than only Indo-Sri Lanka relations) in universities and think tanks in India would also be useful in the post-Covid-19 decade ahead.

The excursion into the history of religion and identity should, however, not distract us from the realpolitik world of foreign policy and its requirements. As recurrent tensions in relations show, cultural diplomacy can help, but will always yield to temporal consideration of national interest as defined by rulers at any given point of time. The strategic importance of Sri Lanka's geographical location makes it a permanent factor in India's security calculations. And the geopolitical reality of India's size and proximity is even more true for Sri Lanka. Both of us, however committed to the spiritual ties that bind us, understand what Cardinal Richelieu, the French clergyman and political leader, is reported to have said: 'Man is immortal; his salvation is hereafter. The state has no immortality, its salvation is now or never.' Covid-19 has highlighted man's mortality, but in the post-Covid-19 world we will have to work for man and state.

Indian security planners recognise that any inimical forces acquiring a strategic presence in Sri Lanka would pose a serious threat to India. While in times past we worried about the VOA and possible US naval presence in Trincomalee, currently, the focus is on China's demonstrable hostility to India, which makes its presence in Sri Lanka, and its activities with security implications for us—all matters of serious concern. Trincomalee, which is one of the world's great natural harbours, has figured in India's history more than is generally known. The British probably were covering up imperial greed when they claimed that they seized it from the Dutch in 1796, as the latter could not guarantee keeping it out of the hands of the French, who were again threatening their control over peninsular India. But, they then used it as one in a chain of bases that kept the Indian Ocean a British lake to secure their Indian empire for over a century. When Japanese Admiral Chuichi Nagumo raided Colombo and Trincomalee in 1942, and sent the British Eastern Fleet scuttling all the way to East Africa, it was a time of major crisis for British India. Only Nagumo's return to the Pacific for the Battle of Midway, where he lost his carriers, averted what Winston Churchill called 'the most dangerous moment' for his country in World War II. Post-independence Sri Lankan leaders, DS Senanayake and Sir John Kotelawala, retained a British military base in Trincomalee till 1956, but this was not a real security concern for India. Thereafter, the policy of non-alignment followed by successive Sri Lankan governments kept the issue of foreign security presence on the island dormant, despite occasional worries about US interest in the old British oil tank farms in Trincomalee, VOA stations, etc.

The expanding activity of China's People's Liberation Army (PLA) Navy in the Indian Ocean since 2008 has created new strategic realities for India to contend with. The Chinese lodgement in Hambantota Port, their stake in the Colombo International Container Terminal—which handles 70 per cent of India's international container traffic—and port visits by Chinese vessels have created legitimate concerns for India in view of China's overweening Maritime Silk Road strategy and its hostility towards India. It would be necessary to maintain regular and frank strategic dialogues with President Gotabaya Rajapaksa and Prime Minister Mahinda Rajapaksa on India's concerns. This will have to be combined with keeping up the close ties between our military forces, of exercises, training and dialogues, and continued intelligence sharing to counter terrorist and other threats. Sri Lanka would not want to get drawn directly into the rivalry between the US and Chinese navies, and has shown wariness about the Quad, which links the United States, Japan, Australia and India. We should prioritise bilateral security cooperation between the Indian and Sri Lankan navies, extending it to trilateral cooperation with the Maldivian forces, including operations on maritime domain awareness, and humanitarian assistance and disaster response (HADR).

Sri Lankan security planners have also not hidden their concern at the prospect of Indian dominance of the Indian Ocean. Security, therefore, has to be woven into a broader framework of maritime cooperation involving not just the navies of both countries, but also the Sagarmala projects, increased use of coastal shipping for moving goods between ports on both sides of the Indian peninsula, and endeavours to harness the blue economy potential of the ocean that links us so closely. The problem of clashes over our fishing trawlers in the Palk Bay has to be converted into an opportunity of cooperation in deep sea fishing. Presently, illegal, unregulated and unreported (IUU) fishing in the exclusive economic zones (EEZs) of both countries—Chinese vessels are reported to be particularly active—pose a threat to the sustainability of both our fisheries.

In responding to the Chinese challenge, we also need to be able to reckon with a phenomenon which Sri Lanka, despite having been an arena of propaganda competitions during the Cold War, did not have to contend with earlier. That is the Chinese Communist Party's insidious and unprecedented 'United Work Front' activity. Earlier, this was used to keep friends in the political leadership, and their families, well supplied and regularly exposed to China through sponsored visits. Now, the emphasis is on influencing national narratives through claims about China's Buddhist legacy and ancient historical linkages (Zheng He et al) and targeting of a new class of young professionals, thought leaders and the media on the inevitability, and benign 'win-win', consequences of China's ascendancy.

To get the Sri Lanka political leadership to keep India's security interests in mind in the post-Covid-19 era, it is necessary to factor in their concerns and interests, whether it is keeping their grip on political popularity, stepping up economic growth and employment or retaining room for manoeuvre in a global order in flux. It bears recalling that in 1952, when the Cold War was raging, the conservative, pro-Western leaders in Colombo entered into the famous 'Rubber-Rice' barter deal with China, even risking loss of US aid at the time. Chinese rice was needed to deal with domestic shortages and expand the popular public distribution schemes of the government; Sri Lanka's rubber got a premium price. So, Sri Lanka forfeited some Western goodwill, but went ahead in an act of independently-minded pragmatic politics, which stood the country in good stead for over a decade. China's standing in the country, thus, predates their current influence-buying operations. But the traditional pragmatism in Sri Lanka's calculations and their independent-mindedness still exists, and must inform our policies. Sri Lankan leaders would be aware of the risks to themselves in the sharpening of China–US competition, and, counter-intuitively, this may give us some options. Despite the setback over the cancellation by Sri Lanka of the pact to operate the East Coast Terminal (ECT), we can continue partnership with Japan on expanding economic opportunities for Sri Lanka.

India cannot avoid involvement in trying to facilitate a peaceful settlement of the Sri Lanka Tamil issue. In doing so, we are faced by the twin problems of general consensus among the Sinhala leaders that devolution of power by implementing the thirteenth Amendment is too difficult politically—and not worth a sustained effort—and the lack of democratically empowered Tamil leaders to negotiate effectively. On the Sinhala side, there is a myopic assumption that, having dealt with the threat of the Liberation Tigers of Tamil Eelam (LTTE), the problem of dealing with Tamil aspirations can be ignored or postponed indefinitely. The militarisation of a once peaceful society, and destruction of civil society institutions, which worried JR Jayewardene, does not seem to concern the present political establishment. (There have also been caustic comments asking how India can espouse devolution abroad when the present Government of India is diminishing the federal authority of Indian states through legislative and administrative encroachment.) On the Tamil side, a generation of elected leaders who carried some weight both in Colombo and Jaffna was decimated by the LTTE, and has not been adequately replaced. Indian policy will have to walk a tightrope between being seen as interfering in a sensitive issue in Sri Lanka's domestic political arrangements and neglecting sentiment in a key state of India. Serious negotiations could help reduce the salience of the issue for domestic politics in India; and we should encourage emerging Tamil political leaders to work towards incrementally changing the status quo through patient and practical negotiations. In India, we also need, someday, to analyse how the LTTE's version of the Sri Lanka Tamil cause came to get a grip on Tamil Nadu's political imagination. Historically, the Jaffna Tamil elites distanced their destiny from that of their counterparts in India, and they were complicit in Sri Lanka passing legislation in 1948, which disenfranchised Indian-origin Tamils in the island. The latter were India's main concern for three decades after independence. It was, of course, the Jaffna Tamil elites who articulated and led the long democratic struggle for autonomy, but they were eliminated—along with much of the Tamil civil society—by the depredations of the LTTE in the longer years of civil war after 1983. Yet, the networks of Sri Lanka Tamil diaspora lobbies, mainly in Western countries, seem to have acquired great influence in media and thought leadership in parts of our country, and projected the LTTE as the 'sole representative voice' of Tamil nationalism.

It should be understood that involvement on the Sri Lanka Tamil issue carries political costs only for India, among all of Sri Lanka's external interlocutors. Voting patterns on United Nations Commission on Human Rights resolutions on Sri Lanka make hardly any difference to public opinion about relations with the Western countries which generate these resolutions, but, they do generate negative reactions against India. A calibrated policy to support gradual movement forward on reconciliation without appearing to interfere in the domestic politics of the country is the only way to make progress. Quiet diplomacy will be required, along with steps which can build confidence in India's ability to be a net security provider to the country, transcending political considerations. The gift of vaccines has been a useful start. Working together on planning to cope with future emergencies, projects under the Coalition for Disaster Resilient Infrastructure, cybersecurity, oceanography using space applications and tackling other cross-border threats are areas in which institutionalised cooperation should be pursued.

Helping Sri Lanka cope with looming challenges posed by Colombo's exposure to foreign debt may also be necessary. In the aftermath of the victorious war against the LTTE, Sri Lanka stepped up its borrowings from international capital markets substantially. So much so that between 2006 and 2020, commercial loans increased from less than 10 per cent to 56 per cent of total foreign debt (Sri Lanka Central Bank data). The borrowings enabled successive governments to continue populist economic policies without tackling structural weaknesses in the economy. Facing a balance of payments crisis in 2015, Sri Lanka obtained an Extended Fund Facility of US$ 1.5 billion from the International Monetary Fund (IMF). In 2021, and years ahead, with large debt repayments due, Sri Lanka's ability to raise resources will be tested. It does not wish to resort to the IMF again and face conditionalities it views as Western impositions. It has used a currency swap facility from India, and is reported to be seeking another; just as it has sought additional financial assistance from China. With trade stagnant and tourist earnings hit by the Covid-19 pandemic, Colombo has resorted to import restrictions, which provide temporary relief, but it will need assistance to stabilise its external balances, and it would be in our self-interest to be part of the solution.

Trade is vital for Sri Lanka's economy—its contribution to the gross domestic product (GDP) has ranged from 55 per cent to 80 per cent since the 1960s. Commercial ties will, therefore, be critically important as post-Covid-19 recovery gets under way. Sri Lanka is one of India's largest trading partners in South Asia; and for the island nation, India is the largest source of imports and third largest destination for exports (after the US and European Union [EU]). Since the India–Sri Lanka Free Trade Agreement (ISFTA) in 2000, trade grew rapidly to almost US$ 5 billion annually, with India exporting 4.1 billion and importing 750 million in 2018. China rivals India as an exporter to Sri Lanka, but lags far behind as an importer. While trade-enhancing measures can be implemented by both sides, in the short term, Sri Lanka's foreign exchange constraints will act as a limitation. Investments from India and joint ventures, which can expand Sri Lanka's exports, need to be kept in focus. There could be opportunities in sectors where investors are shifting production away from China, as well as in the emphasis being placed on security and diversification of supply chains by major economies of the world. Just as we did with tariffs, India should unilaterally make mobility for Sri Lankan professionals easier, give incentives for investment in manufacturing and trade services and respond to Sri Lankan representations on non-tariff barriers believed to be limiting their exports to India. Proposals for economic and technology co-operation agreement (ETCA) or comprehensive economic partnership agreement (CEPA) between the two countries should be taken up again thereafter.

Cooperation on development of energy sources also holds out promise. The major hydropower projects built under the (Western funded) Accelerated Mahaweli Development Program of the 1980s, provide Sri Lanka an impressive 35 per cent of its power requirements, but the country faces challenges in scaling up energy production to meet growing demand in an increasingly urbanised middle-income economy. Heavy imports of coal and oil, including refined products, are not only a burden on the balance of payments, but also a vulnerability from the perspective of energy security. While Sri Lanka has not succeeded in finding commercial quantities of oil so far, the region offshore Mannar should remain an area for active exploration either through incentives to private players or as a joint venture between our public sector companies. The potential cannot be ignored, particularly in view of resources uncovered across the Indian Ocean. Sri Lanka has considerable potential for both solar and wind energy which has been slow to develop; and the national policy ambition of generating 80 per cent of power from renewable sources by 2030 is nowhere near achievement. The target would call for all renewable energy sources to raise their contribution to total power generation from 45 per cent to 80 per cent. As mentioned earlier, large hydro already generates 35 per cent of power and ramping it up further carries too many environmental and financial costs. Wind and solar, therefore, have to scale up from 4 per cent to around 30 per cent if Sri Lanka is to meet its commitments under the Paris Agreement and achieve macroeconomic and security benefits. India has rapidly expanded its solar and wind energy industries, and has provided concessional finance to rooftop solar installations in Sri Lanka. Credits and grants for larger renewable power projects could be considered for the future. As Sri Lanka develops a path towards energy security, the schemes for connecting the Indian and Sri Lankan grids would be seen as viable projects.

The global growth of renewable energy will also raise the criticality of a number of minerals used in the catalysts, permanent magnets, electrodes, special materials, etc. necessary to convert solar and wind energy into electricity. Like India, Sri Lanka could benefit from the world's growing need to diversify its supply chains for critical minerals. Sri Lanka is the source of the purest graphite found in the world; and cooperation on geological surveys on other critical minerals should be looked at. Sri Lanka's beach sands hold substantial potential for rare earth elements. China dominates world production of rare earths and, along with other countries, has shown interest in Sri Lanka's resources. India has experience in the extraction and processing of rare earths and should keep open avenues for cooperation with Sri Lanka

Finally, the future of India's development assistance should be reviewed. As a middle-income country, Sri Lanka's needs are sector-specific. Once our existing commitments on housing, transportation, etc. focused on communities in the north/east and in the south are completed, India could propose schemes like the Rural Technology Action Group Technical programme shared with Bangladesh, which offers new technologies in food processing, aquaculture, environment, textiles, etc to start-ups, non-governmental organisations (NGOs) and small and medium size enterprises (SMEs). Cooperation which brings Sri Lanka's millennials into its orbit, with support for innovation and creative industries, would be beneficial. Traditional development funding should focus on improving the living conditions of the Tamils of Indian origin and enabling them to break out of the confines of tea plantation labour lines to a more inclusive role in Sri Lankan national life. The poor indentured labourers from the Pallar and Sakkiliyar communities from some of the (then) poorest regions of India, helped build the tea-based prosperity of Sri Lanka 150 years ago. After the British left, they were treated as the 'debris of departing empires' in the words of our high commissioner, Thomas Abraham. India would be fulfilling a historic responsibility, as well as creating new avenues for India–Sri Lanka amity, by assisting them more in the post-Covid-19 world.

CHAPTER 5

INDIA–AFGHANISTAN RELATIONS

JAYANT PRASAD

Peace and stability in Afghanistan is the greatest single global security challenge today. The Taliban stormed into Kabul on 15 August 2021 in a stunning campaign in which it took all the thirty-four Afghan provinces, except for Panjshir (which also fell later), starting from Nimroz on 6 August. The US prevarication in the face of the growing ubiquity of the Taliban in Afghanistan and its failure to deal with Pakistan's equivocation has demoralised Afghan patriots and republicans and encouraged the armed opposition (the Taliban and associated terrorist networks). There is a flight of talent and capital from the country; a shrinkage of external assistance and investments; and a collapse of construction, logistics and transportation. Ironically, foreign forces were deployed in Afghanistan on the grounds of both counterterrorism and promoting democracy and human rights. Now, the United States, which spearheaded the deposition of the Taliban government in 2001, has completely forsaken its support for the Afghan people's democratic aspiration.

THE DOHA AGREEMENT

The prime purpose of the February 2020 Doha Agreement was to secure the complete withdrawal of US forces from Afghanistan. It was entitled 'The Agreement to Bring Peace to Afghanistan'. The Taliban's head, Mawlawi Hibatullah Akhundzada, instead described it as the 'Termination of Occupation Agreement'. The agreement neither ensured a ceasefire nor a political process of peace and reconciliation. It was meant to trigger intra-Afghan negotiations, which began in Doha in September 2020, six months behind schedule, and remained virtually stalled since. For the Taliban, the next stage objective was to remove what it described as the puppet regime of collaborators of the foreign forces and restitute Taliban rule. Since the forcible end of the 'Emirate' in Afghanistan in 2001, the important obligations for all Afghans were to defeat and expel the foreign forces and to re-establish the 'Emirate'.[1]

The United States ran out of patience and embraced an exit strategy, which Henry Kissinger famously described earlier as all about exit and not at all about strategy. This abject exit is likely to be a catastrophe for Afghanistan, for the region and the world. India cannot have an exit strategy—it has to necessarily remain engaged with Afghanistan, secure its interests, and extend support and solidarity to its people.

The US troops began to thin out within weeks of the conclusion of the Doha Agreement. One of the first places from where the US military withdrew was in Gardez, Paktia, compromising the security of the region. The outcome was a spike in killings, a growing area of control under the Taliban and greater collection of taxes by it and dramatically reduced intelligence inputs for the Afghan defenders.

Even though the Afghan National Defense and Security Forces were inadequately equipped, while withdrawing, the US forces carted off most of their weapons and supplies. With the US troops gone completely, the Afghan forces collapsed in a very short period, bereft of supply lines, air support, aerial reconnaissance, medevac and ammunition. The cost of deploying a single US soldier is between half a million to 750 million dollars, not counting the cost of logistics and munitions. A small proportion of what the United States had been spending in Afghanistan could have gone a long way in equipping the Afghan Army effectively.

The United States brought down its troops' level and pressured the Afghan government to release 5,000 plus Taliban prisoners, a significant proportion of whom joined the Taliban fighting force. In contrast, according to the former chairman of the Joint Chiefs of Staff, General Joseph Dunford, the Taliban has failed to meet the conditions of the agreement.[2] It has neither reduced violence nor moved towards a ceasefire. It did not sever its ties with al-Qaeda (AQ). Neither did it earnestly engage in the intra-Afghan negotiations. The head of the US Army Central Command, General Kenneth McKenzie, held the Taliban responsible for countrywide attacks on Afghan security forces and targeted assassinations in Afghan cities while sparing US and North Atlantic Treaty Organization (NATO) troops.[3]

The Joe Biden administration first maintained that the Taliban had not held up its part of the bargain made under the Doha Agreement. The White House Press Secretary Jen Psaki said that Biden would not be okay if the Taliban ruled Afghanistan.[4] Although the Biden administration was dissatisfied with the Doha Agreement and President Biden himself promised that the US forces would be withdrawn from Afghanistan in a responsible, deliberate and safe way, contrary to this, the US forces numbering just over 2,500 were pulled out of the Bagram airbase on the night of 1 July, along with about 17,000 US contractors, without as much as informing the new Afghan commander of the base, who discovered that the Americans had left only at daybreak. With the maintenance contractors gone, the helicopters and aircraft given to the Afghan Army were grounded.

The American strategy in Afghanistan remains practically the same across three presidencies, starting with President Obama—*plus ça change, plus c'est la même chose*. While announcing an additional deployment of 30,000 US troops on 1 December 2009, in the same breath, startlingly, Obama prescribed the deadline of July 2011 to begin the transfer of US forces out of Afghanistan.[5] The then Secretary of Defence, Robert Gates, elaborated the fine print of Obama's policy as reversing the Taliban momentum—different from defeating it—and degrading the Taliban to levels manageable by the Afghans.[6] President Obama also conveyed categorically to the Afghan leadership that fighting the Taliban was no longer the responsibility of the United States. US troops had ceased combat operations in 2014. President Trump accelerated the withdrawal process by backing the Doha talks without seeking any guarantees of the Taliban's good behaviour. President Biden only delivered the coup de grâce.

In early March 2021, the US Secretary of State, Antony Blinken, wrote a bluntly worded letter to President Ashraf Ghani that the United States envisages an 'inclusive' government in Afghanistan that will allow the Taliban a 50 per cent share in power.[7] The blueprint for the interim arrangements being discussed by the US Special Representative, Zalmay Khalilzad, envisages an executive, a *shura*, a High Council for Islamic Jurisprudence and a commission to prepare a new constitution, to be followed by 'free and fair' elections. It is difficult to conceive how the Taliban could be persuaded to opt for any elections. In its anxiety to extricate itself from Afghanistan, the United States unwittingly delegitimised the Afghan government by blindsiding it while directly striking a deal with the Taliban. The absence of any compliance mechanism in the Doha Agreement reduced the salience of the few, feeble Taliban commitments.

Since the setting up of the Peshawar-based seven-party alliance government in Kabul in 1992, the establishment of the Islamic Emirate in 1996 and the ouster of the Taliban government in 2001, Pakistan and the United States have played a dominant role in Afghanistan. All other countries, China, Russia, Iran and India included, have a peripheral role, as do Afghanistan's three northern neighbours—Turkmenistan, Uzbekistan and Tajikistan. Post-2001, Pakistan acted as both the firefighter and incendiarist. While assisting the United States, it sheltered the AQ and Taliban leadership and nurtured the bruised Taliban back into a formidable fighting force. At the end of 2001, the leading cadres of both the Taliban and AQ had fled, and it was expected that Pakistan would take care of them. Afghanistan is reaping the consequences of this initial neglect.

In a testimony to the US Congress, the then Chairman of the Joint Chiefs of Staff, Admiral Mike Mullen, underlined that Afghanistan could not be referenced without 'speaking of Pakistan', and that insurgency 'inextricably linked' the two countries.[8] In return for its help in bringing the Taliban to the peace process, Pakistan has been pressing for the recognition of its 'legitimate' strategic interest in shaping the contours of the end-state in Afghanistan, including a lower Indian profile there. Replying to a question on Pakistan seeking to link its cooperation to scaling down India's presence in Afghanistan, a former US national security adviser said: 'You could be handing out free ice cream there and Pakistan would consider it nefarious.'[9]

India's Engagement in Afghanistan

India was in Afghanistan for the same reasons as the rest of the international community—to prevent it from becoming a safe haven for terrorists. When US cruise missiles came down on an al-Qaeda camp near Khost to target Osama bin Laden in 1998, those killed were not Arabs and Afghans, but Pakistan Army personnel and terrorists being trained to fight in Jammu and Kashmir. So, India has a vital stake in Afghanistan's stabilisation.

India's contribution to Afghanistan's reconstruction has many success stories, sometimes underplayed due to the haze of war and the prevailing mood of doom and gloom. India has connected Afghanistan's ring road, from the midpoint of Kandahar and Herat, at Delaram, to southern Iran. Kabul, called 'the capital of darkness', now has a 24-hour Uzbek electricity supply, carried on transmission lines that India has built, along with the largest substation in Afghanistan, just north of Kabul. The Afghan parliament and the Friendship Dam on the Hari Rud River were also built by India.

India's expanding partnership covers all parts of Afghanistan and the entire gamut of development activities—from toilets to transmission lines. These activities span the areas of humanitarian assistance, infrastructure projects, quick gestation small development projects and capacity building and skills development.

India's greatest emphasis has been on human resource development, predicated on the belief that only the Afghans can take care of Afghanistan. India has the largest programme in Afghanistan to train Afghan public servants abroad in specialised institutions—in the same institutions where Indian public servants are trained—and the largest university scholarship programme in Afghanistan, enabling its students to pursue undergraduate and postgraduate studies in India. India's unique selling proposition is building institutions and developing human resources—training Afghan public officials, including from the Election Commission, the Public Service Commission, the Presidency, and Parliament, and India's massive scholarship programme has begun to provide the country with a new generation of educated and skilled workforce.

A Regional Approach to Afghanistan

There has been a greater emphasis on possible regional approaches or regional solutions to the conflict in Afghanistan in recent years. A Regional Economic Cooperation Conference on Afghanistan process started in Kabul as early as December 2005, but with little to show by way of positive outcomes. Afghanistan's membership of the South Asian Association for Regional Cooperation (SAARC) at the New Delhi Summit in 2007 made the association's boundaries contiguous to Iran and Central Asia. The 1998 SAARC Group of Eminent Persons had proposed an Economic Union by the year 2020. The organisation is well short of this lofty goal. The Afghanistan-centred Heart of Asia–Istanbul process, launched by Afghanistan and Turkey, began in November 2011 to promote dialogue and confidence-building measures, has had equally unsatisfactory results.

It is tempting to pursue the idea of Afghanistan's neutrality in conjunction with a regional solution. The Afghans themselves dislike the notion of neutrality or any solution that is imposed on them from the outside. Though attractive to some of Afghanistan's neighbours, the idea must be evaluated in the context of the ascendancy of the Taliban, supported by Pakistan. The concept of neutrality is best suited to a country that is least dependent on external assistance. Afghanistan has a long way to go before it stands on its own feet. Moreover, neutrality entails non-interference—difficult to conceive of in the present circumstances. Neutrality strengthens the idea of demilitarisation, an idea mooted in 2010 by the International Security Assistance Force that was strongly rejected by the then Afghan government on the ground that this would provide a de facto control over the area to Pakistan.

A possible regional solution could be for a group of regional countries, plus the United States and the Russian Federation, committing to protect and guarantee a united, secure, sovereign and pluralist Afghan state. In theory, all regional countries would have a stake in such a solution. Afghanistan's unravelling could undermine Pakistan's political order, presenting a security nightmare for India. Iran, as a Shiite country, cannot countenance Wahabi fundamentalism in its neighbourhood. China, too, cannot be unaffected by the free reign for Islamist terrorists that could link up with disaffected Uighurs. And the three northern countries—Turkmenistan, Uzbekistan and Tajikistan—want peace and stability in Afghanistan to contain the flow of narcotics and terrorism into their territories.

Iran is concerned by its existential struggle against the West. While it views the Taliban as surrogates of Pakistan that could threaten both Iranian interests and those of the Shia community within Afghanistan, it believes that US presence in the country is a bigger threat to Iran than the Taliban. Russia and China, too, wary of NATO's long-term presence in the region, prefer the Taliban. Press reports, sourcing their story from CNN's coverage that cited US intelligence, spoke of China paying bounties for the killing of US soldiers in Afghanistan.[10] China defers to Pakistan in its approach towards Afghanistan, though it is apprehensive about the presence of Uighur militants of the East

Turkestan Islamic Movement in Afghanistan and has even placed its intelligence personnel there. In December 2020, according to its chief, the National Directorate of Security unearthed Chinese spies and arrested and charged ten Chinese nationals for espionage.[11]

Among the more distant countries, only Turkey is taking a greater interest in Afghanistan for projecting a more active foreign policy profile as a problem-solver in the Islamic world. The Saudis, despite some low-level contacts with the Quetta Shura leadership, are reticent about brokering a peace deal, which they have left largely to Pakistan.

A regional solution looks like a non-starter for now. One of its essential prerequisites is intra-regional traction, presently absent. An added problem is that some of Afghanistan's neighbours continue to be a source of the current problems of Afghanistan. Finally, for the regional solution to succeed, Iran has to be persuaded to more constructively engage in the future of Afghanistan, and India must be more involved.

Looking Ahead

The long-term challenge is to make Afghan security and development sustainable even under the present trying circumstances. Afghanistan will be secure if the infrastructure of terrorism in its border regions were to be dismantled. There has never been a truly successful counter-insurgency or counterterrorism operation anywhere in the world so long as support, sustenance, safe havens and sanctuaries are available in the contiguity. The Taliban regime will have to deliver on its promise not to harbour terrorists that act against the interest of other countries. It will also have to respect human rights and form an inclusive government, as it has promised.

Ideally, the Taliban should be persuaded to stand down its fighters for the sake of lasting peace and reconciliation, as happened in Tajikistan and Nepal. In Tajikistan, some 6,000 cadres of the Islamic Renaissance Party (IRP) were absorbed in the armed forces of Tajikistan, and well under 1,000 Maoist combatants of the People's Liberation Army were integrated into the Nepal Army. The Islamic Renaissance Party's leaders were co-opted into the Tajik government. Under the November 2005 12-point understanding, arrived at in New Delhi, seven democratic political parties of Nepal and the Nepal Communist Party (Maoists) decided to establish permanent peace and resolve the armed conflict through an inclusive and democratic restructuring of the state—by agreeing to full democracy, bringing the autocratic monarchy to an end, forming an interim government and holding elections of a constituent assembly.[12]

India signalled its readiness to engage with the Taliban when India's minister for external affairs participated in the inaugural of the intra-Afghan negotiations in Doha. This underlined that India has no reservations in interacting with the Taliban.

Instead of disengaging from Afghanistan, India must persevere with an outlook of the longue durée; patience, perseverance and a durable commitment to the Afghan people. India should contribute to enabling an environment in which the gains made in Afghanistan over the past two decades are not reversed. The international community should consider supporting, not abandoning, Afghanistan, which should neither be partitioned nor handed over to those not accountable to the Afghan people. No single power or group of outside powers should have exclusive or extraterritorial rights, defined in terms of a veto over decisions that Afghans themselves must make, particularly about the type of relations they would like to maintain with any other country or countries.

For Afghanistan's neighbours, the country should cease to be a source of terrorism and narcotics. Instead, it could become a trade, transportation, energy and mineral hub in the region. It could become the crossroads of Asia, linking Iran and Central Asia to China and the Indian subcontinent, as it has been through history.

And, in the area of development, we should forget the notion that development can be brought in from the outside. All the audits point to the fact that the contractors' profits and consultants' fees had soaked up a substantial part of international assistance from the Western countries. Now that the Taliban is in control, the international community's objective should be to secure desirable outcomes, without tangling with processes other than ensuring that the new dispensation acts with moderation and in the interest of the Afghan people. India and the international community must find ways to pursue a differentiated strategy—containing support to terrorist groups and continuing to assist in the development of the country.

The effort to arrive at an inclusive government must carry on. While this must be largely an intra-Afghan process, members of the international community, including India, must encourage and support the process. It should proceed based on the renunciation of violence; inclusiveness; commitment to human rights, democracy and pluralism; and ending ideological and organisational links with terrorist organisations. As Rumi, the great Afghan Sufi sage said in his *Masnawi* over 800 years ago: 'Believe in God, yet tie the camel's leg.'

Endnotes

1. Interview with Zabihullah Mujahid, 24 October 2020, Al-Emarah, http://alemarahenglish. Accessed on 15 March 2021.
2. Hearing on 19 February 2021, on 'A Pathway for Peace in Afghanistan: Examining the Findings and Recommendations of the Afghanistan Study Group'. https://www.congress.gov/117/crec/2021/02/19/CREC-2021-02-19.pdf (accessed on 18 March 2021). Also, see https://timesofindia.indiatimes.com/world/us/joe-biden-would-not-be-okay-if-the-taliban-ruled-afghanistan-white-house/articleshow/81186086.cms. Accessed on 18 March 2021.
3. AFP, 'Taliban "Clearly" Behind Violence in Afghanistan: US'. https://www.barrons.com/news/taliban-clearly-behind-violence-in-afghanistan-us-01613695806. Accessed on 30 March 2021.
4. Press briefing by Press Secretary Jen Psaki. https://www.whitehouse.gov/briefing-room/press-briefings/2021/02/23/press-briefing-by-press-secretary-jen-psaki-february-23-2021/. Accessed on 18 March 2021.
5. 'The New Way Forward - The President's Address', https://obamawhitehouse.archives.gov/blog/2009/12/01/new-way-forward-presidents-address. Accessed on 30 March 2021.
6. See Bob Woodward, *Obama's Wars*, Simon and Schuster, New York, 2010. See also Robert Gates, 'On Afghanistan, Obama was caught between his generals' advice and his advisers' political worries', *The Washington Post*, 14 January 2014. https://www.wsj.com/articles/SB10001424052702303848104579310772780856370. Accessed on 30 March 2021.
7. 'Blinken Threatens May 1 Afghan Troop Withdrawal'. https://foreignpolicy.com/2021/03/08/afghanistan-letter-blinken-ghani/. Accessed on 31 March 2021.
8. See 'Admiral: Troops alone will not yield victory in Afghanistan', http://edition.cnn.com/2008/POLITICS/09/10/mullen.afghanistan/. Accessed on 30 March 2021.
9. Jim Jones to a group of Indians, including the author, Washington, DC, 3 August 2010.
10. CNN coverage of 31 December 2020, https://asiatimes.com/2021/01/why-china-fears-us-withdrawal-from-afghanistan/. Accessed on 30 March 2021.
11. Reuters, 'China "unaware" of any Afghan deportation of Chinese on spying charges', https://www.reuters.com/article/us-afghanistan-china-arrests-idUSKBN29C25U. Accessed on 31 March 2021.
12. '12-Point Understanding between the Seven Political Parties and Nepal Communist Party (Maoists)', https://peacemaker.un.org/nepal-12pointunderstanding2005. Accessed on 31 March 2021.

CHAPTER 6

INDIA AND PAKISTAN: CONTINUITY AND CHANGE AMIDST A PANDEMIC

TCA Raghavan

Those who had anticipated that the multiple crises induced by the Covid-19 pandemic would lead to something new in the India–Pakistan dynamic were not finally disappointed. The announcement on 22 February 2021 by the Indian and Pakistani army headquarters that there had been an agreement on enforcing the November 2003 ceasefire on the line of control (LoC) suggested a thaw, however small, was under way. The attention this drew in both countries underlined the significance of the development. There was inevitable criticism and carping from naysayers on both sides. In India, they wondered at this erosion of the well-thought-out and principled position that, 'talks and terror cannot happen together'; in Pakistan, the criticism from some quarters was equally fierce and centred over the question, 'What about Kashmir?' Such critical views have always emerged in the wake of every India–Pakistan initiative to reset relations on a more positive note. To an extent, the strategic mistrust on both sides is so deep and so old that any prospect of a situation other than that of an undeclared war is alarming.

Yet, these views have their limitations because they base themselves on seeking consistency and a linear trajectory in India–Pakistan relations when, in fact, one has never existed and is also unlikely to.

The 22 February agreement had, in fact, come at the end of a long period which had seen a historically bad relationship plummet to an even lower plateau. The milestones in that process are well-documented: Terrorist attacks at an Indian Air Force base in Pathankot (January 2016), on a military camp in Uri (September 2016) and on a convoy of security personnel in Pulwama (February 2019). The latter two events had seen vigorous countermeasures by India. The Uri attack was responded to by a cross-LoC military operation by the Indian Army, which entered the military lexicon and popular imagination in India as the 'surgical strike' response to Pakistan's provocation. The Uri terrorist attack saw an even more robust response—confined not to a cross-LoC operation but an air strike deep inside Pakistan. The latter's response, in turn, saw aerial clashes between the two air forces—unusual even in the adversarial India–Pakistan context, given that this aerial conflict took place in 'peacetime'.

Terrorist attacks and counterterrorism measures were only one axis of recent India–Pakistan tensions. Legislative changes were enacted by the Parliament of India concerning Jammu and Kashmir (J&K) in August 2019. In particular, these ended the provisions that had hitherto existed under Article 370 of the Indian Constitution and, more significantly, bifurcated the state into two union territories of Ladakh and J&K. In Pakistan, these steps were greeted with outrage and rhetoric at levels that were tantamount to a situation barely short of war. The headlines that encapsulated both this outrage, as also Pakistan's public position on these legislative charges, was 'India annexes Jammu and Kashmir'. To a great extent, the reaction was sentimental and rhetorical, but what underwrote it was also clear enough—Pakistan's deep-rooted sense of entitlement regarding J&K was being rejected by India and, therefore, this had to be resisted. Inevitably, what followed was a vast amount of polemic and counter-polemic, démarche and counter-démarche between both countries internally, bilaterally and internationally.

The net impact of these developments on the security and political axis amounted to a comprehensive negative for India–Pakistan relations as a whole. Diplomatic relations were downgraded to sub-ambassadorial level and the strength of the diplomatic missions was sharply and progressively reduced. India withdrew most favoured nation (MFN) treatment for Pakistan's exports to India, thus ending a non-reciprocal concession it had unilaterally extended to Pakistan for over two decades. The legislative changes made with regard to J&K led to

Pakistan banning all trade with India. A summit of South Asian Association for Regional Cooperation (SAARC), scheduled to be held in Pakistan in 2016, had in any case been put in cold storage after India and some other SAARC members declined taking part on grounds of Pakistan's support for terrorism. The most dramatic impact of this general backslide was on people-to-people and cultural contacts. This field has traditionally been most vulnerable to bilateral tensions and the spike over the past five years led to an almost complete drying up of cross-border movement of people. Rhetoric and counter-rhetoric ricocheted off each other domestically in both countries and also reverberated regionally and internationally in the world press and in different multilateral and intergovernmental fora. All this was accompanied from the second half of 2019 and over 2020 by constant skirmishes on the LoC—the intensity and frequency of these underwrote the high level of tension as equally that the 2003 ceasefire was now largely a forgotten agreement.

These events broadly summarise the India–Pakistan situation around the time the Covid-19 pandemic starting pushing all other news to the margins from around the end of the first quarter of 2020. Yet, this summary of largely negative developments does not do full justice to the texture of India–Pakistan relations even over the past half a decade. This negative chronology from 2016 to 2019 is bookended by two contrarian events and bringing them on to the radar is, therefore, of relevance. Firstly, 2015 ended in the India–Pakistan relationship on a very high and unexpected note. This was on account of a brief, unannounced in advance, visit by the prime minister of India to Lahore to participate in a family function of the prime minister of Pakistan. Critics, of course, scoffed at this personalisation of diplomacy to surmount complex and structural India–Pakistan issues. Nevertheless, the discerning had noted the more obvious takeaway—the two principals were signalling their willingness to wage their personal political capital on an India–Pakistan normalisation process. This was, in many ways, similar to the presence of Pakistani PM Nawaz Sharif at the swearing-in of PM Narendra Modi's first cabinet in mid-2014—the invitation to attend being extended and it being accepted, both marked the event as unusual. For hardliners in both countries, this personal angle as an effort to circumvent difficult issues was a futile effort. But again, there were others who saw the possibilities inherent in major political initiatives of this kind.

The other bookend of the sharp 2016-19 downturn is provided by the opening of the Kartarpur Sahib pilgrim corridor in November 2019. This development followed in the wake of both the heightened military tensions post Pulwama and Balakot, as equally the heightened political and diplomatic rhetoric following the legislative changes with respect to J&K in August 2019. For naysayers in both countries, the high-profile opening of a 'visa-free' corridor had all the ingredients of a maverick and inconsistent decision-making. In Pakistan, many found it difficult to reconcile this agreement with the position taken by its government on J&K post August 2019. In India, similarly, there was the view that a step such as this was fundamentally inconsistent with the tough stance required to counter the threat emanating from cross-border inspired terrorism. The more discerning disagreed and pointed to the most unusual feature of this development. A step forward in people-to-people exchanges that would have been difficult to implement even in the best of times of India–Pakistan relations was being put in place in what was admittedly a very bad phase of bilateral relations. Significant breakthroughs of this kind in the past are associated with periods of upswings in bilateral relations—the Munabao–Khokhrapar rail link in 2006 or the Srinagar–Muzaffarabad bus service in 2005, for instance, took place at a time when India–Pakistan relations were looking better than they had for decades, perhaps ever, and constructive engagement was at a high. The fact that a long-standing demand—considered but not found possible to implement many times earlier—of the Sikh community would be agreed to and implemented by both governments at a time of very high tension and when their relations were minimal is thus both unusual and significant. At the very least then this suggested that the relationship had inherent capacities to surprise. It also highlighted a fundamental feature of India–Pakistan relations—that it would not always move predictably in a linear fashion—either upward or downward.

The pandemic, as it advanced across South Asia, presented India and Pakistan with a fresh set of issues. Quite apart from the huge challenges to lives, livelihood and economy, the epidemic was in the nature of a common threat and one, moreover, being biological in origin, that was unrelated to the entire gamut of their bilateral problems—whether territorial, security or identity related. Could the pandemic provide a platform for India–Pakistan cooperation with a new and desecuritised agenda was an obvious question in the early stages of the pandemic. On March 2020, Prime Minister Modi convened a virtual SAARC heads of government meeting intended to focus on the coronavirus and public health issues. Whatever were the takeaways of this near summit for SAARC as a whole and for India's relations with its other neighbours, for the India–Pakistan dynamic, this virtual meet did not have much impact. Firstly, Pakistan did not attend at head of government level and its representative muddied the waters somewhat by raising the Kashmir issue. Secondly, the first quarter of the year had seen a non-Kashmir issue also adversely impacting the relationship. The agitations in India against the National Register of Citizens (NRC) and the Citizenship Amendment Act (CAA) had fuelled rhetoric of high intensity in Pakistan—both at the political and at the diplomatic levels. This further vitiated relations and the polemics were accompanied by some intense firefights and skirmishes on the LoC. Pakistan also mounted over the year its own campaign accusing India of terrorist acts in its territory—possibly designed to appeal more to its own domestic audience and seeking to establish a moral equivalence with India on the terrorism issue. The net result was that over 2020, the view that a major pandemic could induce elements of change in a historically adversarial and conflict-prone relationship had few takers.

Desecuritisation in an India–Pakistan Context

Historically, attempts to induce non-security elements into the heavily securitised India–Pakistan relationships have faced headwinds throughout. The traditional options—encouraging people-to-people contacts through liberal visas, pilgrimages and cultural exchanges and promoting commercial and economic exchanges and cooperation—have all been attempted on numerous occasions, but have remained fragile and regularly come up against both anticipated and unanticipated roadblocks.

In addition to the broad field of people-to-people contact, there have been, over the past decades, three principal attempts to desecuritise the India–Pakistan agenda. This has been attempted through introducing elements from the non-security domain principally, as a means of reducing the intensity of existing differences. Two of these were failures; one was, relatively speaking, a greater success. The success story was in the division of the Indus system of rivers through a 1960 treaty that pragmatically ring-fenced river water sharing from all the other contestations of India–Pakistan geopolitics, including J&K.

This ring-fencing could not, however, be enlarged or deepened largely as a result of the political turn Pakistan took post 1965 and, especially, after 1989.

The two failures were in the field of energy—represented by the Iran–Pakistan–India (IPI) gas pipeline—and in promoting trade as an instrument of dampening tensions. The reasons for these failures are obvious enough—the gas pipeline proved to be a bridge too far because of the difficulties in combining India–Pakistan issues with the geopolitics of Iran. The trade initiative was also full of promise, but faced the problem that the two economies are basically competitive rather than complementary, and the difference in size meant that balance of trade issues acquired greater prominence than would have been otherwise.

Other contemporary domains of desecuritisation—climate change, glacial melt, water availability, environmental pollution—have developed only a limited traction in the India–Pakistan context, largely because these spillover into the domain of traditional geopolitics and security issues. This means a burden too heavy for the science involved in these issues to bear on its own. It is, therefore, evident that the desecuritisation impulse in India–Pakistan relations has been historically weak, although never entirely absent. The principal feature of India–Pakistan bilateral relations, therefore, is its securitisation.

Current Debates

In the long history of India–Pakistan breakdowns following breakthroughs, how do we contextualise this latest joint decision reiterating the value of enforcing an old ceasefire agreement? The easy option is, of course, to predict its impending breakdown or that it does not reflect or signify any real change. A plausible reason may well be that it is only a tactical arrangement to give the respective militaries a respite from the constant skirmishing that had defined the past few years. The alternative view to these pessimistic assessments looks at other signals—around the time the ceasefire arrangement was announced—that suggested the beginning of a slow thawing and, more importantly, also suggested that the leadership in both countries was now looking ahead and wanting to move on. Thus, the Government of India had convened on 18 February 2021 a meeting of 'regional countries' in which Pakistan also participated[1]. This was *not* a SAARC meeting and, to that extent, there was no reason to have invited Pakistan to it. It was addressed by the prime minister of India, who spoke about cooperation in the public health sector by various means. His remarks also included the following statement: 'If the twenty-first century is to be the Asian Century, it cannot be without greater integration among the countries of South Asia and the Indian Ocean island countries.' The principal point of importance in this is that Pakistan was invited and that it agreed to attend. Given all that had happened in the past four years, it would appear that these moves have some larger significance.

This, of course, leads to other questions on whether this thaw is related to an India–China agreement in the first half of February 2021 on forces pulling back in one sector in Ladakh or indeed to the changes in the United States with a new president in place. Yet others point to a possible role by Gulf states—in particular, Saudi Arabia and the UAE. The rapid progress made by India in its relations with them gives to these countries a key role vis-à-vis Pakistan. Speculation on these issues will continue, and the role of outside actors in India–Pakistan agreements of the past has been discussed many times before. Thus, it has also been argued that both Pakistan and India have tactically manoeuvred their political positioning to take into account this changing external environment so as to be better placed to take advantage of it. Such arguments have value and are not to be discarded or even discounted. Yet, changes in India–Pakistan relations have ultimately to be understood in terms of their own texture and dynamic and can never be understood or fully explained by exogenous factors.

Historically, India–Pakistan relations have moved in a cycle with periodic crests and troughs. Bilateral, domestic, regional and international factors have all played a role in moulding this cyclical behaviour. The differences between the two countries are, as is well known, foundational and these express themselves in territorial and ideological divergences that are not easy to bridge. The most ambitious effort to address these differences by means of a diplomatic process was through the composite dialogue between 2004 and 2009, but it eroded in the face of terrorist attacks which sparked a wave of public and political disillusionment in India that has continued until today. Efforts to improvise a variant of the composite dialogue in 2010 through the 'resumed dialogue' and in 2015 with a 'comprehensive bilateral dialogue' did not, therefore, make much progress. Civil–military tensions in Pakistan also played a major role in ensuring a lack of forward movement. The chances of it being resurrected again are slim. The composite dialogue, nevertheless, represented an effort to confront and address the basic cyclical pattern of the relationship by integrating a confidence-building process with some elements of dispute resolution.

The present effort to break a long impasse has to be viewed neither with excessive optimism nor with cemented cynicism, but rather clinically as a reflection of a fundamental cyclical pattern. The fact that a long downturn punctuated by multiple crises—Uri, Pulwama, Balakot, legislative changes in J&K, etc.—is nevertheless bookended, as noted earlier, by two major attempts to break the existing mould of strategic hostility only confirms this pattern. Similarly, the recent attempts to end the downturn have to be seen in the same context. The challenge ahead for the diplomacy of both countries will be on how to introduce new elements that may desecuritise a heavily securitised relationship. How to moderate the crests and troughs and introduce a more stable pattern, notwithstanding the fact that the stated positions of both countries on key substantive issues will remain far apart, is part of this challenge as indeed it has been for long in India–Pakistan relations.

The most recent moves at tension reduction come in the midst of a major public health crisis. Perhaps cooperation on healthcare issues may offer some possibilities for constructing a platform on which, over time, a larger edifice of stable India–Pakistan relations could be constructed. Whether in the future the two governments will decide to inch forward or be more ambitious remains to be seen. Both sides, however, will be mindful of the deep divisions in their respective world views, of past history and of the pitfalls ahead. The key may well be in visualising a process that is able to surf over the characteristic crests and troughs of their relationship and, thereby, avoid an abrupt derailment.

Endnotes

1. Participating countries were Afghanistan, Bangladesh, Bhutan, Mauritius, Nepal, Pakistan, Seychelles, Sri Lanka and India.

CHAPTER 7

INDIA–IRAN RELATIONS: RIVALRY AND COOPERATION

KC Singh

India and Iran shared a boundary till India's partition in 1947. Consequently, their history is intertwined with long periods of peaceful coexistence, rivalry over contested areas in modern Afghanistan and shared experience of occupation by Mongol invaders or Western colonial powers. Kenneth M Pollack, in his masterly book, *The Persian Puzzle*, on Iran–US relations, concedes at the start that, 'Iran is a maddeningly complicated state and society, and even a cursory understanding of its motives today requires knowing a fair bit about the forces that have shaped the nation over time.' The same can be said of India.

India and Iran are also civilisational states, which gave birth to two ancient belief systems—Hinduism and Zoroastrianism, respectively. While Iran produced the Achaemenid Empire (522-486 BC), which, to quote Pollock again, 'was a superpower like nothing the world had ever seen—with a monotheistic religion, a vast army, a rich civilisation, a new and remarkably efficient method of administration, and territory stretching from Egypt to Central Asia.' Also, not to forget, from the Aegean to India. Almost conquering Greece, it paid the price when Alexander extracted revenge by overrunning it and then arriving at India's doors in 327 BC. While a strong Iran was a menace for the region, a weak Iran allowed invaders to threaten India. The Mongol invasions, emanating from Central Asia, led to pillage and destruction in both Iran and India from the thirteenth century onwards. They destroyed Iran's advanced agriculture infrastructure, and a weakened and divided India was repeatedly invaded and finally subdued by a branch of their descendants in the form of the Mughals.

After centuries of instability, both nations saw stability and prosperity restored as Safavids in Iran (1501-1722) and Mughals in India (1526-1707, the year Aurangzeb died) consolidated power and restored the territorial integrity and military-economic strength of the nations. For a fifteen-year period, when Humayun, having lost his Indian throne, was given refuge by the Safavid Empire, the ancestor of great Mughals imbibed Persian culture, language, art and architecture. Regaining the Delhi throne in 1555, Humayun brought Persian language and influence that runs through two centuries of Mughal rule. Despite many courtiers and generals of Persian origin being Shias in an otherwise Sunni-dominated court, they rose to prominence and even established marital ties with the ruling family. In fact, the Safavid persecution of Sufis in Iran, due to strict enforcement of Shia tenets, saw them gravitate towards the Agra court. Babur, having won the battle at Panipat, is said to have immediately, after entering Delhi, visited the Nizamuddin shrine or dargah of Chishti Sufi Khwaja Nizamuddin Auliya, who hailed from Bokhara. Thus, Humayun was buried in the spiritually blessed vicinity of the dargah.

While this process of cultural osmosis was continuous between Iran and pre-1947 India, as Mughals weakened after Aurangzeb's death, successors of the Safavids in Iran looked to exploit the power vacuum in India. Nadir Shah's invasion of India (1738-40) is a chapter that contemporary Iran likes to avoid discussing. Remnants of Mughal jewels looted during that raid are still displayed in Tehran, although with their provenance undisclosed. The blow that this invasion dealt to the power and prestige of the Mughals opened the door to European colonial gains on the battlefield and eventual occupation of India.

Interestingly, neither nation escaped colonisation, albeit in case of Iran it was informal and more damaging as loss of sovereignty was not even compensated, as in the case of India, by establishment of efficient administration, creation of connectivity through roads and railway lines albeit to enable better exploitation of resources, setting up of a judicial system and trained military and police forces. The nineteenth century Qajar dynasty rulers of Iran faced constant pressure from Russia in the north and the British, then controlling India, from the west and the Gulf in the south. The Great Game of Russo-British rivalry was played out in Iran and Afghanistan. In the process, Iran was constantly exploited, its sovereignty curtailed, its resources and territory controlled. This saga continued till World War II, during which Iran was the only supply route to a Soviet army retreating before the advancing Nazi German forces. British and Americans literally overtook the supply corridor. Although the US played a significant role post-War in getting the Soviets to withdraw troops from north-western Iran, the Iranian popular perception of foreigners manipulating and controlling Iran and its resources dates from 1949. Under pressure from the US and domestic public opinion, the Shah was compelled to allow a free election. The newly created National Front, under Mohammad Mosaddeq, a scion of the Kajar dynasty, captured power. The immediate dispute was over the sharing of oil revenues between Iran and the Anglo-Iranian Oil Company (AIOC). Britain was unwilling to accept a fifty-fifty sharing, as American oil companies had accepted in Venezuela and would again, later, in Saudi Arabia. This perception of a conflict between a covetous foreign power, a popularly elected government representing the will of the people and seeking fair compensation and a ruler complicit with foreign power is constantly replayed in public mind till the Iranian Islamic Revolution in 1979, or even later.

The Korean War in 1950 brought the Cold War politics into bold relief. The US began looking at the Gulf region from the perspective of Soviet containment. The US signed a mutual defence agreement with Iran in 1950. Mosaddeq was overthrown in a coup engineered by America's Central Intelligence Agency (CIA), the task having become easier as he had become dictatorial and isolated. But public recall of the event is of paradise lost due to US interference. Mosaddeq is often upheld as a martyr in the cause of Iranian freedom of governance, his fate symbolising foreign interference. Finally, the Shah led Iran to join the Baghdad Pact of 1955—an alliance of Turkey, Iraq, Iran, Pakistan and Britain. The US was its sponsor, but not a member.

For the next two decades, India–Iran relations were constrained by this Cold War realignment which put India's regional nemesis, Pakistan, at its centre. The Iranian transfer of US-made military equipment to Pakistan during the 1971 India–Pakistan war cast a shadow on relations with India. However, the Shah's leadership of the post-1973 Organization of the Petroleum Exporting Countries (OPEC) cartel to push up oil price, despite US President Richard Nixon writing to dissuade him, and steep rise in Iranian oil revenues encouraged him to diversify Iranian relations. The Shah of Iran visited India in October 1974 on the last leg of a five-nation tour of the Asia-Pacific. This was an attempt to recalibrate relations with India after the 1971 pro-Pakistan tilt. At that stage, India was importing almost two-thirds of its oil from Iran. Also, Iran was flush with funds, and a number of joint ventures in shipping and petroleum refining were initiated after the visit.

However, domestic developments in Iran had already begun to turn popular opinion against the Shah after mishandled land reforms and ill-planned industrialisation. Inflation was kicked off by lopsided government spending on military hardware and ambitious infrastructure upgrade, besides uncontrolled corruption siphoning off revenues. By 1975, forty-five Iranian families controlled 85 per cent of national manufacturing firms. President Richard Nixon cut the Shah a lot of slack on his domestic governance, unlike President John F Kennedy, who had insisted on political and economic reforms. The Nixon Doctrine of 'Twin Pillars'—the outcome of US strategic fatigue after the Vietnam War—positioned Iran and Saudi Arabia as two local policemen to safeguard US interests. This was somewhat similar to the recent Donald Trump–Joe Biden approach of using regional allies, following similar US strategic overstretch after fighting two wars non-stop over two decades. But, the negative aspect of this was that it fed the Shah's megalomania and insecurities and Iran overspent on military equipment and weapons. The resulting economic distortions combined lethally with the Shah alienating all segments of public opinion, ranging from the clergy, big and small landholders and students to the common man. Henry Kissinger, in one of his least perceptive statements, called the Shah 'that rarest of leaders, an unconditional ally'.

The result was first a gradual and then a rapid disintegration of the Shah's military and intelligence organisations. He eventually self-exiled in January 1979, leaving behind a nation in the hands of Islamic revolutionaries under the leadership of Ayatollah Ruhollah Khomeini. Whereas earlier India–Iran relations had the overhang of the Cold War and Pakistan's Kashmir agenda, now the factors got rejigged. India, having the second largest Shia population in the world, automatically attracted the new rulers of Iran, seeking to seize leadership of the Islamic world from the Saudis. Khomeini also brought rabid dislike of the US and Israel, thus putting the Palestinian issue up front. With India, the Kashmir issue was flagged, though Iran mostly balanced its approach, realising the importance of India as a market for its oil, source for technology and, of course, the abode of a large population of Shias. India's Iran policy got complicated by the Iran–Iraq War, started by Iraqi President Saddam Hussein in 1980. Despite taking Iran by surprise after the top Iranian military leadership had been purged and the defence forces were in disarray, Iraq's tactical mistakes allowed Iran to rally its forces for a stout defence. Iraq was seen by India as a reliable, secular and non-aligned Muslim country that fell in a Nasser-inspired Arab group, which balanced those who supported or empathised with Pakistan at the Organisation of Islamic Conference (OIC) on the Kashmir issue. During the eight-year war, India managed to maintain good relations with the two warring nations.

However, the year 1979 brought more than the Iranian Islamic Revolution. In December, the Soviets complicated the geopolitics of the region by intervening militarily in Afghanistan. Thus, both on the eastern and western borders of Iran conflict flared. It had to repel the Iraqi offensive on one side, and on the other, carefully watch as Soviet military faced a hybrid war. The unholy alliance facing the Soviets and Afghan government consisted of Saudi money and Wahabi version of Islam, US weaponry and intelligence and Pakistani leadership in procuring and training recruits produced by multiplying madrasas under the patronage of the Islamist Pakistani President, Zia-ul-Haq. The Iran–Iraq War ended in 1988, after a terminally ill Khomeini was convinced that Iran lacked the resources to do better than retain its territory. Khomeini termed it as drinking from a 'poisoned chalice'. Coincidently, the Soviets announced their exit from Afghanistan on 15 May the same year. The steep drop in oil price had hobbled the finances of all three combat-saddled and oil-producing nations—Iraq, Iran and Soviet Union. In 1980, oil was at US$ 35 per barrel, equivalent to US$ 109 for 2019, inflation adjusted. In 1986, it fell from US$ 27 to US$ 10 or US$ 63 to US$ 23, again, inflation adjusted.

But the consequences for the region were just beginning to manifest. The US lost interest in the Afghan theatre once Soviets accepted defeat and left. But the army of jihadis that had been created now had Pakistani ownership. Plans brewed to capture power and turn Afghanistan into an Islamic Caliphate, which would provide Pakistan the much desired strategic depth. The civil war in Afghanistan (1989-92) after the Soviet withdrawal was followed by fragmentation of governance, as different areas in Afghanistan came to be controlled by warlords. Eventually, from 1994, it led to the rise of the Taliban. Once Kabul fell in 1996, the Pakistani game plan was largely in place, but seeds had been sown of future chaos as the al-Qaeda had embedded itself in Afghanistan, with freedom to operate under the protection of the Taliban.

At that point, the strategic interests of India and Iran converged almost totally as the Taliban targeted Shias and even massacred Iranian diplomats. A joint Indo-Iranian effort commenced to counter them by propping up the Northern Alliance, under the charismatic leadership of Tajik-origin Ahmad Shah Massoud. Indian financial and military assistance was channelled via Iran and Tajikistan. The point man on the Iranian side was Major General Qassem Soleimani—later assassinated in a US drone attack in 2020 in Iraq. In 1998, Prime Minister Atal Bihari Vajpayee, representing the Lucknow constituency that had a large Shia population, formed the government. President Mohammad Khatami, charismatic and reformist, had been the surprise winner of the Iranian presidential election a year earlier.

The two used the new-found convergence of interests to take bilateral relations to a new strategic level. Vajpayee visited Tehran in April 2001. In a talk at the Tehran Chamber of Commerce, he spelt out five key areas for bilateral engagement. One, energy and energy security related projects, including a proposed gas pipeline. Two, flowing from first, downstream petrochemicals, refineries, fertiliser production, etc. Three, doubling of bilateral trade in one year from US$ 1 billion annually, and trebling it in three. A preferential trade agreement was proposed and better banking facilities were stressed upon. Four, information technology, telecommunications, pharmaceuticals, space and oceanography. Five, railways, shipping, foreign direct investment and optimum use of free-trade zones, etc.

But, neither leader imagined that the 9/11 terror attacks on the US later in same year would dramatically alter the regional context. The US intervention in Afghanistan to eliminate the al-Qaeda threat altered the regional geopolitics. India naturally saw this as an overdue recognition of the Pakistan–Taliban–al-Qaeda terror collaboration. Iran initially offered to assist, as, by sheer accident, even their interests coincided with those of the US on the limited point of ejecting Taliban and its terrorist associates from their lair in Afghanistan. But, their interests diverged when it became clear that the US troops were there to stay. Iranian President Mohammad Khatami returned the Vajpayee visit in

January 2003, when he was the chief guest at India's Republic Day celebrations. Although the US attack on Iraq was still two months away, the Delhi Declaration, issued jointly, reflected the altered geopolitics of the region. Both sides affirmed that developments since their Tehran meeting had reinforced their faith in pluralism, diversity and tolerance. Cooperation was desired in science and technology, agreed areas of defence, terrorism, etc. Economic relations were seen as necessary, underpinning to strategic relations. Chabahar Port surfaced as part of the trilateral agreement between India, Iran and Afghanistan. Sensing rising US irritation with Saddam Hussein, a peaceful resolution of the stand-off with Iraq was sought.

Again, in retrospect, the disconnect between the US plans for the region and India–Iran plans for multisectoral and deeper bilateral engagement seems obvious. The US distrust of Iran was going to be a factor restricting India's ability to play along with both parties. If there was any doubt, the revelations about Iran's clandestine nuclear programme later in 2003, while India negotiated a nuclear waiver from the Nuclear Suppliers Group (NSG), put India–Iran relations to a severe test. Although Iran quickly came to the negotiating table and engaged the trio of the UK, Germany and France, India was caught in the crossfire, as it was required to take sides when the issue came before the International Atomic Energy Agency (IAEA).

The issue reached the UN Security Council (UNSC) and a series of resolutions were passed, starting with the UNSC resolution 1696 on 31 July 2006, demanding the suspension of Iranian uranium enrichment. The resumption of Iranian enrichment programme began after the surprise win in presidential election by conservative candidate Mahmoud Ahmadinejad in 2005. The UNSC resolutions kept coming as Iranian recalcitrance persisted, culminating in UNSC resolution 1929 of 9 June 2010, imposing a fourth round of sanctions. India missed getting embroiled in the vote, as it joined the UNSC only the following year. But the India–Iran relations were more or less in cold storage all through the United Progressive Alliance (UPA) government of Prime Minister Manmohan Singh, as focus was on deepening ties with the US, including to get India liberated from the shackles of the four technology-control regimes—Nuclear Suppliers Group, Missile Technology Control Regime, Wassenaar Arrangement and Australia Group. Iran watched ruefully as India, the non-signatory of the Non-Proliferation Treaty (NPT), was mollycoddled while it was pilloried, despite being a signatory. Of course, what Iran ignored was that while it was seen as in breach of its treaty obligations, India was not. Nevertheless, this irritant remained to bug bilateral engagement.

The election of US President Barack Obama brought a fresh approach to the Iranian nuclear issue. In the first of his two-volume memoir, *A Promised Land*, President Obama notes that after gaming military options to stop Iranian nuclear programme, they decided on a two-step approach. One, direct outreach. Thus, in his inaugural address in January 2009, he offered to 'extend a hand to those willing to unclench their fists'. Iranian supreme leader Ali Khamenei's response, he adds, was a blunt no. Matters took an adverse turn when, in June 2009, the re-election of Ahmadinejad as president resulted in widespread protests, dubbed as the Green Movement. The slogan that people adopted was, 'Where Is My Vote?', alleging election fixing. Perplexed over the violent crackdown, President Obama wanted to react strongly, but he explains, 'that my heart was now chained to strategic considerations and tactical analysis'. Step two was to ratchet up sanctions by mobilising the international community to apply multilateral and tough economic sanctions.

Wanting to improve relations incrementally with the US, Prime Minister Manmohan Singh and his successor, Narendra Modi, treated relations with Iran with caution. All the promises voiced in Tehran and Delhi declarations signed by Prime Minister Atal Bihari Vajpayee and President Mohammad Khatami came to nought. The election of liberal and reformist President Hassan Rouhani, opened the possibility of a breakthrough. The late sultan of Oman, Qaboos bin Said, who maintained friendly relations with the Iranian regime, offered to mediate. Through this route, and without informing the UN-mandated group of P5+1 (Germany), the US secretly began negotiating what fructified as the Joint Comprehensive Plan of Action (JCPOA). In September 2013, when President Rouhani came to New York for the UN General Assembly session, though a personal meeting between him and President Obama was deferred, they spoke on the phone.

The US endorsement of JCPOA left Saudi Arabia and the United Arab Emirates—the traditional US allies in the Gulf—seething. Israel was also incensed as the deal was seen as merely postponing the inevitable Iranian desire to have a full enrichment programme, from which they could break out towards nuclear weapons in months. But the US was also calculating the sudden capture of large swathes of northern Syria and Iraq by the Islamic State of Iraq and the Levant (ISIL). The fall of Iraq's second largest city, Mosul, on 4 June 2014, left everyone aghast. Options before the US were to either return troops to the region or unshackle Iran to create local resistance to the Sunni terrorist syndicate, which, unlike al-Qaeda, now controlled territory on its own. Under the deft leadership of Major General Qassem Soleimani—the head of the Quds Force of the Iranian Revolutionary Guard Corps (IRGC)—the Shia militias, Hezbollah volunteers and local armed forces were welded into a force to roll back the ISIS. But it also multiplied Iranian influence in the entire Shia arc, running from Iran through Iraq and Syria to Lebanon.

President Obama's successor, President Donald Trump, during campaigning, called the JCPOA the 'worst deal ever'. On assuming office, he flew to Riyadh to openly back the Saudi–Emirati alliance, forged by the crown princes of the two nations. Following the visit, the six-member Gulf Cooperation Council split, with the Saudis and Emiratis aligning against Qatar on the pretext that it was encouraging the Muslim Brotherhood. Qatar shares its main gas field with Iran and can hardly be antagonistic towards it. Kuwait and Oman maintained neutrality. Beyond the Gulf, Turkey also threw its weight behind Qatar and then put Saudi Crown Prince Mohammed bin Salman in a mess by leaking reports about his complicity in the brutal killing of journalist Jamal Khashoggi in Istanbul. Trump applied even more pressure on Iran to compel it to accept a much more restrictive nuclear deal and curtailed regional ambitions. In a last throw of the dice, on 3 January 2020, Trump authorised the assassination of Major General Qassem Soleimani through a drone strike as he exited Baghdad airport. It was a serious provocation and, perhaps, aimed to provoke Iran to retaliate so that the US and Israel could then defang it by air strikes. Iran did not take the bait.

India, realising that US exit from Afghanistan was inevitable, suddenly commenced its own fence-mending with Iran. Iranian President Hassan Rouhani arrived in India on 15-17 February 2018. Nine agreements, including some memoranda of understanding (MoUs), were signed. Indian focus was on the Chabahar Port, seen as crucial for Indian access to Afghanistan and Central Asia. As has been the routine over the years, oil and gas projects were mentioned, but Iran knows that India will be chary of defying US sanctions. The importance of Iran became self-evident, as possibility arose in Afghanistan of a

Taliban–Pakistan–China axis filling the post-US power vacuum. The Taliban, despite a deal with the US, has not accepted a ceasefire and persists with its standard tactic of talk-and-fight. For India to help the incumbent Afghan government, access to that country is critical, which only Iran can provide.

However, the new factor is an assertive China, with Russia in tow, having its own grand plan for the region. China signing a twenty-five-year deal with Iran, worth US$ 400 billion, repositioned Iran, as US President Joe Biden was still shaping his Iran policy. The size and scope of the deal, if implemented, can remake Iranian industrial economy and infrastructure. China, in return, gets assured supplies of gas and oil. But, historically, Iranians resent being under the thumb of any single country. Iran also has a tendency to attach conditions in small print that can often mire partners in lengthy post-deal negotiations. Nothing is ever final in Iran as there are multiple stakeholders. The voice of the IRGC is the strongest now, as it has intruded into different sectors of the economy, including oil and gas. Iran is using this deal to signal to the US that pressure will be counterproductive, as the gainer shall be China, without Iran being brought to its knees.

China, in turn, is using its ability to defy the US and protect Iran to gain a greater grasp over the Iranian economy, particularly the energy resources. In the last decade—2010-20—China invested only US$ 18.2 billion in Iran, compared to the US$ 30.6 billion in Saudi Arabia and US$ 29.5 billion in the UAE. The US seems to have deciphered the message. The green flag for re-engagement with Iran to bring it back in compliance with the JCPOA indicates that a counterplay has begun. Apparently, the deadlock over who takes the first step has been broken by the US remaining in the background and doing arm's-length negotiations. There may be a two-step process, with some sanctions relief mirroring Iranian movement towards compliance. The complication is due to the Trump administration having loaded the nuclear programme related sanctions on earlier ones for Iranian support to terrorism or its missile programme. Containing Iranian regional role would have to await generation of mutual trust and confidence. The Islamic world is today not only divided between Shias and Sunnis but also between rival groups of Sunnis. Saudi Arabia went public to demand a seat at the table before the JCPOA II is finalised.

All this activity leaves India adrift due to Prime Minister Narendra Modi's excessive hug-and-greet diplomacy with Crown Princes Mohammed bin Zayed of the UAE and Mohammed bin Salman of Saudi Arabia. Iran would have closely read each and every public gesture. The perils of personalised diplomacy became manifest when President Joe Biden won the US election after Modi–Trump hand-holding at political rallies of the Indian diaspora had crossed the normal boundaries of diplomatic conduct. In a sense, the region is back to the 1990s, as Afghanistan again undergoes power transition, not dictated by outsiders, but on the basis of local strengths, including the use of force and violence by incumbents and their opponents wanting to displace them. Another civil war cannot be ruled out. But, Iran is not the Iran of that period, nor is China. For instance, the Taliban and Iran have been maintaining a working relationship. They actually share more in terms of their view of the society and the world than what they disagree on, which, in the past, has been the Taliban's persecution of Shias.

The final question would be whether India can successfully engage different factions in the Islamic world. In the past, India managed to keep out of factional and regional quarrels by not taking sides and mainly ensuring Pakistan did not rally the Islamic nations on the Kashmir issue. A new factor now is the majoritarian politics and agenda of the BJP-led government, especially in its second term. Saudi Arabia and the UAE, under younger leadership, cut India slack on its domestic politics mainly to ensure that India–Iran relations remained limited. But, in the Biden era, even they are scampering to not get isolated when Iran is re-engaged by the US. Where does that leave India? In one of the least free elections and with very low turnout, the Supreme Leader's confidant Ebrahim Raisi was elected as president. He took over on 3 August in the shadow of Taliban's speedy capture of territory as US troop withdrawal speeded up. Taliban 2.0 has de facto captured control of Afghanistan. But unlike the 1990s, Indian and Iranian interests may not converge fully. So far, Taliban have not persecuted Shias. Letting Ismail Khan, strongman of Herat, to seek refuge in Mashhad indicates a new modus vivendi between Iran and the Taliban.

At the moment, the situation is fluid as Taliban is seeking legitimacy and its sponsor Pakistan would encourage good behaviour to facilitate that. US Secretary of State Antony Blinken has spelt twin criteria before recognition: treatment of Afghan people and denial of refuge to terrorists. India would have to lay down even stricter conditions.

Lesson for India is to not take US lead in playing favourites in the Islamic world. The Indian government would also need to rethink its majoritarian domestic politics. With Taliban–Pakistan nexus now entrenched, India's domestic communal fissures could make it vulnerable to foreign meddling. India–Iran relations now face Taliban's shadow. Coming months would show if it helps closer engagement or becomes an irritant.

CHAPTER 8

LOOKING AT BANGLADESH

DEB MUKHARJI

As Bangladesh celebrates fifty years of *Muktijuddho*, or War of Liberation, that led to its emergence as a free nation, it is useful to reflect on its journey so far. The trajectory of its journey has been different and more turbulent than its neighbours, and some understanding of its ethos and compulsions is necessary as we consider India's foreign policy vis-à-vis Bangladesh.

The two successor states to British India had chosen different paths in 1947. India had drawn on its past and had charted a path both inclusive and liberal—some recent shadows notwithstanding. Conversely, Pakistan defined itself in religious terms and seems, even after seven decades, unable to find an identity beyond being 'not India'. India did have a national movement over several decades with many facets, not all pacific, but its final emergence, as also Pakistan's, was negotiated. Thus, of the three successor states today, Bangladesh is the only one to have been born in the maelstrom of genocidal violence through armed resistance, albeit with Indian assistance and intervention.

The conflict with Pakistan arose from charges of economic exploitation and cultural-linguistic assertion, even as common origins remained in the two-nation theory. Mohammed Ali Jinnah's unwise refusal to accept Bengali as a national language, despite being the language of the majority, made the linguistic-cultural identity the defining edge of the popular movement, particularly after '*Ekushe*', the Language Martyr's Day of 21 February 1952, when agitating students were shot dead.

Many Indians believed that 1971 signalled a rejection of the two-nation theory. This was a mistaken assessment of the nearly two-decades-old struggle of the East Pakistanis against Rawalpindi's domination. The Bengali Muslim had played a significant role in the creation of Pakistan. Thereafter, the struggle had been for the linguistic and economic rights of the people of East Pakistan within the framework of Pakistan, until the discourse was changed by Rawalpindi's refusal to accept the results of the 1970 elections and subsequent military action. In the Bangladesh that emerged, Islam and the linguistic-cultural identity could exist in parallel, even as recognition to other religions was accorded. But, this essentially secular identity of Bangladesh in the broadest sense—which had evolved not only through *Muktijuddho* but also through the political and student's movements over the previous two decades—was unacceptable to those steeped in the ideology of Pakistan. Ziaur Rahman made this 'course correction' after taking over power in 1976 with suitable changes in the constitution. The 'Bengali' became 'Bangladeshi' and '*Joy Bangla*' was replaced with 'Bangladesh *zindabad*'. In short, the original Pakistan Resolution of 1940, seeking independent Muslim majority states in north-western and eastern India, was revived. It was the 'end of a betrayal and restoration of the Pakistan Resolution', as 1971 was described by a leading Muslim League politician of earlier days.

While apologists of Zia's moves could argue with some apparent justification that he only formalised what was the reality, the reality is that his legal changes and other moves made it possible for hardcore opponents of the freedom struggle, some with blood on their hands, return to politics. The assassins of Mujibur Rahman and the four Awami League leaders in prison were either rewarded or given safe passage. Zia remains primarily responsible for the culture of impunity that bedevilled Bangladesh for nearly four decades, leading to further violence, including Zia's own assassination, until the present government established accountability. And his attempt to re-Pakistanise the Bangladeshi psyche corroded the self-assurance of the people with regard to their Bengali heritage. A corollary was the shadow on relations with India.

With or without the aberrations introduced by Zia, there were forces at play in Bangladesh inimical to India on principle. A quarter century after liberation, the home minister of Bangladesh—a former chief of air staff—saw the emergence of Bangladesh not due to the freedom fighters or the will of the people, but due to Indian machinations. The clergy would have shared this view. The radical left, who thought that the war of liberation was a bourgeois charade, remained steadfastly opposed to Indian imperialists. Even many freedom fighters of the left, who should have been well aware of the ground situation, averred that India should not have entered the war, which they would have won in due course, establishing a non-bourgeois government. It was, therefore, never going to be easy to create a constructive relationship with India.

It is fitting that there should be celebrations in Bangladesh and India on the fiftieth anniversary of the war of liberation. It is not often that a nation has the privilege of assisting another in gaining its freedom from oppressors. Perhaps understandably, but no less unfortunately, Indians have often tended to see the war of December 1971 through an Indo-Pakistani prism. The role of the Mukti Bahini in wrecking the morale of the Pakistani forces and inflicting losses through relentless actions needs to be underlined. But, while the memory of the collaboration between Bangladesh and India in 1971 should be treasured, it must not detract attention from continued emphasis in promoting bilateral relations between the two countries for mutual benefit. The year 1971 was, indeed, a seminal event in the lives of the two nations. But, it should not be deemed as the cornerstone of our relations. Continued attention to mutual understanding and respect for each other's concerns has to be the bedrock of our relations.

What makes interstate relationships more challenging in South Asia, perhaps most so in the case of Indo-Bangladesh relations, is that these are not abstract formulations decided in the capitals. People need to be carried along and, unfortunately, there is a good deal of historical baggage that exists. Like the villager who noticed my flag and reminded me as I was visiting an old palace that not very long ago people like him would not be allowed to come anywhere near with any footwear. History casts its shadow when a 'Bihari' woman in a hijab sees me in my office in the late '70s and says with regret that our forefathers committed *gaddari* against their *qaum* and we continue to pay the price. A hundred years later, Chittaranjan Das is remembered by many in Bangladesh for the fair deal he attempted to give the Muslims of Bengal through his Bengal Pact, opposed by the Hindu gentry and rejected by the Congress Party. Das's acolytes had been Netaji Subhas Chandra Bose and Sher-e-Bangla Fazlul Huq. When Prime Minister HD Deve Gowda visited Dhaka in 1997 after the Farakka Agreement, riders in medieval armour paraded the streets to remind him that the king of Bengal, Lakshman Sen—a Kannadiga like him—had been defeated by Bakhtiyar Khilji in 1206. Politics and history remain inextricably linked in South Asia.

In another respect, historical baggage is also carried on by the states themselves. India has permitted its domestic politics to influence its relations with both Nepal and Sri Lanka with regard to their minorities. While there are much larger issues between India and Pakistan, the recent tendency to vilify dissenters from government policies as Pakistani agents is another unfortunate development. The issue with Bangladesh is more serious.

Illegal migration from Bangladesh has been a matter of concern in India for many decades. This migration comprises both Hindus and Muslims. Hindus have migrated both due to economic compulsions as also religious maltreatment, while, for Muslims, the reasons have been economic. Some of the migration has been seasonal. The number of such migrants is not known, but speculatively runs into several millions. In the past, different governments in West Bengal and states in the North East have not been averse to such migration for their own political ends, or even labour requirements. It is alleged that illegal Bangladeshi Muslim migration has, and would, change the demographic contours in neighbouring Indian states.

The issue reached a crescendo with the attempted implementation of the National Register of Citizens (NRC) in Assam. After causing considerable disruption, the exercise was abandoned. Simultaneously, in order to protect Hindu migrants, the Indian Parliament passed the Citizenship Amendment Act (CAA) 2019, introducing religion as a factor in the grant of citizenship, which led to widespread protests and whose constitutionality has been challenged in the Supreme Court. It was the occasion for strong language from leaders of the ruling party, describing illegal migrants, read Bangladeshi, as termites and promising their mass expulsion.

There were contradictions in government statements on the CAA, NRC and National Population Register (NPR), and it is possible that the high-decibel exercise was meant for internal political purposes. Nevertheless, since it implied repression of Hindus in Bangladesh and expulsion of millions of Muslims to Bangladesh, it could not but be considered an affront by Dhaka. While public reaction was restrained, several high-level visits were cancelled.

This episode, presently dormant, illustrates the gravity of India's internal politics impinging on foreign relations. Even if the Bangladesh government has been restrained, it would have to take note of the public fury at the Indian charges and potential threats. This does not contribute to a wholesome and constructive bilateral relationship. More importantly, the atmosphere of divisiveness and the shift towards religion-based politics in India encourages similar, but extreme, manifestations in Bangladesh, of which there have been not too distant examples. It also does not make it any easier for any government in Dhaka to engage in a cooperative relationship with India. At the moment of writing, blood has been shed and demonstrations cutting across ideological affiliations continue in Bangladesh over the visit of the Indian prime minister to celebrate the fiftieth anniversary of the war of independence.

The geographical location of Bangladesh makes it India's most important neighbour in terms of security. A radicalised Bangladesh would pose incalculable threats to the neighbouring states of India and to India as a whole. It might be important to recall that as recently as fifteen years ago, a variety of jihadi groups were running rampant in Bangladesh thanks to the feckless attitude of the then elected government. The actions of the present government in uprooting such elements may be commendable, but they do remain in subterranean caverns as shown in the attack on Holey Artisan Bakery in July 2016. Obviously, the people of Bangladesh will choose their government from time to time, but India has to consistently reach out to different sections of Bangladeshi society. While state-to-state relations have to be maintained with utmost cordiality, the larger canvas of cultivating the goodwill of the people must not be lost sight of, and would be an insurance against less sanguine circumstances.

Even though the Awami League that returned to power in Dhaka in 1996 against all odds after twenty-one long years had shown admirable political courage in entering into the twenty-five-year Ganga Waters Treaty with India—putting behind the most significant source of discord—it was too preoccupied with internal issues to progress towards a substantive engagement with India. Possibly, the several changes of government in India at the time also did not contribute towards a sustained policy, even if there was no absence of goodwill. In my view, what marked a paradigm shift in attitudes, expectations and promises was Prime Minister Sheikh Hasina's visit to India in January 2010 after her re-election in 2009. The Framework on Cooperation laid out a vision for the future with no reservations. This visit had resulted in an Indian offer of credit of US$ 1 billion and agreement in diverse fields, ranging from cooperation to fight terrorism to the opening up of routes from Nepal and Bhutan to Bangladesh, supply of electricity from India, opening of border *haat*s etc. Significantly, 'the two prime ministers agreed to put in place a comprehensive framework of cooperation for development between the two countries, encapsulating their mutually shared vision for the future, which would include cooperation in water resources, power, transportation and connectivity, tourism and education. They agreed on the need to operationalise the various areas of cooperation at the earliest.' What was significant about the joint statement was that it stated or implied that our bilateral relations were not a zero-sum game, or merely transactional, but one with prospects of mutual benefit and a vision for the future.

The optimism generated by the visit was carried forward by then Prime Minister Manmohan Singh's visit in September 2011. I had been in Dhaka during such visits in 1979, 1997 and 1999. These did not lack cordiality, but were formal and the substance transactional in nature. Each country had its set positions on issues it considered important—water, trade, migration, terrorism, etc.—and the effort was to gain as much advantage as possible, even if it was only in terms of the language used in joint statements, and not envisage a holistic approach to bilateral relations, or a desire or ability to upgrade it to another level. Even though the visit had the welcome protocol on land boundary, West Bengal's intransigence prevented a resolution over sharing the Teesta waters, which still remains unresolved.

Even when relations between the governments had been frosty in the early years of the century, civil society on both sides had been able to meet and identify diverse areas of cooperation for mutual benefit. Many of these came to be reflected in government policies in more propitious times.

There is a tendency in Bangladesh to look at India and Indian overtures with a degree of caution. It is here that the attitude of governments can make a difference. In discussing issues in the past, much too often they were seen as a zero-sum game. But, the road map laid out in 2010, followed up in 2011 and subsequent interactions have sent positive messages. Prime Minister Narendra Modi has described the present as a golden chapter in Indo-Bangladesh relations.

Academic Dr Sreeradha Datta makes the valid point that since the landmark framework of cooperation signed in 2010, 'the past decade has seen a bouquet of milestones for them. From the first takeaway of energy trade to growing economic ties that is witnessing greater balance of trade than ever before, Indian support of nearly US$ 10 billion has led to a spurt in cross-border infrastructure as well as multimodal transport corridors including coastal shipping, inland water transport, surface transport system including railways being out in place. Undoubtedly, India and Bangladesh have reached a level hitherto unknown. But ironically, a relation that has always been people-centric seemed to have waned in the background, while the state-to-state and government-to-government ties have strengthened.' According to her, 'the political context between India and Bangladesh outweighs all other aspects in their bilateral relations.'[1] This is a disturbing thought and makes it all the more necessary to put in place a framework of interdependence which cannot be easily changed by shifting political sands.

As we look to Indo-Bangladesh relations in the coming years, it would be useful to bear in mind that overcoming all hurdles, Bangladesh has emerged as a significant member of the global community. Its self-assurance is demonstrated by the self-financing of the multibillion-dollar Padma bridge after the withdrawal of the International Bank for Reconstruction and Development (IBRD) from its planned assistance. In recent years, the growth of the gross domestic product (GDP) of Bangladesh has exceeded that of India. In several social indicators, Bangladesh is ahead of India.

It may be noted that recently, the reputed Hudson Institute considered the track record of Bangladesh under different social and economic parameters to qualify it as a 'model for developing countries to follow if they hope to achieve strong economic growth and lift their population out of poverty.'[2]

India's policy towards Bangladesh should reflect the respect due to its achievements as also the consideration due to being a smaller neighbour. There are certain perennials that require continued attention. These may be summarised as follows:

Until a few years ago, India's major concern with regard to Bangladesh was the use of Bangladeshi territory by Indian insurgents. This was often with the connivance of Bangladeshi agencies, as the fortuitous arms seizure off Chittagong in 2004 had exposed. Over the past decade, the Bangladesh government has provided a full measure of cooperation with India on this issue. But dialogue between the security agencies should continue.

Dialogue and exchange of information would also be essential with regard to the activities of jihadi elements that often acquire cross-border dimensions, as the Burdwan incident notably demonstrated. Right-wing Islamic extremism is an existential threat to Bangladesh, with the most dire consequences for India as well.

Sreeradha Datta has pointed out the many positive developments on the economic front. These need to be sustained. The recent opening of the Maitri Setu—friendship bridge—over the Feni River, connecting Tripura to the port of Chittagong, has huge implications for India's North East. At the same time, a World Bank report suggests substantial increases in exports as also national incomes in both countries with free trade and increased connectivity. These possibilities have to be pursued and actualised.

The status of the Hindu minority in Bangladesh—the ostensible backdrop to the CAA—has been a matter of concern in India. The percentage of Hindus in the population of Bangladesh has dipped since 1971. Their physical travails have been highlighted, notably by Bangladeshi writers Taslima Nasreen and Humayun Azad. According to the latest figures, Hindu outmigration from Bangladesh has reduced substantially since changes in the Vested Property Act—a major source of harassment to them—as well as the proactive steps taken by the government. It may be noted that following the exchange of enclaves in 2015, most Hindus in the Bangladeshi enclaves, who had the option of migrating to India for resettlement, chose to stay on. With recent developments in India, it would seem to have lost the moral authority to speak for the minorities in Bangladesh. In any event, it would not be the expression of concern from abroad, which may well be counterproductive, but the ability of the community to assert its lawful rights that would be fruitful.

The issue of alleged illegal migration of Bangladeshi Muslims has caused the most unfortunate ripples in recent months. That such migration has taken place is undeniable. But the numbers seem to have been highly exaggerated. Nor is it acknowledged that such migrants have filled economic needs and have not been a burden on society. The recently aborted NRC exercise in Assam, expected to show a large Muslim migration, showed the opposite. In this connection, a recent comment in the *Indian Express* is relevant: 'In an age of dog-whistle scaremongering, a union minister alleged on February 9 that, "half of Bangladesh will come to India if citizenship is offered." But no crystal ball prediction could be more deluded. This year Bangladesh's economic growth rate has surpassed India. In the last decade, on a range of social development indicators, from infant mortality to immunisation, Bangladesh has fared better.'[3] This issue seems to have been blown out of proportion, owing to internal political calculations, and needs to be carefully handled.

As a riverine country dependent on the rivers, great and small, all flowing in from India, for many aspects of their livelihood, Bangladesh has a critical interest in their flows. Upstream requirements of India are no less important. In the absence of any binding international law on the sharing of common rivers, it is necessary for India to approach the problem with transparency and an open mind. As the Farakka Agreement had shown, answers would lie not with the ministries of water resources, but with political judgement and accommodation.

The idea of a South Asian Association for Regional Cooperation (SAARC) was mooted by then President of Bangladesh, Ziaur Rahman in 1979. A series of discussions at various levels of governments after Zia's assassination in 1981 led to the formation of SAARC in 1985. In any regional grouping, even if the ostensible objectives relate to trade and harmonisation of rules concerned with interaction between states, forward movement is difficult if there is no overarching common vision of the future, let alone perceptions of security. The negative nature of India–Pakistan relations and the overwhelming mutual suspicions would never have made possible for SAARC to deliver on larger objectives, despite the commitment, at least at the early stages of countries like Bangladesh and Sri Lanka. I had been associated with the discussions preceding the formation of SAARC and had felt that this was a useful umbrella under which members could assemble without being overwhelmed by India's presence.

Two other regional associations with which India and Bangladesh are associated are the Bangladesh, Bhutan, India, Nepal grouping (BBIN) and Bay of Bengal Initiative for Multi-Sectoral Technical and Economic Cooperation (BIMSTEC), both emerging in the mid-1990s, perhaps under the compulsions of the hurdles facing SAARC. But movements have not been spectacular.

For reasons of history and shared religion, as also suspicions about India, a section of the people in Bangladesh would look favourably on Pakistan, even as their numbers or influence should not be overestimated. The new 'transactional' generation would probably be indifferent to past associations. But what was, nevertheless, revealing were the massive demonstrations at Shahbag square by apolitical youth in the spring of 2013 demanding, and ensuring, justice for the war criminals of 1971, vividly recalling in speeches and cartoons the atrocities committed by the Pakistan Army and its collaborators. It had been a significant recovery of lost history.

China had recognised Bangladesh on 31 August 1975, a little over two weeks after the assassination of Sheikh Mujib, in whose birth centenary 'China will show the highest respect to the greatest Bengali of all time, Father of the Nation Bangabandhu Sheikh Mujibur Rahman'.[4] Echoing the Indian prime minister, the Chinese diplomat, Li Jiming, also said, 'China–Bangladesh relationship is now at its best time ever in history.' Chinese diplomatic callisthenics have always been admirable and, coupled with a weighted purse, won them dividends. China is the major supplier of arms and equipment to the Bangladesh Army, Navy and Air Force, even if there are muted questions on their cost and serviceability. Bangladesh is a willing member of the Belt and Road Initiative (BRI). China is its largest trading partner with also the largest trade deficit.

It would be futile, even counterproductive, for India to be oversensitive to the increasing Chinese presence in Bangladesh in diverse areas. If there are concerns in Bangladesh and elsewhere about some of the Chinese terms and conditions for engagement and the consequences for overexposure, these have to run their course. Again, to quote Sreeradha Datta, 'In short, within the context of China, nationalist credentials would mean Bangladeshi parties seeking closer ties with Beijing, while in the Indian context, being a nationalist would imply adopting positions that are in opposition to New Delhi.'[5]

The fiftieth anniversary of Bangladesh's war of independence is a good moment to take stock of Indo-Bangladesh relations and look at the future. They have seen several ups and downs over the past half a century, and are, today, at an even keel with cooperation at many levels. It remains for the two governments to build further on existing foundations, with mutual respect and consideration for each other's interests and concerns, for the benefit of the two peoples. Prime Minister Narendra Modi's visit, celebrating the fiftieth anniversary of the liberation war, was an excellent occasion to reaffirm mutual commitments to shared values. The agreements signed on the occasion should serve to reinforce bonds of economy and connectivity. The prime minister has assured that wrinkles in the relationship would be removed. The still-ongoing demonstrations against the Indian PM's visit should give both countries pause to reflect on the importance of ensuring that sensitivities of the people are always borne in mind to ensure secure foundations for the future.

Endnotes

1. Datta, Sreeradha. 'India and Bangladesh: The Rock Solid Neighbours', Vivekananda International Foundation, 17 August 2020. https://www.vifindia.org/2020/august/17/India-and-bangladesh-the-rock-solid-neighbours
2. Newton-Cheh, Nicholas. 'Bangladesh: A Blueprint for South Asia', South Asia Program at Hudson Institute, June 2019.
3. *The Indian Express*, 14 February 2021.
4. Jiming, Li. Chinese Ambassador to Bangladesh. *Dhaka Tribune*, 15 January 2021.
5. Datta, Sreeradha. 'Bangladesh the Much-Coveted Neighbour', Institute of South Asian Studies', 4 August 2020.

CHAPTER 9

INDIA–NEPAL RELATIONS DURING COVID-19 TIMES

Ranjit Rae

Recent months have witnessed unprecedented political turbulence in Nepal. As if the Covid-19 pandemic and its negative impact on the economy and people's livelihoods were not enough[1], Nepal faced serious internal political problems, particularly within the then ruling Nepal Communist Party (NCP). Supported by a pliant president, the then Prime Minister KP Oli took a series of decisions that undermined the Constitution and threw democratic norms to the wind. It is the Supreme Court of Nepal that stepped in, upheld the Constitution and protected democracy. These decisions have had a wide-ranging impact on the domestic political dynamic in Nepal.

Nepal's relations with India, too, have been fraught; they have swung like a pendulum—from a deep freeze and no engagement for the better part of 2020 to a strong upswing in the relationship with a series of high-level visits between the two countries beginning September 2020. The bilateral relationship was buffeted by the internal political turbulence in Nepal with a widespread perception that India was solidly backing the authoritarian regime of KP Oli. China–Nepal ties received a significant boost following the visit of President Xi Jinping to Nepal in October 2019—a presidential visit that took place after twenty-three years. The geopolitical contestation for influence between China and the US has also impacted the domestic politics in Nepal.

A coalition of the CPN (UML) and CPN (Maoist Centre) had coasted to a spectacular victory in the 2017 general elections. Subsequently, with China's blessings, the NCP was formed through a merger in May 2018 of the two parties[2]; the architect of the electoral victory was clearly KP Oli, a polarising leader, who has perfected the art of gaining popular support by raising anti-India rhetoric. The dynamics of the merger, however, required power sharing between the two co-chairpersons of the party—KP Oli and Prachanda—and it was agreed that the prime ministership would be held on a rotational basis while the party would be headed by both leaders. Over a period of time, Oli's autocratic behaviour, unwillingness to adhere to the power-sharing arrangement with Prachanda, or even to consult him and other senior leaders such as former PM Madhav Kumar Nepal on matters of policy and appointments; the amassing of coercive powers of the state within the prime minister's office; and strengthening the prime minister's powers over appointments to constitutional bodies[3], including the all-powerful Commission for the Investigation of the Abuse of Authority (CIAA), led to a growing mistrust and alienation between the two leaders and the effective creation of two rival factions within the NCP. Earlier, Oli had also brought in an ordinance that made it easier for political parties to split, but this was withdrawn in the face of protests.

During the early part of 2020, Oli also tried to buttress his credentials as a strong nationalist leader—someone who could stand up to India—by redrawing the map of Nepal, incorporating several Indian territories, including Kalapani, Lipulekh and Limpiyadhura, a move that was provided parliamentary cover by a two-thirds majority. India had produced a new map in November 2019 following the reorganisation of Jammu and Kashmir into two union territories. Nepal objected to this map, even though it did not reflect any change in India's international borders from the previous maps, on the grounds that Kalapani was shown as part of the Indian territory. Kalapani is a long-standing territorial dispute originating from differences with regard to the source of the river demarcating the boundary between the two countries—the Mahakali—which needs resolution through dialogue. Oli has compounded matters by expanding Nepalese claims significantly by including other territories, including the famous Lipulekh Pass, used by pilgrims and traders since ancient times for the sacred Kailash Mansarovar Yatra, thereby making the issue more intractable.

As the bilateral relationship deteriorated, Oli added fuel to fire by making several unfriendly comments and unfounded allegations vis-à-vis India. He made fun of the Indian national emblem—Ashoka's lion capital—by asking whether India's motto is *Satyameva Jayate*—truth will triumph—or *singhameva jayate*—might (lion) will triumph[4]. He said that the Indian virus was deadlier than the Chinese one[5]. Oli publicly alleged that India was destabilising his government[6], thereby implying that his opponents within the NCP were acting at the behest of India; this attracted a sharp retort from the Prachanda–Madhav Kumar Nepal faction. Oli argued in a public speech that Lord Ram was born not in India but in the real Ayodhya, which was in Nepal[7]. On International Yoga Day, 21 June 2021, Oli asserted that yoga was developed in Nepal and not in India[8]. As someone who has mastered the art of anti-Indian rhetoric for political benefit, Oli perhaps had hoped that the same tactic would again strengthen his support base. Instead, it severely damaged the bilateral relationship with India without shoring up Oli's position within his own party or indeed in the public.

Some of these developments, particularly the 'cartographic assertion'[9], angered India, with virtually all high-level engagement between the two countries going into a deep freeze.

China's expanding engagement was another complicating factor in India–Nepal relations. For several years, particularly since 2016, the Chinese had been very comfortable with Oli, who was responsible for far-reaching decisions, including participation in and strong support to China's Belt and Road Initiative (BRI), and the agreement between the Chinese and Nepalese communist parties signed in September 2019. This was capped by the visit of President Xi Jinping to Nepal in October 2019. Today, China is not merely engaged in undertaking projects under the awkwardly named Nepal–China Trans-Himalayan Multidimensional Connectivity Network[10], some of which are a part of the BRI and covers, roads, rail, digital connectivity in addition to development of land ports at the border. What is new and striking is the extent to which China is involved in the domestic politics, particularly with regard to the communist parties in Nepal. It is widely believed that the Chinese facilitated the unification of the erstwhile communist parties into the NCP[11]. As differences mounted within the NCP between the Oli and Prachanda–Madhav Kumar Nepal factions, there was a high-profile telephone conversation between President Xi and President Bidya Devi Bhandari of Nepal[12], followed by shuttle diplomacy by the Chinese ambassador in Kathmandu to patch up matters between the two factions. It appeared that the Chinese goal was to ensure that the NCP remained united at all costs.

India had been watching the developments in Nepal with growing concern. The no-dialogue situation was creating a vacuum that was being filled by others, notably China. Further, India's significant bilateral cooperation programme was affected as mechanisms responsible for ensuring efficient implementation remained in abeyance. The Oli government was also coming under attack domestically for its inability to begin talks with India on the boundary. (PM Oli had made several rhetorical statements that he will get the territory back from India[13].) It is in this context that the first signs of a rapprochement became evident with PM Oli's phone call to PM Narendra Modi on Independence Day in 2020. India reciprocated in full measure with a series of high-level visits in quick succession. The head of the Research and Analysis Wing (RAW) made a high-profile and visible visit in September, followed by the army chief and the foreign secretary during the last four months of 2020.

Thereafter, the foreign minister of Nepal visited India for a meeting of the Joint Commission in January 2020. Though the agreed minutes did not make any reference to the question of talks on the boundary dispute or on the acceptance of the report of the Eminent Persons Group—the group was established to prepare a road map for India–Nepal relations in the future, including on the contentious 1950 Treaty of Peace and Friendship between the two countries, but the report is yet to be accepted by the two governments—the commission undertook a comprehensive review of the overall bilateral partnership and cooperation programme, including the all-important 5040 MW Pancheshwar multipurpose hydroelectric project. Subsequently, Nepal has also granted the Lower Arun hydroelectric project to India—the Indian company Satluj Jal Vidyut Nigam Ltd (SJVNL) is already executing the Arun-III hydropower project on the upper reaches of the same river.

India's rapprochement with the Oli government coincided with a growing isolation of PM Oli within his own party. The decision of the Constitutional Bench of the Supreme Court in February 2021 to overturn the first dissolution of the Pratinidhi Sabha (December 2020) on the grounds that this was unconstitutional, came as a blow to the Oli government. (Historically, Nepal has been plagued by considerable political uncertainty with short tenures of governments. It is against this background that the new Constitution makes it very difficult for a sitting prime minister to dissolve the house, unlike in other democracies such as India or the UK. House dissolution can only be undertaken after all possibilities for the formation of an alternative government, as listed in Article 76 of the constitution, are exhausted).

A separate decision of the Supreme Court in March 2021—restoring status quo ante prior to the merger of the CPN (UML) and NCP (Maoist Centre)—to say the least an unexpected decision, however, seriously complicated the politics of the communist parties in Nepal and strengthened Prime Minister Oli's position. Whereas in the erstwhile NCP, Oli had been reduced to a minority, following the Court's decision, Oli now headed the CPN (UML), the single largest party in parliament with 121 seats out of a total of 275. His bête noire in the party, Madhav Kumar Nepal, who had joined forces with Prachanda and his band of Maoists in the united NCP, was reduced to a much weaker position.

Following the restoration of the lower house, Oli lost a vote of confidence as a section within his own party in addition to the NCP (Maoist Centre), a faction of the JSP and the Nepali Congress (NC) did not support him and a faction of the JSP abstained. Though Oli resigned, since the opposition headed by Sher Bahadur Deuba of the NC was unable to forge a majority, Oli was again appointed prime minister as the leader of the single largest party in the house. Thereafter, he refused to seek another vote of confidence and, without resigning, recommended to the president that clause 76 (5) of the Constitution be activated, wherein, any member of the house who can gather a majority can form a government. In another words, without creating a vacancy in the post, a search for a new prime minister was launched. The president provided only one day for the establishment of a new government. In dramatic developments, within the prescribed time frame, Sher Bahadur Deuba was able to garner 149 signatures of MPs against a requirement of 136 for a majority, and accompanied by several former prime ministers, including Prachanda, Madhav Kumar Nepal and Baburam Bhattarai submitted the list to the president. Meanwhile, Oli, who at a press conference the same day had said that he did not have the majority, submitted letters from himself as leader of the CPN (UML) and Mahant Thakur, leader of JSP claiming support of 153 members (121 of the CPN (UML) and 32 of the JSP) despite the fact that the Madhav Nepal faction of the CPN (UML) and the Upendra Yadav–Baburam Bhattarai faction of the

JSP had declared support for Deuba, to the president. The president, instead of inviting Deuba to form the government, rejected both claims on the ground of overlapping names; the Oli led cabinet thereafter recommended dissolution of the house for a second time and announced general elections, a decision that was endorsed by the president late in the night of 21 May 2021. This decision was challenged by a host of writ petitions in the Supreme Court.

In a historic judgement on 12 July 2021, a constitutional bench of the Supreme Court unanimously decided to restore the lower house for a second time; furthermore, the court replaced KP Oli with Sher Bahadur Deuba as prime minister. The court also decided that the actions of the president are subject to judicial review and it is the responsibility of the court to correct presidential actions that are not in conformity with the Constitution. Finally, the judgement pronounced that under Article 76 (5) of the Constitution, members of parliament would be sovereign in deciding who to support as prime minister and party whips would not apply. The judgement, with far-reaching ramifications changed the political course of the country. Deuba was appointed prime minister (this is the fifth occasion when he has become prime minister) and secured a thumping majority with 165 members supporting him, including 22 from the CPN (UML) and both factions of the JSP. He is expected to lead a stable coalition; if however, the coalition unravels due to poor management, general elections could conceivably be held earlier than scheduled under Deuba's leadership.

The US–China rivalry is also playing out in interesting ways in Nepal. The US, under its Millennium Challenge Corporation (MCC) programme, has agreed to provide a US$ 500 million grant to Nepal for the development of roads and electrical transmission lines. This programme has further increased the differences within the communist camp. The NCP (Maoist Centre) and the Madhav Kumar Nepal faction of the CPN (UML) are opposing it on the grounds that it is part of the Indo-Pacific strategy of the US, which, in their perception, is to 'contain' China[14]; Prime Minister Deuba and former PM Oli are in favour of it. Even though the grant will provide the much needed infrastructure for the development of Nepal and strengthen its power connectivity with India, the fact that key communist leaders are opposed to it clearly demonstrates the growing clout of China.

For India, the ongoing domestic turmoil has created several dilemmas. India is wary of the consolidation and dominance of the communist forces in Nepal, a development that has the solid backing of China and has resulted in a significant expansion of China's role in Nepal. Historically, it is the royalists and leftists that have been the most ardent exponents of anti-India nationalism in Nepal. A dissolution of the NCP into its erstwhile constituents—CPN (UML) and NCP (Maoists)—should reduce the salience of the left parties in Nepalese politics and provide greater space to democratic forces, including the NC and the JSP. This would also represent a setback for China that has invested considerable energy in bringing various communist groups together. However, one should not underestimate China. Even though they may have suffered a temporary setback, China is a long-term player and is there to stay. Nepal is likely to see both political fragmentation and new alignments in the run up to general elections, likely to be held in early 2023, before the house completes its scheduled term of five years.

India would also like democracy and rule of law to flourish in Nepal; India views these as a prerequisite for stability, peace and prosperity in the country. The new constitution was forged in a crucible of violence and bloodshed and contains key elements from the solemn agreements that ended the Maoist insurgency and the Madhesi *andolans*—agreements that in one way or the other were facilitated by India. Already, in the face of the ongoing uncertainty in Nepal, demands for a restoration of a Hindu *Rashtra* and/or the monarchy have been raised. Influential political leaders are wary of the federal project contained in the constitution. Though the constitution was not fully accepted by all sections of Nepal's diverse society, a reopening of some of these deeply contested issues could again plunge the country into turmoil.

The perception in Nepal was that India was strongly backing the unpopular Oli regime—a regime that had blatantly violated the constitution to save itself. India's primary and limited objective was seen as neutralising communist and Chinese influence rather than supporting constitutional governance. Such a tactical approach without regard to its long-term implications is bound to complicate India's engagement with Nepal. Traditionally, India has always sided with the people's aspirations in Nepal. We have supported movements for progressive change, inclusive democracy and constitutional governance. While we naturally need to work with the government of the day, this should not imply a reduction in our engagement with other political actors, including those opposed to the government.

India needs a clear long-term strategy for Nepal. There is a close civilisational connect that provides a strong foundation for the relationship. This has been built upon through various connectivity initiatives—roads, rail, digital; in the energy sector—including hydropower and oil; development of border infrastructure; and close cooperation between the security and police forces between the two countries. The grant of a large number of doses of the Covid-19 vaccine has generated significant goodwill in Nepal. No other country can match India's engagement with Nepal. Having said that, at an incremental level, there is a growing Chinese presence; for instance, China contributes more foreign direct investment (FDI) to Nepal as compared to India. Massive connectivity projects under BRI have been agreed. And, following India's inability to supply additional Covid-19 vaccines in the face of domestic requirements, China has stepped in with its own supplies.

India needs to address the challenge posed by the expanding Chinese footprint. This requires stepping up and improving our own project implementation efforts. We need to speed up the development of Nepalese hydropower potential, including through cooperation with third countries, since this will strengthen the integration of the two economies for mutual benefit. Projects, such as the Pancheshwar multipurpose hydropower project, should be viewed strategically. Pancheshwar will transform the nature of the relationship between the two countries, even as it leads to massive development of Nepal's poor far western region and the Kumaon region in India. Accordingly, India should be generous in resolving some of the contentious issues, such as calculation of existing consumptive usage of water from the Mahakali River by the two countries, so that the detailed project report (DPR) can be finalised and project implementation can begin.

We also need to strengthen our engagement with like-minded countries. In Nepal for instance, during the Maoist insurgency, regular exchanges with countries such as the US and UK contributed towards a more coordinated international approach that was aligned to our perceptions.

India is already a strong supporter of the Indo-Pacific strategy and is an active member of the Quad grouping, which includes US, Australia and Japan, and has only recently met at summit level[15]. Even as the South Asian

Association for Regional Cooperation (SAARC) has lost steam, we have stepped up our engagement in the Bangladesh, Bhutan, India, Nepal (BBIN) grouping and the Bay of Bengal Initiative for Multi-Sectoral Technical and Economic Cooperation (BIMSTEC) as well as the Association of Southeast Asian Nations (ASEAN). India is working to strengthen subregional and regional connectivity through the development of several infrastructure projects that will eventually link South Asia with ASEAN.

Lastly, even as our relations with China are fraught, we should not rule out the possibility of India and China sharing respective assessments about the situation in Nepal. At a fundamental level, both countries would like to see stability in Nepal. Turmoil and instability would make Nepal susceptible to inimical external influences. China worries about the role of Western countries and non-governmental organisations (NGOs) with regard to the Tibetan issue. India worries about growing proselytisation efforts, especially within Nepalese *janjati* communities as well as exploitation of the open border by inimical forces; the memory of the hijack of IC 814 from Kathmandu to Kandahar is still fresh in memory. Such convergences could be built upon in the future, once bilateral ties with China improve.

With a new government in place in Nepal, led by the Nepali Congress, a party with old fraternal links with India, this is an appropriate time to re-invigorate and step up bilateral cooperation and engagement. Subject to the vagaries of the Covid-19 pandemic, a visit of Prime Minister Deuba to India could provide such an opportunity.

Endnotes

1. See https://www.worldbank.org/en/news/press-release/2020/10/08/covid-19-impact-on-nepals-economy-hits-hardest-informal-sector
2. Baral, Biswas. 'Nepal Left Parties Merger: How the Political Behemoth Came to Life', *The Wire*, 18 May 2018.
3. Oli government issues ordinance on Constitutional Council Act amid crisis in ruling party', *The Kathmandu Post*, 15 December 2020. See also, Anil Giri, 'Appointments to constitutional bodies receives widespread flak', *The Kathmandu Post*, 4 February 2021.
4. Joshua, Anita. 'Nepal rubs it in with "satyamev"', *The Telegraph*, 19 May 2020.
5. Chaudhury, Dipanjan Roy. 'Indian coronavirus more lethal than Chinese: Nepal PM KP Sharma Oli', *The Economic Times*, 21 May 2020.
6. Sibbal, Siddhant. 'Nepal PM KP Sharma Oli blames India of conspiring to topple his government': Zee News, 28 June 2020.

7. 'Lord Ram born in Nepal: PM Oli ignites new row with stunning claim on Ayodhya', *Hindustan Times*, 14 July 2020.
8. 'PM KP Sharma Oli claims Yoga originated in Nepal, not India.' PTI, 23 June 2021.
9. Ministry of External Affairs, 'Official Spokesperson's response to media queries on the revised map of Nepal released by Government of Nepal', 20 May 2020.
10. 'New Blueprint for Trans-Himalayan Project to come up during Xi's Nepal visit: China', *The Business Standard*, 9 October 2019.
11. Gupta, Shishir. China's move to play political broker in Nepal not working, 29 December 2020, *The Hindustan Times.*
12. President Bhandari holds phone conversation with Xi Jinping', Onlinekhabar, 28 April 2020.
13. We Will Get Territories Back from India: Nepal's PM Oli', The Wire, 10 January 2021.
14. Giri, Anil. 'NCP task force suggestion throws future of MCC into confusion', *The Kathmandu Post*, 25 August 2020.
15. The first Quad Summit of heads of state/government of Australia, India, Japan and the US was held virtually on 15 March 2021.

CHAPTER 10

INDIA'S RELATIONS WITH BHUTAN IN THE POST-COVID-19 ERA

VP Haran

India–Bhutan relations are unique and based on history, geography, culture and religion. Trust, understanding and sensitivity to each other's interests and concerns underpin these relations. India enjoys tremendous goodwill in Bhutan and so does Bhutan in India. Bilateral relations are an example of how the two countries that are vastly different on various parameters can coexist peacefully and work together for mutual advantage. Cooperation during the Covid-19 pandemic strengthened these relations further.

Bhutan handled the Covid-19 situation extremely well, with His Majesty the King of Bhutan Jigme Khesar Namgyel Wangchuck and Prime Minister Dr Lotay Tshering actively leading the efforts. PM Narendra Modi spoke to His Majesty the King of Bhutan on 18 September 2020 and conveyed India's readiness to support Bhutan's fight against Covid-19. India facilitated the movement of essential goods, medicines and medical equipment, and the evacuation of the Bhutanese in India. A new land customs station (LCS) was opened at Ahllay in Bhutan—near Phuentsholing in Bhutan and Jaigaon in West Bengal—for movement of goods to Bhutan after the closure of the LCS at Jaigaon due to the pandemic.

As a practical manifestation of India's Neighbourhood First Policy, India handed over 150,000 doses of Covishield vaccine to Bhutan on 20 January

2021, just four days after the roll out of the vaccine in India. India has also committed to meet the entire requirement of Bhutan for vaccinating a target population of 533,500. India's gesture and the warm acknowledgement of the same by Bhutan reflect the close and friendly relations between the two countries. The challenge lies in ensuring that relations stay the course in the post-pandemic era.

In the present, fast-changing world, the younger generation, with education and exposure to the outside world, TV, Internet and social media, have a wider horizon. Their hopes and aspirations are different from the earlier generation. This is, no doubt, part of the evolutionary process, but the pace of evolution has quickened in recent decades. Bhutan is not an exception. The young Bhutanese have their views and expectations. They may be aware of the importance of India's contribution to Bhutan's development and security, but may not attach the same importance to it as the elder generation. Certain basic assumptions in relations may not hold true in the longer term. Already, some have a different view on important elements of Bhutan's foreign policy. In this background, India and Bhutan should be working to establish long-term interdependencies to underpin the close relations. This is possible through further strengthening mutually important security cooperation; consolidating and intensifying economic cooperation, for which the hydropower sector offers immense potential; revitalising cooperation in the education sector; and further nurturing people-to-people contacts.

PM Modi's Visit

Frequent contacts at the highest levels is the hallmark of India–Bhutan relations. The Bhutanese PM Dr Lotay Tshering took part in the swearing in ceremony of PM Modi in May 2019. Modi visited Bhutan in August 2019, a few months after taking over as prime minister for the second term. Ten memorandums of understanding (MOUs) in the fields of space research, education, information technology (IT), power and aviation were signed during the visit. Modi said that the outcome of the visit would enhance the bilateral ties. Bhutanese prime minister observed that India and Bhutan may vary in size, but their beliefs, values and motivation are the same. There is now a lull in contacts due to Covid-19. His Majesty the King was invited to visit India on mutually convenient dates, when PM Modi spoke to him in September 2020.

SECURITY COOPERATION

The bilateral security cooperation predates establishment of formal diplomatic relations in 1968. India has been providing training and equipment to the Royal Bhutan Army since 1962. Security of the two countries is interlinked with connectivity provided by the narrow Siliguri corridor being critical for both North East India and Bhutan. The India–Bhutan Friendship Treaty of 2007 provides in Article 2 that the two countries 'shall cooperate closely with each other on issues relating to their national interests. Neither government shall allow the use of its territory for activities harmful to the national security and interest of the other.' Security cooperation has been proceeding smoothly, and is more essential now in the face of increasing challenges posed from the north of Bhutan.

The 699 km-long India–Bhutan boundary has been demarcated, excepting for the tri-junctions in the west and the east, determination of which needs to be done in consultation with China. The 470 km-long Bhutan–China boundary is yet to be finalised despite twenty-four rounds of boundary talks. Two sections of the boundary are disputed—495 sq km in the Pasamlung and Jakarlung areas in the north and 269 sq km, including the strategically important Doklam plateau (89 sq km), in the west. In 1988 and 1998, the two countries had agreed to maintain peace and tranquillity in the border areas, pending final settlement of the boundary question and to maintain status quo till then. Despite the agreements, China has been nibbling at Bhutanese territory.

In a major move in June 2017, China sought to extend the road from Chumbi Valley to the north of Doklam plateau to the south. According to Bhutan and India, the Bhutan–China boundary runs along the ridge to the north of the plateau. China claims the plateau and asserts that the Jampheri ridge to the south of the plateau is the boundary. The importance of access to Jampheri ridge lies in the fact that from the ridge one can get a clear view of movement along the Siliguri corridor, which would be hugely advantageous should any trouble break out. India intervened physically to stop the road construction, as it violated the 2012 agreement between special representatives of India and China that status quo would be maintained till the tri-junctions were determined in consultation with Bhutan. India, in consultation with Bhutan, carried out negotiations with China. The stand-off was resolved on

29 August, with India and China agreeing to pull back their troops and equipment from the stand-off point.

Since then, China has been more active along the border with Bhutan. It has established permanent facilities in northern and eastern Doklam, and is present there now throughout the year, whereas, before 2017, there was no permanent presence of its People's Liberation Army (PLA) on the plateau. In a meeting of the Global Environment Facility (GEF) in June 2020, it claimed that the Sakteng Wildlife Sanctuary in eastern Bhutan, well away from the border with China, is a disputed area, though in the 24 rounds of border talks, China had never mentioned it as a disputed area. More recently, China has built settlements in Pangda village near Doklam, which maps indicate is in Bhutan. Bhutan may not be able to counter Chinese moves at the border. India's interests are directly involved since it is near the tri-junction area.

Developments on the ground indicate that China does not attach importance to dialogue to settle the boundary dispute, and is determined to move ahead unilaterally to change the status quo along the border, bilateral agreements notwithstanding. It is necessary that India and Bhutan hold regular consultations to periodically assess the evolving situation, as this issue is of vital security interest to both the countries. Available options could be assessed for their feasibility and effectiveness. These options include holding trilateral dialogue with China to settle the issue of tri-junctions, particularly in the Doklam area, as envisaged in the 2012 agreement between special representatives of India and China; strengthening Bhutanese army's presence in the southern part of Doklam plateau; and establishing Bhutanese army posts on Jampheri ridge. The two countries should also decide in advance on how to respond to any fresh moves by China at the border, as time would be of the essence in countering Chinese moves.

Economic, Commercial and Development Cooperation

Bilateral Trade

The scope for increasing bilateral trade, which was US$ 1.01 billion in 2018-19, is limited, as India already accounts for nearly 90 per cent of Bhutan's foreign trade. There is potential for increasing imports of dolomite, cement and mineral products from Bhutan, and this must be explored.

Indian investments in Bhutan account for less than a third of the total foreign direct investment (FDI) in Bhutan. From July 2007 to March 2019, investment from India was US$ 50 million. Indian industry should be made aware of the advantages of investing in Bhutan—Bhutan's liberal FDI policy, free trade and double taxation avoidance agreements with Bhutan, power at lower rates than in India and a huge market next door, with good connectivity from potential industrial areas. The Indian industry should be encouraged to look at Bhutan as an investment destination.

New Land Customs Station

Ninety per cent of Bhutan's external trade passes through the Jaigaon LCS located in the narrow and crowded Jaigaon market. For long, Bhutan had been requesting to shift the LCS to opposite to Bhutanese town, Ahllay so that heavy industrial raw materials and products could move directly to and from the Pasakha industrial area to India. With the Jaigaon LCS closed due to the pandemic, India allowed transport of goods through Ahllay in Bhutan, by establishing a new LCS near Jaigaon. This has since been converted into a full-fledged LCS and is open for Bhutan's trade with other countries. India should move quickly to establish a modern LCS there, with all facilities, to facilitate Bhutan's external trade.

Development Cooperation

Since 1961, when Bhutan launched its five-year development plans, India has been its most important development cooperation partner. For the initial two plans, India contributed the entire plan outlay. Over a period of time, Bhutan has been able to meet much of the requirement for funds for the plans. India's contribution is now down to 14.5 per cent of the outlay, with a commitment of Rs 4500 crore for the twelfth five-year plan. Rs 400 Cr has also been made available as transitional trade support facility to help the Bhutanese industry to adjust to the loss of competitiveness in the Indian markets following the implementation of the goods and services tax (GST). It is the most successful development cooperation programme that India is implementing anywhere, due inter alia, to active cooperation of the Government of Bhutan. Our support should continue till Bhutan desires our help and guidance.

Hydropower Cooperation

The hydropower sector is critical to Bhutan's growth. Bhutan has an estimated hydropower potential of over 30,000 MW. Of this, it is technologically and financially feasible to develop 23,760 MW. Less than 10 per cent of this is being exploited now. According to Bhutan's twelfth five-year plan document, the sector accounted for 13 per cent of the gross domestic product (GDP), 10 per cent of national revenues and a third of its exports revenue in 2017. In 2020, when the economy was ravaged by the pandemic, the only sector that remained unaffected was hydropower. Power generation went up by over 31 per cent, thanks to increased rainfall and the Mangdechhu power plant, which was commissioned the previous year, operating at full capacity.

Till 2006-07, three major hydroelectric power projects (HEPs)—Chukha (336 MW), Kurichu (60 MW) and Tala (1,020 MW)—were commissioned with India's assistance. The projects were mutually beneficial, with India getting renewable power at reasonable tariff and Bhutan boosting its GDP, revenues and export earnings. The contribution of these projects to the Bhutanese economy encouraged it to seek to expand cooperation in this sector. So far, the projects are run-of-the-river type and eco-friendly, and involve minimal human displacement.

India and Bhutan signed an agreement on cooperation in hydropower sector in July 2006, with India committing to set up additional hydropower capacity to enable Bhutan to export 5,000 MW power by 2020. At the request of the newly elected PM of Bhutan, this target was raised to 10,000 MW by 2020, during the visit to Bhutan of former PM Manmohan Singh in May 2008. Successful completion of this target would have helped Bhutan to become a middle-income country by now. But, progress on ground has fallen far short of commitments.

The only project that has been commissioned since the agreement is the Mangdechhu plant (720 MW) in 2018. Two other projects—Punatsangchhu I (1,200 MW) and Punatsangchhu II (1,020 MW)—have got delayed due to geological issues. Safety of the under-construction Punatsangchhu I dam came into question following land subsidence on the right bank in 2013. Despite best efforts, the problem is yet to be resolved. Alternatives are being explored. This would delay the project further. The only other project that has been taken up is the Kholongchu project (600 MW), for which the foundation stone was laid in 2014, but work has not started on the ground.

The earlier projects were being executed on an intergovernmental basis, and Kholongchu was the first project under the joint venture (JV) model with an Indian public sector undertaking (PSU)—Satluj Jal Vidyut Nigam Ltd (SJVNL) in this case. Three other projects had been identified for execution under JV model. Its experience, so far, on the JV model has prompted Bhutan to convey that it would prefer the intergovernmental model for the remaining projects.

Following the experience gained in the hydropower sector, Bhutan would now like to go in for the 2,560 MW Sankosh storage project, which would earn revenue and foreign exchange throughout the year and facilitate generation during peak hours—which will earn higher revenues. The proposed dam site on the Sankosh River is in the same valley and on the same river as Punatsangchhu I and II projects and close to the border with India. Punatsangchhu becomes Sankosh after the Dagachhu River joins it downstream from the Punatsangchhu II project site. Given the geological issues faced in the other two projects on the same river, and the recent incident in Uttarakhand state, it is necessary that proper assessment be made first on whether, geologically, the mountain on the right bank is stable enough to permit a huge reservoir.

Bhutan is concerned about project delays, cost escalation and mounting hydropower debt. Cost escalation is more due to the approval of cost without providing for cost escalation during the construction period. It should worry India more since price for power is fixed on cost plus basis.

The total public debt of Bhutan as on 30 September 2020 at 120.8 per cent of GDP (2020-21) is high but not worrisome. The external debt is 116.3 per cent of GDP, of which 72 per cent is owed to India in rupees, for hydro projects. External debt service was 6.1 per cent of exports revenue in 2019-20, but will go up from 2020-21, as repayment of the Mangdechhu project loan commences. Debt repayment commences only after the project starts generating revenue. Concerns of a section of the Bhutanese on the debt issue needs to be clarified proactively.

The International Monetary Fund (IMF) and the World Bank—which had gone into the issue of Bhutan's hydropower debt serviceability—noted that construction and financial risks are borne by India, which assures the market for all surplus power. Tariff is fixed at cost plus 15 per cent net return. The joint analysis concluded that risk of debt distress is moderate in Bhutan's case.

Some in Bhutan are of the view that India is not paying the market price for power from Bhutan. They compare the export price with what is charged for the retail consumers in India, what India charges for export to other countries and the peak hour rates quoted in the Indian Energy Exchange. What is not factored in are the cost of transmission, transmission loss and cross-subsidisation of power among different consumers in India. Further, the peak hour rates in the exchange is for a few blocks of fifteen minutes each during a day and the average rate is much lower.

Another issue is the 10 per cent interest charged on hydropower loan. Steep downwards revision of this rate is called for, in line with recent market trends. This would bring down the cost of hydropower projects and make Bhutanese power more competitive. There is need to work out a weighted average price for Bhutanese power, as project-wise price creates confusion.

There are other issues that would be of concern to Bhutan. Indian power plants are operating at around 60 per cent capacity, since capacity expansion has outpaced growth in demand for power. Also, the rate for power is coming down in India, with recent auctions in Gujarat for solar power discovering a price of around Rs 2 per kWh. Bhutan may be concerned about continued demand for Bhutanese power in India.

The rules on cross-border trade in electricity, drafted by India with the aim of liberalising power trade in the Bangladesh, Bhutan, India, Nepal (BBIN) region, would have achieved the opposite result, since it did not provide for sale through power exchange and to third countries through India. Strict conditions on ownership of power plants raised doubts on whether power from the planned JV projects could be exported to India. These concerns have since been addressed, but, in the process, more than two years were lost.

Many of the above issues are serious and merit detailed discussion at the highest levels, given that hydropower trade is possibly the most important vehicle for strengthening economic links and interdependence. The discussion should also focus on the churn in the Indian power market, reasons for delays in taking up power projects under the agreement, debt issue and problems encountered in execution of projects and work out a realistic schedule for achieving the target of 10,000 MW power export.

Education and Training

Cooperation in the education sector over the last 70 years was an important vehicle for creating trust and people-to-people goodwill between the two countries. The earlier generation was educated in India or was taught by Indian teachers, which is remembered to this day. Over the last twenty years, our contribution in this sector has come down steeply. This was partly due to the establishment of quality institutions in Bhutan. The abolition of seats reserved for Bhutanese students in leading institutions in India and decline in the number of teachers deputed by India have also been responsible for declining cooperation in this crucial sector. This needs immediate attention. The request of Bhutan for teachers in higher educational institutions should be handled expeditiously. Fully paid scholarships should be made available in leading institutions, including in professional courses, for Bhutanese students with good academic record.

During the 2019 visit of PM Modi, the two PMs inaugurated the interconnection between Bhutan's Druk Research & Education Network and India's National Knowledge Network, providing access to Bhutanese scholars to the vast information and research material available in the Indian network. More such initiatives should be planned.

India should extend assistance for setting up training institutions in Bhutan to facilitate upgradation of skills in diverse fields. The Chiphen Rigpel (Total Solutions) project (2010-15) for human capacity development in the IT sector was a huge success—imparting IT skills to a quarter of the population of Bhutan belonging to different sections of people, ranging from school students to teachers, government officials and elected representatives. Similar projects should be implemented as part of development cooperation programme. Investment in education and training will deliver returns for a long time, by way of goodwill towards India.

Culture

Since Guru Padmasambhava carried the message of the Buddha to Bhutan in the eighth century, religion and culture have been an important bond and brought the two countries closer. Importance of culture and religion in bringing the people of the two countries closer is recognised and every effort is made to nurture and strengthen relations in these areas. The Nehru–Wangchuck Cultural Centre in Thimphu is playing an important role in this area. The annual Mountain Echoes literary festival in Bhutan is the catalyst for bringing together writers, artists, scholars and poets of the two countries on one platform and promotes friendship and understanding. The India–Bhutan Foundation has facilitated cultural events and visits by artists and supports seminars and academic exchanges. These are valuable initiatives that need to be nurtured carefully and supported further so that there is full appreciation of the importance of close relations in both the countries.

Relations Post-Covid-19

Addressing the students of the Royal University of Bhutan in August 2019, PM Modi, in a message of friendship and cooperation, said, 'As Bhutan soars high in its endeavours, your 1.3 billion Indian friends will not just look on and cheer you with pride and happiness. They will partner you and share with you and learn from you.' This approach underlies our bilateral cooperation and has been reciprocated in good measure by Bhutan and, hence, the success in our bilateral engagements.

Cooperation during the pandemic has strengthened the bond between the two countries. Receiving the vaccine consignment at Paro airport on 20 January 2021, Bhutanese PM, Dr Tshering, applauded the gesture of India and said it was a gift from a trusted friend. He added, 'It is the display of altruism at best, and an exhibit of India's sincerity in the relationship we cherish.' The statement is as much a reflection of the traditional goodwill that India has enjoyed in Bhutan as it is on our gesture of sharing vaccines and medical supplies with other countries in these trying times. India had supplied 550,000 vaccine doses to Bhutan earlier in 2021, which enabled it to give the first shot of vaccine to over 90 per cent of its targeted population by April 2021. We were not able to supply the doses for the second shot due to subsequent political and pandemic developments in India. Bhutan struggled to get vaccines from other sources. We should have worked out a way to supply the vaccine requirement of Bhutan without having to lift the export ban on vaccines. Relations are, no doubt, strong and friendly at present and both countries are conscious of the need for them to stay that way in the longer term, in common interest.

This would require careful nurturing of relations and strengthening of interdependencies through joint efforts in fields such as hydropower, education and training, as also on security-related issues in the wake of Chinese aggression along the borders of both the countries.

CHAPTER 11

INDIA–CHINA RELATIONS IN THE POST-COVID-19 WORLD

NEELAM D SABHARWAL

MILITARY STAND-OFF IN 2020

The India–China relationship, rebuilt in 1988 on the promise of the two countries to work together to make it the Asian century, became the first and the most serious casualty of Covid-19. The unprecedented scale of the People's Liberation Army (PLA) build-up and its coordinated intrusions across the line of actual control (LAC), at multiple points in eastern Ladakh, resulting in a loss of twenty Indian lives—the first in forty-five years—has profoundly disturbed the relationship. The PLA advanced to the post-1962 line to claim sovereignty in the Galwan Valley and prevented Indian patrols from accessing their traditional patrolling points in Depsang, Hot Springs, Gogra, Demchok and around Pangong Tso.

India's resolute military and diplomatic response has ensured a negotiated solution to the crisis. As a first step, simultaneous disengagement on both banks of Pangong Tso was completed in February 2021, on the basis of 'matching' concessions by each side. India vacated strategic Kailash Heights on the Southern Bank as part of this deal. However, all other friction points remained unresolved. It has taken a total of twelve rounds of military level talks besides political level dialogue to see both sides disengage and agree on buffer zones in the Galwan Valley, the site of the June 2020 clash, disengagement from Patrolling Point 17 in Gogra and a limited new agreement reached on 4-5 August 2021.

The conflict has not ended yet. More than a year after the clash at Galwan Valley, efforts to resolve the border crisis continue to move slowly. The next round of talks is expected to discuss patrolling Point 15 in Hot Springs, Demchok, where Chinese ingressions were relatively smaller in numbers than the deployments in Pangong Lake. There is also no indication yet that Beijing is ready to discuss the strategically significant Depsang Plains where Indian patrols are presently blocked from patrolling. India's immediate priority is to seek disengagement and full de-escalation from all friction points, withdrawal of some new forward deployments close to the LAC and restoration of status quo ante on the border.

India has conveyed its view to the Chinese side that continuing impasse along the LAC was 'visibly impacting the relations in a negative manner'. External Affairs Minister S Jaishankar reiterated the imperative of early restoration of normalcy on the border to his Chinese counterpart at their meeting on the sidelines of the Shanghai Cooperation Organisation (SCO) in Dushanbe in mid-July 2021. Foreign Minister Wang Yi's position in contrast has been to argue that 'border issue was not the whole story of the bilateral relationship'. He called on both sides to place the border issue 'in an appropriate position' and it should be addressed while the two countries need to 'expand the positive momentum of bilateral cooperation and create favourable conditions to resolve differences through negotiation'.

How the 'solution' in the remaining areas in Ladakh and the 'favourable conditions' are defined and what will be acceptable to India to stabilise relations is not clear, considering the depth of ingressions by the PLA, and claims of 'sovereignty' by China. What is also not clear is whether the use of the buffer zone model by both sides ceasing patrolling in disputed areas is a temporary measure for maintaining peace or is being considered as a permanent arrangement and when and how status quo ante might be restored.

Though the developments in the spring and summer of 2020 came as a surprise, the transition from engagement and coexistence in the post-1988 era to conflict and confrontation did not happen suddenly. The relationship had been eroding since 2012, when China's more assertive drive for regional domination started making India's task to balance its high-stake security and economic interests vis-à-vis China more complicated.

Why the Change in China's Stance?

China's military stance in eastern Ladakh came as part of a pattern of aggressive posturing and military exercises earlier in the Senkaku Islands, Hong Kong, South China Sea and Taiwan Straits. Initially, these seemed to be diversionary tactics by a beleaguered China, under domestic criticism at home and growing international sentiment seeking accountability for its culpability for Covid-19. This may have been the trigger, but China had specific objectives in each theatre. In the case of military action in eastern Ladakh, it could only be located in China's end game with India.

China's reasons it was understood were its objection to India's build-up of its border infrastructure in forward areas in the last two decades. The catch-up by India was disturbing its dominance in access, logistics and military preparedness since 1962. The road building in high-altitude locations, particularly the new road, the Darbuk-Shyok-Daulat Beg Oldie road, together with construction and operationalisation of advanced landing grounds near the LAC would have been seen as closing the gap by India.

But the pattern of military build-up and multiple intrusions in Ladakh hinted at a yet larger objective. The territorial advances suggested that these pre-meditated and well-planned moves were waiting to happen, to deliver the political message China had decided to convey.

Why it assumed urgency can only be understood in the larger geopolitical context of China's deteriorating relations with the US. Though India is not seen as a threat to China's rise in the world, China has not been able to break free from its mindset to view India as part of the US containment strategy against it since the fifties. India's improved ties with the US through the 1980s was an important consideration for China to seek an improvement in its relations with India to keep it bolstered against a possible convergence with USA. The growing bipartisan consensus on strategic ties with India in Washington in recent years was seen as aimed against China.

Post-Covid-19, China saw calls for decoupling by US businesses and shift of manufacturing lines to other destinations, including India, as hostile moves threatening and undermining China's domination of global supply chains and thwarting its ambitions in the race for technological primacy.

China decided to show the US its limits in checkmating it while reminding the traditional allies and new partners of the downside of acting against

China's will. The unmistakable message to India was twofold—China's ability to create embarrassment on the border at will and a warning that India should desist moving closer to the US.

China's strategic calculus behind the 2020 military incursions in Ladakh may be seen as much for advancing its territorial objectives on the LAC and thwarting India's infrastructural build-up as for diverting India from its more balanced strategy, in both the maritime domain and continental security. By keeping it mired in managing its border security, China hoped to diminish India's value as a strategic partner for the US in the Indo-Pacific.

Viewed thus, Beijing sees little incentive for LAC clarification or an early border settlement, as an unresolved border serves its strategic objectives. By advancing its physical claim to its preferred position in the western sector, China has also been able to change the status quo on the LAC.

Chinese military action in Ladakh and its consequences have raised questions about its policy objectives and how it views relations with India. These developments have unravelled many assumptions in India's own China policy and introduced new uncertainties and rivalries. What has happened on the LAC is clearly not merely a military stand-off. China's disregard of commitments to minimise troop levels in border areas and breach of agreements has left the status quo built over thirty years disrupted. The power differential has given rise to a more intractable China, relations with which can no longer be handled by the 1988 template.

1988 Policy Framework: Decades of Stability

The 1988 policy framework known also as the Rajiv Gandhi–Deng Xiaoping template marked a fundamental shift in India's approach to India–China relations and settlement of the boundary question. Both sides agreed its prior settlement would no longer be a prerequisite for full normalisation of relations. The decision to revive ties in all fields was predicated on ensuring the sanctity of LAC would be observed and the undertaking by the two sides to maintain peace and tranquillity along the LAC pending a fair, reasonable and mutually acceptable final resolution of the border.

This came in the background of the boundary question holding up full normalisation of ties, even though ambassadorial relations were restored in 1976. It took an exchange of foreign minister-level visits in 1979 and 1981 and eight rounds of annual official level talks between 1981 and 1987 at vice minister-level, before the first prime ministerial visit could take place in 1988. By that time, it was clear that a common understanding of the politically sensitive boundary issue could not be found and neither side was in a position to achieve an acceptable settlement, but both sides needed peace on the border.

Despite the criticism today that it was China's self-interest in seeking improved relations with India, this understanding has provided almost three decades of relative stability to the relations. From India's perspective, foremost, was a cooling down of a volatile India–China boundary and minimisation of military adventurism in its periphery. Peace was maintained on the border for almost a quarter of a century.

The Agreement on Maintenance of Peace and Tranquility along the line of actual control (LAC) signed three years later, in 1993, formalised in an international treaty a bilateral commitment by the two countries to maintain status quo on the border and speed up the clarification and confirmation of the LAC. The more detailed listing of military confidence-building measures (CBMs) followed in the 1996 Agreement, which added limits on the size and nature of exercises and use of arms. With increased patrolling by the two sides, a protocol was developed in 2006 for defining the procedure for restraint in such situations.

The summit-level political interactions in the initial phase saw benefits for India in its immediate neighbourhood. While continuing its strategic relations with Pakistan, a moderation of China's public posture provided India the breathing space in its neighbourhood. China showed a more even-handed treatment of the Kashmir issue by correcting its tilt towards Pakistan in terms of its public statements and quiet pressure to desist from carrying through anti-India resolutions in the United Nations Commission on Human Rights (UNCHR) in the mid-1990s. This was evidenced again in Pakistani Prime Minister Nawaz Sharif's visit during the Kargil crisis in 1999, when, instead of assistance, he was advised to de-escalate the situation and pull back troops.

The two countries were able to overcome the hiatus in relations, following India's calling out 'China threat' as the reason for its nuclear tests in 1998. Moves towards normalisation picked up momentum and boundary negotiations saw some progress, too. The establishment of the Special Representatives mechanism in 2003 was a hopeful sign of the seriousness of the Chinese side for a border settlement. The give and take in the leadership exchanges brought a formal recognition by China of Sikkim as a part of India. Bilateral exchanges expanded in all areas. China became one of India's largest trading partners, a very significant source of investment and, perhaps, even of technology, a partner in infrastructure projects and a very substantial destination for tourism and education.

With both countries rising almost simultaneously and sensing an improvement of India–US ties, China agreed, in 2005, to India's proposal for an Agreement on Political Parameters and Guiding Principles for the Settlement of the India–China Boundary Question. From China's viewpoint, a fulfilment of its major objective was in the progressive acknowledgement by India of Tibet as part of People's Republic of China (PRC).

This was also the period when both countries saw a shared world view on global issues, like climate change, and in forging groupings like the Russia–India–China trilateral, Asian Infrastructure Investment Bank (AIIB) and Brazil, Russia, India, China, and South Africa (BRICS). In a move to prevent Delhi from aligning too closely with Washington, a strategic partnership was offered by Beijing in an agreement formalised on the understanding that both countries will not look upon each other as a threat.

Widening Power Differential: Early Signs of Strains

In early signs of a changing balance of power, a shifting position on boundary settlement by a vastly more powerful China was detected. It reneged on the 2005 Agreement by reclassifying Arunachal Pradesh as Southern Tibet and stepping up infrastructure build-up along the LAC and in Tibet. Yet another irritant was added by introducing stapled visas for residents of Jammu & Kashmir and by blocking listing of terrorists in the United Nations Security Council (UNSC) repeatedly.

Trade and investment became a contentious issue, with India's trade deficit in a total two-way trade of US$ 92.68 billion rising to an unsustainable US$ 56.77 billion. The expanding demands of India's growth opened up to Chinese companies in infrastructure building, power generation and telecommunications. China, as the largest trading partner in goods for India, wiped out many indigenous Indian industries without showing any reciprocity to companies with world-class standing in sectors like pharmaceuticals and information technology (IT). A perception started gaining ground in India about the one-sided and limited benefits of engagement with China.

The exponential growth of the Chinese economy and the global financial crisis in 2008 marked China's transition from a regional to a global power and its emergence as the rising challenger to the US in the Asia-Pacific. This also saw a corresponding shift in its foreign policy priorities and perceptions about India as a possible new partner of America in the region.

Unencumbered by the need to converge with the Western model of capitalism and democracy, China, with its one-party rule and increasingly more authoritarian polity, was emboldened to engage with the world on its own terms. This mood coincided with the leadership transition in China in 2012 and emergence of a powerful Xi Jinping, and his 'China Dream'. In a departure from political and economic policies put in place in the post-Mao era, Xi Jinping began scripting a new narrative of China as a great power and made no secret of its aspiration for global leadership.

This newfound confidence started impacting relations with all other countries. But nowhere was the challenge to regional security felt more than in the Asia-Pacific, where China believes its impressive accumulation of economic and military power entitles it to claim predominance in the region and equal status with the US globally. This meant displacing the US as the leading power and containing its peer rivals—Japan and India—by seeking to impose a hierarchical order. In the maritime domain, China started creating artificial islands in the South China Sea as new geographical facts and the Association of Southeast Asian Nations (ASEAN) was faced with these new moves as non-negotiable 'core interests'.

India's ties with China entered a more difficult phase. By 2012, border incidents started becoming more frequent and larger in scale than before and began to coincide with high-level visits. India's improved capabilities and mechanisms put in place since the agreement of 1993 helped in early resolution of stand-offs in Depsang (2013), Chumar (2014) and Doklam (2017), the longest which took 72 days to resolve. It could only be defused on the basis of limited disengagement at the stand-off point. A more assertive China not only tested India on the border but began to undermine Indian interests in South Asia and the Indian Ocean Region. China's position started hardening on boundary settlement to retain the ambiguity of an unsettled border as a leverage and reduce its incentive to maintain peace.

It is in the maritime domain, however, where the rising interest of both countries came to be perceived in direct competition. China saw a connection between the US pivot to Asia and the Quad (United States, Japan, Australia and India) and India's greater focus on maritime security. Whereas, India sees its maritime policy on top of its security agenda, given its vital dependence on maritime traffic. Around 90 per cent of its trade by volume and 77 per cent in value are seaborne. Traditional threats from Pakistan and a more assertive China in South China Sea, with its base in Djibouti, would, no doubt, have been factored in India's considerations while developing a maritime partnership with the US, but India neither sought obstructing China's strategic requirements nor posed a threat to its use of sea lines of navigation.

China's inroads in India's South Asia neighbourhood and the Indian Ocean escalated with Xi's decision to use China's economic strength to build alternate connectivity and financial arrangements under its unilaterally conceived multi-country infrastructure project—the Belt and Road Initiative (BRI). But for India, the China–Pakistan Economic Corridor (CPEC) through Pakistan-occupied Kashmir (PoK), and huge financial investments in it as its 'flagship project' were a violation of its sovereignty.

More importantly, this marked the re-emergence of Pakistan as the fulcrum of China's new geopolitical game in the region. If this meant a commitment to ensure Pakistan is equipped with the capabilities it needs to play the role it is expected to, China has not been averse to making known publicly how much more one-sided its policy has become on India–Pakistan issues. China repeatedly blocked Masood Azhar—leader of the Pakistan-based Jaish-e-Mohammad (JeM)—as a terrorist through 2016 and 2017, and earlier opposed India's membership of the Nuclear Suppliers Group (NSG) in 2015. China's offensive though futile moves in the UNSC to introduce resolutions against India's sovereign action to abrogate Article 370 in the reorganisation of Jammu & Kashmir in 2019 reinforced the existing perception of China–Pakistan nexus working to thwart India's interests.

A more competitive India–China relationship emerged. India opposed China's Belt and Road Initiative, raised barriers to Chinese investment and technology and consulted more closely with major powers in the Indo-Pacific.

These developments ended up straining relations between the two nations, even as PM Modi and President Xi Jinping, both confident in the value of personal diplomacy, started on a high note and met eighteen times. But China's long-term objective of politico-military containment of India, through a strategic relationship with Pakistan and close ties with Nepal, Sri Lanka, Bangladesh and Myanmar; a militarily aggressive posture on the border; and opposition to India at regional and multilateral forums on its NSG membership, began to overshadow the goodwill built over the years.

In the interest of maintaining a stable relationship, the two leaders displayed maturity in rethinking the future of their relations at Wuhan Informal Summit in August 2018 by downplaying the challenges after a new low was reached at Doklam. Some positive gestures were made by India by distancing official association with Tibetan anniversary events, showing more mindfulness of China's stakes in the BRI and China's concerns about the emerging security relationship with Australia, Japan and the US—the Quad countries. The Mamallapuram dialogue in 2019 was part of striving for more balanced India–China ties.

A Stalemate and a New Equilibrium: Some Projections

The way forward will be shaped by how the present stand-off is resolved. India is clear that 'the border and the future of the ties cannot be separated'. In his recent interaction with Foreign Minister Wang Yi, Minister of External Affairs (EAM) S Jaishankar underlined again that ties cannot be reset as long as there were tensions on the border caused by Chinese aggressive actions. India is unambiguous in emphasising the centrality of the border, while China has taken the position to delink the border from overall relations, suggesting the two sides move on. The ongoing de-escalation and disengagement on the LAC in the western sector will have to find a mutually acceptable solution.

Having achieved its objectives on the border, China is inclined to delink the boundary question from the overall relations. For India it is neither an acceptable basis nor will it be possible to return to business as usual. At the same time, China is continuing to step up building new permanent airbases and air defence units closer to the LAC since Doklam crisis in 2017. India has been moving rapidly to upgrade its own infrastructure to close this gap. The result is an entirely changed security dynamic along the LAC which calls for new protocols and confidence-building measures as both sides gradually resume patrolling in buffer zones.

In the absence of a satisfactory progress on restoring status quo ante of April 2020 and the LAC continuing to be heavily militarised, India will be looking at ways to cope with a stalemate in its relations with China as a consequence of Chinese military action in eastern Ladakh. India must also recognise that the multiple challenges posed by a more assertive China, presently in an adversarial mode, will need to be confronted by both internal and external balancing A new equilibrium has to be found in each country's need to engage, while being cognizant of the areas where the two sides will compete.

China Challenge

With China's growing military power, India has to be ready to face a more assertive PLA on the border. An effective military balance will have to be maintained by India to deter any adventurism. A new modus vivendi will have to be based on an assurance that China is not pursuing a policy of continuing confrontation with India and the two sides do not have to face each other as antagonistic adversaries on their periphery. This will depend principally on how China views its relationship with India, but will also depend on India to demonstrate the potential value of maintaining good relations with it and the ability to press its point of view that peace and tranquillity on the border can only be maintained through a commonly agreed LAC.

The military actions have brought to the fore a growing perception of China as the only major power which is not reconciled to India's rise. The negative trends in relations have also given rise to an impression of India's reduced salience in Chinese foreign policy priorities. Strong public opinion against China has called for a review of some fundamental postulates of India's China policy, to end the policy of strategic autonomy and one-China policy. There is also pressure to use the Tibet card and lessen economic dependence on China.

Whereas, the Chinese strategic experts, echoing the Ministry of Foreign Affairs' line that 'the border issue should not be linked with bilateral relations' are arguing for early resumption of trade and economic exchanges. While there is no disagreement the relationship must be underpinned by a sound economic basis, but it cannot be one-sided. The unsustainable trade imbalance has shown the rise of China as an 'opportunity' for India was an unrealistic assumption, which saw it as a competitor and had no interest in powering its economic growth.

Some lessons will have to be drawn from past mistakes in allowing Chinese firms a free run in the Indian market without linking it with China's behaviour on issues of India's core concerns. The decoupling measures by the government to reduce economic dependence by restricting Chinese investments, banning Chinese apps and cancelling contracts have been welcomed. How far will this be sustainable in light of the latest import figures from China for January to December 2020 as US$ 58.71 billion remains to be seen. The government is positioning for the longer run by adopting a strategy of 'self-reliance'. India will have to engage China in a serious dialogue on developing a mutually productive trade and investment partnership in the future.

It is self-evident that China has surged ahead of India on every indicator in the last decade and is the pre-eminent power in Asia, which cannot be ignored or dealt with as in the past. It must also be recognised that a heightened profile of China as a regional and global power, and a widening asymmetry in power, will be a constant factor in India–China relations for the foreseeable future.

How, then, should India deal with a powerful China at its doorstep? Accelerated efforts to strengthen internal capabilities will be the foremost priority, but should India be resigned to a subregional role until a notional time in the future when it has equipped itself with economic, military and technological strength to deal with the Chinese on equal terms?

Clearly, a policy of drift does not serve India's security interests. India will be looking at other options, particularly as it is not fighting a lonely battle. Other countries, too, are trying to come to terms with a more powerful China and its military actions, and punitive trade measures are leading to a crystallisation of new partnerships with global and regional powers.

India's ties with the US are expected to expand most significantly, which will be an essential partner in the development and transformation of India. The Modi government has overcome its hesitation in seeking closer ties in the defence, intelligence sharing and security domain. India is no longer diffident about institutionalising the quadrilateral alliance with America, Japan and Australia and now sees the Quad as essential to ensuring a multipolar Asia.

India's security concerns are not just in the Indo-Pacific, where it has convergences with the US. These will need to be built in the continental domain, where our principal security concern lies in an unsettled border with China. The security cooperation in the Quad is already underpinned by a set of four bilateral logistics, communication and intelligence-sharing arrangements.

By the decision to hold a virtual summit of the burgeoning group high on the agenda, the Biden administration has signalled a more robust response to an aggressive China and the importance it is attaching to Quad at the centre of the strategy for a free and open Indo-Pacific. Though principally designed as a partnership for balancing an aggressive China, the Quad leaders have a larger vision and would like to see the grouping as described by PM Modi as a 'force for global good'. The March 2021 summit decided to advance cooperation in vaccines, critical technologies and climate change.

Useful discussions continued on deepening cooperation in the Quad during Secretary of State Antony Blinken's first visit to India in August 2021, which added a new focus on economic and business ties. The partnership may take time to evolve its full agenda and emerge as a coherent grouping capable of forging a multilateral coalition to effectively balance China, but what is important are indications that Beijing is beginning to take note of the implications for its regional and global prospects.

India will get a stronger hand by playing a more central role in the region. It will be the biggest diplomatic challenge for India to walk the tightrope between the US and China, towards the creation of a multipolar Asia, without which, as EAM S Jaishankar, has said, '...a multipolar international order would be difficult to sustain'. As a rising power in its own right, with an aspiration to develop and influence geopolitical outcomes in Asia and beyond, it remains in India's interest to engage with China and strive to find a sound and realistic long-term basis for its relations. It will be important for both India and China to not allow their relations to rupture and, instead, build on the conviction that their rise can be mutually supportive. The challenge for India will be to develop new terms of engagement in bilateral relations, based on its national interest, in the larger global context.

CHAPTER 12

INDIA'S ACT EAST POLICY IN THE POST-PANDEMIC WORLD

GURJIT SINGH

The impact of the Covid-19 pandemic led to a reassessment by many countries and regional groupings of their national security concerns. Countries now look at a wider set of issues to find a determination of their national interests. This has led to loosening of some relationships, strengthening of sectoral partnerships and broader definitions of security perceptions.

India's Act East Policy (AEP) has been in force since 2014. Mainly, it covers countries of East and South East Asia as well as Oceania. Institutionally, it covered ASEAN, the East Asia Summit (EAS), the ASEAN Regional Forum (ARF) countries, Indian Ocean Rim Association (IORA) and Bay of Bengal Initiative for Multi-Sectoral Technical and Economic Cooperation (BIMSTEC).

On the economic side, this included the free trade agreements (FTAs), comprehensive economic partnership agreements (CEPA), Regional Comprehensive Economic Partnership (RCEP) and the emerging trilateral partnerships for resilient and strategic value chains. In no other region have so many different criss-crossing engagements emerged.

Beyond this, India has vigorously pursued the concept of the Indo-Pacific and the Quad. These required greater cohesion and coordinated engagement in 2020, coinciding with the rise of the pandemic.

Be that as it may, it is the revision of the extant strategic balance and efforts to unilaterally alter it by China that have led to reassessment of much of the strategy of the AEP. This is accentuated by the pandemic. Chinese engagement has expanded trade, investment and economic cooperation even after the pandemic. A similar reorientation by countries of the region, including those in ASEAN, East Asia, Australia and the permanent members of the UN like China, Russia and the US, has occurred.

The focus of international strategic attention is now strong enough for the enunciation of new Indo-Pacific policies by France, Germany, the European Union (EU), the Netherlands, besides Canada. The focus of international interest and challenges has shifted due to the developments in the region extending into the Pacific. The main challenge is of China, which has undertaken confrontation and contestation with countries of the region, including some member states of ASEAN, India, Japan and Australia. China's avoidance of commitment to international rules and treaties has led to a challenge to the regional order. It is clearly seeking to acquire control over maritime routes, island territories, access and resources based on its own perception—for example, using the nine-dash line—rather than following the international law.

The economic dimension has seen China increasing its domination through trade, investment and development cooperation in the region to create an area of economic hegemony. China has vigorously utilised all the rules of international trade in its favour and gone beyond them aggressively to secure a larger share of economic activity in the region.

It has used the Belt and Road Initiative (BRI) and the Asian Investment Infrastructure Bank (AIIB) to good advantage. Besides, the expansion of China's economic engagement has continued efficiently even after the pandemic, leading other partners to believe that besides the strategic challenge, the issue of economic domination also needs to be effectively countered.

Another area of concern and reaction to the pandemic is the innovation and distribution of the vaccine and the building of national public health capacities to face the impact of the pandemic. In many countries, the availability of appropriate medicines, protection equipment, testing facilities, intensive care units and emergency hospital capacity, besides human capacity to deal with the pandemic, were in short supply. This led to a reassessment of regional supply chains, since the lockdowns that were caused by the pandemic led to disruption of supplies at critical times. The consequent human and social impact, as well as the crisis for the public health systems, is a major security challenge. While openness was demanded in trade and investment, the closing down of national borders due to the lockdown and the 'me-first' approach of countries to control access to critical medical supplies dented the regional cooperation idea which was seen as the hallmark of this region. The vaccine development by China, Russia, Europe and India has brought in new elements of strategic engagement. The US offered 23 million vaccine doses to ASEAN, of its global export of 110 million doses, by August 2021, showing the strategic importance of vaccines.

During 2020, online summits were held among and with ASEAN, the EAS, the Asia-Pacific Economic Cooperation (APEC) members and many on bilateral levels. Most countries are now focusing on new ways to hasten the capability to deal with the pandemic and adopt cooperation to reduce dependence on China-based supply chains. Reduced dependence, rather than decoupling, is among the efforts undertaken to create alternative chains for provision of critical supplies to deal with the situation created by the pandemic.

India's Act East Policy

India announced its Look East Policy (LEP) in 1992. It became a sectoral dialogue partner of ASEAN. The LEP was aimed at maximising the gains of India's economic reforms through better integration with the growth areas in East and South East Asia. In 2014, it was reformulated as the AEP and brought about greater strategic considerations over the economic rationale for its origin.

During the evolution of this policy, the situation to the east of India altered rapidly. India became a charter member of the EAS in 2005 and initiated free trade and economic engagement with several countries. India was not a member of APEC but built upon its dialogue partnership with ASEAN and membership of the ARF and EAS. During this period, it enhanced its leadership of IORA and BIMSTEC and participated in RCEP.

In this interregnum, China successfully altered the terms of engagement in a fulsome manner, be it trade, investment or aggressive expansion into the South China Sea. China's rise was anticipated, and its failure to abide by international norms and practice was neither benign nor adequately challenged.

By 2015, ASEAN had evolved into three communities dealing with political and defence, economic and socio-cultural themes. India engaged

ASEAN mainly on economic and social-cultural matters, but with the AEP, it brought in a larger strategic dimension. At the twentieth anniversary summit of ASEAN–India partnership in 2012, a strategic partnership was enunciated and, by the time of the twenty-fifth anniversary summit in 2018, substantive discussions on maritime security were in place.

When the Covid-19 pandemic hit the region hard in 2020, India's engagement was intensive, but it had withdrawn from RCEP in November 2019. This created a perception of doubt about India's AEP. The pandemic renewed challenges of Chinese expansion, and despite India's economic withdrawal from RCEP, it received demands for greater cohesion and regional cooperation in the region. The development of vaccines to deal with Covid-19 by India added a new push to this effort. In this, the participation in an FTA was not the highest priority, the development of a vaccine was.

The AEP has a rules-based friendly engagement with the region at its core. ASEAN centrality is kept in focus, and an adherence to the ASEAN-centered institutions to the east of India is maintained. In several of its international engagements, like the EAS, the India–ASEAN partnership and ARF among others, India retained its commitment to ASEAN centrality, including in Prime Minister Narendra Modi's definitive enunciation at the Shangri-La dialogue in June 2018.

As part of its AEP, the EAS is the most important engagement that India has. The importance of the EAS is that it brings the leading players of the region into one annual summit along with the US and Russia. The original inclusion of India was a recognition of its LEP and the balancing role vis-à-vis China. As China's aggressive posture has enhanced, the importance of India has risen. India has taken the lead under the EAS in dealing with malaria, which can be expanded into a wider effort to deal with pandemics and strengthen public health capacities and availability of medicines and devices in the region. India initiated the Nalanda University project as part of the EAS; since it is based on voluntary contributions, a large number of countries have not been forthcoming. Nalanda University has the capacity of becoming a light house project (LHP) for socio-cultural interaction, coinciding with the expansion of education, research and capacity building as well as peace efforts in the region.

The ARF is a larger grouping and, unlike the EAS, only meets at the level of ministers and senior officials. It is basically a security related engagement and

India needs to use it more to identify the risks of dealing with China since the forum is larger and has many countries which are less ambivalent about China than ASEAN is. The ARF has been on a backburner for India mainly because it has been treated as a part of international security and not the AEP. Among all other institutions in the region, this is the only one which brings in other South Asian countries, including Pakistan, Sri Lanka and Bangladesh. India has begun to pay greater attention to this now.

The India–ASEAN dialogue partnership is a unique one and continues to meet at varied levels—ambassadors, senior officials and ministers—and at Summit level. In fact, so diverse is this relationship that there are nearly thirty mechanisms between India and ASEAN to fulfil its robust Action Plan which has five-year terms. India has provided a substantial funding for implementing the programmes under this. While the partnership is intense, its implementation and the results leave much to be desired. A critical stock-taking of the grants provided to ASEAN for two decades is urgently required. Most ASEAN countries have better economic standards than India and should contribute substantially to this partnership rather than depend solely on India to be a donor. This one-sided partnership needs alteration, and if that happens, perhaps the projects, too, would be better thought-out and have more coherent results.

India has contributed to the ASEAN effort to narrow development gaps in Cambodia, Laos, Myanmar and Vietnam (CLMV countries). These efforts have been lauded but their results remain uncertain. Most projects do not have business plans and remain dependent on Indian funding in perpetuity or the projects close down since local governments do not invest ownership in them.

With Myanmar and Vietnam, there are important strategic partnerships of substantive diversity. However, with Cambodia and Laos, the expansion of the relationship has not taken place due to the sheer domination by China and the willing closure of space for Indian interests in these countries. It is time for a realistic assessment of the grant programmes and concessional lending to Cambodia and Laos unless they provide entry points for Indian business on a preferred basis. The extension of the trilateral highway beyond Myanmar and Thailand to these countries needs reconsideration. There does not appear to be any economic rationale for the entry of Indian goods and services through the highway into Cambodia and Laos. With Vietnam, the engagement can best be invested in through the maritime route.

Papua New Guinea and Timor-Leste are two developing countries which are candidates for ASEAN, and in partnership with whom, India can expand its grant programmes in lieu of Cambodia and Laos. Timor-Leste has been inundated by Chinese investment but remains open to Indian interest, while Papua New Guinea has shown palpable warmth for India.

There are other organisations which impact the region in which ASEAN centrality was not the major issue. India's AEP used these organisations to some extent. The BIMSTEC was a collaboration between South and South East Asia, keeping the Bay of Bengal as the common factor. All SAARC members, except Maldives, Afghanistan and Pakistan, were part of it. Myanmar and Thailand are in it too. It was sometimes seen as an alternative to a dysfunctional SAARC. The trilateral highway project that India offered to ASEAN overlapped with BIMSTEC, but there was never any certainty about how much India would invest in this concept, leading to muted responses from most participants. India should be the driver of this grouping in harmony with AEP.

Similarly, the Indian Ocean Rim Association (IORA), created in 1997, was revitalised by India under its chairmanship in 2012. The trilateral discussions with Indonesia and Australia helped to give the organisation a cohesive approach, particularly in the region east of India. The resurgent IORA contributed to initial steps to develop the Indo-Pacific concept; the coordination between India, Indonesia and Australia can now be enhanced, but the focus of IORA, due to rotation of Chairs, has shifted to Africa, West Asia and the Western Indian Ocean (WIO) in which India has stakes. With France now formally joining IORA, there is scope for India, France and Japan to coordinate their activities in the WIO.

The hegemonic intent of China in the South China Sea region required several countries to come together to counter the impact strategically, economically and physically. Several ideas about the Indo-Pacific emanated, including from Indonesia in 2012, and were presented to the EAS. The Chinese abhorrence of the Indo-Pacific concept, supported by Russia, made ASEAN member states reassess their outlook. The ASEAN Outlook on the Indo-Pacific, announced in 2019, is a non-realist one, and seeks to accommodate China without the means to make it abide by preferred principles.

Finally, it was left to India, Japan, USA and Australia to formulate a robust Indo-Pacific policy. This is because the strategic value of the region has enhanced economically, strategically and tactically. The new great game is indeed a maritime one and is being played in the Indo-Pacific with a specific focus on the South China Sea. Indian interest has taken this to the east coast of Africa, while the United States interest takes the concept well into the Pacific. This concept has now been adopted by several countries. This region is likely to remain the centre of attraction in the years ahead and, though ASEAN is geographically at its centre, it dilutes ASEAN centrality because the Indo-Pacific is a realist concept while ASEAN is a liberal rule-focused organisation.

The re-emergence and consolidation of the Quadrilateral Security Dialogue—or the Quad—between India, Japan, USA and Australia is among the salient features of the Indo-Pacific construct. The Quad started as a strategic concept to counter the hegemonistic intentions of China, and is now moving towards more functional and economic collaboration based on strategic considerations to balance, if not counter, the Chinese domination of South East Asia. The Malabar Exercise now includes all Quad members and meetings are more regular, including at the level of ministers. For the present, the anxiety on 'what will China think' has been evaded and all Quad members seem to engage fully.

The Security and Growth for All in the Region (SAGAR) and the Indo-Pacific Oceans Initiative (IPOI) are two broad constructs through which India has sought to engage the Indo-Pacific countries with a functional approach. This is a direct alterative to the Chinese pushy approach and seeks partnership and collaboration in areas of importance to all. The seven pillars of IPOI provide opportunities for regional partners to engage India on an even footing. This includes maritime security and disaster risk management; illegal, unreported and unlicensed fishing; and other non-traditional threats. These can certainly be a basis for collaboration at trilateral or plurilateral level without being prescriptive. The development and distribution of the Covid-19 vaccine, and its future expansion and adaptation, can be a useful part of such partnership ahead.

Economic Issues

On the issues of trade, Japan has assumed leadership of the Trans-Pacific Partnership (TPP) since USA withdrew from it. Japan has played a major role in ensuring that the RCEP was finally concluded in 2020. The absence of the United States and India from either group has given rise to concerns that both of them are strategically active in the region, but absent from the RCEP and TPP structures. This creates a shadow on the level of commitment.

Japan is now working on an expansion of these trading blocs in the region by bringing together the members of RCEP, TPP and North American Free Trade Agreement (NAFTA) into a new FTA for the Asia-Pacific through APEC. Since India is not a member of any of these, it risks being left out of these arrangements and needs to consider how new strategic and resilient value chains will be established without preferential access to countries of the region.

What Next?

What can India do to make its AEP more effective and secure the goals for which it looks East? It needs to understand that 'looking East' now includes looking at USA and China. India's participation in the new developments in the Russian Far East are a sign of this realisation. The 'looking East' will also be useful when India will be able to use the polar route when the Arctic ice caps melt enough for international shipping. Strategically and functionally, the ambit of the Indian Navy and economic and technology outreach will need to go well beyond ASEAN into a wider concept of the East which includes the Pacific and Arctic oceans. At the same time, the Indian Ocean to the west will require a more robust and focused policy to the east and southern African region. Already, Mozambique, Tanzania and Ethiopia are among the biggest beneficiaries of Indian credit lines in Africa. Functional naval cooperation with two of them and the island countries of Mauritius, Seychelles, Comoros and Madagascar are quite robust, too.

India needs to enhance the perception of its partnership with the region. Elaborate mechanisms for collaboration exist particularly with ASEAN, but these have not generated the structure necessary to balance China. Several ASEAN countries continue to believe that there is too little of India and too much of China in their midst. Indian efforts through EAS and ASEAN, as well as BIMSTEC, have included the trilateral highway and several other projects to build capacity and outreach among ASEAN countries. However, inadequate partnership-building has prevented effective implementation. What is started, never seems to finish or attain the goals which are set out.

In this, the ASEAN countries are also responsible, as most of them are happy to receive Indian support and participation in projects, but would not do enough on their part to ensure the success of the projects. India needs to show greater intent and demonstrate effective implementation to retrieve lost ground. A frank discussion with ASEAN countries is necessary to reformulate the approach and implementation of plans for joint projects.

A comparison with China becomes obvious in this context. It is not as if Chinese projects are always successful or do not have problems or delays. The Chinese advantage is its deep pockets, ability of quick decision-making and rapid-fire announcements to keep the momentum with them. India, Japan, Australia and USA, through various trilateral dialogues, have attempted to undertake sustainable and quality projects in the region. Efforts between Australia, USA and Japan have started in this direction; the going has been tough due to lack of cohesion in their systems. A partnership with India could bring lower costs, efficiency and better results since India's engineering, procurement and construction (EPC) capabilities are of high quality. Indian skills and capacity building can provide a dose of realism into such plurilateral efforts, which will create bankable and sustainable projects. Most of all, India must insist on business models for new projects whether under grant or credit.

India has a US$ 1 billion line of credit on offer for infrastructure in ASEAN countries. Using this as a basic contribution, India should discuss with Japan and Australia, as well as France, some joint ventures which will focus on digital connectivity, public health related value chains and skill-development embedded in a wider infrastructure strategy. A combined effort with seed funding from India will give an opportunity to discuss new projects with countries of the region, and allow Indian companies to join hands with Japanese and Australian companies to undertake projects for mutual benefit. This will require a 'Think Regional, Implement Bilateral' approach to avoid overlapping procurement issues. At present, more than new credits, a greater foreign direct investment-led approach is necessary, for which India's private sector needs momentum and initiative.

India enunciated the Nalanda University as an EAS project. This project brings forth the essential spiritual, educational and capacity-building aspects, which, by themselves, are a challenge to the Chinese way of doing things. Indian efforts to work this project out and make it a centre of learning for East and South East Asia with modern and traditional subjects at a much larger scale is currently visible. India needs to avoid the impression that it undertakes major initiatives and then allows them to flounder.

ASEAN members have suffered immensely due to Covid-19, with depletion of their usually robust economies. The benefits of globalisation, like tourism flows (including from China) and investments, have stumbled. They, too, need a panacea and, hence, India and its assimilation into regional value chains (RVCs) could be welcomed. ASEAN has taken for granted the large inflows of Indian tourists and the open skies for its airlines, which contribute to strong hubs in Singapore, Kuala Lumpur and Bangkok. A similar trait holds for ASEAN ports, particularly in Singapore. Can these be leveraged better?

The development of the Indian vaccines and India's ability to be a leading manufacturer contribute to a new idiom of cooperation under the AEP. China moved faster and engaged many ASEAN countries into its vaccination programme, including testing. Ultimately, no single source of the vaccine will be enough for any major country and India will, thus, have space for expansion. Creating strategic value chains, collaborative efforts and new matrixes of cooperation will be the hallmark of the post-pandemic AEP. This will be balanced by a heavier imprint on maritime issues in the region with others, if possible, and by itself if necessary.

CHAPTER 13

INDIA AND JAPAN IN THE POST-COVID WORLD

Deepa Gopalan Wadhwa

The India–Japan relationship has rapidly matured in the two decades of this century to become one of the most consequential relationships of Asia and its extended remit of the Indo-Pacific. Former Japanese Prime Minister Shinzo Abe, one of the principal architects of the relationship, maintained that 'a strong India was in the best interest of Japan, and a strong Japan in the best interest of India'. This convergence of interests is not limited to the bilateral, but also to the changed security environment and balance of power consequent to the rise of China. Prime Minister Narendra Modi's vision of the relationship, as expressed during his first visit to Japan as PM in 2014, was that it would 'exercise a profound influence in shaping the course of Asia and our interlinked ocean regions'.

These two statements explain the rationale of the India–Japan Special Strategic and Global Partnership, which is supported by common values and practices as democracies, converging perceptions of threats to the regional security environment, self-evident complementarities of respective economic strengths and needs, and shared aspirations for a greater role and say in international affairs. Additional factors which are likely to sustain this special partnership in the post Covid-19 era are widespread domestic goodwill and bipartisan political support in both countries; our growing ties with the US of which Japan is an alliance partner; continued unrelenting, aggressive Chinese actions threatening the territorial integrity of both countries; realisation of the need to retool existing supply chains to reduce dependence on China; and the institutionalisation of the Quadrilateral Security Dialogue, known as the Quad, in which both are stakeholders and which seeks to offer an alternate option for a peaceful, prosperous, open, inclusive, stable, and rule-based regional order.

To promote cooperation and understanding in the political, strategic, security, economic, and cultural fields, a comprehensive, multilayered architecture of dialogue is in place, covering an ever-widening agenda of subjects, with annual prime-ministerial summits at the apogee, followed by a 2+2 defence and foreign ministerial dialogue and other ministerial and official interactions. In the area of defence and foreign policy, besides 2+2 ministerial-level dialogue, there is the strategic dialogue between foreign ministers, Foreign Office consultations, a defence policy dialogue, the national security adviser (NSA)-level dialogue and staff talks across the three services and coastguards.

This institutionalisation of dialogue lends structure, periodicity and dynamic content to the bilateral engagement. During the last year, while most meetings have been held virtually, External Affairs Minister S Jaishankar undertook a visit to Tokyo in September 2020 for a meeting of the Quad foreign ministers and also to meet with his counterpart, Toshimitsu Motegi, for the thirteenth India–Japan Strategic Dialogue. The predictable annuality of prime ministerial summits has been affected due to the Covid-19 pandemic, with the last summit having been held in October 2018, but Prime Minister Modi and Yoshihide Suga have held three telephonic 'mini summits' since PM Suga's assumption of office to maintain the momentum of the relationship. The two leaders also met at the virtual Quad summit on 12 March 2021 at which they decided to work together on tangible outcomes for the stability and prosperity of the Indo-Pacific, and are likely to meet in person at the Quad summit in Washington on 24 September 2021, even as PM Suga is set to demit office shortly as new elections to the LDP leadership and the Diet are imminent, and he has decided not to be a candidate in the light of his perceived inability to control the spread of the pandemic and a consequent drop below acceptable levels of his popularity ratings.

The Covid-19 pandemic that has seminally changed the world, adversely affecting personal destinies, the global economic order and politics within and between countries, has brought into focus issues such as the resilience of global supply chains, access to health-related global goods and advantages of digitisation and innovation, especially for delivery of public services. In the India–Japan context, the pandemic has also provided opportunities for cooperation as Japan launched a US$ 2.2 billion fund for supply chain diversification to help Japanese companies reshore and shift production lines out of China and back to Japan. Around US$ 220 million of this is earmarked for companies seeking to move production to members of the Association of Southeast Asian Nations (ASEAN), India and Bangladesh. This has coincided with the Indian government's AatmaNirbhar Bharat Abhiyaan and there are apparent synergies which can be achieved. The Japan Bank for International Cooperation (JBIC) has entered into loan agreements of US$ 2 billion with the State Bank of India in recent months to support manufacturing and the supply chain of Covid-19-affected Japanese carmakers in India under the AatmaNirbhar Bharat initiative. The healthcare crisis caused by the Corona virus has elicited a budget support of Rs 7500 crore and a Rs 150 crore grant from the Government of Japan for India, and a loan of Rs 2,000 crore from Japan International Cooperation Agency (JICA), as crisis response support to mitigate adverse socio-economic impacts.

Japan has also proposed a trilateral Supply Chain Resilience Initiative (SCRI) with Australia and India at a meeting of commerce ministers of the three countries in September 2020 as the countries faced heightened tensions with China, with the pandemic exposing vulnerabilities of overdependence on China for production and supply chains and highlighted the need for de-risking and geographical diversification to build resilience against exogenous and unanticipated shocks. One of the tangible outcomes of the Quad summit of 12 March 2021 has been a working group set up for cooperation among the Quad members to expand access to Covid-19 vaccines among Indo-Pacific countries, with production in India and funding by Japan.

With India's foreign policy priorities being security, economic development and a global role commensurate with its size and contributions, there are clear synergies with Japan's own interests and priorities. As the political relationship is secured by a special strategic partnership and the supporting framework is in place, going forward in the post-Covid-19 era, the areas of cooperation which will hold the most potential of mutual benefit can be identified as the deepening of bilateral security and defence ties, with tri- and plurilateral cooperation with like-minded countries as exemplified by the Quad; investments in modernising the infrastructure in India, including development of the North East and strategic connectivity to neighbouring geographies and the ASEAN; and enhanced Japanese foreign direct investment (FDI) directed at the domestic market and global value chains, as also collaboration in frontier technologies to stay ahead in the technology race.

Security and Defence Ties

Strategic convergence between India and Japan has been a strong driver of the partnership in this century as the regional security environment deteriorated primarily due to the rise of Chinese assertiveness and our immediate neighbourhoods affected by the inimical policies of North Korea for Japan, and Pakistan in the case of India. Bilaterally, the convergence has been manifest in a steady accretion in defence and security ties beginning with the 2008 Joint Declaration on Security Cooperation, which has matured to the annual defence ministers' meetings and exercises across all three wings of the military and the coast guard.

Both countries have, in recent years, incrementally deepened cooperation through agreements extending to areas such as transfer of defence equipment and technology as Japan loosened self-imposed restraints under Prime Minister Shinzo Abe, exchanges on maritime domain awareness and the Reciprocal Supply and Services Agreement signed in September 2020, commonly referred to as ACSA or Acquisition and Cross Servicing Arrangement, to facilitate mutual logistics support and interoperability between navies. Naval exercises such as the bilateral JIMEX, the co-option of Japan as a permanent member of the Indo-US Malabar exercise, the Shinyuu Maitri exercises between the air forces, the Dharma Guardian exercise between the Indian Army and the Japanese Ground Self Defence Force for joint training in counterterrorism and jungle warfare, and the Sahyog-Kaijin exercise between the coast guards are carried out on an annual basis and with increasing remit and intensity.

These exchanges provide an established framework for continuing cooperation in the security area, even though there has been a mismatch of expectations in the area of defence acquisitions due to pricing and transfer of technology issues for the sale of the ShinMaywa US-2 amphibious aircraft and

Soryu submarines by Japan. However, under an agreement between the Defence Research and Development Organisation (DRDO) of India and the Acquisitions Technology Logistics Agency (ATLA) of Japan, there is ongoing cooperation in research in robotics and unmanned ground vehicles for military use.

India and Japan also discuss security cooperation within two trilateral mechanisms with the US and Australia, respectively, and as members of the Quad. After a false start in 2007, and some preliminary hesitations after its revival in 2017 by former PM Shinzo Abe, the grouping has progressed from ad hoc meetings of officials and foreign ministers to the virtual summit on 12 March 2020 among the leaders of the four countries who agreed to work together on non-traditional threats, such as vaccine production for Covid-19-hit countries of the Indo-Pacific, climate change and critical and emerging technologies. There is little doubt that China's post-pandemic actions in Ladakh for India, and its belligerence in the maritime and air space around the disputed Senkaku Islands of Japan, as also retaliatory trade actions against Australia and deteriorating relations with the US, have been the galvanising factors in the evolution of the Quad into a grouping with a structure, agenda, planned meetings and substantive programmes, which seeks to achieve the joint vision of a free, open and inclusive Indo-Pacific.

Cooperation in Infrastructure Development

Japan, which has been extending development assistance to India since 1958, is today India's leading bilateral donor with cumulative official development assistance (ODA) of US$ 56 billion, a position it is likely to keep with the addition of new areas such as projects in the North East and the Andamans. Japanese development cooperation assistance in India stands apart on four important counts. The first, that it is directed to national areas of priority and fulfils nationally determined needs such as infrastructure upgradation. The second is the large scope and scale of projects that are meant to deliver transformative outcomes. Examples of these are the Western Dedicated Freight Corridor (WDFC) from Dadri in Uttar Pradesh to Navi Mumbai in Maharashtra, which aims to decongest 70 per cent of India's rail freight network and drastically shorten time taken for movement of goods from weeks to days. The freight corridor is to be the spine of the Delhi–Mumbai Industrial Corridor, said to be one of the world's largest infrastructure projects with an estimated outlay of US$ 100 billion, planned with eight new smart cities covering seven states. There is also the Chennai–Bengaluru Industrial Corridor, which will upgrade infrastructure along the route linking several industrial zones and Metro projects in several cities that seek to emulate the success of the Japanese-built Delhi Metro. The third is the terms of loans that cannot be matched by other global lending institutions. An example being the loan for the Ahmedabad–Mumbai high-speed rail project of US$ 12 billion which carries an interest rate of 0.1 per cent and repayment period of fifty years with a fifteen-year moratorium. But the project will require procurement from Japan of rolling stock, signalling, telecommunication and other equipment benefitting Japanese companies and advancing Japan's promotion of exports of infrastructure systems as a means to revitalise its own economy and create interdependencies with partner countries. The fourth is the trust factor that makes Japan the favoured partner to undertake projects in politically sensitive and strategically important areas, such as the north-eastern states and the Andaman and Nicobar Islands.

This derives from the desire of both countries to cooperate in shaping the geo-economics of the Indo-Pacific with an eye on consequent strategic gains. Synergies are, thus, being developed between India's Act East and Neighbourhood First policies and Japan's Free and Open Indo-Pacific vision. India's Act East Policy seeks to link the North East through greater connectivity and commerce with the countries neighbouring the region, such as Bhutan, Nepal and Bangladesh and through Myanmar to South East Asia. Japan also has undertaken complementary projects of multimodal physical infrastructure in these countries and is also committed to the development of India's north-eastern states for reasons of history, ethnic comfort and its strategic location. The Act East Forum led by the Japanese ambassador in India and the Indian foreign secretary was set up following a decision taken at the prime ministerial summit and has met with regularity to review and recommend cooperation projects in the region. One such project, in the news recently as the foundation stone was laid by PM Modi, is to be the longest bridge over the Brahmaputra connecting Dhubri in Assam with Phulbari in Meghalaya, and funded by JICA, which when completed in 2026-27 will reduce the distance between the two points from 250 kms to 19 kms and facilitate the movement of goods and people greatly, enhancing connectivity between the two states.

Another sensitive geography of strategic importance where India has been traditionally wary of foreign presence but has opened to Japan is the Andaman and Nicobar Islands, regarding which conversations to upgrade civilian infrastructure were initiated some years ago and a Japanese company, NEC, has built India's first submarine optical fibre cable system covering 2,300 kms from Chennai to the islands. A first ever ODA project in the islands by Japan was announced in March 2021 as a grant of US$ 36 million to install a battery energy storage system to utilise renewable energy and provide stable energy supply. Given the importance of the islands in India's defence and security and its geostrategic location at the mouth of the Strait of Malacca which makes it ideal to track naval movement, this project between India and Japan could be a precursor to future security cooperation, especially post the signing of Acquisition and Cross Servicing Arrangement which envisages access to each other's naval facilities.

Investment and Trade Relations

Complementing economic strengths and needs have been a key driver of the India–Japan relationship. There is no doubt that the lure of the growing heft of the Indian market—the single largest after China—and Japan's financial and technological capacities provided a strong impetus to the reset of relations in 2000. A Comprehensive Economic Partnership Agreement (CEPA) was signed in 2011 to boost trade and investment between the two countries, which, however, has not delivered the anticipated fillip to the economic relationship.

Bilateral trade was a mere US$ 16.95 billion in 2019-20, with Indian goods accounting for 0.7 per cent of Japanese imports. The trade balance has also been widening in Japan's favour from US$ 3.54 billion in 2010-11 to US$ 7.91 billion in 2018-19. The expectations from CEPA are clearly still to be realised. For example, though imports of generics from India are identified in CEPA as a priority which will be accorded national treatment in approvals, etc., Indian pharma has got less than 1 per cent of the US$ 87 billion market which still relies on the US and Europe for sourcing imports despite the price differential. A study by Indian Council for Research on International Economic Relations (ICRIER) in May 2020 says that sixty-four non-tariff barriers were raised by Japan against our main export products. Similarly, despite Japan being the second largest market after the US for IT and IT enabled services, only

2 per cent of our exports go to Japan. While it is a fact that only 10 per cent of Japan's IT needs are outsourced offshore, China receives 50 per cent of the share. The areas that need to be worked on are now well-known ten years after the signing of CEPA, but both countries seem to be unable to transcend the impediments of regulations, systems, perceptions and inconsistent quality.

The FDI from Japan has done better and cumulatively stands at US$ 34 billion since 2000, making it among the top five investors in India. There are now 1,441 Japanese industrial establishments in India, but this compares poorly with the staggering figures of over 30,000 companies in China and around 13,000 in ASEAN, of which 4,000 are in Thailand. In annual surveys conducted by JBIC, India moved in 2014 as the most favoured country for investments in the medium term and has stayed at the top positions ever since. But, this has not helped to get a bigger share of Japan's total FDI. With India seeking to increase domestic production under the Make in India and AatmaNirbhar Bharat initiatives, five sectors for Japanese FDI which can help India's aims for self-sufficiency and also to be part of global value chains are the automotive industry, electronics and electronic systems, pharmaceuticals and medical devices, textiles and food processing. Forty per cent of Japanese companies present in India are known to solely produce for the domestic market, while 60 per cent also export goods manufactured in India. With the move to diversify China-dependent supply chains, it is necessary, to begin with, to target moving production especially for products manufactured by Japanese companies in China for the Indian market. We also need to attend to the genuine problems of doing business in India raised by Japanese companies related to the regulatory framework, land, labour and poor infrastructure.

Both governments have been conscious of the need to boost economic relations and prime ministerial summits have produced platforms to narrow perception and information gaps, as well as find solutions to issues. One of these, the India–Japan Industrial Competitiveness Partnership, led by respective ministers of investment and trade, seeks to identify and mitigate challenges of specific sectors. India has set up twelve Japanese industrial townships with developed infrastructure and special incentive packages to create conducive ecosystems for Japanese companies. Japanese companies have invested in skilling of Indians by setting up thirteen India–Japan Institute of Manufacturing and Japanese Endowed Courses in leading engineering colleges.

A recent and promising area of Japanese interest has been the start-up ecosystem in India with investments from Japanese private equity and venture capital funds having grown from US$ 2 billion in 2015 to US$ 15 billion in 2020 according to estimates. The over 100 technology-based start-ups in sectors such as e-commerce, enterprise, transport related technologies and biotech have helped to create twelve out of the twenty-nine unicorns in India. A Japan–India start-up hub has been set up with a permanent office in Bengaluru to facilitate business collaborations and investments between the two countries.

Another area of India–Japan economic collaboration with potential, which has been talked about for a while without much actualisation is businesses and projects in third geographies. The prime ministerial summit in 2018 identified projects in Myanmar for housing, education and electrification in the Rakhine state; road and rail construction in Bangladesh; development of liquefied natural gas (LNG) related infrastructure in Sri Lanka, which has run into problems with the current Sri Lankan dispensation; and a cancer hospital in Kenya. Both countries seek to provide an option different from China's Belt and Road Initiative (BRI) with responsible debt financing and respectful of the priorities of the recipient states. In the context of Africa, it is believed that optimal advantages can be achieved through industry-led collaborations and an India–Japan Business Platform has been established to develop industrial corridors and networks in the region.

Going forward, an important area of India–Japan ties is going to be a collaboration in frontier technologies, as both countries watch the advance of China as a technology superpower seeking to dominate and lead in certain areas of critical technologies which impact geopolitics and national security. Projects have been initiated for collaboration in areas such as 5G technology, artificial intelligence, Internet of Things (IoT), cybersecurity, space and production of critical material like rare earths. A Japan–India Digital Partnership memorandum of understanding (MoU) was signed at the last prime ministerial summit in 2018, recognising the complementary nature of strengths of India in IT and software and Japan in hardware and electronics and seeking to expand cooperation in IT, digital technologies, information and communications technology (ICT) and start-up promotion. Projects have since been taken up under the digital partnership involving government entities and private companies. Some examples are the Rakuten–Jio collaboration in 5G development and joint research in artificial intelligence (AI) between Indian Institute of Technology-Hyderabad (IIT-Hyderabad) and the National Institute of Advanced Industrial Science and Technology of Japan. An MoU on ICT was signed on 15 January 2021 to enhance cooperation in 5G technology, telecom security, submarine optical fibre cabling to remote islands, and broadband connectivity platforms in unconnected high-altitude areas, all of which have a bearing on national security. Besides AI and 5G, India and Japan have had a cybersecurity dialogue and have finalised a cybersecurity agreement to be signed soon.

The partnership between India and Japan has matured in the last two decades, and now covers an exhaustive agenda covering areas of compelling mutuality of interests which have a bearing on national security, regional and international stability, and economic growth. With institutional structures in place, political convergence and public goodwill, the task is to finally leverage the 'unparalleled potential', as PM Modi said, of our ties.

CHAPTER 14

QUAD AND INDO-PACIFIC CONSTRUCT COME OF AGE

VISHNU PRAKASH

'World's two largest democracies...(we)...bridge the Asia-Pacific and Indian Ocean region...(we agree that) a closer partnership between the United States and India is indispensable to promoting peace, prosperity and stability in those regions.... We affirm the importance of safeguarding maritime security and ensuring freedom of navigation and overflight throughout the region, especially in the South China Sea.... We call on all parties to...pursue resolution of territorial and maritime disputes through all peaceful means....'[1]

The leaders 'exchanged views on the impact of China's actions on peace and prosperity in the Indo-Pacific region and the world...including the use of economic and other forms of coercion. (They) oppose any unilateral attempts to change the status quo in the East China Sea...(and) reiterated (their) objections to China's unlawful maritime claims and activities in the South China Sea... and reaffirmed (their) strong shared interest in a free and open South China Sea governed by international law, in which freedom of navigation and overflight are guaranteed.'[2]

Excerpts from the two joint statements above, both involving the US—the first with India in 2015 and the other with Japan in April 2021—span a period of just five years. While there is barely an allusion to China in the first, the angst against China is clearly palpable in the second. It also reflects an unusually swift, yet significant, change in the nomenclature from Asia-Pacific to Indo-Pacific, signifying a reconfiguration of the geostrategic and geo-economic equations, with far-reaching implications.

This was the consequence of the undisguised Chinese belligerence—military and economic—against one and all, under the watch of President Xi Jinping who assumed office in 2010-12. Surprisingly, the land of Sun Tzu simultaneously opened multiple fronts by waging aggression against most of its neighbours. Economic heft, military muscle and growing stature made it difficult for Beijing to contain its expansionist instincts. The ease with which it managed to militarise the South China Sea (SCS) and stake a claim on 80 per cent of the resource-rich and strategically vital region whetted its appetite for more.

The US, Japan and even Australia came to realise that it could not be business as usual with China, and also that individual push back would not be that effective. Like-minded democratic countries needed to join hands to dampen extraterritorial ambitions of China. And, hence, the search for a new paradigm which is taking shape in the form of the Quadrilateral process (Quad for short), comprising the US, Japan, Australia and India. The Quad, thus, constitutes the core, nucleus or implementation arm of the Indo-Pacific construct.

For the US, the Asia-Pacific region traditionally extended up to China in the east, but excluded India which was bracketed under South Asia along with countries in the Indian subcontinent. With the rise of India on the one hand and emerging strains in the Sino-US relations on the other, for reasons alluded to above, the Barack Obama administration in November 2011 declared a 'strategic pivot to Asia[3]—to generate confidence in America's future leadership role in this region'.

The administration also began using the term 'Indo-Asia-Pacific' along with 'Asia-Pacific' when referring to a broader region bound by the Pacific Ocean and the Indian Ocean. In October 2010, then US Secretary of State Hillary Clinton described the importance of the 'Indo-Pacific basin…to global trade and commerce.'[4] However, Indo-Pacific (IP) is not necessarily an American coinage, nor does it mean the same thing to every nation.

The term Indo-Pacific has been in use among scholars of international relations and geopolitics since the first decade of this century, around the same time as China's rise[5]. Addressing the Indian parliament in August 2007, Japanese

Prime Minister Shinzo Abe envisaged the 'dynamic coupling' of the Pacific and the Indian oceans or 'Confluence of the Two Seas' to further freedom and prosperity of a 'Broader Asia' without actually calling it Indo-Pacific.

A maverick and iconoclast, Donald Trump, who succeeded Obama in January 2017, was quick to sense the enormity of challenge from China and the importance of the Indo-Pacific construct. During his first visit to East Asia as the president in November 2017, Trump gave the Indo-Pacific region (IPR) the much-needed visibility and endorsement. In Vietnam, he was honoured to be in the 'heart of the Indo-Pacific' and used the term ten times in his address at the Asia-Pacific Economic Cooperation (APEC) CEO summit[6]. In Tokyo, he celebrated his 'first visit to the Indo-Pacific region' as US president.

Thus, the credit for energising the Indo-Pacific and creating a buzz around it goes to Trump, who publicly called out Chinese aggression and 'unfair trade practices' that resulted in 'enormous trade deficits' for the US, adding that the 'United States will no longer turn a blind eye to violations, cheating or economic aggression. Those days are over.' As with many other developments in the world today, the trigger for Indo-Pacific, too, is the change in the American stance and the rise of China[7].

India's position on the Indo-Pacific region was authoritatively expounded by Prime Minister Narendra Modi at the Shangri-La Dialogue in Singapore on 1 June 2018, in one word 'SAGAR' (Ocean)—an acronym for Security and Growth for All in the Region': 'India's own engagement in the Indo-Pacific region—from the shores of Africa to that of the Americas—will be inclusive. The Indo-Pacific is a natural region. ...India does not see the Indo-Pacific region as a strategy or as a club of limited members. ...And by no means do we consider it as directed against any country. ...It stands for a free, open, inclusive region, which embraces us all in a common pursuit of progress and prosperity. It includes all nations in this geography as also others beyond who have a stake in it.'[8] For good measure, the prime minister observed: 'No other relationship of India has as many layers as our relations with China.... Our cooperation is expanding. Trade is growing. And, we have displayed maturity and wisdom in managing issues and ensuring a peaceful border. ...I firmly believe that, Asia and the world will have a better future when India and China work together in trust and confidence, sensitive to each other's interests.'

There is no agreed definition of the IPR. It is conditioned by the size, geographical location, security matrix and strategic calculus of each nation. New Delhi views it as the logical step beyond the Act East Policy and a transcending of the confines of South Asia.[9] Former National Security Adviser Shivshankar Menon nuances it further: 'I try, but don't always succeed, to use Indo-Pacific for the continuous maritime space, Asia for the continental landmass, and Asia-Pacific for both, to include the land and sea. Definition of I-P and A-P remains fluid, varying from person to person, country to country.[10]'

For India, unlike the US, the IPR is a vision, a consciousness and a sense of belonging in the belief that the destiny of the IPR nations is interlinked. The US essentially sees it as a strategy, but without officially calling it as such.

And there lies (or lay) India's dilemma! India believes that the security and prosperity of all the IPR countries, including China, are interlinked. Other Quad countries, especially the US, essentially regard the IPR as 'Asia-Pacific minus China plus India'. Japan and Australia, too, subscribe to this outlook. To a large extent, India's position is dictated by geography. It is the only Quad country with a (3500 km long) land border with China. New Delhi, therefore, walked the tightrope from day one, not wanting to tread on any toes.

India was (is?) regarded as the most hesitant Quad member, even though India's External Affairs Minister S Jaishankar maintains that we 'drove the revived Quad arrangement'[11]. But for Prime Minister Shinzo Abe's persuasion and his warm equation with Prime Minister Dr Manmohan Singh, India may not have agreed to the first ever Quad meeting at officials' level in Manila on 25 May 2007.

There was no joint statement. India did not issue any press release at all. There was no mention of China anywhere. As if apologetic for having had the meeting, the participants appeared anxious to dispel any notion that it had anything to do with China. All the same, Beijing let its disapproval be known to the capitals concerned. Soon thereafter, the Japanese Prime Minister quit on health grounds, there was a change of guard in Australia and India heaved a sigh of relief.

This was the time when India was trying to secure a clean waiver from the Nuclear Suppliers Group (NSG) to emerge from the nuclear cold and also operationalise the landmark bilateral 123 nuclear deal with the US (clinched in October 2008). China and India still harped on being the twin engines of growth in Asia. The ritual reference to the 'Peaceful rise of China' was still a norm.

Fast forward to 2017. The world looked decidedly different. Gone was the charade of 'peaceful rise'. Beijing had a new emperor since 2012 in the form of Xi Jinping who was busy selling the dream of 'rejuvenation of the great Chinese Nation'. Aggression against neighbours became the order of the day. The template was test driven, without much resistance in militarising and staking a claim over most of the South China Sea. Tokyo, Canberra and Washington, all found themselves on the receiving end.

Shinzo Abe, the moving force behind the Indo-Pacific vision and Quad, was back as prime minister since 2012. Sino-Japanese ties were getting increasingly tense. In September 2010, a Chinese fishing trawler rammed into two Japanese patrol boats in Japan's territorial sea surrounding the disputed Senkaku Islands[12], which are administered by Japan. From 14 September 2012, Chinese government vessels started to enter Japan's contiguous zone almost daily[13].

Further east, Australian PM Malcolm Turnbull, in the saddle since 2015, turned out to be a pragmatist. First, he refused to join the Belt and Road Initiative (BRI). Second, Australia's '2017 Foreign Policy White Paper' was forthright: 'Australia is particularly concerned by the unprecedented pace and scale of China's activities. Australia opposes the use of disputed features and artificial structures in the South China Sea for military purposes'.

Third, there was growing concern in the country about Beijing using its Australian proxies to colour the academic and political discourse in its educational institutions as well as the parliament. Reflective of a steely resolve to safeguard its autonomy, security and values, Canberra went public, notwithstanding the economic cost. In 2017-18, Australian exports to China stood at US$ 123.3 billion or 30.6 per cent of its total exports.

The political and strategic landscape in and for India had similarly undergone a sea change. After thirty years of coalition governments, Modi, a homespun political leader, was swept to power in May 2014, armed with a decisive popular mandate. He was not bashful about reaching out to China and President Xi. However, the Chinese leader had other plans. Incursions across the line of actual control (LAC) started morphing into standoffs more frequently, including the one at the India–Bhutan–China tri-junction near Doklam that took seventy-three days to be resolved in August 2017.

India agreed to the revival of the Quad after a gap of nine years, and the second official-level meeting was held in Manila in November 2017, on the margins of the East Asia Summit. Even if a one-way street, India was still very cautious about Chinese sensibilities. The meeting was termed as India–Australia–Japan–US Consultations on Indo-Pacific. There was no mention of Quad or security, nor was there any consensus on a joint statement.

True to its wont, China failed to appreciate India's restraint. To New Delhi's dismay, Beijing reacted strongly against its decision in August 2019 to amend Article 370 of the constitution, revoking the special status of Jammu and Kashmir and making it a union territory of India. It led the charge at the UN Security Council against India. India now had no hesitation to the elevation of the Quad dialogue to the level of foreign ministers, which took place in New York in September 2019 on the margins of the UN General Assembly.

Next came the India–China armed standoff at multiple points in Ladakh in early May 2020 (still continuing). During the night of 15-16 June 2020, China's People's Liberation Army (PLA) troops launched an unprovoked assault on a small Indian army unit in Galwan (Ladakh), resulting in twenty fatalities on the Indian and many more on the Chinese side. The die was cast.

Two Quad ministerial meetings followed in quick succession at Tokyo (physical) in October 2020 and in February 2021 (virtual) convened by the new US Secretary of State Antony Blinken. Much to the relief of partner nations, the Biden administration made the Quad the cornerstone of its Indo-Pacific policy and that, too, within two months into his presidency. India was now ready for a summit-level meeting, convinced that the answer lay in collective security.

Ambassador Shyam Saran presciently notes, 'One should thank the Chinese for helping India to "overcome the hesitations of history" and put the Quad at the centre of its Indo-Pacific strategy.... In terms of their combined economic and military capabilities, the Quad members are more than a match for China.'

The first ever joint statement adopted by the Quad leaders noted, 'We strive for a region that is free, open, inclusive, healthy, anchored by democratic values, and unconstrained by coercion.'[14] China was not mentioned, but the implications were clear.

All the same, China wants nothing to do with the architecture, convinced that it is meant to contain it. Beijing's attitude and response have evolved over time from dismissing it as 'seafoam', to disparaging it as 'Asian NATO' and finally engaging in platitudes, which it does with aplomb, consequent to the Quad summit.

'China has always been a builder of world peace…(and)…firmly upheld the UN-centred international system…based on international law, not the one defined by individual countries to maintain their hegemony. …Certain countries should shake off their Cold War mentality and ideological prejudice, refrain from forming closed and exclusive small circles,' intoned the Chinese foreign ministry spokesperson[15].

However, India was put in a different box. 'China and India are each other's friends and partners, not threats or rivals, so the two sides need to help each other rather than undercutting each other, should intensify cooperation rather than harbouring suspicion of each other,'[16] observed Chinese Foreign Minister Wang Yi, barely a week before the Quad summit, exposing the hollowness of the assurances and pledges of the Middle Kingdom.

That Quad's agenda is still evolving is absolutely natural. Yet, it is evident that the Quad will not just confine itself to maritime security and preserving a rule-based order in the IPR, but it will also take on crisis management be it related to healthcare, humanitarian assistance and disaster relief (HADR) or climate change.

In a significant move, the leaders agreed that Japan and the US will finance the production of one billion doses of Covid-19 vaccines by India by 2022 for being supplied to needy nations. The Quad 'will only succeed if it serves a more substantive purpose.'[17] At the same time, it is as important not to overload the agenda so that its primary focus does not get diffused.

Two related issues are those of expansion of the Quad and that of Quad Plus. Both these aspects need to be addressed clinically, as they would have a bearing on its strength and vitality. Therefore, given its challenging and action-oriented agenda, only those states that have the ability and willingness to add real value should be invited in.

The sole country that is Quad-ready at present is France. Even though the joint statement issued by the Quad leaders stipulated against an expansion for the time being, that should not be a real hindrance as and when it is decided to induct France. It has 1.5 million citizens on island territories and 93 per cent of its exclusive economic zone (EEZ) of more than 11 million sq km is in the IPR.

Since the outbreak of the Covid-19 pandemic, virtual Quad meetings were hosted by Washington and New Delhi, to which a number of other countries, such as South Korea, Israel, Brazil, the Philippines, Indonesia, Vietnam, New Zealand, Singapore, Taiwan, France and Sri Lanka, were invited, which are loosely bracketed as Quad plus states.

Some of them, like South Korea, Vietnam and the Philippines, have been victims of Chinese aggression, yet are loath, except for France, to give any cause for complaint to 'Emperor' Xi. The way forward is to have issue-based engagements with them to strengthen their negotiating leverage vis-à-vis China. The Quad should display the flexibility to work in different segments with different players. This should enhance its attractiveness. Vietnam and Indonesia could be among the early subscribers to the vision of the Quad, at least in principle.

Consequent to the Quad leaders meet, China is likely to shift gears and tactically switch to a mix of carrot and stick, to fracture the IPR and Quad unity. Amenable (especially Quad plus) nations could be lured into distancing themselves from the Quad. China's financial and military muscle is enough to be both persuasive and dissuasive. Its influence in the region is best not underestimated.

China will do its best to derail the Indian locomotive. The fact remains that the gap in comprehensive national power between the two countries is substantial and growing. India has made a determined effort to improve infrastructure along the LAC and in its north-eastern region. China is not standing still either.

Fortunately, Beijing is at loggerheads with most of its neighbours due to President Xi's unbridled ambition. Military aggression apart, China is trying to ensnare dozens of developing countries in a web of debt, in the garb of providing developmental assistance through the highly opaque and exploitative BRI. Its cover-ups, denials and machinations have subjected the world to a devastating healthcare crisis, the after-effects of which will last for years. Little surprise, therefore, that the Chinese stock is at an all-time low across the world.

'We believe in a region governed by rules, not power,' said Australian Minister of Foreign Affairs Marise Payne. There is a growing realisation amongst law-abiding nations of the need for a new and credible security architecture to deter China, stemming from the belief that even if China cannot be contained, it can be restrained.

However, the Quad is still susceptible to the conflicting foreign policy objectives of each country. Despite the inclusive rhetoric and phraseology of a 'free and open Indo-Pacific', America's leaders sometimes betray a preoccupation with the Asia-Pacific at the expense of the Indian Ocean.[18] Protecting Taiwan from Chinese armed action could be the acid test for the Quad in the coming years. If the Quad rises to the challenge, it would become a grouping to be reckoned with.

India appears to have taken the strategic decision to embrace the Quad. But what about its policy of retaining strategic autonomy? Such a posture is meant to enhance, not restrict, India's elbow room. Did India have any difficulty in concluding a treaty of peace, friendship and cooperation with the erstwhile USSR in 1971? The fact remains that India has always taken decisions in national interest.

That said, India is not counting on any foreign boots on her hallowed grounds. Diplomatic, military hardware and intelligence support itself would be quite valuable. This would increase the uncertainties and cost of any misadventure for Beijing. However, it remains to be seen if India would be willing to commit military resources beyond its extended neighbourhood. Would it have the flexibility of opting out in certain situations? Many more volumes in the IPR and Quad saga have yet to be written. All eyes are now on the first-ever in-person Quad Leaders' Summit at the White House on 24 September.

Endnotes

1. US–India Joint Strategic Vision for the Asia-Pacific and Indian Ocean Region, January 2015, https://www.mea.gov.in/incoming-visit-detail.htm?24728/USIndia+Joint+Strategic+Vision+for+the+AsiaPacific+and+Indian+Ocean+Region.
2. US–Japan Joint Leaders' Statement: 'US–Japan Global Partnership for a New Era', April 2021, The White House.
3. The American Pivot to Asia, by Kenneth G Lieberthal article for Brookings Institute, www.brookings.edu/articles/the-american-pivot-to-asia/.
4. 'Indo-Pacific: Can an Idea Shape Geopolitics?' by Dhruva Jaishankar, https://www.ispionline.it/en/pubblicazione/indo-pacific-can-idea-shape-geopolitics-20712.
5. 'The geopolitics of Indo-Pacific: How India and others interpret the term', *The Indian Express*, by Nirupama Subramanian https://indianexpress.com/article/explained/the-geopolitics-of-indo-pacific-explained-how-india-and-others-interpret-the-term-5807991/.
6. Remarks by President Trump at APEC CEO Summit, Da Nang, Vietnam, on 10 November 2017, https://asean.usmission.gov/remarks-president-trump-apec-ceo-summit-da-nang-vietnam/.

7. Jaishankar, S. *The India Way*, HarperCollins India, pp. 14, 18–4.
8. Prime Minister's Keynote Address at Shangri-La Dialogue, 1 June 2018, https://www.mea.gov.in/Speeches-Statements.htm?dtl%2F29943%2FPrime+Ministers+Keynote+Address+at+Shangri+La+Dialogue+June+01+2018#.YH2sfJLLK5c.twitter.
9. Jaishankar, S. *The India Way*, HarperCollins India, pp. 14, 18–4.
10. Tweets from Shivshankar Menon @ShivshankaMenon on 16 April 2021, in response to a query by this author @AmbVPrakash.
11. Jaishankar, S. *The India Way*, HarperCollins India, pp. 14, 18–4.
12. 'Boat collisions spark Japan–China diplomatic row', BBC, 8 September 2010, https://www.bbc.com/news/world-asia-pacific-11225522.
13. 'Trends in Chinese Vessels in the Waters Surrounding the Senkaku Islands', - Press release by Japanese foreign ministry https://www.mofa.go.jp/region/page23e_000021.html.
14. Quad Leaders' Joint Statement: 'The Spirit of the Quad', 12 March, 2021, https://www.mea.gov.in/bilateral-documents.htm?dtl%2F33620%2Fquad+leaders+joint+statement+the+spirit+of+the+quad#.YH8dbMSNMX0.twitter.
15. Foreign Ministry Spokesperson Zhao Lijian's Regular Press Conference on March 15, 2021, https://www.fmprc.gov.cn/mfa_eng/xwfw_665399/s2510_665401/2511_665403/t1861145.shtml.
16. 'China and India are friends, not rivals', CGTN, 7 March 2021, https://news.cgtn.com/news/2021-03-07/China-and-India-are-friends-not-rivals-Wang-Yi-YrbhF5nHWg/index.html.
17. 'Over time … perception that India is at best an illiberal democracy could lead to weaker ties', 6 December 2020, https://timesofindia.indiatimes.com/blogs/talkingturkey/over-time-perception-that-india-is-at-best-an-illiberal-democracy-could-lead-to-weaker-ties/.
18. 'A Rules-Based Order for the Indo-Pacific?' by Dr Peter Harris, Air University USA https://www.airuniversity.af.edu//Portals/10/JIPA/IndoPacificPerspectives/Harris%20-%20Intro.html.

CHAPTER 15

INDIA–US RELATIONS: PROGNOSIS FOR THE BIDEN ERA AND BEYOND

ARUN K SINGH

India–US relations in the Biden years will no doubt be impacted by the vision the new administration lays out for its global role and challenges, especially in the wake of the precipitous withdrawal from Afghanistan, and its attendant domestic political consequences for the president, and international implications for US credibility.

On 3 March 2021, the White House issued an 'Interim National Security Strategic Guidance'[1], pending a more detailed policy document projected for later in the year.

The document captured the essence of overall approach articulated over the past year or so by candidate and now President Joe Biden, Secretary of State Antony Blinken, National Security Advisor Jake Sullivan and Secretary of Defense Lloyd Austin, among others.

It sought to distinguish itself from the Trump administration and provide the organising principles as the incoming administration and its officials hit the ground.

In the face of the mounting economic, technological and military challenge from China; Trump-disrupted relations with allies in Europe and Asia; continued instability in West Asia; and healthcare and economic disruption caused by the Covid-19 pandemic, the document declared that 'this moment is an inflection point. We are in the midst of a fundamental debate about the future direction of our world'.

The document gave an insight into the third major reordering of international relations that the US was attempting since the Second World War, even before the post-Afghanistan withdrawal, new challenges revealed themselves more clearly. The first was marked by the Cold War; 'containment' of the erstwhile Soviet Union, global rivalry for influence against communism; establishment of multilateral institutions, such as the International Monetary Fund (IMF), the World Bank, and General Agreement on Tariffs and Trade (GATT), to deepen US/Western linkages with other economies. It ended, in US perception, in its victory with the defeat and dissolution of the Soviet Union in 1991. Of course, the period witnessed several failures for the US, including in Vietnam, Korea, etc.

The second was marked by the US-led effort to seal its preponderance through globalisation of production and trade, declaration of 'end of history' with the stage ostensibly set for a US-led 'liberal international order', setting up of World Trade Organization (WTO), coercively and militarily imposing its unilateral preferences in Serbia/Kosovo (1999), Iraq (2003), and then through use of economic sanctions against Iran, Russia, etc. when the limits of military strategies became apparent. The US, again, cannot claim unvarnished success in this phase since its policies facilitated the rise of China as a rival, its military interventions in Iraq and Afghanistan did not lead to social and political stability; under its watch Syria and Libya have become quagmires, and international terrorism continues to be a major threat. Domestically, within the US, globalisation-induced stagnation in the 30 to 40 per cent of the population led to the rise of Trump and sharpening of systemic racism.

The effort, in this third iteration, was to organise allies, partners and rules for trade and technology access to deal with China's rise and its own unilateral assertions in South and East China seas, on line of actual control (LAC) with India, in Europe and elsewhere, and to make foreign and trade policy choices more acceptable to the wider American society, to the electoral advantage of the Democratic Party.

China

China was identified as the main global rival and described as having 'rapidly become more assertive...the only competitor potentially capable of combining its economic, diplomatic, military and technological power to mount a sustained challenge to a stable and open international system'. On 3 March itself, previewing the release of the report, Blinken gave a speech titled, 'A Foreign Policy for the American People', where he described the US relationship with China as the 'biggest geopolitical test of the twenty-first century'.[2]

In an article I wrote in February for the Institute of China Studies[3], I gave a detailed assessment of the Biden administration's approach to the challenge from China; its search for a strategy factoring in cooperation, competition and confrontation; the prevarication of several of its European and Asian allies; and the likely Chinese countervailing strategies.

Domestic political compulsions and the US effort to preserve its preeminence in global context will drive a search for partners and institutional architectures in the 'Indo-Pacific' to 'shape the environment around the rise of China'. The guidance declared that US will 'deepen partnership with India'. The new team has repeatedly emphasised the relevance of the Quad with Japan, India and Australia. On 12 March, the four countries held a virtual summit meeting, the first time at this level, and in an early phase of the new administration, revealing the priority it attaches to this grouping in its Indo-Pacific strategy. Secretary Blinken had also held a foreign minister level meeting in February. The March summit resulted in several concrete decisions—a joint effort to produce one billion Covid-19 related vaccines for supply in the Indo-Pacific region and setting up joint working groups on climate and on new and emerging technologies.

These will provide India the opportunity to explore further the deepening of defence cooperation and technology partnerships and explore 'trusted, secure supply chain' relationships.

TRADE AND ECONOMIC ISSUES

One distinguishing feature of this guidance, particularly from that of even the Obama administration, was the manner in which it elaborated on the planned approach to international economic engagements.

Issued under authority of the US president, it asserts that the US, in its international engagements, would 'redefine America's interests in terms of working families' livelihoods, rather than corporate profits or aggregate national wealth'.

Clearly, Joe Biden has absorbed the lesson from the Trump victory in 2016, and the latter having got 74 million votes in 2020, 11 million more than in 2016, despite all the criticism of his polarising and whimsical behaviour and decision-making. In the globalisation of production and trade, led by the US since the dissolution of the Soviet Union in 1991, US economy benefitted in the aggregate, the elite benefitted, but 30 to 40 per cent of the population in the middle saw their wages stagnate, longevity come down and death rates and drug addiction go up. This was the segment drawn to Trump, and has largely remained loyal to him since. He continues to dominate the Republican Party, despite his electoral loss, and has raised prospects of a 2024 rerun.

At her confirmation hearing in the US Senate on 25 February, the nominee for US Trade Representative (USTR), Katherine Tai, said that the US would not only be seeking efficiency in global production through trade policies and negotiations, but would also be adopting a 'worker-centric' approach.[4] This echoed the comments of her Trump presidency predecessor, Robert Lighthizer, who had criticised the unbridled pursuit of efficiency for the offshoring of US jobs.

The interim guidance went on to declare that US would 'only pursue new trade deals after...investments in American workers and communities'. During the campaign, Biden had repeatedly promised that any new trade deals would come only after an increase in competitiveness of the American workers through investments in infrastructure, skills and technology. In his 3 March speech, Secretary of State Blinken had articulated that the US would 'fight for every American job, and for the rights, protections and interests of all American workers'.

While not adding new tariffs so far, unlike Trump, Biden has not rescinded the earlier ones as yet, except the ones worked out through mutual concessions with the European Union (EU), and has issued executive orders calling for 'Buy America'.

The guidance also says that 'in today's world, economic security is national security'. This is a theme oft repeated by the new National Security Advisor Jake Sullivan. There is intensified search for 'trusted, secure supply chains', to break the Chinese current advantages in rare earths, pharmaceutical ingredients and emerging technology areas such as artificial intelligence (AI) and 5G.

Interestingly, in response to a question, Tai said that she preferred the term 'reshoring' to 'onshoring', since the former allowed for trusted supply chain relationships.

In March itself, the Office of the USTR had issued a fact sheet on the president's trade agenda, asserting, inter alia, that: 'President Biden will pursue a fair international trading system that promotes inclusive economic growth and reflects America's universal values...trade policy must respect the dignity of work and value Americans as workers and wage-earners, not only as consumers...trade agenda will support long-term investments to strengthen domestic production of essential medical equipment, expand industrial capacity and bolster preparation to tackle future public health crises.... Trade must protect and empower workers, drive wage growth, and lead to better economic outcomes for all Americans.... Workers will have a seat at the table as the Biden administration develops new trade policies that promote equitable economic growth by including strong, enforceable labor standards in trade agreements that protect workers' rights and increase economic security...trade agenda will include the negotiation and implementation of strong environmental standards that are critical to a sustainable climate pathway.... The Biden administration recognizes that China's coercive and unfair trade practices harm American workers, threaten our technological edge, weaken our supply chain resiliency, and undermine our national interests.... Policies that promote equitable global economic growth and increase global demand benefit American workers, manufacturers, farmers, ranchers, fishers and service providers by expanding the customer base. The trade agenda will include a review of existing trade programs to evaluate their contribution to equitable economic development, including whether they reduce wage gaps, increase worker unionization, promote safe workplaces, tackle forced labor and exploitative labor conditions, and lead to the economic empowerment of women and under-represented communities'.[5]

These comments reveal the trend in the new administration's approach to trade and economic relationships.

There is an inherent opportunity for India to further rework its geo-economic engagement with the US to its economic and geopolitical advantage. The two countries should consider starting a strategic commercial dialogue, going beyond the USTR's normal preoccupation with market access issues based on current patterns of production. New areas of supportive interactions should be explored in emerging technologies through in-depth dialogue between business and governments in both countries. The US could benefit from India's skilled workforce and tech entrepreneurs in meeting the Chinese competition. The existing Global Comprehensive Strategic Partnership provides the framework for trusted, secure supply chain arrangements. The US has variously described India as a 'pre-eminent US partner in the Indo-Pacific'[6], a 'net provider of security' in the region, and that it sees the rise of India to be in its own interest. It should, therefore, allow sufficient space for the Indian industry in the new reordering. As India looks to expand output through production-linked incentives, or attract foreign investment, access to major markets would incentivise business.

At the Tai hearing, Senator Cornyn of Texas, co-chair of the Senate India caucus, called for building a strategic economic partnership with India. The moment must be seized by both sides. Otherwise, we would remain bogged down, like the senators from Montana, Louisiana and Washington did, in talking about market access for apples, pulses and shrimps. The growing strategic partnership would not have the ballast of a more solid economic interlinkage.

Afghanistan/Pakistan

Decisions on Afghanistan would also have a bearing on India's security.

The document had reiterated that 'the United States should not, and will not, engage in 'forever wars'', the US would work to 'responsibly end America's longest war in Afghanistan, while ensuring that Afghanistan does not again become a safe haven for terrorist attacks against the United States'.

As vice president in the Obama administration, Biden had pushed for substantial drawdown of US military presence. President Obama eventually did not go along with this advice, mindful of negative political blowback for him from any subsequent terrorist attack on US soil, or a collapse of the Afghan governance structure that the US had spent 'blood and treasure' building since 2001. Trump, on the other hand, had come into office promising to end US military presence there. Even he could not bring the number below 2,500, despite an agreement with the Taliban, since there was not much progress in the intra-Afghan reconciliation talks, and Taliban violence against Afghan civilians and government targets had continued.

Given his own inclinations, Biden projected that he had inherited this situation, and a 1 May ostensible deadline for withdrawal of all US troops as per the US–Taliban agreement, which he later delayed to end-August.

While undoing Trump's rejection of the Paris 2015 climate agreement, and restarting talks with Iran to try and resurrect the JCPOA, Biden decided to use the Trump agreement on withdrawal to implement his own policy preference. Initially, the administration indicated that it was reviewing the specific commitments made under the agreement by both sides. Clearly, it was in a bind. If it withdrew, as it eventually did, without progress in reconciliation, and with continued violence, there could be no guarantee that its counter terrorism requirements would be addressed. If the Afghan governance structures collapsed, as it did, there would be a major dent to US credibility in the international context. On the other hand, if it did not, it would own the next phase of the strategy in Afghanistan. The Taliban had indicated that if US did not meet its deadline, it may once again start attacking US forces. US would then have to also escalate and counter attack. Biden did not want to go down this path.

Various US efforts to minimise the negative consequence of a withdrawal came to naught. In May, US came up with three planks of a new approach: calling for an intra-Afghan summit in Turkey, with presence of top leaders of all major factions; asking the UNSG to convene a meeting of foreign ministers of US, Russia, China, India, Iran and Pakistan to get a regional buy in to the process; presenting a US drafted reconciliation framework document to speed up negotiations between the Taliban and the Afghan government and others. In a letter to Afghan President Ghani, Secretary Blinken sought to generate pressure on him for compromise by writing that 'we are considering full withdrawal of our forces by May 1st, as we consider other options' and added to it by suggesting that after US withdrawal 'the security situation will worsen and that the Taliban could make rapid territorial gains'.[7] Ghani resisted power sharing with the Taliban or creation of an interim governance structure, arguing that any such framework should emerge only through an election. Eventually, the Taliban made rapid gains throughout the country and moved into Kabul on 15 August. US had to evacuate a large number of US nationals and Afghans who had worked with the US presence for the past two decades. US could not avoid images similar to its withdrawal from Saigon in 1975, giving a sense of leaving under pressure and in disarray, even though it could claim a major logistical achievement in terms of number of people moved out in a short span of time. Manner of US exit, nature of subsequent Taliban governance structure announced, have led to questioning of limits of US power and its international credibility.

Pakistan did not find any mention in the guidance. Historically, the US–Pakistan relationship has oscillated between incentivising and pressurising, depending on whether the US is valuing or is frustrated with the cooperation it is getting from Pakistan for its objectives, initially against the Soviet Union, and later in the Afghanistan context. Today, Pakistan will be valued if it can deliver on a successful counterterrorism strategy through the Taliban, since terrorist groups and other entities supported by it have come into the power structure in Kabul. It will be criticised and demands will be made within the US system for scaling back of support if it fails. India will need to carefully watch as this dynamic plays out, making sure that it is able to preserve the US relationship and also prevent Pakistan from getting any assurances against India's interests. The US will continue to find a need to engage with Pakistan because of its nuclear weapon capabilities and presence of terrorist groups in the Af-Pak region.

Other Issues

Several other issues would also impact the relationship in the ensuing period.

The Biden administration is expected to continue a hard-line approach to Russia, despite engagement on arms control issues. There are no current prospects of a rollback of any of the sanctions imposed. Disagreements on Ukraine; perceptions related to Russian cyber hacking of US political, economic and government entities; and treatment of political opponents will hinder any overall positive movement. Russia recalled its ambassador for 'consultations' after Biden referred to Vladimir Putin as a 'killer' in a TV interview. There had also earlier been a build-up of Russian forces along the Ukrainian border, prompting statements of concern from the US, France and Germany. This will be a challenge for India, since major defence purchases from Russia, including of the S-400, will come under adversarial scrutiny, especially as India does more and more with the US in framework of the Indo-Pacific and gets more defence supplies, technology and intelligence sharing. Russia, on account of its own China related strategies, has continued to oppose any strategic framework based on the 'Indo-Pacific' construct. It would be important for the US to recognise its own interest in allowing geopolitical space to India, mindful of its historical relationship with Russia, nearly 60 per cent of defence inventory being of Russian origin, and so as not to reinforce history-based suspicions and perceptions in India of the US being an unreliable partner. A recent US seventh fleet 'freedom of navigation' activity off Lakshadweep, unilaterally asserting US interpretation of international law, in violation of Indian provisions, and making a public statement of it, has reminded of past US challenges to India's national interests.

India would also need to watch carefully how US advocacy on climate change plays out. Biden had called a summit of major economies and "emitters" on 22 April.[8] His cabinet-level Special Envoy John Kerry has been calling for 'enhanced ambitions'. India has been proactive in rapidly increasing renewable energy, including wind and solar, in its energy mix. It has also taken several initiatives, including the International Solar Alliance and Coalition for Disaster Resilient Infrastructure. As the debate progresses on this, it would be important that the principle of 'common but differentiated' responsibility is kept firmly in view, along with that of historical emissions, climate justice and need of developing countries for access to technology and finance for mitigation and adaptation.

In sections of the Democratic Party in the US, there is criticism of some of the actions of the Indian government on Citizenship Amendment Act (CAA) 2019, National Register of Citizens (NRC), J&K etc. The US faces its own challenges of systemic racism and voter suppression. The two governments would need to navigate any differences, keeping in mind the overall strategic convergence. The Biden team has said that any differences on these issues would be addressed as a 'dialogue among friends'.

Prognosis

The overarching priority for the US to deal with the economic, technological and military challenge from China will provide the convergence for advancing the US–India Global Comprehensive Strategic Partnership. Businesses and governments in both countries could usefully seize this moment to build new, trusted and secure supply chain relationships, including in new and emerging technologies. This would deepen economic interlinkages to the geo-economic advantage of both. Both would also gain by managing their differences on Russia or Afghanistan by showing understanding also for their varying domestic and geopolitical compulsions.

Despite his victory in November 2020, Biden faces some domestic headwinds. The senate is evenly divided, and conservative Democratic senators are joining Republicans in holding back progress on some of the progressive agenda that Biden supports on the economy, infrastructure, voting rights, etc. There is a growing humanitarian and political crisis of illegal immigrants from Guatemala, Honduras and El Salvador turning up on the US–Mexico border, prompting criticism of the administration as being 'soft' on the issue. Former President Trump continues to dominate the Republican Party and Republican fundraising. Republican majority legislatures in several states have passed legislations restricting voting facilitation and sustaining the partisan projections of a 'stolen election' in 2020. There is talk of Democrats losing control of the senate and, perhaps, even the House in the 2022 mid-term elections. Trump could make a renewed bid for the presidency in 2024. Should all that happen, there would be another turnaround in many of the US domestic and foreign policies. But, approach on China, Russia, and Afghanistan/Pakistan can be expected to continue. So would the approach to the India relationship, which has enjoyed bipartisan consensus since 2000, through Republican and Democratic administrations.

ENDNOTES

1. Biden, Joe. 'Interim National Security Strategic Guidance', 3 March 2021. https://www.whitehouse.gov/wp-content/uploads/2021/03/NSC-1v2.pdf
2. Blinken, Antony. 'A Foreign Policy for the American People', 3 March 2021. https://www.state.gov/a-foreign-policy-for-the-american-people/
3. Singh, Arun K. 'US–China Relations in the post-Trump Phase', *ICS Analysis*, no. 128 (February 2021) https://www.icsin.org/uploads/2021/02/24/5d73d221fbebf85d3187a344502e132f.pdf
4. 'Hearing to Consider the Nomination of Katherine C. Tai, of the District of Columbia, to be United States Trade Representative, with the rank of Ambassador Extraordinary and Plenipotentiary', United States Senate Committee on Finance, 25 February 2021. https://www.finance.senate.gov/imo/media/doc/Katherine%20Tai%20Opening%20Statement%20for%202.25.2021.pdf
5. 'Fact Sheet: 2021 President's Trade Agenda And 2020 Annual Report', Office of the United States Trade Representative, accessed 9 March 2021, https://ustr.gov/sites/default/files/files/reports/2021/2021%20Trade%20Agenda/Online%20PDF%202021%20Trade%20Policy%20Agenda%20and%202020%20Annual%20Report.pdf
6. 'Secretary Blinken's Call with Indian External Affairs Minister Jaishankar', United States Department of State, accessed 9 March 2021, https://www.state.gov/secretary-blinkens-call-with-indian-external-affairs-minister-jaishankar/
7. Blinken, Antony. 'Letter to Ashraf Ghani'. https://tolonews.com/pdf/02.pdf
8. 'US: Joe Biden Signs Climate Directives, Announces April Summit', *Deutsche Welle*, 27 January 2021. https://www.dw.com/en/us-joe-biden-signs-climate-directives-announces-april-summit/a-56365062

CHAPTER 16

INDIA–RUSSIA RELATIONS: OPPORTUNITIES AND CHALLENGES

PS Raghavan

A few years ago, a senior Indian dignitary was holding forth to Russian President Vladimir Putin on the decades of India–Russia friendship. The latter interrupted him to say that, while we should celebrate the achievements of the past, the health of the relationship depends on the strength of the current and objective conditions for its future development. Analysts would say this hard-headed approach is typical of a leader with a background in an intelligence service, but in the shifting sands of modern global geopolitics, more and more world leaders are evaluating their international relationships through this prism.

The strong performance of India–USSR relations, the precursor of India–Russia relations, during the Cold War years, is undeniable. In many ways, it continues to shape India's foreign policy choices and constrains some of its actions.

The vibrancy in the relationship dates back to the 1950s, when post-Stalin Soviet leaders reached out to India. Since then, the USSR extended support to India in international forums on Jammu and Kashmir and other issues of core political and security concern. The USSR used its veto in the United Nations Security Council (UNSC) five times to block resolutions that would have hurt India's interests. The developing nexus between Pakistan and Russia's then arch-rival China, as well as Pakistan's accession to US-led military alliances, cemented

Russian support for India. This support included extensive military assistance and capacity-building for newly independent India's infrastructure industries. Close people-to-people linkages developed, including educational and cultural exchanges.

After a decade of relative uncertainty following the end of the Cold War, the advent of President Putin to office and crystallisation of India's concept of a multipolar world order led to a new phase of India–Russia strategic partnership. In a major speech to the Indian Parliament during his first visit to India, President Putin reiterated the convergence of Russian and Indian political and security perspectives, declaring that a strong relationship with India was a foreign policy priority for Russia, and that it would not be affected by any of Russia's other relationships, in Asia or elsewhere.

At Russia's initiative, a Russia–India–China (RIC) ministerial dialogue mechanism emerged to articulate the aspirations of these countries for multipolarity in the world order. A Brazil–Russia–India–China—BRIC, later BRICS, with the admission of South Africa—summit level dialogue was initiated to push for democratisation of the global economic and financial architecture, though it developed later into a platform to also express shared political perspectives.

India also showed sensitivity to core Russian interests. When the US and its allies denounced Russia's 'annexation' of Crimea in 2014, India found a way of expressing 'understanding' for the Russian interests that drove its policy. India also distanced itself from the subsequent 'unilateral' Western sanctions against Russia, announcing publicly that it would not be party to any sanctions that are not authorised by the UNSC.

India–Russia defence cooperation surged, as India acquired an array of advanced weapons platforms for its army, air force and navy. Russian collaboration in India's nuclear power industry commenced in 1998, when India was still under sanctions for its nuclear tests earlier that year. The collaboration—involving Russian technology, fuel and credit on attractive terms—intensified after the Nuclear Suppliers Group (NSG) approved, in 2008, a dispensation for India to get international cooperation in civil nuclear energy. Mutual investments in hydrocarbons was another success story. Indian firms have an estimated investment of about US$ 15 billion in Siberian oil and gas fields. Russia's largest investment abroad is a US$ 13 billion project in downstream hydrocarbons projects in India.

Changes in the external environment naturally impacted on the relationship. Russia's relations with the US and its allies, already deteriorating from 2008, reached near-breakdown in 2014, after the 'annexation' of Crimea. A concerted Western campaign was launched to politically isolate Russia and impose a range of economic sanctions, including asset freeze and visa denials to Russian officials and oligarchs, financing restrictions and technology denial. The scope of the sanctions increased progressively in response to alleged Russian 'transgressions', like actions in eastern Ukraine, chemical poisoning of an ex-Russian spy in England, 'meddling' in the US presidential elections of 2016 and many others. The range extended from primary sanctions—applicable to the territories, technologies, financial instruments and currencies of the sanctions-imposing countries—to secondary sanctions, by which entities in a third country—whether ally, partner or adversary—would be blocked from doing business with a US entity (individual or corporate) if they engaged in 'significant' defence or energy cooperation with Russia. Actions to restrict Russian influence in different geographies and Russian pushback against these actions eventually resulted in political or military confrontations, directly or through their respective proxies, from Venezuela to Afghanistan, and from the Baltic, Black, Mediterranean and Caspian seas in the west to the South China Sea and Sea of Japan in the east.

This Cold War-like situation impacted both India–Russia and India–US relations. India–US relations surged in the early 2000s, contemporaneously with the strategic partnership with Russia. The cobwebs of the past—the US 'tilt' towards Pakistan in the 1971-72 India–Pakistan confrontation, the US–China détente and the draconian US-led technology-denial regimes following India's nuclear tests in 1974 and 1998—were cleared by recognition of new opportunities. The US was attracted by the trade and investment opportunities in the expanding Indian market for civilian and military products. India welcomed US goods, technologies, investments and weapons systems that would diversify its arms inventory, which was solely Soviet/Russian till then. The US also saw a strong, democratic India as a potential counterpoise to a fast-rising China, which would soon threaten US global dominance.[1] The India–US nuclear deal, which led to a progressive lifting of US sanctions, opened the door to a major expansion of India–US civilian and military cooperation. US defence exports to India surged from near zero to about US$ 20 billion in a decade.

As India–US relations intensified, so did the pressure on India to support the international initiatives of the US, particularly in the UNSC (when India was a non-permanent member in 2011-12) and the Organisation for the Prohibition of Chemical Weapons (OPCW). Even more, the US tried to restrain India from obtaining major Russian weapons systems. It was suggested that India could be subjected to secondary sanctions, envisaged for 'significant' defence cooperation, if it purchased the S-400 air defence system. As the India–China military standoff in Ladakh dragged on for months in 2020, senior US officials—including the outgoing US ambassador to India—and sections of the Indian media and academia urged India to make the 'strategic choice' of an unequivocal alignment with the US as the only viable course to meet the Chinese challenge. India resisted many of these pressures, including by concluding the contract for the S-400 missile system. Nevertheless, Russia sees with caution an increasing Indian tendency to support US initiatives or equivocate on matters relating to it in international forums. Its concern is also that the confidentiality embedded in the India–US defence agreements and their intensifying military-to-military cooperation would inhibit purchase of Russian hardware and, equally, compromise security of Russian technologies vis-à-vis its adversary.

China figures differently in the calculations of India and Russia. The Russia–China strategic partnership developed rapidly after they resolved their border disputes in the early 2000s. As two large neighbours, with complementarities of economic, energy and military technology interests, their cooperation grew apace—simultaneously with the intensification of the India–Russia and India–US partnerships. India–China relations also thawed initially, but developed frictions, which progressively worsened over the years, with India's concerns over the Belt and Road Initiative (BRI) and the China–Pakistan Economic Corridor (CPEC), China's support for Pakistan on terrorism-related issues and its blocking of India's membership of the NSG. A military standoff near the India–Bhutan–China tri-junction in 2017 was followed three years later by a more protracted, more tense and more deadly boundary confrontation in Ladakh. Meanwhile, as the Russia–West frictions worsened, the Russia–China embrace tightened, as Russia looked to China for closer economic cooperation and political support in multilateral forums like the UNSC. Political cooperation expanded. Chinese investment was wooed in strategic economic sectors, including in the Russian Far East and the Arctic region. Defence cooperation deepened and diversified, with Russian transfers to China of advanced military technologies, joint military exercises, naval drills and air patrols, and intensive sharing of military intelligence. As US–China relations hit turbulence in the latter years of the Donald Trump presidency, the Chinese commitment to the embrace increased. Though both countries have denied that they were moving towards a military alliance, President Putin said, in October 2020, that it was not inconceivable.

Russia's growing engagement with Pakistan and collusion with it to develop closer links with the Afghan Taliban are relatively new developments. Russia–Pakistan relations have warmed up in recent years, as Pakistan–US relations cooled and Russia–China relations intensified. Political exchanges have increased. Pakistan has voted with Russia—against Western countries—on issues in multilateral forums. Military-to-military links have been established, including joint military exercises and training in defence institutions. Some military hardware has also been supplied—most recently, attack helicopters—though Russia has kept this sphere of cooperation in check, in consideration of the damage it may do to military sales to India.

Pakistan has facilitated Russia's contacts with the Taliban in the effort to generate an 'intra-Afghan' consultative process, separate from that promoted by the US special envoy. They have coordinated with China on this. As Russia's influence with Afghan political groups grew, the US used this leverage to further its agenda of creating conducive conditions for early international troop withdrawal. Russia justified its presence in Afghanistan by the need to protect its territory from infiltration of terrorists/extremists through the porous Afghan borders with Central Asia. Russia sees Western activities on Afghan borders as an extension of efforts to create problems on its periphery across Europe and Asia.

These developments of the past decade pose major challenges for India–Russia relations over the next decade.

The principal one is the Russia–China partnership. There are objective political and economic complementarities driving this partnership. However, their chequered history of rivalries and territorial disputes had caused Russia to restrict mutual dependence to acceptable levels. The pressures caused by unremitting tensions with the West may be weakening this resolve. If these tensions ultimately drive Russia into an alliance with China, in which it would inevitably be a junior partner, it would impact very adversely on India's interests. Despite the recent reference to a possible alliance by Putin, Russia's ambitions to be an independent pole in a multipolar world may prevent this, unless it becomes politically unavoidable.

A second challenge is the threat from US sanctions to India–Russia defence cooperation. Despite continuing efforts to diversify its military acquisitions, about 60 per cent of the weapons systems and equipment in India's arms inventory is of Russian or Soviet origin. Their maintenance and upgrading needs continued bilateral commitment. Russia has been willing to supply its latest military equipment as well as engage in joint research and development of technologies. The US has openly said that its Countering America's Adversaries Through Sanctions Act (CAATSA) is designed to wean countries away from Russian equipment and towards those made by the US. India is already increasing its imports from the US. Accelerated delinking from Russia would increase financial liabilities and defence vulnerabilities in the immediate term. Indian diplomacy with the US continues to stress that degrading its defence capability would undermine the strength of India–US cooperation in the Indo-Pacific.

The Indo-Pacific poses another challenge to India–Russia harmony. The waters of the Indian and Pacific oceans carry 90 per cent of India's foreign trade, including most of its energy supplies. Their marine resources feed the economy of the littoral states. India's 7,500 km-long coastline has to be protected from arms, drugs and human trafficking. The Indian peninsula abuts the busy commercial sea lanes of the Indian Ocean, strategically located between its eastern and western 'choke points'. Warding off political, economic and military dominance of these waters by China is, therefore, a principal Indian strategic objective. It is pursued through an energetic 'Act East' initiative for bilateral and multilateral partnerships with regional countries, which also feel threatened by Chinese assertive actions, like its unilateral 'settlement' of maritime territorial disputes and punitive sanctions against countries that offend it, and using debt diplomacy in BRI projects, like the Maritime Silk Road, to establish Chinese-controlled ports on the Indian Ocean—from China to Africa. India's partnership with the US, Japan and Australia, in the 'Quad' dialogue and the Malabar joint naval exercises have drawn the strongest Chinese and Russian ire.

Russia sees this as a US-led conspiracy to draw India into a quasi-alliance that would disrupt the India–Russia partnership.[2] India's diplomacy with Russia seeks to convey that the effort to restrict Chinese hegemony in the Indo-Pacific should also be in Russian interests as a Pacific power. India's investment in a line of credit of US$ 1 billion in the Russian Far East for the development of its natural resources and the activation of a marine trade corridor from Vladivostok to Chennai serve to emphasise this point. Russia's resistance to this argument stems from the aggressive rhetoric of the Trump administration's Indo-Pacific strategy, which advocated a muscular military posture and hinted at the objective of regime change in China. The Biden administration has moderated the rhetoric somewhat, emphasises the non-military nature of the Quad and stresses that it seeks a cooperative order. This naturally does not convince China that it is not the target of a containment strategy. As long as the US–Russia relationship remains mired in hostility, it is difficult to convince Russia that it is not a collateral target. A modicum of a thaw in US–Russia relations could catalyse a more benign Russian attitude towards Indo-Pacific initiatives.

A further challenge to the India–Russia relationship comes from prevailing unhelpful stereotypes about each other, as reflected in sections of their media, academia, business communities and even political circles and officialdom. The view (quoted earlier) that India should make a 'strategic choice' flows from assessments that Russia's interests are so tied up with those of China—and by extension Pakistan—that it can no longer be a true friend of India. This view is reinforced by the narrative that Russia has been significantly weakened by Western sanctions and its own economic infirmities. On the Russian side, many analysts describe India–US relations in the same way that Indians describe the Russia–China relationship—an erstwhile friend, hobnobbing with a current adversary. There is an unwillingness or inability to understand the motivations of India's Indo-Pacific activities. In Indian industry, Russia is still associated with the clunky technologies of the Soviet era. Indian businesses, especially those with bitter experiences from the chaotic 1990s, worry about the business ethics in Russia. Most Western sanctions against Russia are currency-, sector- or technology-specific, providing scope for circumventing them legally. While businesses from the sanctions-imposing countries do so, Indian trade promotion agencies have chosen to look elsewhere. On the other side, Russians are theoretically aware of India's economic progress, but cannot bring themselves to believe that the country in which their forefathers helped set up basic industries, now exports innovations and technologies to many developed countries. A couple of failed Russian investment projects in India have provided the alibi for Russian businesses to avoid investments in India. This smugness of mutual ignorance explains the paltry bilateral trade and investment exchanges, other than in hydrocarbons. Academia and media in both countries take their analysis of each other from Western sources, which accentuates the distortion of perceptions.

At their annual summit meetings, the leadership of both countries have had frank discussions on the divergences in their outlook. They have endorsed the strategy of broad-based, multisectoral economic cooperation to enhance mutual stakes in the bilateral partnership so that they can cope with differences of outlook on some issues. The transition from the past that India–Russia relations have to make is to recognise that there is no exclusivity of relations in this confused post-Cold War order. Countries join to promote shared interests, and join with other countries to promote other interests. Partnerships remain vibrant if the partners respect the core sensitivities of each other. This independence of action is essential for a country working towards a multipolar world order. This is what rules out an alliance, or even a quasi-alliance, for India with the US—or, for that matter, with Russia.

Mutually shared interests with Russia are of weighty consequence. The importance of defence cooperation has already been highlighted. Nuclear energy cooperation has been beneficial and continues to have great prospects for further expansion. For energy-hungry India, the hydrocarbons investments are important for energy security. Supply chain disruptions during the Covid-19 pandemic underlined the importance of diversifying procurements of raw materials. With 30 per cent of the world's natural resources, Russia is an obvious target for sourcing some of resource-hungry India's needs.

From a broader perspective, geographical realities need recognition. India's Indo-Pacific interests have informed its policies and partnerships in the maritime domain. The vast continental space to India's north and northwest present both formidable security challenges and valuable economic opportunities. The Chinese influence in Central Asia is of no less importance to India than its domination of the Indian Ocean. Central Asia borders Afghanistan, Iran and Pakistan-occupied Kashmir. It is a part of the Shanghai

Cooperation Organisation (SCO), which India joined in 2017. The region is, today, dominated by Russia and China, with an unwritten understanding that Russia would underwrite the security of the region, while China would provide the economic support. The increasing Chinese influence in this region may be undermining this understanding. It is important for India to be present in the region to monitor the Russia–China dynamics in it. The multimodal trade and transportation corridor from India's west coast to Afghanistan and Central Asia, through Iran, would provide the vital connectivity to sustain this presence through mutually beneficial trade and investment. As Central Asia seeks to increase its independence from Russia and China, it would welcome this independent access to the sea and the link with India, with which it has had cultural links from the time of the Silk Road.

There are other geopolitical realties. Much as India is discomfited by the intensity of Russia–China relations, it has to remain engaged with Russia to ensure that its stakes in relations with India will restrain it from taking actions inimical to Indian interests. India needs credible assurance that Russia–China defence cooperation will not compromise the effectiveness of weapons systems that Russia supplies to India. Russia also has extensive presence in the politics and energy of West Asia; its actions in this region impact on the security, energy and consular interests of India.

The India–Russia relationship will continue to be influenced by the current churn in global geopolitics. The US, as the pre-eminent global power, seeks to prolong its unipolar dominance. China is almost alongside it in economic terms and not far behind in many civilian technologies. It seeks to leverage these strengths to expand its political influence. To some extent, it has been helped by the US and major European countries taking their eyes off this ball, mesmerised by the commercial opportunities in China. The other strategic mistake of the US has been equating the threats from Russia and China. Sustained hostility towards both runs counter to the geopolitical wisdom that a superpower divides its adversaries by tactically partnering with the lesser one to secure its support (or at least neutrality), so that it can focus its energies fully on the major threat. Henry Kissinger followed this course in the 1970s by opening a channel to China—then the lesser adversary. There were a number of domestic and trans-Atlantic factors that prevented such a 'reverse-Kissinger' US strategy. Many remain relevant even today. It remains to be seen whether the Biden administration reviews the current US strategy. It is also debatable whether the time for a 'reverse-Kissinger' has not decisively passed.

In the absence of a settled post-Cold War order, a number of middle and major powers are jostling for political and economic space. West Asia is in a state of flux—the realignments engineered by the Trump administration and the resurgence of Turkey, bolstered by its military success in the South Caucasus, could upset the Saudi Arabia-led Islamic order. Even as the Biden administration sets out to repair the trans-Atlantic partnership, it is threatened by divisions within. Brexit apart, there are fault lines within Europe—north–south economic disparities, east–west social divides and differences on political and energy policies that reflect positioning for political and economic influence in the region.

The above are external variables, whose course can influence Russian behaviour vis-à-vis India, and vice versa. There is at least one other internal imponderable in the India–Russia relationship. While successive Indian governments have pursued a consistent policy towards Russia (with variations of nuance), President Putin has been almost the sole determinant of Russia's external strategy for the past two decades, setting the priorities and dictating the tactics. Though he has got himself the constitutional right to conceivably win two more terms, it is not clear if he will use it. We may then see a leadership transition that may result in a recalibration of Russia's foreign policy in response to the emerging trends outlined above.

The vibrancy of India–Russia relations over the next decade would, therefore, depend both on how their governments implement their stated intentions—dealing with the headwinds of perceptions—and on the responses of both countries to changes in the external environment.

ENDNOTES

1. Rice, Condoleezza. *No Higher Honour* (Simon & Schuster, 2011), p. 437.
2. Lavrov, Sergey. Remarks at the General Meeting of the Russian International Affairs Council, 10 December 2020. https://russiancouncil.ru/en/analytics-and-comments/analytics/remarks-at-the-general-meeting-of-the-russian-international-affairs-council/?sphrase_id=72773010. Accessed on 5 August 2021.

CHAPTER 17

INDIA–CENTRAL ASIA: FRATERNITY FOREVER

Vinod Kumar

Prime Minister of India Narendra Modi, in his 7 July 2015 address at Nazarbayev University, Astana (now Nur-Sultan), Kazakhstan, noted that Central Asia has been a region of continuous engagement with India since human civilisation began.[1] Drawn by history and goodwill and as a neighbour, he was in Central Asia to write a new chapter in an ancient relationship.

The historic visit by Prime Minister Modi to all five Central Asian countries—Kazakhstan, Kyrgyzstan, Tajikistan, Turkmenistan and Uzbekistan—in 2015 heralded the rejuvenation of India's relationship with the region. Regular visits have been taking place since then. An India–Central Asia ministerial dialogue has been initiated and there is focused attention on expanding and diversifying cooperation in all areas, including economic engagement, connectivity, and security. India's membership of the Shanghai Cooperation Organisation (SCO) in 2017 has provided it an additional framework to engage with the Central Asian countries. There is interest from both sides and there is great potential to develop a mutually beneficial relationship with the region.

Despite our historical linkages with Central Asia, following the disintegration of the Soviet Union in 1991, Indian engagement with the region remained limited. The independence of Central Asian countries coincided with the commencement of economic reforms in India and consequent focus on economic relationships. The constraints of connectivity with the region, banking issues and local currency regulations were among the factors inhibiting any major enhancement of trade and investment.

Notwithstanding these factors, India and the Central Asian countries continued to work towards developing a mutually beneficial relationship. During his visit to Kazakhstan in June 2002, Prime Minister Atal Bihari Vajpayee, in his opening remarks at the press conference in Almaty, described Central Asia as the extended neighbourhood of India, linked through ties of history, culture and spirituality. He added that India wished to strengthen ties with the region, imparting a multi-dimensional character to them, calling it the new Silk Route Initiative of India's foreign policy that would seek to build a new Silk Road of friendship and cooperation between India and Central Asia.[2]

Another important initiative was India's Connect Central Asia policy, unveiled by Minister of State for External Affairs E Ahamed in his address at the First India–Central Asia Dialogue among academic institutions in June 2012 in Bishkek, Kyrgyzstan. He stated that the policy was based on political, economic and people-to-people engagement with Central Asian countries, both individually and collectively.[3]

The period since 2015 has witnessed regular visits by heads of state/government, ministers and officials, reactivation of existing bilateral mechanisms and creation of new ones. A number of agreements have been signed with these countries in the areas of trade, science and technology, energy, information technology (IT), space cooperation, education, defence, security, etc. Even while Covid-19 travel restrictions have been in place, India has held virtual summits and meetings at ministerial and other levels. Several initiatives have been taken to improve connectivity with the Central Asian countries. Defence and security cooperation has been expanded and joint military exercises have taken place with several countries in the region. India has also revived its agreement for receiving supply of uranium from Uzbekistan, making it the second country after Kazakhstan from the region to supply uranium to India for its energy needs.

The renewed interest in enhancing mutual cooperation and consultations on important regional issues manifested in the creation of a new dialogue mechanism with the Central Asian countries at the initiative of Uzbekistan and India. The first-ever India–Central Asia Dialogue at the foreign ministers' level was held in Samarkand, Uzbekistan, in January 2019. External Affairs Minister of India Sushma Swaraj led the Indian delegation to the Samarkand Dialogue, which was attended by foreign ministers of all five Central Asian countries. The foreign minister of Afghanistan also participated in a special session devoted to connectivity. During the Samarkand Dialogue, several initiatives were taken to enhance cooperation. India proposed the setting up of the India–Central Asia Development Group at the government level to take forward the development partnership between India and the Central Asian countries. India also proposed setting up of the India–Central Asia Business Council, formed by a leading chamber of commerce and industry of each country and comprising of business communities as members.[4]

On 6 February 2020, the India–Central Asia Business Council was launched in New Delhi. The Federation of Indian Chambers of Commerce and Industry (FICCI) has been nominated as the chamber from India. In his address at the launch, Minister of External Affairs S Jaishankar noted that despite India's excellent bilateral relations with all the Central Asian countries, its combined trade with the region was still below US$ 2 billion per annum, and hoped that the council would be able to encourage more trade with Central Asia, promote investment and look at various collaborative opportunities in fields that have not been tapped so far.[5] The second meeting of the India–Central Asia Business Council, held in a virtual format on 28 October 2020, agreed to constitute four joint working groups (JWGs) on energy (oil and gas and renewable energy); agriculture, food processing and textiles; tourism and air corridors and, finally, pharmaceuticals, life sciences and healthcare. Hopefully, the JWGs will come up with concrete proposals that can be put into action in a post-Covid world.

The second India–Central Asia Dialogue, hosted virtually by India on 28 October 2020, signalled the intention of the participating countries to continue discussions and collaboration through the platform. The foreign ministers of Kazakhstan, Tajikistan, Turkmenistan and Uzbekistan and the first deputy foreign minister of Kyrgyzstan participated in the dialogue with the acting foreign minister of Afghanistan joining the second session as a special invitee. India offered a US$ 1 billion line of credit to Central Asian countries for priority development projects in the fields such as connectivity, energy, IT, healthcare, education, agriculture, etc., as also grant assistance for implementation of high-impact community development projects (HICDP) to further socio-economic development.

The SCO has emerged in recent years as an important regional organisation. Along with Pakistan, India became a full member of the SCO in 2017 at the meeting of the heads of state of the SCO in Astana, which was attended by Prime Minister Narendra Modi. India hosted the SCO heads of state meeting for the first time on 10 November 2020 in a virtual format. The SCO meetings provide additional opportunities for India to continue its engagement with the Central Asian countries at the head of state/government and other levels of government. The Tashkent-based SCO Regional Anti-Terrorist Structure (SCO RATS) is a useful mechanism in our efforts to combat terrorism. India has participated in SCO's biennial counterterrorism peace mission military exercises. Despite Pakistan's occasional attempts to create unnecessary controversy, such as by displaying an incorrect map at the virtual meeting of SCO national security advisors (NSAs) in September 2020, prompting the Indian NSA to leave the meeting, India remains committed to fruitful collaboration within the SCO. The organisation has a value addition aspect to India's relationship with the Central Asian countries.

A quick assessment of India's relationship with individual Central Asian countries is in order here. Kazakhstan is India's largest trade and investment partner in Central Asia. The annual trade turnover is more than US$ 1.5 billion, which includes importing of crude oil amounting to over US$ 1 billion per year. There is potential to enhance mutual investment. Currently, Indian investment in Kazakhstan is over US$ 400 million and Kazakhstani investment in India is over US$ 60 million.

Kazakhstan is also the biggest supplier of uranium to India. The two sides are discussing a quantitative increase of uranium supply for the period 2020-24 over the contract for 5,000 tonnes during the period 2015-19. The visit of the defence minister of Kazakhstan to India in April 2021 provided the two countries the opportunity to discuss the possibility of a defence industrial collaboration and an increase in the scope and content of joint KAZIND military exercises. India has been actively participating in, and supporting, the Conference on Interaction and Confidence-Building Measures in Asia (CICA), set up through the initiative of Kazakhstan.

With Kyrgyzstan, both countries are looking at enhancing bilateral trade which is currently to the tune of US$ 30 million. The joint special forces exercise—KHANJAR—initiated in 2011, has become an annual feature. Despite the Covid-19 pandemic, the two-week eighth KHANJAR exercise was conducted in April 2021 in Bishkek.

Tajikistan has been a strategic partner of India's in the region, especially in the context of Afghanistan. Bilateral trade has been fluctuating between US$ 20 million and US$ 75 million in recent years. During his visit to Tajikistan in March 2021, Minister of External Affairs S Jaishankar stated that while the bilateral strategic relations have grown and expanded over the years, there is potential for further strengthening of economic cooperation.

Turkmenistan was declared a permanently neutral country by the United Nations (UN) in 1995. Turkmenistan partnered with Afghanistan, Pakistan and India in the TAPI gas pipeline project, sometimes referred to as the Peace Pipeline or the Silk Route of Gas, which endeavours to lay pipes that traverse over 1,800 kms to bring gas from Turkmenistan to Afghanistan, Pakistan and India. Bilateral trade between Turkmenistan and India fell from a high of US$ 115 million in 2015-16 to US$ 38 million in 2019-20. The hope is that trade will pick up again after the Covid-19 pandemic is over.

Uzbekistan, which borders all the other Central Asian countries and Afghanistan, is a major strategic partner for India. The two countries have set a target of US$ 1 billion in trade, which is currently at about US$ 350 million. India and Uzbekistan have agreed to start negotiations for a preferential trading arrangement. Indian states have also been exchanging delegations with Uzbekistan in order to promote trade and investment. The state of Gujarat has a memorandum of understanding (MoU) with the Uzbek province of Andijan, and several trade and investment initiatives have taken place between them. India has active defence and security cooperation with Uzbekistan. During the Indian defence minister's visit to Uzbekistan in 2019, the two countries signed MoUs on military medicine, military education and training and capacity building, and India offered a concessional line of credit of US$ 40 million to Uzbekistan for procurement of goods and services from India. The first India–Uzbekistan joint military exercise DUSTLIK was also held during the visit. DUSTLIK II was held in Uttarakhand in March 2021.

At the India–Uzbekistan virtual summit between President Shavkat Mirziyoyev and Prime Minister Narendra Modi on 11 December 2020, the nine agreements/MoUs signed included HICDPs. The Indian side confirmed the approval of a US$ 448 million line of credit, which is being extended for four developmental projects in Uzbekistan focused on road construction, sewerage treatment and IT. India welcomed the Uzbek proposal to hold a trilateral dialogue among India, Iran and Uzbekistan to promote connectivity through the Chabahar Port. India also requested Uzbekistan to consider joining the International North-South Transport Corridor (INSTC), which would further improve connectivity in the larger Eurasian space.

Since 2016, Uzbekistan has tried to work with other Central Asian countries to improve bilateral relations and connectivity. India has participated in Uzbekistan's regional initiatives on Central Asia and Afghanistan. External Affairs Minister Dr S Jaishankar participated in the international conference on regional connectivity organised by Uzbekistan in Tashkent in July 2021. The conference—Central Asia and South Asia Regional Connectivity: Challenges and Opportunities dwelt on subjects like economics, culture, security and connectivity. President Shavkat Mirziyoyev, at the conference, proposed an annual inter-regional forum to discuss economic cooperation and investments among the countries of the two regions. Dr Jaishankar underlined that connectivity efforts must be based on economic viability and financial responsibility. He stated that the Chabahar Port provides secure, viable and unhindered access to sea to the Central Asian countries. It would be useful to pursue the shared desire for greater connectivity and collaboration despite the changed scenario in Afghanistan in September 2021 with the Taliban taking control of the country.

The Covid-19 pandemic has also provided opportunities for mutual assistance and support. India provided vaccines and medical supplies to Kazakhstan, Kyrgyzstan, Tajikistan and Uzbekistan and, in the spirit of friendship and cooperation, Kazakhstan provided masks and respirators, and Uzbekistan oxygen concentrators to India as it dealt with its second wave of Covid-19 cases.

It is noteworthy that India and the Central Asian countries continued their physical and virtual engagements despite the Covid-19 pandemic. While political relationships continue to be close and cordial, India needs to work with the resource-rich Central Asian countries to realise the full potential of its mutually beneficial economic engagement. India's bilateral trade of about US$ 2 billion with the Central Asian countries comprises mainly of import of oil and uranium from Kazakhstan, and exports of pharmaceuticals to the region. India needs to explore innovative ways to expand its commercial and economic relationship. This can include investments in sectors, especially the resources sector, that may not be oriented towards export to India but for local consumption and export to third-party countries. The number of campuses of Indian universities and presence of Indian hospitals may be expanded further in the region.

Connectivity should be another area of focus in the coming years. Rather than being overly concerned with the connectivity projects of other countries, we should focus on projects of interest to us. We should work on and promote the INSTC to make it seem more attractive and involve the Central Asian countries in the Chabahar Port. India's membership in the Ashgabat Agreement offers it the opportunity to be involved in the creation and interlinking of transport and transit corridors in Eurasia. Given the intransigence by Pakistan, it makes sense to connect with Central Asia through the maritime route via Iran.

India should also look into connecting with Central Asia and beyond through the Chabahar Port using existing and proposed rail networks through northern Afghanistan and Uzbekistan. With Asian Development Bank (ADB) assistance, Uzbekistan Railways has already built a rail link up to Mazar-i-Sharif in Afghanistan. This can now link up with the proposed Herat–Mazar-i-Sharif rail corridor in Afghanistan, which Iran has expressed readiness to build, and the proposed Tajikistan–Afghanistan–Turkmenistan (TAT) railway. Uzbekistan has good rail and road connectivity with other Central Asian countries and with Russia and Europe. India can consider establishing some presence in the Uzbek border town of Termez, which can be useful for its trade and transit requirements in the future. The developments in Afghanistan pose challenges but we need to have a long-term view on connectivity. We should not put all the eggs in the short-term basket as connectivity projects do take a long time to materialise.

Following the above-mentioned Uzbek proposal at the virtual summit between Prime Minister Narendra Modi and President Shavkat Mirziyoyev, the first Trilateral Working Group Meeting between India, Iran and Uzbekistan on the joint use of Chabahar Port was held virtually on 14 December 2020. The meeting, jointly chaired by the secretary of the Ministry of Ports, Shipping and Waterways of India, the deputy transport minister of Uzbekistan and the deputy transport minister of Iran, discussed joint use of the Chabahar Port for trade, transit and enhanced regional connectivity. During the Covid-19 pandemic, the Chabahar Port has played a significant role in the region with regard to delivering humanitarian assistance.

It may be mentioned here that, in February 2021, Pakistan, Afghanistan and Uzbekistan signed a road map for a rail project from Tashkent to Peshawar through Kabul. The project may potentially be funded by the World Bank and other financial institutions. This ambitious project will reduce substantially both the time and cost for cargo transport between Pakistan and Central Asia, potentially making the Gwadar Port a competitor of the Chabahar Port.

While working on ways of expanding our economic engagement and connectivity, we should not lose sight of our historical and cultural connections. Academic exchanges and institutional linkages in recent years have been growing; more Indian students are going to Central Asia and Central Asian students coming to India. Mutual tourism was also expanding pre-Covid. These indicate opportunities for strengthening our people-to-people contacts.

India has supported observing the year 2021 as SCO Culture Year to mark the twentieth anniversary of SCO. The National Museum of India has developed the first online SCO exhibition on the SCO member countries' shared Buddhist heritage. Indian and Central Asian institutions may focus on the role of Central Asia in the spread of Buddhism. The erroneous narrative of the Silk Route needs to be rectified, and in this context the contribution of the Kushan Kingdom in connecting India's maritime trade to the land routes of Central Asia and the role of the Indian and Sogdian businessmen need to be highlighted. India and Central Asia have enormous mutual goodwill. Their shared interest in partnership and collaboration is a strong indicator that their relationship will expand further post-Covid-19 for the mutual benefit of their peoples.

Endnotes

1. Manohar Parrikar Institute for Defence Studies and Analyses, 'Address by Prime Minister Shri Narendra Modi at Nazarbayev University, Astana, Kazakhstan', 7 July 2015. https://idsa.in/resources/speech/narendra-modi-nazarbayev-university-astana-kazakhstan-july-07-2015

2. Government of India, 'Opening remarks of Prime Minister Shri Atal Bihari Vajpayee at the Press Conference in Almaty', 5 June 2002. https://archivepmo.nic.in/abv/speech-details.php?nodeid=9128
3. Government of India, 'Keynote Address by MOS Shri E. Ahamed at First India–Central Asia Dialogue', 12 June 2012. https://www.mea.gov.in/Speeches-Statements.htm?dtl/19791/
4. Government of India, 'Statement by External Affairs Minister at the First Session of the India–Central Asia Dialogue', 13 January 2019. https://www.mea.gov.in/Speeches-Statements.htm?dtl%2F30905%2FStatement_by_External_Affairs_Minister_at_the_First_Session_of_the_IndiaCentral_Asia_Dialogue
5. Government of India, 'Address by External Affairs Minister on the occasion of the launch of the India–Central Asia Business Council, FICCI', 6 February 2020. https://www.mea.gov.in/Speeches-Statements.htm?dtl/32365

CHAPTER 18

INDIA'S RELATIONS WITH THE GULF REGION

Anil Wadhwa

The Historical Context

India's historical relations with the Gulf region go back to the Indus Valley and the Dilmun civilisations located on the island of Bahrain and the adjacent shore of today's Saudi Arabia. The two civilisations enjoyed flourishing trade, which they monopolised between Mesopotamia and the Indian subcontinent. Traders from present-day Yemen and Oman were dominant, and Yemen was particularly famous for its frankincense and myrrh. The Gulf—in particular Oman—became a natural connection for trade of the Indian Ocean between India, the Middle East and East Africa. By the end of the first millennium CE, trade with India was the economic backbone for the Arabian Peninsula. More than a thousand years ago, most commodities were transported from India, and cash and its equivalent barters flowed back from the Arabian Peninsula to India. The centuries that followed were marked by the rise of the pearl industry, the British colonisation of India and the Trucial States and the discovery of oil in the Gulf. Today, the Gulf Cooperation Council (GCC) states have once again become a formidable bloc of trading partners for India. The British controlled their relationship with the Gulf from the Bombay Presidency—assuming the defence of Oman in 1829, the Trucial States in 1835, Bahrain in 1861, Kuwait in 1899 and Qatar in 1916. And, until the late '60s and early '70s, the Indian rupee was legal tender in Oman, Qatar, Bahrain, Kuwait and the UAE.

Traders from India sailed in dhows, riding the winds, and exchanged foodstuff, silk, raw materials, jewellery and spices for pearls, dates and incense. This trading relationship, according to documented evidence, was over 4,000 years old. Many Indian traders settled in the Gulf and the Arabs settled on the coast of India in places like Malabar. After India gained independence from the British, and the Gulf states discovered oil, both increased their mutual dependence and ties flourished in this extended neighbourhood of India. Ideologically, however, the Gulf monarchies moved closer to the West while non-aligned India was seen as proximate to the communist Soviet Union, creating a mismatch in perceptions of each other. The Arab–Israeli war of 1967 and the Soviet presence in Afghanistan in 1979 saw the Gulf monarchies getting even closer to the United States, the West as well as Pakistan, and Saudi Arabia emerged as a de facto leader in the Gulf due to its size and oil reserves.

In modern times, the Indo-Gulf relationship, which was based on trade, cultural ties and diaspora, which migrated over the years in search of employment to this region, has become multifaceted. The relationship has now expanded to energy security for India and food security for the Gulf, as well as cooperation in defence, cybersecurity, counterterrorism and mutually reinforcing investments, and has lately seen a push in vaccine diplomacy from India. Today, India engages with each of the Gulf states across the board in areas of mutual strengths and complementarities.

The Evolving Relationship

During the latter half of the twentieth century, India was looking at the Gulf from the prism of being a source of employment for its migrant labour and, later, for its white-collar executives in companies which required management expertise at reasonable salaries. This period also saw Indian oil and gas imports from the region grow steadily, on the back of economic and social change in India, especially after it unleashed reforms in the economy in the last decade of the twentieth century. The Gulf 'oil boom' can be traced back to the 1970s, and, in the initial years, many migrants from India clamoured to go to the Gulf especially from Kerala and the southern states. In the process, the Gulf states also benefitted tremendously from their services, hard work and business ethics. Indians, in fact, amount to around one-third of the total workforce in the region. At the same time, militancy and cross-border terrorism launched by

Pakistan continued to grow, and the Gulf states, unaffected during that period by terrorism or radicalism, went along with anti-India resolutions piloted by Pakistan in the Organisation of Islamic Cooperation (OIC) which were barely debated or updated, looking at the issue from the prism of the Muslim ummah.

Commencing from just over one million in the 1980s, the Indian population in the Gulf had surged to 3.5 million in 2005, and is between 6.5 million to 8 million today. Indians work at every level in the GCC—as blue-collar workers, professionals and entrepreneurs as well as successful CEOs of large companies owned by Arab sheikhs. Indian doctors, engineers and chartered accountants are the backbone of Gulf economies. This was also the period of high growth in India's energy imports from the Gulf. Between 1990 and 2013, India became the third highest consumer of energy in the world, and this led to a surge in oil and gas imports—and half of India's needs were met from the Gulf countries by 2012. By 2019, India's energy dependence on imports rose to 84 per cent, out of which half was imported from the Gulf countries. Today, India imports more than 80 per cent of the crude it processes and, in 2019-20, imported 227 million tonnes of crude oil worth over US$ 101 billion.

Consequently, while India's political relationship with the Gulf monarchies during the Cold War, leading up to the dissolution of the Soviet Union, remained lukewarm, the economic relationship was beginning to make its way steadily upwards. By the beginning of the twenty-first century, India's exports to the Gulf countries surpassed those to the European Union. In 2019-20, India's trade with the Gulf was roughly US$ 140 billion, which comprised close to 20 per cent of India's total trade. During April to January in the financial year 2020-21, India's exports to the bloc amounted to US$ 21.74 billion, with the main items being mineral fuels, apparel, gems and jewellery, and electrical machinery. During the same period, India's imports from the GCC were worth US$ 45.7 billion. The economic relations have evolved, but so has the political relationship.

Arab Spring Uprisings

The Gulf monarchies, partners of the GCC, which came into existence in 1981, have their foundations built on a social contract between the ruling families that are supposed to provide security and welfare in terms of education, healthcare and employment in return for loyalty and obedience by the subjects.

This arrangement rode well on the back of steadily rising oil prices even as the monarchies grew more profligate and veered from the ideal governance model in the early part of the twenty-first century. By 2010, the region saw uprisings driven by the desire to replace tyrannical rulers and crony capitalism by accountability, transparency and popular decision-making. The food crisis resulting from rising prices after the world economic crisis of 2008, coupled with rising poverty and use of coercion by the ruling class led to the youth coming together. By 2012, the ruling class in most of the Gulf had bought over those who rebelled by doling out largesse from their oil revenues and had managed to suppress the Shia minority in Bahrain with Saudi military force. The Arab Spring uprising resurfaced in 2018-20 in the larger Middle East region, but it has so far spared the countries of the Gulf.

The Arab Spring uprisings have also given rise to the rivalry and deepened fault lines between the supporters of political Islam lead by Turkey and Qatar and those who want to defend the monarchy at any cost from such influences like Saudi Arabia and the UAE, which are also supported by Egypt. In the larger region, Iran, which was already at loggerheads with Saudi Arabia as part of a Shia–Sunni divide, is seen as a supporter of Qatar, Turkey and the Houthi rebels in Yemen against Saudi Arabia and the UAE who wanted to restore a friendly regime in neighbouring Yemen. This resulted in death and destruction of a high magnitude which is continuing to wreak havoc on the hapless population of Yemen, despite a recent outreach and halt in bombings by Saudi Arabia and the UAE. The two waves of Arab Spring have reshaped individual attitudes, political systems, ideologies, and, consequently, the way in which countries of the region view the world. A 2019-20 Arab opinion poll showed that 70 per cent of the population favoured democracy, and 58 per cent felt positively about the uprisings. It is, therefore, a matter of time before the popular uprisings resurface in some form or the other and the Gulf countries, therefore, have to be prepared and brace themselves for such a situation.

The Regional Security Environment

Of greatest impact in the changing relationship has been the deterioration in the regional security environment, especially during the first decade of this century. The expanding presence of al-Qaeda, strengthening of the Taliban in Afghanistan, unrest in Yemen, sectarian violence in Pakistan and its abetment of cross-border terrorism and hosting of training camps for terrorists on the Indo-Pak line of control have convinced countries like Saudi Arabia that their monarchy and those of the other Gulf states should not continue to have a blind eye to these developments. At the same time, Indian naval and military power has continued to grow, and India's handling of cross-border terrorism emanating from Pakistan as well as its resilience has been seen as a plus by the Gulf monarchies, who have been heavily dependent on expensive US and Western armaments to defend their royals and borders.

A trend of greater engagement with the Gulf has been pursued in full force by Prime Minister Narendra Modi, once his government assumed power, starting in 2014. The next two years and beyond saw extensive engagements with the UAE, Saudi Arabia, Qatar and Bahrain. Since 2015, Prime Minister Modi's engagements in the Gulf have raised the Indian profile in the region, made India more acceptable as a player, and have laid the ground for a greater security role for India in this region which has faced a lot of turmoil. India has reached out to major regional powers and has even successfully managed to maintain friendly relations with those countries that are at odds with each other.

In 2015, the Crown Prince of Abu Dhabi Sheikh Mohamed bin Zayed Al Nahyan, was hosted in Delhi by a large business delegation. The crown prince was also the guest of honour at India's Republic Day celebrations in January 2017. Riding on the back of civilisational links, it was not too cumbersome for India and the Gulf countries to agree on substantial agreements in the economic, security and cultural sphere. There was a common bond of the threat from terror, radicalisation of the region, promotion of dialogue, based on inclusiveness and moderation for which the Gulf states, affected severely by the presence of the Islamic State of Iraq and the Levant (ISIL) in Iraq and Syria, saw in India a role model.

Defence ties have gained by leaps and bounds—and have included agreements on defence dialogues, training, joint exercises, joint maritime operations, supply and joint development of arms and ammunition. The emerging security and regional order were largely responsible for GCC states looking at India with a new prism and moving beyond trade and investment to deepen security and strategic arrangements. India and Saudi Arabia, for instance, first signed a memorandum of understanding (MOU) on defence cooperation in 2014. Then, there were visits by PM Modi to Riyadh in April 2016 and by the Saudi

Crown Prince and Defense Minister Prince Mohammed bin Salman to New Delhi in February 2019. India and Saudi Arabia now have a Joint Committee on Defence Cooperation, and both have agreed to training officers from the Royal Saudi Armed forces at Indian defence training institutes—the first group of Saudi cadets started their training at the National Defence Academy in Pune in 2017.

By 2019, Saudi Arabia and India had moved on to collaborate in joint defence production of spare parts for naval and land systems and develop their supply chains. Maritime security has now been enhanced with the Saudis—the Indian navy and coast guard interact with their Saudi counterparts and Indian naval ships have started calling regularly at Saudi ports. The naval and army chiefs from India have both visited the kingdom.

The army chief, General MM Naravane, also visited the UAE in December 2020 signalling that India sees the UAE as a growing defence market, providing opportunities for collaboration. At the IDEX military exhibition in the UAE in 2017, the Indian Ordnance Factory Board signed an agreement to supply ammunition to the Emirati Army. The UAE had already expressed its interest back in 2018 (during its participation at the Defence Expo in Chennai) in buying the Akash surface to air missile system, the Astra 70 km range air-to-air missile (which can be fitted on the Mirage aircraft) as well as the cruise missile, Brahmos. Caracal International of Abu Dhabi has emerged as the cheapest bidder for supplying close quarter carbines to the Indian Army. The two sides have agreed to explore possibilities for cooperation in the areas of defence manufacturing and space exploration and have strengthened links in maritime security. India and UAE navies conducted their first naval exercise—Gulf Star I—in 2016, the air force exercises were held in 2017, and, in the same year, the air force delegations of the two sides discussed logistics and technology cooperation related to equipment.

The Gandhi Peace Prize for 2020 has been conferred on Sultan Qaboos Al Said, and this will go a long way in further consolidating the relations between India and Oman. The navies of India and Oman have been conducting joint exercises since 2017, and army exercises have been added to this cooperation. Through an annex to the existing MOU on military cooperation, Oman has given India access to the Duqm port for logistical support and turnaround for military vessels—facilitating India's outreach in the Indian Ocean. The Royal

Navy of Oman partners with Indian Navy's anti-piracy mission and Indian naval ships are regularly welcomed by Oman for overseas deployments. India offers training facilities for Omani officers at the Indian National Defence Academy, and all three wings of the armed forces conduct joint exercises with each other. Oman is already buying spare parts for some of its military equipment from the Indian public sector undertakings (PSUs), and has expressed interest in joint production of defence equipment with Indian companies.

The cooperation with Bahrain is mainly focused on internal security areas, and there is regular coordination in cybersecurity, countering terrorism and countering radicalism. Space technology and maritime security cooperation have been discussed. The US Navy's Fifth Fleet, located in Bahrain, is key to the Persian Gulf, which is also important for India's energy security.

On 4 March 2021, the Indian Air Force successfully culminated its participation in Exercise Desert Flag at the air force base in Al Dhafra, UAE. Five other nations—the UAE, US, France, Saudi Arabia and Bahrain—took part in the exercise, with Jordan, Greece, Qatar, Egypt and South Korea participating as observers. The objectives of the exercise were to expose participating forces to deployment in a large formation, improve tactical capabilities and make progress in interoperability, along with fostering friendlier relations and understanding between the participating forces. The UAE and Indian naval forces teamed up with their French counterparts for the first ever trilateral exercise—Varuna—in the Gulf of Oman and the Arabian Gulf from April 25-27, 2021. Both Saudi Arabia and the UAE have expressed interest in acquiring the indigenous Akash air defence missiles systems and Brahmos supersonic cruise missiles.

The UAE's Foreign Minister Sheikh Abdullah Bin Zayed Al Nahyan was in India in January 2021, just two months after External Affairs Minister S Jaishankar's visit to the UAE in November 2020. More than 38,000 Indian companies are registered with the Dubai Chamber of Commerce and Industry and this time the focus was on enhancing bilateral economic cooperation.

To add to this cooperation, there has also been a meeting of minds on intelligence sharing, counterterrorism and adoption of technologies and information exchange among the security agencies. A visible effect of this cooperation is the help rendered by the Gulf monarchies, like Saudi Arabia, the UAE, and Oman, to India in handing over fugitives from law who had carried out bombings in India; information exchange on terror groups and ISIS recruitment operations by Saudi Arabia, Qatar and Bahrain which helped India considerably in stemming the tide of recruitment for radicalisation. On its part, India has helped the Gulf nations through maritime patrols and search and rescue operations carried out by its navy in the Arabian Sea and the seas adjoining the Gulf right up to the African shores, and providing safe passage to commercial shipping by interdicting piracy operations in the region.

The Covid-19 pandemic has served to forge even more closer links between India and the Gulf states. India has extended support to the countries in the region by providing hydroxychloroquine tablets to the UAE, Saudi Arabia, Bahrain, Oman and Qatar; sending a fifteen-member medical team to Kuwait, and another team of eighty-eight medical and healthcare professionals to the UAE to help fight the pandemic; thus, reinforcing its image of a reliable friendly country in an hour of crisis.

The Future

In order to diversify the economic relationship, India and the Gulf countries will need to continue investing in infrastructure development in both India as well as the Gulf region. Saudi Arabia and the UAE have already invested heavily in the petrochemicals segment in India. Indian companies, such as HCL, L&T and TCS are potential investors in large projects in energy, transportation, food processing and information technology in the region.

Qatar is the largest supplier of liquefied natural gas (LNG) to India, accounting for over 50 per cent of India's LNG imports. India also imports ethylene, propylene, ammonia, urea and polyethylene from Qatar. The political instability in the Gulf and the volatility and uncertainty in supplies will mean that India will need to diversify its sources of energy imports. India has recently been critical of Organization of the Petroleum Exporting Countries (OPEC) and Saudi output cuts aimed at increasing oil prices, as well as the differential prices for Asian vis-à-vis the European buyers and has suggested that India will look for energy alternatives to Gulf oil—its main source of crude. The Saudi oil minister's response that India dip into its oil reserves which were filled up by cheap oil imports during the crash in oil prices last year has not gone down well with India. If, and when, the sanctions on Iran are lifted, Indian refineries would like to go back to importing more oil from Iran. Similarly, traditional suppliers like Iraq and the UAE will always be favoured. Venezuela and Libya could become active again, in case they manage political stability. However, the US, Guyana and African countries like Equatorial Guinea and Nigeria have emerged as new sources of energy, and Australian LNG imports could go up with shipments to the east coast of India as new terminals like Ennore come up and the energy distribution networks to the hinterland are developed. Already, the Indian government has asked state-run oil companies to renegotiate term contracts with Gulf-based producers and rope in private refiners to collectively bargain for better deals with OPEC producers. If Indian refineries diversify and cut reliance on Gulf oil, the imports from Saudi Arabia could be cut by a quarter.

The countries of the region are also trying to develop sectors other than oil, whose future is uncertain as other sources of energy gain prominence. Indian companies there are ideally placed to invest in roads, airports, housing and other infrastructure construction; banking; power distribution; and water and solar power projects. India can become a long-term source of food and pharmaceuticals to the Gulf, riding on its success as a vaccine producer and exporter. Conversely, India's recent initiatives in setting up mega industrial manufacturing corridors, including the Delhi–Mumbai Industrial Corridor, and the Digital India and Make in India projects have attracted countries like the UAE to finance ports and shipping and other infrastructure projects which are bound to provide high returns. The recent production-linked incentive (PLI) scheme announced by the Indian government will also gain attention for Gulf states' investments in manufacturing in India. There is a significant hunger for investment in infrastructure in India which the GCC can tap into in collaboration with Indian companies. Investing in India will provide long-term benefits to the GCC states, with its market of 1.3 billion people.

India is reconsidering a free trade agreement (FTA) with the GCC. A framework agreement of economic cooperation between India and the GCC was signed in 2004 that provided for both the parties to consider ways and means to extend and liberalise trade. Two rounds on the FTA were also held in 2006 and 2008. Preliminary analysis suggests that tariff liberalisation in an additional 1,100 products like leather and plastic goods, washing machines, air conditioners, refrigerators, spices, tobacco, cotton fabrics, textiles and iron and steel will push up Indian exports while India will need to give tariff concessions for petroleum and fertiliser products to the GCC. India will gain most from the liberalisation of Mode 4 in services facilitating the movement of professionals and by the liberalisation of long-term visas to the Gulf countries.

According to the World Bank figures, 3.8 per cent of India's gross domestic product (GDP), or US$ 83 billion, is in the form of remittances from its people abroad. Since around one-third of the workforce in the Gulf is from India, their remittances back to their home states are important for a number of families back home. However, post the onset of the Covid-19 pandemic and the economic difficulties facing the Gulf states, it is disconcerting that the number of retuning Indians continues to grow. If it were not for a slow but steady revival in the migration of Indians who had to abandon their jobs abroad or lost work in the last one year, there would be serious problems in terms of remittances to India and its foreign exchange reserves. The return of Indians to their jobs is mostly to the Gulf where recovery is faster than other parts of the world. The northern states of Uttar Pradesh, Bihar, Rajasthan, and Tamil Nadu in the south have now emerged as major source of blue-collar workers to the Gulf, after the decline in migration from Kerala and Andhra Pradesh. The economic slowdown, fluctuating oil prices and hardening of labour policies in the Gulf can be expected, leading on from an indigenisation drive. Indian authorities in the states would do well to skill and train workers migrating to the Gulf countries so that they do not necessarily end up only in low-paying, labour-intensive and dangerous jobs. The Indian consulate in Dubai, for instance, is planning to work with key stakeholders in making sure that the workforce from India in the UAE can be upskilled and retrained for the job requirements in the post-Covid-19 scenario. India and the UAE have also jointly initiated a pilot project for skill certification for the mobility of workers under the Harmonised Framework for Skill Recognition and Certification.

India is increasingly being seen as a 'net security provider' in the region, although Indian authorities themselves use this term rather sparingly. India now has strategic partnerships with Oman, Saudi Arabia and the UAE, and has entered into a military training and cooperation agreement with Qatar. Defence exercises, regular Indian ship visits, training of Gulf armed personnel need to be continued and strengthened. All the GCC countries are members of the Indian Ocean Naval Symposium (IONS) set up in 2008. India needs to strengthen its naval presence in Bahrain and enhance its anti-piracy operations, which it is engaged in since 2008 in the region, especially off the coast of Somalia.

India should continue its policy of non-intervention, and continue to be non-prescriptive in its dealings with the Gulf monarchies, concentrating on issues like money laundering, counterterrorism, human trafficking and coastal defence. The turnaround agreements for ships in Duqm with Oman should be replicated with other countries of the region. Agreements on extradition and transfer of sentenced prisoners should be concluded and refined with all GCC countries. The GCC countries are now increasingly aware of the dangers of radicalisation and terrorism to their countries, and this is a growing area of cooperation. Comprehensive security dialogues between the national security advisers or the national security council secretariats must move forward quickly. There is a potential to enhance cooperation in defence manufacturing and exports. These countries are interested in munitions, small arms, shipbuilding, unmanned platforms and armoured vehicles—all of which can be offered by India. The Gulf countries must be encouraged to invest in the Indian defence industry in cooperation with reputed international defence companies.

As India moves forward with its policies of comprehensive engagement with the GCC countries, it will, no doubt, have an eye on the economic and security inroads by China which has also launched a major diplomatic effort in the region. The diminishing interest and engagement of the US in the region has opened the field for countries like China and Russia to enter the vacant space. China already has abundant energy and economic linkages with the GCC countries. China is eyeing a free trade agreement with the GCC since 2004. It has just signed a comprehensive long-term cooperation agreement with Iran, which envisages US$ 25 billion worth of Chinese investments in energy, transport, ports, power and infrastructure over the next two decades. This comes on the back of a defence cooperation agreement with Iran. It has sought GCC interest through its Belt and Road project in the region. Chinese presence and connectivity projects in Iran could put pressure on Indian plans of developing the Chabahar port for connectivity with Afghanistan and Central Asia. China's priorities in the region are energy, trade and infrastructure development, and the nuclear, space and renewable energy fields in which it seeks to dominate equipment sales and lucrative contracts.

To a lesser extent, Russia is also getting involved much more in the region. It is bound to play a major role in the security order in the Gulf and is eyeing a share of the arms market. Its expanding ties with Iran are part of this strategy.

Russia hopes to export equipment and machinery, transport vehicles, precious metals, and metallurgical and agricultural products to the region along with grain, precious stones and metals and, like in China's case, the growing market for equipment and technology in nuclear and space fields.

The Abraham Accords under the Trump administration have opened up the normalisation process between Israel and the UAE, with far-reaching implications for the region. Bahrain and Morocco were the other countries which joined in this process of thaw with Israel. While this will increase the contradictions within the Arab states on the stance to be taken vis-à-vis Israel, and while Saudi Arabia waits and watches as the process unfolds, the divide between Iran and the UAE, as well as between Iran and Saudi Arabia, has got sharper. These events have coincided with a significant deterioration of Pakistan's relations with the region—especially with the UAE and Saudi Arabia.

A major development in the region is also a declaration of the reconciliatory peace process between Yemen—controlled by the Houthis supported by Iran—and the UAE and Saudi Arabia. If the process can lead to peace in the region, then Saudi Arabia and the UAE will be free to pursue more productive economic engagements. Yet another recent event of significance was the olive branch extended to Qatar by the other GCC states—mainly Saudi Arabia and the UAE—resulting in the GCC states coming together again in January 2021, although deep scars remain, and the divide has resulted in ideological camps which would be difficult to dislodge. India has welcomed this development of reconciliation and rapprochement between the GCC states in the interest of stability in the region. By lifting the air and sea blockades, Saudi Arabia and the UAE will stem the flow of funds from the new axis of Qatar, Turkey and Iran, which had emerged after the 2017 break of relations with Qatar. India will need to navigate carefully through this web of complex relationships. India will do well to focus on fast-tracking existing projects, such as the delayed US$ 44 billion mega refinery in Maharashtra with the partnership of Saudi Arabia's Aramco and UAE's ADNOC, and re-engage in areas of growing importance to the GCC, like healthcare, nuclear and space cooperation and support the GCC states in their aspirations through the Indian Ocean Naval Symposium and the Indian Ocean Rim Association (IORA). The UAE is the current chair of the IORA, where it is focusing on maritime security and safety, facilitation of trade and investment, cultural initiatives and tourist exchange, women's empowerment and increasing momentum for the blue economy. These policies are in close alignment with India's aims of making the Indian Ocean a safe and flourishing corridor of trade and connectivity in close coordination with other Quad countries—the United States, Australia and Japan.

Unlike the past, when national and global security were associated with threats of violence and terrorist attacks, today, food and financial security, as well as healthcare, are all fast-growing security concerns, and India has emerged as a solid partner of the Gulf states in all these fields. Normalisation of intra-Gulf relationships as well as normalisation of relations between some key Gulf states and Israel has thrown up new opportunities. This has been boosted by the opportunities provided to Indian companies by the postponed Dubai expo in October this year, as well as the FIFA World Cup scheduled in Qatar in 2022. Standing up for the sovereignty of the Gulf states and resisting the forces of destabilisation should be the focus of India's attention with the Gulf countries. In this fast-changing scenario, India will have to ensure that its own sea lanes of communication are secure, its transportation and connectivity projects and initiatives are not compromised, and, above all, its energy security and the security of its expatriates and compatriots in the Gulf is maintained.

References

1. Singh, Manjari. 'India–Persian Gulf Relations: From Transactional to Strategic Partnerships', *CLAWS Journal*, Summer 2020.
2. Ahmad, Talmiz. 'The Enduring "Arab Spring": Change and Resistance', *Indian Foreign Affairs Journal*, vol. 15(April-June 2020): 91-107.
3. Onley, James. 'Britain and the Gulf Sheikhdoms, 1820-1971: The Politics of Protection', occasional paper no 4, Center for International and Regional Studies, Georgetown University School of Foreign Service in Qatar, 2009.
4. Ahmad, Talmiz. 'India and West Asia: Promoting security in a turbulent region', In *India's Foreign Policy: Surviving in a Turbulent World*, ed. Arvind Gupta and Anil Wadhwa (Sage, 2020).
5. India Global Business, 'India's deep defense Cooperation in the Gulf', December 2020. https://www.indiaglobalbusiness.com/industry/defence/indias-deep-defence-cooperations-in-the-gulf
6. Sunej, Kritika. *Economic Times*, 11 April 2021.
7. India Global Business
8. Ibid
9. Ibid
10. Ibid

11. Quamar, Muddassir. 'Growing Indo-Gulf Defence Cooperation and Future Prospects', www.raksha.anirveda.com
12. Ibid
13. Siddiqui, Huma. 'India becoming preferred partner for developing defence industries in Gulf countries', *Financial Express*, 11 April 2019.

CHAPTER 19

WEST ASIA: CHANGES AND CHALLENGES

ANIL TRIGUNAYAT

Over a decade ago, the Arab Spring brought West Asia and North Africa into a renewed focus. The systemic challenges faced by a disenfranchised and disgruntled people led to revolutions, revolts and mutiny all at the same time. Some succeeded, most did not; but, they became trailblazers for the Arab world, especially the monarchies and outdated despotic regimes. In countries like Tunisia and Egypt, the protests and the outcome were sui generis leading to the quick removal of autocratic rulers like Ben Ali of Tunisia and Hosni Mubarak of Egypt. In some other countries like Libya, Syria and Yemen, external interventions provided the requisite thrust to the protesters as the revolution became virulent and violent. Libyan dictator Muammar al-Gaddafi had to go in a horrid manner, and most rejoicing Libyans called it a justice well-deserved. Ali Abdullah Saleh was deposed in Yemen. Bashar Assad of Syria got saved by Russian and Iranian support and intervention. But, all these countries are yet to get back to normal and several remain hotspots and theatre of geopolitical competition, defying a peaceful resolution and way forward. People continue to suffer and hope for better times. While Tunisia, after several quick political changes, remains a partial success story, Egypt has virtually taken a 180 degree turn with the army-supported Abdel Fattah al-Sisi remaining in charge after the first democratically elected government of President Mohammed

Morsi—of the Muslim Brotherhood—was removed. The Gulf monarchies launched reforms and paid dividends and doles to assuage their disgruntled citizens. Algeria, Lebanon and Sudan are witnessing somewhat better and less violent outcomes—often termed as Arab Spring 2.0—with long-time leaders having been removed under public pressure. The cinders inflamed by the Arab Spring continue to simmer.

The Arab Spring also witnessed a major interventionist and military dimension of the Gulf Cooperation Council (GCC) countries, especially of the Kingdom of Saudi Arabia, the United Arab Emirates (UAE) and Qatar, along with USA and other Western countries especially in Libya, Syria, Tunisia, Egypt and Yemen. The old rivalries like that of Saudi Arabia–Iran–Israel got further accentuated, especially as the US, under then President Barack Obama, finalised the Joint Comprehensive Plan of Action (JCPOA)—a nuclear deal with Iran easing sanctions in 2015. An irritated Saudi Arabia-led Sunni coalition marched to Yemen where the Houthis have been militarily supported by Iran. Proxy wars elsewhere continued for ensuring geopolitical influence. The JCPOA was short-lived as President Donald Trump not only withdrew from the deal but also imposed severe sanctions on Iran and secondary sanctions on those trying to help Tehran or trade with it. This heightened tension became really bilateral between Washington and Tehran, which nearly led to a full-fledged war as Trump's maximum pressure tactics to bring Iran to the table to negotiate the JCPOA afresh with additional constraints pertaining to its missile capacities and proxied interventions through its 3H—Houthis, Hamas and Hezbollah—as its Islamic Revolutionary Guard Corps (IRGC) Ground Forces and other affiliated groups continued to straddle across Iraq, Lebanon, Yemen and Syria. Tehran refused to budge despite economic difficulties and excessive exposure to the Covid-19 pandemic. It was partially helped by China, Russia and E3 countries—France, Germany and Italy—who were part of the JCPOA. But, the instability and browbeating nearly brought the region to the threshold of a disastrous war many a time which everyone in the vicinity feared.

The departure of President Trump and declaration by President Joe Biden that he would like to return to JCPOA was a welcome move, as he called the withdrawal from the nuclear deal dangerous and disastrous. While the key objective remains the containment of Iran's quest for nuclear weapons, the Biden administration agreed to return to the negotiating table without any pre-conditions and, in early days, adhered to both pressure and persuasion by resorting to diplomacy and military responses where required. However, Iranian leadership remained intransigent by incrementally increasing its enrichments thresholds while keeping the door ajar for negotiations. High-decibel mutual recriminations have been common, as Iran is heading towards a more conservative leadership, especially after the elections in June 2021. Consequently, Ebrahim Raisi, a conservative yet pragmatic leader was elected. He did however support the return to JCPOA without any changes in the goalposts. But expecting that the future US administrations will not go back on it is untenable. Even though the window for negotiations is slowly closing, Iran can ill afford to let the opportunity pass by due to its severe economic, pandemic and unemployment situation leading to public outcry and demonstrations, whereby, it badly needs sanctions to be lifted. Saudi Arabia, the UAE and Israel, while calibrating their policies to avoid confrontation with the Biden administration, are worried and want their point of view represented at the renegotiations. Tehran is obviously insisting on lifting of all sanctions imposed by Trump and not changing the goalposts and redlines. Yet, some US actions, like the removal of Houthis from the list of terrorist organisations, non-insistence on sanctions on Iran in the UN, suspension of sale of F35s to the UAE (which was eventually lifted) and 3,000 missiles to Saudi Arabia and acceptance of European invitation for starting the talks with Iran are the confidence-building measures (CBMs) that Iranian leadership duly acknowledges. But, these would not serve their own interests if they continue with their interventionist policy in the region and threat of further enrichment beyond the nuclear threshold.

The onset of Turkey in the region was a game changer. President Recep Tayyip Erdogan, following his ambitious agenda of neo-Ottomanism and the quest for Islamic leadership, securitised his foreign policy by quick military interventions with the support of the country's equally sanguine parliament. It established a base in Qatar as soon as the Saudi-led blockade of Qatar began in June 2017. Likewise, it sent forces to Libya to counter General Khalifa Haftar's aggression onto Tripoli in 2019-20. Tripoli would have fallen to Haftar's forces but for the Turkish intervention. It continued to be a part of the problem in Syria where it often confronted Russia, the primate power. They were on opposing sides in Libya as well as in Nagorno–Karabakh and the Eastern Mediterranean, but Putin and Erdogan were able to find a modus vivendi as US appeared to be withdrawing from the region. However, the delicate balancing remains precarious as Ankara, being a NATO member, also faces some disgruntled Europeans, including Greece—its historical rival in the Mediterranean. However, Turkey is trying to extract some mileage from the European Union (EU), as it has been sidelined by them for too long. Hence, Erdogan's decision to buy a Russian S-400 missile system and independent foreign policy moves and interventions are also being seen as Turkey's desire to carve its own sphere of influence while acquiring greater negotiating leverage with other powers.

The Arabs have their own problems, not only with Iran but also among themselves. Saudi Arabia, being the largest regional economy and military, wishes to exert its unquestioned leadership role among the Sunni countries as the King remains the custodian of the two holy mosques. They feared the fallout of the Arab Spring, as the monarchs were not ready for the democracy people wanted. Hence, Muslim Brotherhood and Islamists also became the major targets after their comprehensive victory in Egypt. Turkey and Qatar continued to support the Brotherhood leadership and used their powerful media outlet—Al Jazeera—to foment trouble. Hence, in June 2017, Saudi Arabia, the UAE, Bahrain and Egypt broke off diplomatic relations with the tiny but rich state and enforced a blockade. Qatar also has close relations with Iran, sharing its biggest gas field. Tehran came to its immediate assistance despite being under sanctions itself. Fortunately, Trump and his son-law, Jared Kushner, during the last weeks of his presidency, managed to persuade Saudi Arabia and the UAE, Bahrain and Egypt to lift the blockade against Doha, which was officially agreed at the forty-first GCC summit at Al-Ula, the ancient city of Saudi Arabia.

One of the key imperatives for all US administrations, more so of President Trump, had been the security of Israel and ensuring a techno-military edge for it in the region. Hence, President Trump, in his wisdom, launched an imbecile 'Deal of the Century' after burning bridges with the Palestinians that included shifting of the US embassy to Jerusalem—a de facto recognition of the holy city as capital of Israel as well as recognising the continued illegal settlements—and withdrawing of funds to United Nations Relief and Works Agency (UNRWA) along with closing PLO office in Washington. It failed, having been totally one-sided. But, it was good enough to create a wedge in the already donor-fatigued Arab world, and ipso facto made Iran, Turkey and Pakistan as the overt champions of the Palestinian cause. This was further accentuated when Trump facilitated normalisation of implicit ties between the UAE, Bahrain and Israel through 'Abraham Accords' and later with Sudan and Morocco. Others may follow suit.

Saudi Arabia, if left to Crown Prince Mohammed bin Salman (MBS), would have liked to also normalise ties, as its facilitation and already closer security and intelligence ties with Tel Aviv as well as permission for its air space to the Israelis attests to its desire. But, due to the reluctance of King Salman (being the custodian of the two holy mosques) and fear of the Arabian street with no tangible benefit by immediate normalisation and considering it a possible carrot for not so positive Biden presidency, the Saudis have decided to test the waters and wait for an explicit advantage to emerge before a formalised recognition of the diplomatic ties with Tel Aviv. They have begun to discuss with others, like Egypt and Jordan, to work out some rapprochement between President Mahmoud Abbas of Palestine and Israeli PM Benjamin Netanyahu, before an international conference on Palestine is organised under the aegis of President Biden. However, to avert the fifth elections in two years and in the aftermath of fourth Israel–Hamas war, an unusual coalition government led by ultra conservative Naftali Bennett and liberal Yair Lapid, with the support of an Arab Party (Ra'am) has formed a government with a fragile majority. Hence, exit of Netanyahu may tamper some approaches and if the Biden administration does take the lead and the Palestinians, especially Al Fatah and Hamas are able to patch up their differences, one could witness some rapprochement on the Palestine issue. But too many ifs and buts there!

Saudi-led coalition against Houthis in Yemen is losing steam and the Saudis wanted some resolution before Biden kicked in and human rights issues become prominent. Russia has emerged as a major power broker with its reinforced regional position in Syria and Libya and enhanced engagement with major players in the region, including Iran, Saudi Arabia, the UAE and Turkey. China has carried on and reinforced its strategic economic outreach in the whole region and maintained close ties with Saudi Arabia, the UAE, Iran, Oman, Israel and others, most of whom are its Belt and Road Initiative (BRI) partners. Next step is militarisation of its assets in the region. Eyebrows were raised when a Sino-Iranian comprehensive deal of nearly US$ 400 billion was announced for strategic projects.

Domestically, nearly all regional countries are on the edge as Arab Spring 2.0 has been at play, and with reduced hydrocarbon revenues, adversely impacted regional economies due to Covid-19 and expensive adventurism by some combined with popular discontent has the potential for internal disturbances, which might be further exacerbated by the already existing Abrahamic religious competition and discord and the Shia–Sunni divide.

Unless the Biden administration takes a more balanced strategic, non-partisan view (though unlikely), we are witnessing the emergence of a loose alliance of China, Russia, Iran, Pakistan, Turkey and Qatar (CRIPTQ)—an outlier—even if they have a competing dynamic with one or the other in diverse theatres in the region vis-à-vis an emerging Israel-centric Arab grouping supported by the US and Europe. The developments in Afghanistan with the withdrawal of US troops and the resultant security void, CRIPTQ may have found another strategic ally in Taliban-led Kabul.

India's Choices

From our perspective, the Middle East is not only our extended neighbourhood, but is also the most important one which was taken for granted as far as high-level visits and interactions were concerned. After Indira Gandhi's visit in the early 1980s, high-level bilateral visits rarely took place until Dr Manmohan Singh visited Oman, Qatar and Saudi Arabia during 2008-10 which, indeed, changed the focus—converting the relationship into a strategic one from a buyer–seller and Pakistan-centric approach towards the region. Prime Minister Narendra Modi understood the exceptional importance of relations with the Middle East that included Israel, too. Hence, a rounded and balanced relationship was to follow. Modi converted the 'Look West' policy to 'Link and Act West' policy through his first visit to the UAE followed by those to Qatar and Saudi Arabia as well as Iran in the first two years of his period in office—August 2015 to June 2016—and to Israel in 2017 to celebrate the twenty-fifth anniversary of diplomatic relations. He visited Palestine and Oman separately. He also became the most decorated Indian leader by these countries, and the relationship has moved into a real strategic orbit with greater focus on security in all its ramifications—from maritime to defence to cyber to counterterrorism, technology, economy and investments. This was evident in their reaction to the abrogation of Article 370, repatriation and extradition of wanted criminals and terrorists and the Pulwama and Balakot attacks—even if they would prefer a state of peace between India and Pakistan, overtly, most countries in the region wish to partake in the Indian opportunity and want to see India play a greater role in the region.

Trade and investments have witnessed an unprecedented interest and growth, especially from GCC countries. Saudi Crown Prince MBS during his visit to India, declared their intention to invest nearly US$ 100 billion, and he committed to investing US$ 75 billion in Indian infrastructure and capital markets and strategic reserves and refineries. They expect greater Indian participation in their 2030 Vision. For the first time, a memorandum of understanding (MoU) between an Indian consortium—ONGC Videsh Limited (OVL), Bharat PetroResources Limited (BPRL) and Indian Oil Corporation Limited (IOCL)—and Abu Dhabi National Oil Company (ADNOC) was signed, which allowed the acquisition of 10 per cent participating interest amounting to US$ 600 million in Abu Dhabi's offshore Lower Zakum concession for forty years. They also remain our major trading partners. Similarly, Saudi Aramco, in partnership with ADNOC of UAE, had entered in a joint venture with an investment of US$ 44 billion in the Ratnagiri Refinery and Petrochemicals Ltd (RRPCL) project. In fact, the UAE has emerged as the third largest and Saudi Arabia as the fourth biggest trading partners of India. Our collaboration in the multilateral domain remained robust even during the pandemic, especially as India assisted Saudi Arabia during its presidency of the G20. Our Vande Bharat and Vaccine Maitri initiatives were greatly appreciated and valued by the leadership in the region.

The low oil prices and the pandemic have not really prevented the inflow of investments from the region. It was flattering to note that the four-year old Reliance JIO technology platforms recently attracted investments of over US$ 20 billion, of which Mubadala Investment Company (1.85 per cent) with US$ 1.2 billion; Abu Dhabi Investment Authority (ADIA) (1.16 per cent) with US$ 750 million; and Public Investment Fund of Saudi Arabia (2.3 per cent) with US$ 1.5 billion were the prominent partners for the rollout of 5G and related infrastructure.

Region: West Asia-GCC—India's Exports Values in US$ million

S. No.	Country	2018-19	2019-20	% Growth
1.	Bahrain	742.14	559.09	-24.66
2.	Kuwait	1,333.92	1,286.56	-3.55
3.	Oman	2,246.31	2,261.81	0.69
4.	Qatar	1,611.16	1,268.35	-21.28
5.	Saudi Arabia	5,561.72	6,236.86	12.14
6.	UAE	30,126.73	28,853.59	-4.23
	Total	**41,621.97**	**40,466.26**	**-2.78**
India's Total		**330,078.09**	**313,361.04**	**-5.06**
% Share		**12.6097**	**12.9136**	

Imports from GCC

Region: West Asia-GCC

S. No.	Country	2018-19	2019-20	% Growth
1.	Bahrain	539.63	421.50	-21.89
2.	Kuwait	7,430.82	9,573.80	28.84
3.	Oman	2,759.00	3,669.33	33.00
4.	Qatar	10,721.70	9,685.98	-9.66
5.	Saudi Arabia	28,479.21	26,857.37	-5.69
6.	UAE	29,785.33	30,256.65	1.58
	Total	**79,715.68**	**80,464.64**	**0.94**
India's Total		**514,078.41**	**474,709.27**	**-7.66**
% Share		**15.5065**	**16.9503**	

Source: Ministry of Commerce & Industry, www.tradestat.commerce.gov.in

Hence, the foregoing developments in the region would also impact India's strategic interests that have been predicated on cultivating bilateral relationships, which, from all accounts, are possibly at their best. But, in a fast-moving, volatile region, being agile, proactive and on the toes always helps. We also need to mull over our role as partial regional and bilateral security provider and a trustworthy interlocutor in regional affairs where it is warranted, expected and feasible in terms of our own national interests. Perhaps, we could consider the following:

- While the bilateral relations in the context of energy security and diaspora welfare, increasing stakes in India through investments, especially from the Gulf countries, must continue apace with high-level monitoring mechanisms, it would be desirable to develop trilateral arrangements to work together in third countries, especially in Africa in the food security domain. Israeli technologies, Arabian funding and Indian expertise do provide a feasible and mutually beneficial combination.
- Crude oil is likely to be shadowed by gas, and for its economic progress in the medium term India needs to ensure long-term uninterrupted supplies at a reasonable cost. It may be useful to explore a buyers' cartel with China, Japan and South Korea and some others which could provide the requisite negotiating leverage.
- As West Asian countries are key to our maritime security, especially in the context of Indo-Pacific construct, it would be useful to double up our efforts to create structural arrangements, including naval ports and assets in case of need. For the time being, anti-piracy operations, joint exercises and capacity building have provided the requisite landscape. We could examine the possibility of exploring Socotra Port in Yemen with the UAE and establish a strong asset base in Duqm, Oman as well as in Aqaba at Red Sea in Jordan, where they have a desire for increased collaboration with India. Some of these countries have good leeway in East Africa and in the Horn, and a joint demarche could yield qualitative dividends under the Security and Growth for All in the Region (SAGAR) policy or the Indian Ocean Rim Association (IORA) or our own military and naval doctrines.
- Defence arrangements and partnerships should be taken a step forward for joint ventures, research and development and manufacturing and servicing of equipment. Saudi Arabia and the UAE have been keen, and Oman has been an old partner in this domain. Recent first visit of the chief of army staff to Saudi Arabia and the UAE should have cemented the contours of future cooperation in this domain after the minister of external affairs visit and high-level interactions and bonhomie between Prime Minister Modi and the regional leadership. The Sino-Pak axis in these countries will have to be contended through smart venturing and

mutually beneficial planning as both Saudi Arabia and the UAE have huge regional ambitions and targets.

- Iranians are unhappy, as we reduced our oil imports to nearly zero and failed to stand up to Trump's bullying, but the recent contacts and meetings at the level of foreign and defence ministers may have assuaged them. While we cannot turn the wheel but the Chabahar activity could still lead the way. Happily, India has begun to deliver on that front. As such, we need to work out bilateral mechanisms, banking channels and special purpose vehicles (SPVs), which could be made immune from unilateral sanctions by keeping them in a different financial and insular banking orbit.
- Turkey will remain a challenge with China and Pakistan in the region, and we have no option but to compete with them for every inch of influence lest they are able to undercut the Indian goodwill. Currently, the going is good for us and we must flow with the tide.
- Cooperation in counterterrorism, intelligence collaboration and futuristic ventures must be given prominence. Several of the regional countries are moving fast for artificial intelligence (AI), Industrial Revolution 4.0, outer space missions, nuclear and renewable energy, data management and information and communications technology (ICT) and medicine and healthcare, where we have a clear advantage and which must be leveraged by creating viable partnerships on an urgent basis through dedicated and time-bound task forces with relevant actors being represented. Technological alliances will help reap the new opportunities.
- Laudably, India evacuated a large number of Indians from the region under Vande Bharat Mission, but as many of these countries are technologically revving up their industry and enterprise, it would be necessary to retrain our workforce to avail of the goodwill for India.
- With over nine million Indians in the region, any spiralling conflict will pose an unprecedented challenge for the government that has to be ready for any eventuality at all times. While standard contingency plans are in place and may be scrambled at a short notice, it might be useful to assemble a standing group of former ambassadors and

defence attachés as well as intelligence officers who have experience in conflict zones and were instrumental in prior evacuations, etc. They could have a monthly meeting (or as and when required) with the minister of external affairs or the foreign secretary, chairing with other senior officers from line ministries at the latter's convenience so that a dynamic assessment of the situation could be made and prompt action could be formulated.

- Social media could be exploited for the psychological conditioning of Muslim youth averting radicalisation and inducement to rivalries between various Islamic factions. Greater surveillance of Muslim youth travelling to West Asia in close collaboration with the agencies from the target countries could be considered. Likewise, our agencies have to be far more focused on the infusion of Takfiri ideologies propagated by militant groups like ISIS and al-Qaeda. The Singapore model, as well as anti-Takfiri Amman Message advanced by King Abdullah II of Jordan, along with that of our own local schools, like those run by Deobandis, could be studied in greater detail. We also need to keep track of funds coming from the Middle East and being utilised to radicalise the youth. It would be useful to seek the assistance of religious leaders to create a correct narrative and promote peace and harmony in the society apart from aggressive developmental initiatives and job opportunities for the youth.
- We should be part of major regional meets and arrangements and should not shy away from taking risks and initiatives to justify our position, as the competition is becoming severe and space crowded, especially as US security umbrella appears to be closing. Perhaps, it will be useful to start Track 1.5 or Track 2 with the major countries in a regional format with dedicated think tanks or West Asia experts to always have an extensive outreach and live connects with the influential segment of eminent persons across the spectrum—from business to military to politics. Special envoys mechanism may be reintroduced with specific mandates and missions.
- Of late, pursuant to the 'Link and Act West' policy of PM Modi, India's prestige and strategic importance has significantly increased in the

region, especially with the GCC leadership. This was also reflected in their responses to the abrogation of Article 370 and the Pulwama and Balakot strikes as well as in the Organisation for Islamic Cooperation (OIC). For the first time, the Indian Foreign Minister—late Sushma Swaraj—was invited to address the ministerial in Abu Dhabi much against the protests of Pakistan. Thus, a sea change in attitude, largely positive, is witnessed on India's core issues. However, to sustain this is imperative that India, assiduously and smartly, plays the card and fact that it is the second largest Muslim nation in the world. Of course, the Indian government has to remain vigilant and take decisive action against anti-Muslim rhetoric and fake news, often perpetrated from across the border and by some vigilante groups in the country.

- From India's perspective, the Strait of Hormuz and the Gulf supply lines and anti-piracy operations will remain important. West Asia's inclusion in India's canvas of Indo-Pacific gives it a greater leeway to extend its strategic outreach with key players in the region through bilateral and regional alignments before it is too late.
- India should be able to work with regional powers for ensuring maritime security. The issue of freedom of navigation and sea lines of communication (SLOCs) is vital in the Gulf for India's energy security and other interests. Informal coalitions with countries like Russia, Qatar, Turkey, Oman and Iran on one side and the US, Israel, Saudi Arabia and the UAE on the other could provide the exit ramps. Iran must be part of the solution.
- As the situation in Syria, Iraq and Libya is likely to improve in 2021, we must focus on reconstruction projects and position ourselves from now on. In my view, Jordan could play a significant role in outreach to Syria and Iraq and, given its strategic location and web of preferential trading arrangements, a free trade agreement (FTA) would be desirable to access regional and external markets by Indian companies in special economic zones (SEZs), as is being done by some textile groups there.

West Asia remains in the throes of reformed evolution and bitter rivalries, which may have far-reaching consequences for its security, stability and sustainability. As the US, hitherto a major arbiter of regional security, becomes less invested in the region and emerges as a competitor in the oil supply chains, greater heft of China and Russia will evoke enhanced competition for resources and influence. The new power dynamic and shifts among traditional rivals and competitors, combined with superpower geopolitics, could pose some serious policy choices for countries like India. Simply hedging may not remain an option any longer.

CHAPTER 20

INDIA AND AFRICA: SHARED DESTINY

Ruchi Ghanashyam

'Location, location, location' was the slogan coined by Harold Samuel, founder of Land Securities, one of the United Kingdom's largest property companies. The slogan describes the three things that matter in property.[1] Translating that slogan onto the world atlas, Africa's location would certainly come out a winner. With a map of all the continents kept flat, from Australia in the east to the Americas in the west, Africa appears in the middle; Europe to its immediate north, Asia and Americas just across the ocean to its east and west, respectively; and Australia, its south-western neighbour. Even the continent of Antarctica is just a few hours by air.

Penguins and seals can be seen on Africa's southern tip, the continent is the largest home for the Big Five, the must-see iconic megafauna on the wish list of wildlife enthusiasts and tourists—lions, leopards, elephants, African buffalo, and rhinoceroses.[2] Given Africa's rich wildlife, there are other fives in the wildlife circuit; the Little Five and the Shy Five.[3] Africa's wildlife resides in the midst of one of the world's richest and diverse flora and fauna. The African continent is home to a large proportion of the world's natural resources, both renewable and non-renewable; arable land, water, oil, natural gas, minerals, forests and wildlife. It has around 65 per cent of the world's arable land and 10 per cent of internal renewable fresh water sources. Africa is home to about 30 per cent of the world's mineral reserves, 8 per cent of the world's natural gas, 12 per cent of the world's oil reserves, 40 per cent of the overall gold and accounts for

90 per cent of its chromium and platinum. The continent accounts for the largest reservoir of cobalt, diamonds, platinum and uranium.[4]

Africa is home to a large population of young people. By the year 2030, it is expected to host nearly 46 per cent of the world's youth, creating an enormous need for jobs, food security and overall development at a much faster pace than before. Sub-Saharan Africa also has a very high concentration of the world's poor with around 40 per cent of people living under the poverty line[5]. More than 30 per cent of the 830 million people worldwide suffering from insufficient food supply live in Africa. In addition, undernourishment in the continent increased from 234.6 million in 2016 to over 256 million in 2018.[6] Sub-Saharan Africa has a high rate of education exclusion. According to the United Nations Educational, Scientific and Cultural Organization's (UNESCO's) Institute of Statistics, 60 per cent of the population between the ages of 15 and 17 were not in school.[7] With the Covid-19 pandemic, these statistics can be expected to get worse.

Use of Artificial Intelligence

The adoption of artificial intelligence (AI) strategies in the continent can help in achieving quicker and easier access to services like healthcare and education, while bringing higher efficiency in productivity. It has the potential to end unemployment and underdevelopment.[8] Development of AI is lagging in Africa primarily due to low Internet penetration. Barring a few countries, the application of AI has yet to develop strongly across the continent and there is unequal Internet penetration across the continent. The lack of information and communication infrastructure in most countries remains the primary challenge.[9] Africa also lags behind in key aspects of e-trade readiness, including connectivity, payment solutions, trade logistics, Internet security and legal frameworks. Most African countries lack fundamental data, which slows down the ability to formulate evidence-based policies in the area. While the continent has progressed in several areas, it will need to increase its efforts in the penetration of emerging technologies and AI to achieve the UN's sustainable development goals (SDGs) by 2030.

From Nigeria to Kenya, and Rwanda to Ghana, tech innovation is expanding across multiple sectors in Africa, including energy, healthcare and agriculture. The continent has seen tremendous growth in terms of AI for SDGs, in particular with healthcare, agriculture, education and sustainable housing. The number of tech hubs has grown in Africa in recent years. Exploring the role of artificial intelligence and emerging technologies in addressing global challenges, AI Policy Labs, a London-based global public policy think tank, has put together some examples of these innovations and launched an Africa-specific programme exploring AI and technology for development in the continent. Such efforts are being made by other institutions as well.

India can partner Africa in its efforts to fulfil critical infrastructure needs, including in areas like reducing the cost of data and increasing access to fixed line broadband, spurring corporate ventures in tech ecosystems and providing the citizens of Africa with the skills contributing to digital transformation. India's National Strategy for Artificial Intelligence envisages using the Indian ecosystem as an 'AI garage' for emerging and developing countries. India provides a unique opportunity for organisations to develop scalable solutions; a solution for the Indian population could possibly be customised and rolled out to African nations. Given the commonality of challenges, AI-based solutions developed in India for key sectors, such as agriculture, education and mobility, could be adapted for use in Africa.[10] This would be in line with the ten guiding principles that will dictate India's engagement with Africa, outlined by Prime Minister Narendra Modi to the Ugandan parliament in July 2018, where he promised to harness India's experience with the digital revolution to support Africa's development, help improve delivery of public services, extend education and healthcare and spread digital literacy among others.[11]

Combating Climate Change and Its Consequences

Climate change and its implications are a serious cause of concern to both India and Africa. At the third India–Africa Forum Summit in Delhi in 2015, visiting leaders backed PM Modi's call for a 'comprehensive' agreement on climate change at the Paris Climate Conference or the Twenty-first Conference of the Parties (COP21) in Paris.[12] The ten guiding principles that PM Modi highlighted in Uganda included a commitment to address the challenges of climate change through India–Africa partnership and to work together to improve Africa's agriculture.

Approximately 70 per cent of the population in sub-Saharan Africa depends on forests for their livelihood. Unfortunately, a significant share of these resources is used unsustainably. It is estimated that Africa loses US$ 195 billion annually of its natural capital through illicit financial flows, illegal mining, illegal logging, illegal trade in wildlife, unregulated fishing, environmental degradation and loss among others.[13] Harnessing its vast resources sustainably would benefit the continent in the short as well as long term.

Africa hosts one of the world's most precious rainforests, second only to the Amazon rainforest. Around 22 per cent of Africa consists of forest and woodland. According to one estimate, around 3 million square kms of Africa is covered by rainforest. African forests are especially important from a human standpoint because of their timber and water resources, and as reservoirs of outstanding biological diversity. Unfortunately, African rainforests are poorly studied, only a small percentage is protected and deforestation claims them at a rate of 0.3 per cent every year. This rate is lower than the speed of deforestation of other major forests, but greater losses are likely if logging for timber continues without replacement plantation or if palm oil production expands to keep pace with the growing global demand.[14]

Desertification is an area of concern to Africa. Drought, overpopulation, over-farming, deforestation and climate change are amongst the prominent causes of destruction of fertile land, causing desertification. The Sahel region of Africa, the area between the Saharan desert and the Sudanian savanna, is most vulnerable to desertification. One ambitious initiative started in 2007 to reduce desertification in Africa is the Great Green Wall, which, when completed, is likely to be the largest living structure on the planet, spanning more than 4,500 miles across the entire Sahel. It is hoped that planting trees will combat desertification, create jobs, improve food security and bring migrated populations back home. It hopes to restore 100 million hectares of currently degraded land, sequester 250 million tonnes of carbon and create 10 million green jobs by 2030. India's tree and forest cover increased by 0.8 million hectares between 2015 and 2017.[15] At the high-level segment of the fourteenth session of the Conference of the Parties (COP) to the United Nations Convention to Combat Desertification (UNCCD), PM Modi announced that India will raise its ambition of restoring 26 million hectares by 2030 from the hitherto committed 21 million hectares.[16]

Water scarcity (water stress or water crisis) was listed by the World Economic Forum in 2019 as one of the largest global risks in terms of potential impact over the next decade. Climate change, combined with pollution, has added to the excessive demand for water by a growing global population and its needs for agriculture and industrial development. Sub-Saharan Africa has the largest number of water-stressed countries on the planet and about 30 to 40 per cent of Africa's population is estimated to be living in a water-stressed environment.[17] According to findings presented at the 2012 Conference on 'Water Scarcity in Africa: Issues and Challenges', it was estimated that, by 2030, 75 million to 250 million people in Africa will be in intensive areas of high water stress.[18]

India, too, has a serious desertification and water stress challenge. According to a 2016 report by the Indian Space Research Organisation's (ISRO's) Space Applications Centre, desertification is under way across 96.4 million hectares, totalling around 30 per cent of the country's land area[19]. A NITI Aayog report, titled 'Composite Water Management Index', states that, 'India is undergoing the worst water crisis in its history. Already, more than 600 million people are facing acute water shortages.' The crisis is set to get worse and by 2030, the country's demand for water will be twice the available supply, creating a severe water crisis for millions of people. India has shown concern for altering land degradation in the country by developing policies and soil preservation programmes. Over centuries, India developed traditionally community-driven expertise to manage drought[20] and floods, rivers, lakes, wetlands and other water bodies. Africa, too, has traditional knowledge for survival in a land faced with water stress. Given its scientific advancements, India is using remote sensing and space technology applications for land restoration. With assistance via cost-effective satellite technology, India could help other countries by establishing land restoration strategies. The Ministry of Jal Shakti has been set up in India to recognise the value of water in all forms and preserve and strengthen existing water resources of India. A national Jal Jeevan Mission (Mission Water is Life) aims to provide safe and adequate drinking water through individual household tap connections by 2024 to all households in rural India, with focus on recharge and reuse through grey water management, water conservation and rainwater harvesting. Based on a community approach to water, it hopes to make water a priority for everyone.[21]

Given the shared problems faced by India and countries in Africa, and the several initiatives under way on both sides, avenues need to be found for experience sharing in these areas. South-South and trilateral cooperation would be widely and mutually beneficial. An event on 'Economic Recovery: Toward a Green, Resilient, and Inclusive Future', at the World Bank's Spring Meetings in April 2021, underlined that as countries rebuild their economies after Covid-19, it is of significant importance to look at the unique opportunity to build a framework for a green, resilient and inclusive future.[22]

Focus on Agriculture

Africa has 25 per cent of the world's arable land. Yet, it contributes only 10 per cent of the global agricultural output. Around 60 per cent of the world's uncultivated land is also in Africa. There is, thus, an enormous potential for growth of agriculture in Africa. An ambitious study envisages increasing African agricultural output to US$ 880 billion in the next nine years—by 2030. It is not an unreasonable objective, given the vast uncultivated fertile land, availability of many sources of water and plentiful rain in parts of equatorial Africa.

In order to achieve the potential, several challenges need to be overcome, requiring enormous investments in a number of areas. The first would be for Africa to bring potentially cultivable land under cultivation and convert it into a productive asset. The challenge is that even though agriculture comprises almost 23 per cent of the gross domestic product (GDP) of sub-Saharan Africa, over 60 to 70 per cent of the population consists of farmers with small holdings. African agriculture also needs modernisation to realise its potential. Sub-Saharan Africa has a very low usage of fertilisers—17 kg of fertiliser per hectare of arable land as compared to 135 kg across all crops used globally. High fertiliser prices, caused mainly by limited production and high logistics costs, hold back the African farmers' usage of fertiliser. Better and more skilful use of pesticides and farm equipment would also help raise productivity. A McKinsey & Company report, titled 'Winning in Africa's agricultural market', estimates[23] that sub-Saharan Africa will need eight times more fertiliser, six times more improved seed, at least US$ 8 billion of investment in basic storage and additional investments in cold chains for horticulture or animal products. Investment of about US$ 65 billion in irrigation would also be required to fulfil its agricultural promise. Much investment will also be needed to develop basic infrastructure, such as roads, ports and electricity. Indian companies have shown their utility through supply and installation of water pumps and drip irrigation systems in some

African countries. They have familiarity with somewhat similar challenges in parts of India. Given the condition of the average Indian farmer, Indian companies are also better suited to find solutions in tune with African challenges. Joint venture fertiliser projects using the naturally available phosphates and natural gas in African countries can be mutually beneficial.

With around eight billion people on the planet, ensuring global food security is going to remain a priority, especially in a post-Covid-19 world economy. A focus on African agriculture, notwithstanding the challenges, would help pull out vast numbers from poverty in Africa, thus, contributing to the achievement of SDGs there. India can share its experience and expertise to aid Africa's efforts, and Indian companies need to look at the many opportunities that exist in this sector of potential future growth.

India–Africa Links

India is bound with Africa through multiple threads going deep into history. Trade relations during the Harappan civilisation between Egypt and Kathiawar are suggested by two terracotta figurines, one resembling a gorilla and the other a mummy, being found at Lothal.[24] Prior to the Dutch settlement of the Cape Colony in 1852, Indian merchants were actively involved on the eastern coast of South Africa. A proportion of slaves imported into the southern tip of Africa, in and around the Cape, were from parts of southern India. Many of the slaves were kidnapped and had no identity as Indians. They were subsumed into the 'Cape Coloured' and Cape Malay communities. White Afrikaners may also have had some Indian slave ancestry. Former South African President FW de Klerk revealed in his autobiography, *The Last Trek: A New Beginning*, that one of his ancestors was a female slave from India, called Diana of Bengal.[25] There was also reverse traffic from Africa to India. The Siddi community or 'Afro-Indians', believed to be mainly of Bantu origin and living in parts of west and south India, form the African diaspora in India. African-origin people played a significant role in India from seventh century onwards, especially after the Arab Islamic conquest of the subcontinent and in the Delhi Sultanate. Much of the rather large Indian diaspora in east and southern Africa came in the nineteenth century as indentured labour while some came as traders.

The more recent history of the nineteenth and twentieth centuries is one where both India and Africa underwent similar painful experiences of colonialism, racial prejudice and economic exploitation. There is a special place for Africa in the history of India's freedom struggle that was transformed after the return of Mahatma Gandhi from South Africa. Gandhi's method of peaceful resistance, or Satyagraha, was developed during his struggle against racial discrimination in South Africa.

Having experienced similar discrimination, Africa's struggle for liberty was seen in India as a reflection of its own struggle for freedom. India's independence from the mighty British Empire inspired leaders in Africa in their respective struggles, just as India's development under a democratic dispensation and its membership of the G20, is encouraging for Africans today. Close bonds were forged between builders of modern India and African leaders striving to break free from the yoke of colonialism. Diplomatic relations between India and Nigeria, Ghana and Madagascar were established even prior to their independence. India was at the forefront of convening the Asian-African Conference in Bandung in 1955. [26]

Despite being a poor, newly independent nation, India stood with the South African people against the apartheid regime. India imposed a trade embargo on apartheid-era South Africa, followed by a complete diplomatic, commercial, cultural and sports embargo, and worked for imposition of comprehensive international sanctions against South Africa. India placed apartheid on the agenda of the United Nations in the very first session of the United Nations General Assembly (UNGA). The African National Congress maintained a representative office in New Delhi from the 1960s onwards. During the Namibian liberation movement, the first SWAPO (South West Africa People's Organization) embassy was set up in India in 1986, which spurred international support for Namibian independence.

India's support to Africa could be seen in its participation in the United Nations peacekeeping missions in Congo, Somalia, Liberia, Burundi and Sudan, and support to African Union initiatives to bring peace to Somalia and Mali, among others. India has shared its military training facilities by training African military officers in Indian institutions as well as by deputing training teams to other countries. India assisted in setting up defence academies in countries such as Nigeria, Ethiopia and Tanzania. Air Commodore Jaswant Singh of the Indian Air Force, for example, laid the foundation of Ghana's air force as its first chief of air staff from May 1959 to August 1960. [27]

India came forward as a first responder in crisis situations through its Operation Sahayata to assist cyclone-hit Mozambique in 2019 and Operation Vanilla to provide relief to flood victims in Madagascar in 2020, apart from the many efforts of humanitarian assistance and disaster relief missions that India has undertaken in Africa.[28] In the first year of the Covid-19 pandemic, twenty-five African countries received medical aid from India, consisting of supplies of essential drugs, including hydroxychloroquine or HCQ, and sixteen other essential drugs, including life-saving antibiotics, with around 150 tonnes of medical aid worth nearly US$ 10 million delivered to the African countries.[29]

India–Africa trade grew from nearly US$ 52 billion in 2010-11 to under US$ 70 billion in 2019-20, with growth in exports in both directions during this period. Africa's market share in 2020 stood at a healthy 8 per cent of India's overall import basket, while India contributed roughly 9 per cent of Africa's total imports from outside the continent. The Duty Free Tariff Preference (DFTP) scheme announced by India extends duty-free access to 98.2 per cent of India's total tariff lines and is availed by thirty-eight African countries. India offers the third largest market for Africa's commodities and products, while the continent has become a major market for Indian products.[30] With cumulative investments of over US$ 54 billion, Indian investment has created thousands of jobs for local citizens. Indian companies present in Africa vary from energy, mining, telecommunications to IT-enabled services. The key sectors of Indian investments in Africa are agriculture, healthcare and pharmaceuticals, textiles, automobiles, banking and financial services, information technology, energy and infrastructure.[31]

There is also investment from Africa into India. Mauritius is a major contributor of foreign direct investment (FDI) into India, at times accounting for almost 40 per cent of the total FDI inflows to India.[32] Morocco and South Africa are also large investors. Over the years, investments from South Africa brought companies like Tiger Brands, Airports Company South Africa, Bidvest, SAB Miller, FirstRand Bank, Standard Bank, Old Mutual, Anglo-American, Sasol and Nando's to the Indian market. Morocco has invested in the manufacture of phosphate in India, with a large investment by Zuari Maroc Phosphore in the earlier state-run Paradeep Phosphate Ltd.

Over two-thirds of India's lines of credit (LOCs) in the past decade have been offered to African countries—close to 200 development projects in forty-two African countries, valued at close to US$ 12 billion, being implemented under Indian LOC. The schemes include drinking water to irrigation initiatives, solar electrification to power plants, transmission lines, technology parks and railway infrastructure. They extend to power projects and dams in Sudan and Rwanda, water treatment in Tanzania, sugar factories in Ethiopia, and technology parks in Mozambique and Swaziland. The presidential palace in Ghana, the National Assembly building in The Gambia, and the Mahatma Gandhi International Convention Centre in Niger—completed in just fourteen months—hold pride of place amongst the Indian projects in Africa. Grants in aid worth more than US$ 700 million are being used for projects in infrastructure, connectivity, skill development, security, and healthcare sectors.

A fundamental constituent of India's development assistance to Africa has been its capacity development. The Indian Technical and Economic Cooperation (ITEC) programme, launched as far back as 1964, shares India's lessons in development with other developing countries and continues to remain an important pillar of Indian development cooperation programme. Around ninety-eight Indian institutions run training courses in fields such as agriculture, food and fertiliser, engineering and technology, and environment and climate change. Furthermore, the ITEC manages defence training programmes, study exploration journeys, assistance for disaster relief, deputation of Indian experts abroad and project-based cooperation. Africa is a key beneficiary of the programme with nearly 50 per cent of the ITEC slots reserved for countries from the region.[33]

India and France launched the International Solar Alliance (ISA) in 2015 to enhance use of solar energy, reduce dependence on fossil fuels and reduce emissions that cause global warming. Thirty-five African nations are listed amongst the seventy-five countries who have signed and ratified the ISA Framework Agreement, as per the official website. It is estimated that half of the around US$ 94 trillion worth of infrastructure that will be built till 2040 will be made by developing countries. The Coalition for Disaster Resilient Infrastructure, or CDRI, an Indian initiative, seeks to establish a network to popularise good practices and develop appropriate standards to manage infrastructure development and protect precious investments in infrastructure against cyclones, tsunamis and other natural disasters.[34]

FROM HOPELESS CONTINENT TO RISING AFRICA

In May 2000, Africa was described as 'The Hopeless Continent' on the cover page of the respected magazine, *The Economist*. An article described the situation in Africa as a continent ravaged by war, famine and disease: 'Floods in Mozambique; threats of famine in Ethiopia (again); mass murder in Uganda; the implosion of Sierra Leone; and a string of wars across the continent. The advanced golden age has seen an increase in disaster than hope for Africa. Worse, the few candles of hope are flickering weakly.' Africa certainly seemed like a continent with no hope. Eleven years later, in its December 2011 issue, the magazine's cover featured a boy flying a rainbow-coloured kite of the shape of the continent, with the title 'Africa Rising'. One of the articles recalled that Nigerian cement tycoon Aliko Dangote had overtaken Oprah Winfrey as the richest black person in the world, and included Ghana, Ethiopia and Mozambique amongst the fastest growing economies in the world.[35]

Over the first twenty years of the new millennium, the GDP in sub-Saharan Africa tripled. According to a report published by the International Monetary Fund (IMF), sub-Saharan Africa's growth saw an increase from 3 per cent in 2018 to 3.7 per cent in 2020, and saw a GDP expansion of 7.3 per cent in 2019 from 6.6 per cent in 2018.

In 2020, Africa's GDP was US$ 2.6 trillion. The average per capita income, adjusted for inflation and purchasing power, more than doubled, life expectancy in the region increased by more than ten years with a rise in healthy life expectancy at birth by 9.1 years—from 46.1 years to 55.2 years in 1990 to 2017, respectively; infant mortality rates almost halved and literacy rates increased by 8 per cent. Sub-Saharan Africa has seen a double fold increase in its basic literacy skills—among the younger population by 75 per cent and the older population sees an increase by 35 per cent. This increase translates to 136 million more Africans being able to read and write since the year 2000. In recent years, many of the world's fastest growing economies have been in Africa and the combined GDP of the continent is around US$ 2.6 trillion. By 2030, Africa will represent almost a quarter of the world's workforce and consumers. With fifty-four countries, over a billion people, a youthful demographic and an abundance of resources, a rising Africa will possibly represent the hopes of the entire planet.

The continent has also been relatively better off vis-à-vis the Covid-19 pandemic. Despite the emergence of a deadly variant in South Africa with its vicious impact, the situation in most African countries at the end of the first year of the pandemic did not deteriorate as envisaged at the beginning of the pandemic.

Africa is focused on the sage advice given by Ghana's first president, Kwame Nkrumah: 'It is clear that we must find an African solution to our problems, and that this can only be found in African unity.' The African Continental Free Trade Area (AfCFTA), first adopted by the African Union (AU) in March of 2018, is the largest in the world in terms of the number of participating countries since the formation of the World Trade Organization (WTO). The new free trade area will abolish 90 per cent of tariffs on goods traded between member states, and by the end of 2030, a further 7 per cent of tariffs that remain on 'sensitive products' will be removed. A United Nations report has predicted that the AfCFTA could increase intra-African trade by upward of 50 per cent within just a few years. After the final 10 per cent of tariffs are removed, that number will likely double, possibly adding billions to the continent's economy. The AfCFTA predicts a rapid increase in its manufacturing results by US$ 1 trillion, generating 14 million jobs by 2025.[36]

India and Africa Must Join Hands

India has remained committed to Africa in its foreign policy since independence. Successive governments have found ways to enhance the mutually strengthening partnership between India and Africa. India–Africa Forum Summit, last held in October 2015 in New Delhi had participation by the fifty-four countries of Africa, with forty countries represented at heads of state/government/vice president level. The summit continued the tradition of friendship, mutual understanding, and cooperation between India and Africa. At the 2015 summit, India announced a doubling of the number of scholarships to 50,000 over five years, including by adding new schemes exclusively for African students and scholars. Thousands of African students study in India at any point of time, and along with the thirteen current or former presidents, vice presidents and prime ministers in Africa who have studied or trained at institutions in India, form a strong bridge between India and Africa. India's development partnership will continue to be guided by Africa's priorities, relying on African talent and skills, building local capacity and creating local opportunities.

The Covid-19 pandemic has once again highlighted the need for focusing on sustainable development. Combating climate change, addressing water scarcity and achieving sustainable agricultural growth would benefit not just Africa but also the planet itself. Both Africa and India need to embrace new ways of the future and develop skills to deal with artificial intelligence in an increasingly digital world. By working together, India and Africa can hope to fulfil their shared destiny.

ENDNOTES

1. Costa, Al. 'Location, Location, Location!', *StartUps Magazine*. https://startupsmagazine.co.uk/article-location-location-location
2. Langley, Liz. 'What are Africa's Big Five? Meet the continent's most iconic wildlife', *National Geographic*, July 2019. https://www.nationalgeographic.com/animals/article/africa-big-five-safaris-lions
3. Bowen, J. Big 5, 'Little 5, Ugly 5, Shy 5, and Impossible 5.' *Travel Africa Magazine*, July 2020. https://travelafricamag.com/bigfive/
4. United Nations Environment Programme, 'Our work in Africa'. https://www.unep.org/regions/africa/our-work-africa
5. Schoch. Marta and Lakner, Christoph. 'The number of poor people continues to rise in Sub-Saharan Africa, despite a slow decline in the poverty rate', World Bank, December 2020. https://blogs.worldbank.org/opendata/number-poor-people-continues-rise-sub-saharan-africa-despite-slow-decline-poverty-rate
6. Begashaw, Belay. 'Strategies to Deliver on the Sustainable Development Goals in Africa', Brookings Institute, January 2020. https://www.brookings.edu/research/strategies-to-deliver-on-the-sustainable-development-goals-in-africa/4
7. United Nations Educational, Scientific and Cultural Organization, 'Education in Africa, Sustainable Development Goals, 2021'. http://uis.unesco.org/en/topic/education-africa
8. University of Pretoria, 'Artificial Intelligence for Africa: An Opportunity for Growth, Development and Democratisation, Access Partnership'. https://www.up.ac.za/media/shared/7/ZP_Files/ai-for-africa.zp165664.pdf
9. Travaly. Youssef and Muvunyi, Kevin. 'The Future is Intelligent: Harnessing the Potential of Artificial Intelligence in Africa', Brookings Institute, January 2020. https://www.brookings.edu/blog/africa-in-focus/2020/01/13/the-future-is-intelligent-harnessing-the-potential-of artificial-intelligence-in-africa/
10. NITI Aayog, 'National Strategy for Artificial Intelligence #AIFORALL, Discussion Paper, June 2018. https://niti.gov.in/writereaddata/files/document_publication/NationalStrategy-for-AI-Discussion-Paper.pdf
11. Mishra, A. 'The Ten Guiding Principles for India–Africa Engagement: Finding Coherence in India's Africa Policy,' Observer Research Foundation, July 2019. https://www.orfonline.org/research/the-ten-guiding-principles-for-india-africa-engagement-finding-coherence-in-indias-africa-policy/
12. India–Africa Forum Summit, Reinvigorated Partnership - Shared Vision. Delhi Declaration, 26-29 October 2015. http://www.mea.gov.in/Uploads/PublicationDocs/25980_declaration.pdf

13. United Nations Environment Programme, 'Our work in Africa, 2021'. https://www.unep.org/regions/africa/our-work-africa
14. Swanborough, J. 'Africa's Tropical Rainforests are the Lungs of the Earth, And We're Killing Them.' World Economic Forum, November 2016. https://www.weforum.org/agenda/2016/11/deforestation-africa-palm-oil/
15. Nunez, Christina. 'Desertification, Explained', *National Geographic*, May 2019. https://www.nationalgeographic.com/environment/article/desertification
16. 'UNCCD COP14 Highlights: India will put an end to single-use plastic in the coming years, says PM Modi', *The Indian Express*, September 2019. https://indianexpress.com/article/india/unnccd-cop-14-live-updates-pm-narendra-modi-5978501
17. 'Water Scarcity in Africa: Issues and Challenges', Green Tumble, September 2015. https://greentumble.com/water-scarcity-in-africa-issues-and-challenges/
18. 'Water scarcity'. United Nations Department of Economic and Social Affairs, International Decade for Action 'Water for Life' 2005-2015. https://www.un.org/waterforlifedecade/scarcity.shtml
19. Kumar, Chethan. 'Over 29 per cent of India's land degrading', *The Times of India*, 5 July 2016. https://timesofindia.indiatimes.com/home/environment/Over-29-per-cent-of-Indias-land-degrading/articleshow/ 53068475.cms
20. NITI Aayog, 'Composite Water Management Index', August 2019. http://social.niti.gov.in/uploads/sample/water_index_report2.pdf
21. Jal Jeevan Mission, Department of Drinking Water and Sanitation, Ministry of Jal Shakti. https://jaljeevanmission.gov.in
22. World Bank, 'Economic Recovery: Toward a Green, Resilient and Inclusive Future', April 2021. https://live.worldbank.org/economic-recovery-green-resilient-inclusive-future
23. Goedde, Lutz; Ooko-Ombaka, Amandla and Pais, Gillian. 'Winning in Africa's agricultural market', McKinsey & Company, February 2019. https://www.mckinsey.com/industries/agriculture/our-insights/winning-in-africas-agricultural-market
24. Leshnik, Lawrence S. 'The Harappan "Port" at Lothal: Another View', *American Anthropologist*, vol. 70, no. 5, 1968, pp. 911–22, *JSTOR*. www.jstor.org/stable/669756 Accessed 1 June 2021
25. Bystrom, Kerry. 'A "New" South African Family Romance', In: *Democracy at Home in South Africa. Gender and Cultural Studies in Africa and the Diaspora*, 2016 (Palgrave Macmillan, New York). https://doi.org/10.1057/9781137556929_2
26. Venkatachalam, Meera and Modi, Renu. 'A look at how India's Africa strategy is working', The Conversation, March 2019. https://theconversation.com/a-look-at-how-indias-africa-strategy-is-working-113658
27. Beri, Ruchita. 'India: Providing for Peace in Africa', Ministry of External Affairs, Government of India, 25 October 2015. https://www.mea.gov.in/in-focus-article.htm?25966/India+Providing+for+Peace+in+Africa
28. 'Humanitarian Assistance and Disaster Relief to Mozambique-Operation Sahayta,' Press Release. Ministry of External Affairs, 23 March 2019. https://www.mea.gov.in/press-releases.htm?dtl/31174/Humanitarian_Assistance_and_Disaster_Relief_to_MozambiqueOperation_Sahayata_2019
29. Chaudhary, Dipanjan Roy. 'India to despatch key medicines to 25 African states on goodwill mission', *The Economic Times*, April 2020. https://economictimes.indiatimes.com/news/politics-and-nation/india-to-despatch-key-medicines-to-25-african-states-on-goodwill-mission/articleshow/75422868.cms?from=mdr

30. Siddiqui, Huma. 'India–Africa trade touches US$ 62.66 billion for 2017-18, increases 22%', *Financial Express*, January 2019. https://www.financialexpress.com/economy/india-africa-trade-touches-62-66-billion-for-2017-18-increases-22/ 1444750/
31. Khurshid, Ehtesham. 'Make in India: The Case for Africa', Invest India, June 2019. https://www.investindia.gov.in/team-india-blogs/make-india-case-africa
32. 'US replaces Mauritius to become 2nd biggest FDI source for India during April-September 2020', *Financial Express*, November 2020. https://www.financialexpress.com/economy/us-replaces-mauritius-to-become-2nd-biggest-fdi-source-for-india-during-april-september-2020/2139218/
33. Indian Technical and Economic Cooperation Programme, Ministry of External Affairs. https://itecgoi.in/about
34. Prime Minister announces Coalition for Disaster Resilient Infrastructure at UN Climate Action Summit 2019, Press Release. Ministry of Home Affairs, September 2019. https://pib.gov.in/PressReleaseIframePage.aspx?PRID=1586051
35. Adewunmi, Femi. 'How The Economist Changed its Tune on Africa' How We Made it in Africa, December 2011. https://www.howwemadeitinafrica.com/how-the-economist-changed-its-tune-on-africa/14001/
36. 'African Continental Free Trade Area Completes First Month of Trading' Policy Brief, International Institute of Sustainable Development, February 2021. https://sdg.iisd.org/commentary/policy-briefs/african-continental-free-trade-area-completes-first-month-of-trading/

CHAPTER 21

POTENTIAL UNREALISED: THE SAGA OF INDIA–EU TIES

Manjeev Singh Puri

It was a beautiful morning in New York in August 2013 when I received a call to say that my name had been cleared to be the next ambassador of India in Brussels. This was incredibly special as I would be following in the footsteps of my father who had been the ambassador there when I joined the Indian Foreign Service (IFS) in 1982. And, in the annals of the IFS, one of the rare instances of both father and son serving as ambassadors in the same mission. A very proud moment for us as a family.

When my wife and I got to Brussels in January 2014, one noted that there was hardly any change in the chancery—indeed, I have photographs at the same desk in the ambassador's office with basically the same arrangement as my father. There were also a couple of local officials from his time. I am sure they were confused on how to place me! And, at Bharat Bhavan, the ambassador's residence, one moved to the master bedroom from the beautiful guest room with a view overlooking the garden and long driveway that I had occupied while visiting my father prior to joining the IFS.

The European Union (EU) is a union of twenty-seven countries (following Brexit) and forms a massive common market with a combined gross domestic product (GDP) nearly that of the US and full mobility for people within the union covering most of Europe. Apart from a customs union, many of the countries use a common currency—the Euro—with a European Central Bank, and have a common visa—*Schengen*—regime for non-EU citizens. In recent years, the EU project has been under severe challenge with nationalist impulses coming in several of its countries as benefits of globalisation appear to peter out for many; but, other than the UK's leaving, such fissiparous tendencies are not to the fore.

The EU is unique with several facets of a 'state', even though sovereignty rests with the member states, who are also responsible for national security. It operates through a system of supranational institutions and intergovernmental negotiated decisions of its member states. It also has its diplomatic peculiarities. Heads of missions present—or used to, at least in my time—separate credentials to the presidents of the European Council and the European Commission. And summits with the EU are not one-on-one, but have a double-headed representation.

India and the EU

On the surface, India and the EU share an array of similarities, including continental-scale economies and a bewildering cultural, linguistic and religious diversity framed in democratic structures. They are also two critical pillars in maintaining a multipolar world that is of strategic interest to both.

However, they couldn't be more different. The vastly different levels of economic development, Europe's history of colonisation—and now purveying itself as the paragon of individual rights—and enlightened governance underscore these dissimilarities. Vis-à-vis India, Europe needs to reconcile to its relative global decline and a growing India. There is also a lack of geographic proximity and geopolitical distancing with preoccupation of both sides with their neighbourhood and reaching out to the most important global players.

The EU remains among India's largest economic partners, both in terms of trade and investment and home to a large Indian diaspora. It is also the go-to place for the development of Indian industry standards. However, India has largely reset its relationship with the United States and, with growing economic and political relations, including the groundbreaking civil nuclear deal and defence cooperation, the US looms even larger on the external political canvas of India. There is also China with a huge growth in India–China trade and even investment. There has also been huge diversification of India's trade towards the Association of Southeast Asian Nations (ASEAN) and the Gulf. China is also now critical for the EU, becoming one of its top trading and investment partners. India, on the other hand, has only remained among the EU's top ten trading partners and even lagged behind countries such as Brazil in attracting European foreign direct investment (FDI).

Both sides recognise the benefits of closer cooperation and collaboration and are in a strategic partnership since 2004, but have been unable to realise the high potential of their ties. Some of the reasons are systemic, with both sides underinvested or otherwise preoccupied. Perhaps, a couple of anecdotal stories may help understand the dilemma.

Before proceeding to Brussels, I called on then President Pranab Mukherjee and Prime Minister Dr Manmohan Singh. It struck me that even though economics and trade really underpinned the India–EU ties and were the bedrock of the EU, politics and EU incorrigibility was what was underlined to me.

On the EU side, José Manuel Barroso, the then president of the European Commission, told me that he did not understand India even though he had co-led the EU in seven summits with India. His first summit with India was in September 2005 and it followed an EU–China summit in Beijing. UK PM Tony Blair (at that time there was no permanent president of the European Council and this role was performed by the leader of an EU member state in rotation) and he were representing the EU. Apparently, the Chinese ensured that in all manners, the two EU representatives were treated as equals, but in India, in Barroso's perception, Blair was the only toast of the town. Barroso was not angry, but confused.

Strategic Partnership

The first India–EU Summit was held in Lisbon in 2000 with then Prime Minister Atal Bihari Vajpayee, and it was agreed that India would be one of the ten strategic partners of the EU. The India–EU Strategic Partnership was launched at the fifth summit held in The Hague in 2004 where Prime Minister Manmohan Singh led the Indian delegation for the first time.

In the years that followed, India–EU ties grew with increase in volume of trade and investment in absolute terms and the establishment of a myriad of intergovernmental discussion mechanisms, covering most facets of international cooperation. These included dialogues at foreign minister level, secretary-level discussions and a host of dialogues, including in areas such as human rights, migration and visa and consular matters. The discussions on human rights invariably show up the EU as intrusive, apart from pushing name and shame action in the developing world.

Joint working groups were also set up in subjects as diverse as agriculture, telecommunications and information technology, pharmaceuticals and biotechnology, food processing, environment and customs cooperation. Most of the focus in these groups was technical. Climate change, clean energy, energy efficiency and renewable energy—in particular solar energy—were furthermore subjects of major discussions, though, in general, while small bilateral programmes were invariably agreed, major divergences remained on issues of intellectual property rights (IPR) and mitigation in greenhouse gases (GHGs) emissions.

A major development was a decision by both sides to enter into a Bilateral Trade and Investment Agreement (BTIA). This was taken in 2006 but has still to see the light of the day.

Forward movement on the strategic partnership required both political and security cooperation and deepening the trade and investment ties. Neither of these saw significant progress in the coming years and the annual summits were given a go-by. The eighth—and last—summit under the United Progressive Alliance (UPA) government was held in 2012. No summits were held thereafter for four years. Indeed, even though 2014 marked the tenth anniversary of the India–EU Strategic Partnership Agreement, neither India nor the EU took any initiative to commemorate this milestone.

At that time, matters were also compounded by a bilateral India and Italy matter involving two Italian marines. The marines were on board an Italian oil tanker at the height of the piracy menace off the coast of Somalia and killed two Indian fishermen while their vessel was off the coast of Kerala. Their detention in India led to a major diplomatic stand-off with the European Parliament also weighing in.

The National Democratic Alliance (NDA) government took over in India in 2014 and Narendra Modi became the prime minister of India. European countries were among the first visited by him and all efforts were made to convene the India–EU Summit. This was proposed for 2015, but did not materialise as Federica Mogherini, an Italian and the then high representative of the EU for foreign affairs, was not willing to countenance the custody of Italian marines in India.

The summit was finally held in March 2016 and saw an agreement for the European Investment Bank (EIB) to invest in the Lucknow Metro project. This was a game-changer, marking the entry of one of the world's largest multilateral financing institutions in India's quest for infrastructure development. Personally, for me, this was, indeed, a proud moment.

The Covid-19 pandemic did not prevent India and the EU in continuing with their summits and the fifteenth summit was held virtually in May 2020. It identified several new areas for cooperation, including maritime security, and the two sides agreed to strongly push the BTIA with ministerial-level interlocution.

Security Cooperation

Critical for India is cooperation to combat terrorism. This remains peripheral to the agenda of the EU, which had even fallen short in its condemnation of the 26 November 2008 terrorist attacks in Mumbai, where European lives were also lost. The EU is, furthermore, limited because instrumentalities of hard counterterrorism and cooperation, including intelligence sharing, are with EU member states. Moreover, India's proposals for agreements with the Europol (the EU's coordinating police organisation) to cover counterterrorism and on mutual legal assistance have not seen the light of the day even after being pursued for years.

The above having been noted, India and the EU have witnessed some security cooperation: One area, ironically (given the Italian marines case), is related to anti-piracy operations off the coast of Somalia. Both the Indian Navy and a special task force of EU Naval Force—the Atalanta Task Force—were in operation in the Arabian Sea and cooperated with each other. Similarly, the EU cooperated with India in dealing with the Maoist insurgency in Nepal and its aftermath.

Again, a simple reason is that national security issues are not in the ambit of the EU, but are national concerns of the EU member states or subordinated to the North Atlantic Treaty Organization (NATO). And this scenario has remained no matter certain signs of European security activism in the EU, with the presence of a high representative for foreign affairs and security policy in its highest management structure. Moreover, till quite recently, in the context of the in-your-face rise of China, India's most important security concerns didn't directly impinge the EU and even those with China were overshadowed by the huge economic gains that were coming the way of the EU and its member states.

The EU has also not been unkind to Pakistan, extending its special Generalised Scheme of Preferences Plus (GSP+) to Pakistan at the end of 2013—giving a special boost to the Pakistani economy, no matter its sketchy human rights record and abetment to terrorism.

Parliamentary Exchanges

Parliamentary exchanges were envisaged to invigorate bilateral ties between India and the EU. To this end, the European Parliament established a separate delegation for relations with India as early as 2007 and members of the European Parliament (MEPs) in this group have always been active and generally supportive of India. However, the European Parliament is a very large institution, and with no Euro party ever having had a clear majority, dealmaking—both inter-party and intra-party—has always been the case, providing opportunities, especially on foreign affairs, even to individual MEPs with agendas.

The single biggest contributor to keeping things in India on an edge as far as the EU is concerned has been Kashmir—also literally the main objective of the perambulations of a few MEPs, in earlier years from the UK—a couple were of Pakistani origin, but others came from areas with a predominant presence of people of Pakistani origin. Human rights issues, including caste and women's issues, also brought India on and off into focus in the European Parliament, particularly in its Foreign Affairs Committee. In this context, Covid-19 forestalled the adoption of another resolution in the European Parliament critical of India on its handling of Kashmir issues and the Citizenship Amendment Act (CAA).

Trade, Investment and Economics

India–EU trade has grown impressively over the years, from €4.4 billion in 1980 to €100 billion in goods and services in 2020, making it one of India's principal trading partners and export destination. The EU is also one of India's largest sources of foreign investment and technology transfer, accounting for around 20 per cent of inflows into India.

A fundamental component of the strategic partnership is to build and develop closer trade and economic relations. Indeed, with trade and the common market being the core competence of the EU, this had to be the area where an invigorated partnership would really add new meat to the traditional ties between India and Europe.

A trade and investment agreement would benefit the EU with better access to a huge and rapidly growing market and, for India, particularly assist with technology and innovation access that could qualitatively upgrade the Indian economy. An investment agreement could also propel investments from the EU to India, especially with the abrogation of the Bilateral Investment Protection Agreement system by India in 2017 and bilateral investment treaties with individual countries not having taken off.

Global Issues

The new millennium saw recognition of India's transit from being a developing country to a large economic power that had already declared itself in possession of nuclear weapons. France invited India to the outreach of the G8 Summit hosted by it in 2003. In a formal sense, this signalled India's arrival on the global scene and Europe's acceptance of the same, perhaps, also symbolised by the invitation to Prime Minister Modi to participate in the G7 Summit in the UK in June 2021.

As an emerging power, reform of the structures of global governance are of overarching importance for India, but the EU has found itself unable to take a clear view. One of the reasons is that bodies such as the UN Security Council (UNSC) and the Bretton Woods Institutions are favourably disposed towards Europe, and a restructuring would necessarily rebalance influence even if the emerging powers only want to be co-opted into the West-led system and take a realistic, rather than idealistic, approach. Moreover, the UK and France are permanent members of the UNSC and, while Germany is an obvious contender, Italy and Spain do not countenance this.

Climate change is the defining issue of our times. The EU has been the standard bearer for strong GHGs mitigation action by all countries, paying only lip service to the principle of common, but differentiated, responsibility. India, as a major and growing economy, was very much a target of their efforts despite its per-capita emissions being among the lowest in the world. Perhaps, the high point of European pressure was at the Conference of the Parties of the UN Framework Convention on Climate Change (UNFCCC) held in Copenhagen in December 2009 where then Prime Minister Dr Manmohan Singh had to personally intervene and make clear to then US President Barack Obama—who then conveyed the same to European leaders—that GHG reduction targets were out of the question for India given its development imperatives.

India's strong stakeholding at the UNFCCC—held in Paris in December 2015—that led to the Paris Accord and its massive drive to push renewables, should lead to greater accommodation for India's development imperatives by the EU in the coming years. But, competitive global economics are unlikely to diminish their push to bring India into a tighter GHG limitation, if not reduction, hoop in the coming decades itself.

On the international peace and security front, the revolutions unleashed in North Africa by the Arab Spring in 2009-10 saw the UNSC, under strong European pressure, adopt resolutions that allowed military intervention and brought about regime change in Libya. The Libya resolutions were not vetoed by Russia and China, but five countries, including India, abstained. While Germany was one of the countries that abstained, the EU and European countries kept up the pressure on India to be willing to do more for international peace and security—code words for allowing intervention. In later months, several attempts were similarly made in Syria and the doctrine of non-interference in internal affairs was severely challenged. The Syria resolutions, however, did not find favour with Russia and China, and the security mess in North Africa and West Asia continues to remain. It also helped foster ultra-dangerous terrorism in the form of Islamic State of Iraq and the Levant (ISIL) and European nations found themselves engulfed in waves of refugees from North Africa and Syria.

Underperformance

The ambitious India–EU strategic partnership has been long on shared fundamentals and abstract political objectives, but short on specifics and deliverables and devoid of timelines. Under this burden of faith, both the EU and India have found it difficult to commit to a clear-cut common agenda with specific goals. And there are fundamental deficits on both sides that impede their explicit or implicit global power ambitions as well as their abilities to effectively work together.

In the case of the EU, the deficit is first and foremost a matter of capabilities. Brussels spelled out its vision for a strong EU role in global governance, yet it continues to lack the competencies necessary to fully exert itself on most political and security matters. For India, foreign policy is an integral part of its agenda with the EU while the EU's focus is invariably on trade, economy, global issues and development partnership.

Another issue is India's internalising the place of common institutions and its member states within the EU construct. A case in point used to be the UK, with which India's ties are deep-rooted in every sense of the term, including the presence of a large diaspora. Similarly, with France, there are substantial economic ties, including defence purchases, and across-the-board investments in India from Germany, making them significant players in the Indian domestic scene itself. The case with other European countries, including from the erstwhile Eastern bloc, is no less.

The EU construct, moreover, is such that most matters of interest to Europeans in India are really in the domain of member states and are pushed by them individually. On the other hand, matters of interest to India in Europe invariably fall in the competence of the EU and require action both in European capitals and Brussels. Indian understanding of the relevant influence of the EU and its member states in these matters often exaggerates the role of the member states, especially the bigger ones, but they rarely deliver—or really can't, as even smaller states can block forward movement given the constant need for inter-country compromise within the EU. The salience of Brussels in moving things in the EU needs to be far better understood and appreciated. Moreover, as far as India is concerned, export-oriented and overseas action has a relatively small economic footprint, and the main preoccupations of line ministries are for overseas action in India, which are met by the EU member states.

There is also substantial presence of all these countries in India also in terms of their diplomatic representation. This often shaded the EU presence, and the actions by the EU representation were either trade-centred or symbolic, such as leading a group of European envoys to make a démarche. At the same time, India, too, had a large diplomatic presence in the capitals of these countries. The net result of all of this was an overbearing importance of India's bilateral links with major European countries. The EU was invariably 'incorrigible' and Blair had to be the toast of the town.

The Potential Must be Realised

India and the EU will meet at the summit in Portugal in 2021. This would be a special summit where leaders from EU countries would also participate—a clear signal of recognition in the EU to India's growing importance and strategic relevance. Though a golden opportunity for Prime Minister Modi for reaching out to the Europeans across the board, it is also time for concrete action and realisation of the India–EU potential. Both sides must, of course, play to the strength of the other. For the EU, this certainly needs to be India's economy and international place, including for a multipolar world that is critical also for Europe. India needs to focus its attention on the EU's competencies in investment, trade and the economy, and leverage these without letting politics over-dominate the discourse. A few more microns of skin would also not hurt in dealing with EU's incorrigibility of preachiness.

Postscript

The recent months have seen a somewhat buoyed EU because of an improvement in its most important traditional trans-Atlantic ties with the US following the election of President Biden. Furthermore, it is now exhibiting a greater realisation about Chinese aggressiveness, including from its Belt and Road Initiative activities in Europe. This has, of course, been buttressed by the negative perceptions about China among the European people from Covid-19. Accordingly, the EU has also announced a policy on Indo-Pacific, emphasising a 'a free, open, inclusive and rules-based Indo-Pacific space'. This is a matter of significant interest to India.

Bilateral India–EU ties also appear to be experiencing a bump following a virtual summit of PM Modi with all the twenty-seven leaders of EU countries held in May 2021. This was only the second time that the EU had offered such an all-encompassing format to a foreign leader—the earlier occasion being with President Biden in March 2021. The Chinese had been keen on such an all-Leaders' Meeting with the EU in September 2020 but, ironically, Covid-19 prevented it from taking place!

The Leaders' Meeting agreed to restart negotiations on trade and investment, which have been stalled for years, and have them overseen by a high-level interaction at ministerial level. The joint statement mentions separate trade and investment agreements, a useful approach given that bilateral investment protection agreements were terminated by India in 2017 and there has not been much success in signing new bilateral investment treaties. The key of restarting the trade and investment agreement needs to be turned decisively and economics harnessed to realise the potential of India–EU ties.

CHAPTER 22

INDIA–UK RELATIONS POST BREXIT

YK Sinha

Almost six months after the momentous Brexit referendum, UK Prime Minister Theresa May laid out the contours of what she hoped would be a post-Brexit 'Global Britain' at a speech at Lancaster House on 17 January 2017[1]. Listening to the speech, one wondered whether such an ambitious agenda would mitigate the unravelling of the symbiotic ties that bind the British Isles with the continent, notwithstanding a long and chequered history. Moreover, the impact of Brexit on our bilateral relations remained imponderable. It was somewhat reassuring that PM May specifically referred to India twice in her speech—first in the context of the UK being one of the most multicultural members of the European Union (EU), with so many friends and relatives from across the world; and second, perhaps more importantly, in the context of future trade ties. That India, the former jewel in the British crown, was an alluring partner, there was little doubt, given the focus that successive British prime ministers have imparted to relations with India. While some in the UK harked back to the days of imperial glory by referring to the possibility of an Empire 2.0, most realised the significance of cultivating an emerging India—about to overtake the UK in terms of gross domestic product (GDP)—as a cherished strategic partner.

After four years of tortuous negotiations and a few false dawns, the UK finally left the EU on 31 December 2020, but only after a bitter wrangling both within the country and during talks with the EU, costing two prime ministers their jobs. The stage is set for the UK to embark on what promises to be a difficult and arduous journey towards becoming a truly global Britain. India looms large in this regard. The three visits of Prime Minister David Cameron and one of Theresa May to India, reciprocated by two visits of Prime Minister Narendra Modi to the UK, have laid the foundations of a new chapter in India–UK relations. Prime Minister Boris Johnson has always been an ardent advocate of closer bilateral ties, even in his earlier avatar as foreign secretary. His ability to think out of the box, take calculated risks and propensity to fashion unconventional outcomes is matched by a strong, committed and visionary interlocutor on the Indian side.

On 4 May 2021, at a virtual summit between the two prime ministers, India and the UK issued a comprehensive Roadmap 2030 that will form the bedrock of an enhanced, re-invigorated relationship. The four key pillars that will propel these ties are health, trade and investment, defence and security and climate change and clean energy. These pillars will subsume the wide canvas of cooperation that already exists and is enumerated in some detail in the Roadmap. A quantum leap in relations was predicated on a series of prime ministerial visits in 2021, commencing with Prime Minister Boris Johnson's visit to India in April, followed by Prime Minister Modi's visits to the UK for the G7 Summit in the summer and UN Climate Change Conference (COP26) in Scotland in December. However, the first two visits had to be substituted by virtual interactions, owing to the rampant Covid-19 pandemic. These interactions provided ample opportunities to flesh out the details of an even stronger and closer partnership. The visits to India of Foreign Secretary Dominic Raab in December 2020, International Trade Secretary Liz Truss and Business, Energy and Industrial Strategy Secretary Alok Sharma—who is also the COP26 president—in February 2021, have been useful in the lead up to the summit-level interactions.

The dynamics of India–UK relations have often been shaped by a long, complex and bitter past, replete with the depredations of almost two centuries of colonial rule and the saga of India's freedom struggle that led to India's independence in 1947. The modern relationship, which rests on the sinews of a contested history, has evolved into a vibrant, multifaceted and mutually beneficial partnership, encompassing almost all spheres of human endeavour, notwithstanding the ghosts of the past. While India–UK relations are marked by cordiality, a similar worldview and a mutual commitment to democracy and the rule of law, we have often found ourselves on opposite sides on issues, particularly during the Cold War. In the post-Cold War period, there has been a greater confluence of views and interests. The role of the 1.5 million Indian diaspora residing in the UK, often referred to as the living bridge, in nurturing, sustaining and fostering the robust relationship between the two countries, should not be underestimated.

Re-engaging India and the UK's Tilt to the Indo-Pacific

In June 2019, the House of Commons Select Committee on Foreign Affairs came out with an important report entitled, 'Building Bridges: Reawakening UK–India Ties', containing a set of noteworthy conclusions and recommendations for the UK government and the Foreign and Commonwealth Office (FCO)[2]. The report concedes that, 'the UK needs to adjust its strategy to India's enhanced influence and power: we should do more to respond to India's priorities, and should communicate our own objectives more clearly. As the UK leaves the EU, our foreign policy priorities will change.' Specifically, the report recommends that, 'the Government should make greater efforts to engage with Indian ministers, officials and non-governmental opinion leaders on defence, around UK interests in the Indian Ocean. These efforts may be boosted by greater engagement with third partners such as France and Japan, which have established joint initiatives with India in the region.' The report further recommends that, 'the FCO should ensure that the overarching objective of building a closer relationship with India is front-and-centre in Government efforts to enhance bilateral defence ties. As with other areas of UK–India relations, this will require an effort to address India's priorities, such as developing Indian domestic defence production, rather than simply presenting UK objectives. In defence industry cooperation with India, the Government should aim to build a partnership, rather than merely pursuing a transactional, buyer-seller relationship. This is likely to include efforts to increase joint manufacturing and technology transfers, within the restrictions set by the UK's international obligations, and closer cooperation on cyber security. In its response to this report, the FCO should set out the steps the Government is taking to achieve this.'

The report is significant as it also contains recommendations regarding a wide spectrum of issues like support for a permanent UN Security Council seat for India and a closer engagement with the Commonwealth, including envisaging a leadership role for India in the organisation. It also recommends a more active engagement with the Indian diaspora. The report concludes by stating: 'The story of the UK's recent relationship with India is primarily one of missed opportunities. In all fundamental respects, the UK is well placed to capitalise on a mutually beneficial relationship with India—so it is a disappointing reflection on recent UK governments that we have been losing out in term of influence and trade. There are certain practical steps the Government must take to reset its relationship with India, in particular making it easier for Indians to visit the UK and to work or study here. But it is also vital that the Government sets the right tone and sends strong messages. The UK is ready to do business with India, and to work together bilaterally and in multilateral forums as a partnership of equals. In an increasingly unstable world threatened by autocratic states with contempt for the rules-based international system, it is more important than ever before that the UK and India support each other—and our mutual allies. These messages are not complex but they are essential. The Government now needs to communicate them clearly and make sure that their words are backed by actions.'

Policy Exchange's Indo-Pacific Commission, chaired by Right Honourable Stephen J Harper, former prime minister of Canada, came out in 2020 with a useful interim report titled, 'A Very British Tilt, Towards a new UK Strategy in the Indo-Pacific region'[3], which highlights the salience of countries in the region, particularly India, in three broad policy areas—Indo-Pacific trade, economics and technology developments; Indo-Pacific domestic and international politics and diplomacy; and Indo-Pacific defence and security issues. The report provides holistic recommendations and a list of possible UK initiatives and integration activities. While seeking to place the Indo-Pacific in a geostrategic construct and enumerating the shared assumptions that the UK has with its closest regional allies—US, Australia and Japan—the report states: 'They all recognise the deepening of engagement with India as fundamental to an evolved geostrategic architecture in the Indo-Pacific.'

Striking a discordant note, Chatham House, in a research paper published in January 2021 titled 'Global Britain, Global Broker: A Blueprint for the UK's Future International Role'[4], seemed to question India's credentials as a viable and credible partner, sparking a degree of consternation and even some mirth amongst Indian analysts. The author seems to have been carried away by a prejudiced and jaundiced view of India, fashionable in some circles in the UK, and actively promoted by some so-called intellectuals of Indian origin. The report clubs India along with Russia, Turkey and Saudi Arabia and calls them 'the difficult four'. The author argues that India's complex, fragmented domestic politics has made it one of the countries most resistant to open trade and foreign investment and goes on to make highly objectionable and gratuitous observations about India's political milieu, displaying both appalling arrogance and ignorance of ground realities.

Prime Minister Boris Johnson, in a landmark statement to the House of Commons on 16 March 2021 on the integrated review of security, defence, development and foreign policy, outlined the UK's tilt towards the Indo-Pacific, setting at rest speculation about the direction that UK will take in a post-Brexit world. The 111-page review of UK's defence, security, development and foreign policy, titled, 'Global Britain in a Competitive Age'[5], released subsequently by the government, allayed some of the doubts and misapprehensions in this regard.

The UK's foreign and security policy tilt towards the Indo-Pacific does not abandon its traditional trans-Atlantic moorings, nor does it forsake its European linkages. The US continues to remain the UK's most important strategic ally, and Russia its most acute threat. While China, India and Japan are recognised as the three principal powers in the Indo-Pacific, the matrix under which each of these powers are treated differs. Economy, security and civilisational values influence the desire to deepen engagement in the Indo-Pacific. Over the years, the UK military presence in the region has diminished considerably, even though it has now seven 'permanent points of presence' in the Indian Ocean—in Bahrain, Oman, Kenya, Brunei, Singapore, Diego Garcia and Qatar. The new aircraft carrier, Queen Elizabeth, is deploying in the Indian Ocean for the first time this year. It remains to be seen how the UK will join and coordinate activities with other countries in the region and from outside. France is already active in the region and is conducting naval exercises with the Quad—United States, India, Australia and Japan. The UK is yet to address its cooperation with groupings like the Quad and the absence of any mention of the Quad in the review detracts from the focus on the region that it sought to impart. However, the Roadmap 2030 modestly concedes, 'India and the UK will work in strategic partnership to strengthen efforts to tackle cyber, space, crime and terrorist threats and develop a free, open and secure Indo-Pacific region.'

On the other hand, the UK's recognition that China poses a threat and challenge to its security, prosperity and values, while at the same time expressing willingness to engage China at multiple levels, reveals a shift from the halcyon period of engagement under the David Cameron–George Osborne combine. 'In effect, the UK's approach to China appears to be compete where necessary; cooperate where possible; counteract when necessary.'[6] This dovetails well into the Quad's approach to China. The UK needs to shed its hesitancy of the past and play a more active role in conjunction with the Association of Southeast Asian Nations (ASEAN) and the Quad. Coordination and cooperation between India and the UK could spearhead the latter's sustained engagement in the region, with a more substantial presence on the ground.

Trade and Investment

While outlining the review in the parliament, Prime Minister Boris Johnson described India as 'the largest democracy in the world' and an 'international actor of growing importance'. An important pillar of the renewed engagement with India is trade and investment. The current levels of trade remain rather modest, notwithstanding high-level dialogue between the relevant ministries, departments and apex business organisations on both sides. It is estimated that India's trade in goods and services with the UK expanded from US$ 21.9 billion in 2015 to US$ 26.7 billion in 2020. Trade in services constituted a significant part of the total trade. In terms of investment, the UK ranks sixth with a cumulative investment of around US$ 29.5 billion, about 6 per cent of all foreign direct investment (FDI) into India. On the other hand, despite Brexit, the UK remains one of the top destinations for investment in Europe for India.

During the virtual interaction between the two prime ministers on 4 May 2021, a declaration for the launch of an enhanced trade partnership was made with the intent to negotiate a comprehensive free trade agreement (FTA) to unlock bilateral trade and commercial relations, including consideration of an interim trade agreement for delivering early gains. India and the UK also agreed to facilitate market access in specific sectors of mutual interest and set an ambitious target of more than doubling the bilateral trade by 2030.

A joint working group is already in place to explore the contours of a possible bilateral FTA. The thirteenth meeting of the India–UK Joint Economic and Trade Committee (JETCO) was held in London in July 2019. While both sides noted the expansion of bilateral trade by 27 per cent over the previous three years, they looked forward to 'exploring the building blocks that would allow for more ambitious trade arrangements in the future'. A sector-driven approach that identified key areas, like advanced manufacturing, renewable energy, information communications technology (ICT), life sciences, healthcare, food and drink, animal husbandry, dairy, fisheries and so on, imparts a more focused approach to the bilateral economic engagement. The progress made on the implementation of the recommendations of the India–UK Joint Trade Review agreed at the twelfth JETCO in London in January 2018 would help in identifying key areas and product lines on both sides that would need to be pushed. The review would also help in eliminating any policy or procedural roadblocks that are identified. This would constitute an essential building block towards an FTA.

It is estimated that there are around 572 UK companies in India, with a combined turnover of Rs 3,390 billion, ninety-one of which have a turnover of more than Rs 500 million and growth above 10 per cent. The total tax paid by UK companies in India in 2019-20 was Rs 173 billion. These companies directly employ 416,121 people. The leading sectors in which the UK companies have invested are industrial (22 per cent); business services (21 per cent); technology (13 per cent); and consumer and retail e-commerce (10 per cent).[7]

A similar study conducted by Grant Thornton estimates that there are around 842 Indian companies in the UK, with a total turnover of GBP 41.2 billion, employing 110,793 people and having paid almost GBP 462 million as corporation tax. The leading sectors of investment are technology and telecoms (38 per cent); pharmaceuticals and chemicals (15 per cent); engineering and manufacturing (14 per cent); and business services (11 per cent).[8]

An important segment is the small and medium enterprise (SME) sector in both countries. There are major new opportunities for investment and technology tie-ups, which could broaden cross investments in both countries. This sector should be of special focus in the burgeoning business partnership between the two countries. In September 2017, the Indian High Commission in London launched an 'Access India' programme to attract and assist British

SMEs in investing in India. The UK India Business Council (UKIBC) was the knowledge partner in this venture with Invest India as a partner from the Indian side. Such initiatives need to be encouraged and sustained on both sides, particularly since both economies boast of a large and vibrant SME sector.

Both economies rely substantially on their service sectors, and while both countries will focus on enhanced market access for their products and services, for India, the importance of greater and easier access for skilled professionals, as well as students, would be important. The decision by the UK to revert to a two-year post-study work visa for international students is a welcome development. However, much more needs to be done, particularly with respect to easier access for Indian professionals, such as doctors, engineers and those in the ICT sector, etc. India will continue to insist on Mode IV access in negotiating an FTA with the UK. This would not be easy, given UK's priorities. A white paper on immigration, titled 'The UK's Future Skills-based Immigration System' unveiled at the end of 2018, outlines how the UK plans to regulate migration after Brexit[9].

An MoU on India–UK Migration and Mobility Partnership was concluded as an outcome of the virtual interaction between the two prime ministers in May 2021. This seeks to facilitate legal movement of students and professionals and also enhance cooperation between India and UK in combating illegal migration. The MoU creates a new scheme for exchange of young professionals under which every year up to 3,000 young Indian professionals can avail employment opportunities in the UK for a period of two years without being subject to labour market test.

While London is undoubtedly one of the leading global financial centres and Brexit is unlikely to change that, it will face a huge challenge in case there is a flight of capital after Brexit. A number of Indian companies, particularly public sector undertakings (PSUs), have raised rupee-denominated bonds, popularly called masala bonds, in the London Stock Exchange. The UK's credit rating has been cut, and given that most buyers of the bonds are from the EU, there is nervousness around these bond issuances. However, with the UK joining the International Solar Alliance in April 2018, the possibility of raising green bonds in the London Stock Exchange should be explored, particularly since climate change and clean energy form an important pillar of the bilateral engagement.

India is one of the largest exporters of IT-enabled services, and the sector has significant exposure to the European market, especially the UK. The UK accounts for about 17 per cent of India's total IT exports. India's IT prowess can be married with the UK's fintech expertise, creating an environment of innovation and avenues for future growth, including incubating start-ups, where both have a significant presence. A joint declaration of intent between India and UK was announced in May 2021 which aims to deepen cooperation on emerging technologies, digital infrastructure and data policies. An MoU on cooperation in the field of telecommunication/ICT was also concluded.

While there are numerous challenges, there are also huge opportunities for Indian companies. A study carried out by the Commonwealth Secretariat after the Brexit vote[10] identified thirteen new products which India can export to the UK. It estimated market access of around US$ 2 billion for these products. A well-negotiated bilateral trade arrangement between the UK and India has the potential to increase bilateral trade by 26 per cent. In fact, the report says that the UK and India can secure a far-reaching deal which will see the value of British exports to India rise from GBP 4.2 billion to GBP 6.3 billion, an increase of GBP 2.1 billion, or 33 per cent. Imports from India by the UK will rise by around GBP 1 billion. The UK's balance of trade could improve, even though it may still be in favour of India.

Science and Technology and R&D

The considerable cooperation between the two countries in science and technology, and in critical areas like digital technology, artificial intelligence, public health, education, etc. is particularly noteworthy and needs to be nurtured and strengthened. In particular, the education sector in India would greatly benefit from collaboration with niche British institutions of higher learning, which continue to attract droves of Indian students. Another area of cooperation is the Coalition for Disaster Resilient Infrastructure (CDRI), of which UK is a founding member.

In November 2020, Prime Minister Johnson announced the UK's ambitious plan for a Green Industrial Revolution, including ending the sale of new petrol and diesel cars by 2030—putting the UK on course to be the first G7 country to decarbonise road transport—and new measures to establish world-leading industries in carbon capture and storage, and hydrogen[11]. The ten-point plan will mobilise over GBP 12 billion of government investments and aims to spur over three times as much private sector investment by 2030, to build the green jobs and industries of the future across the UK and around the world. On the other hand, India has made remarkable progress on developing some of the most affordable renewables in the world—even during the pressures of lockdown—and set an impressive target to generate 450 GW of renewable power within a decade. With both countries in the forefront of ensuring a greener future for posterity, collaborations in this endeavour will only further enhance global efforts to mitigate the impact of climate change. The fascinating story of an IIT, Kharagpur, alumnus, the late Lord Kumar Bhattacharyya, setting up the Warwick Manufacturing Group in Coventry, where both JLR and Tata electric vehicles have undergone trials, is a testament to the limitless opportunities that exist.

Scientists from both countries have forged a partnership to tackle chronic air pollution, which is impacting the health of more than twenty million people in Delhi, a city plagued by some of the worst air pollution in the world. Air quality experts from the University of Manchester, along with their counterparts from the Ministry of Earth Sciences, the Indian Institute of Tropical Meteorology and IIT Madras in India, are conducting a study to identify the causes behind the crisis and develop viable and lasting solutions. A similar collaborative arrangement in the form of a memorandum of understanding (MOU) signed by British Water, cGanga—a think tank set up by the Ministry of Drinking Water and Sanitation of India and the National Mission for Clean Ganga (NMCG), with a planned investment of US$ 200 billion—would make it easier for UK technology companies in this vital sector to enter the Indian market.

While the Covid-19 pandemic has had a global impact and changed the way countries and societies do business, the UK and India have shown the way through an alliance in the production and distribution of the Oxford-AstraZeneca vaccine, both in India and in the UK. An MoU in the field of medical products regulations between the UK's Medicines and Healthcare Products Regulatory Agency (MHRA) and India's Central Drugs Standard Control Organisation (CDSCO) and another MoU on pharmacopoeial cooperation between the Indian Pharmocopoeia Commission (IPC) and British Pharmocopoeia (BP) was concluded in May 2021. The robust science and technology cooperation manifests in programmes like the Bhabha–Newton Fund, and forms the basis of collaboration and cooperation in the future. Such joint endeavours are likely to form the cornerstone of the India–UK engagement in the post-Covid-19 world.

Obstacles

While transforming bilateral relations, we also need to be mindful of some of the impediments that impact adversely on our ties. The anti-India activities of Khalistanis, Kashmiris and Pakistanis in the UK are a source of constant friction. While it is hoped that violent demonstrations and attacks on the Indian High Commission in London and its consulates general cease, the propensity of various pressure groups to lobby British members of Parliament to debate purely domestic policies of India does not create a conducive environment for an enhanced sustained bilateral engagement. Of late, this trend has increased, and is likely to invite reciprocal actions in legislatures in India over issues such as the prevalence of racism in the UK. Another sticking point is the perception in India that Indian fugitives from law are able to live with a certain degree of impunity in the UK, given the abysmal track record of their extradition to India. From the UK side, illegal immigration and retrospective taxation on British companies are sticking points. Both these issues are being addressed.

Almost on cue and as a supposed curtain-raiser to Prime Minister Boris Johnson's the then impending visit to India, the Diplomatic Editor of *The Guardian*, in an article on 6 April 2021 titled, 'UK faces difficult path as it resumes courtship with India',[12] vents his angst and regurgitates the motivated and tiresome criticism levelled against India and its democratically elected government. He ruefully concedes, 'the perilous courtship is back on'. His carping and hand-wringing would normally be ignored, but since such an insidious piece reflects a certain mindset and contrarian point of view, it begets the question, whether some in the UK are really interested in an enhanced partnership with India or is that dependent on their personal predilections about the type of government they want in India? Fortunately, it is not they, but the people of India, who elect their government!

Conclusion

Brexit constitutes an important landmark in the UK's recent history, and is both a challenge and an opportunity for its partners, particularly those outside Europe. The salience of India has been reinforced, given the size of its economy, its growth and the large market that it offers. On the other hand, the UK continues to remain a preferred partner in a gamut of activities. The Covid-19 pandemic has opened up further avenues of engagement and 2021 so far has been an eventful year for bilateral ties. The prognosis for the future is bright and is predicated on whether both countries are able to leverage their strengths and complementarities and seize the opportunity that beckons with the UK leaving the EU.

The views expressed in the article are personal and of a retired diplomat, and do not reflect the views of the Government of India.

ENDNOTES

1. Prime Minister Theresa May's Speech at Lancaster House on 17 January 2017. https://time.com/4636141/theresa-may-brexit-speech-transcript/
2. House of Commons Select Committee on Foreign Affairs, 'Building Bridges: Reawakening UK–India ties'. https://publications.parliament.uk/pa/cm201719/cmselect/cmfaff/1465/146511 htm
3. 'A Very British Tilt', Interim report by Policy Exchange's Indo-Pacific Commission. https://policyexchange.org.uk/wp-content/uploads/A-Very-British-Tilt.pdf
4. Chatham House, 'Global Britain, global broker: A Blueprint for the UK's Future International Role. https://www.chathamhouse.org/2021/01/global-britain-global-broker International Role
5. 'Global Britain in a Competitive Age: the Integrated Review of Security, Defence, Development and Foreign Policy,'. https://www.gov.uk/government/publications/global-britain-in-a-competitive-age-the-integrated-review-of-security-defence-development-and-foreign-policy
6. Roy-Chaudhury, Rahul. 'Understanding the UK's "Tilt" Towards the Indo-Pacific', *The Wire*. https://thewire.in/diplomacy/uk-indo-pacific-india-us-china-japan
7. Grant Thorton Bharat, 'Britain Meets India: Latest trends on UK investment in India', Confederation of Indian Industry. https://www.grantthornton.in/globalassets/1.-member-firms/india/assets/pdfs/britain_meets_india_report-february_2021.pdf
8. Grant Thorton Bharat, 'India meets Britain tracker: The latest trends on Indian investment in the UK, 2020', Confederation of Indian Industry. https://www.grantthornton.co.uk/globalassets/1.-member-firms/united-kingdom/pdf/publication/2020/india-meets-britain-tracker-2020.pdf
9. 'The UK's future skills-based immigration system'. White Paper on immigration. https://assets.publishing.service.gov.uk/government/uploads/system/uploads/attachment_data/file/766465/The-UKs-future-skills-based-immigration-system-print-ready.pdf
10. 'Brexit: Opportunities for India, Commonwealth Secretariat Trade Competitiveness Briefing Paper. https://thecommonwealth.org/sites/default/files/inline/TCBP_Paper%2001_Brexit%20Opportunities%20for%20India.pdf
11. 'The Ten Point Plan for a Green Industrial Revolution.' https://www.gov.uk/government/publications/the-ten-point-plan-for-a-green-industrial-revolution/title
12. Wintour, Patrick. 'UK faces difficult path as it resumes courtship with India', *The Guardian*. https://www.theguardian.com/uk-news/2021/apr/06/uk-faces-difficult-path-as-it-resumes-courtship-with-india

CHAPTER 23

INDIA AND THE UN IN THE POST-COVID-19 WORLD

Asoke Kumar Mukerji

The role of India and the United Nations (UN) in the world after the Covid-19 pandemic revolves around the implementation of the objective of 'reformed multilateralism', which was highlighted by India during the high-level meetings held in 2020 to mark the seventy-fifth anniversary of the founding of the UN. In this article, it is proposed to look at this topic from the perspective of India's stakes in the system of modern multilateralism, and the role that 'reformed multilateralism' will play in catalysing the transformation of India and the UN in the twenty-first century.

Background

More than a century ago—in June 1919—India became a founder member of the modern multilateral system as a signatory to the Treaty of Versailles, which created the League of Nations.[1] Among the steps taken by India during its membership of the League, the signing of the Kellogg–Briand Pact on 27 August 1928 continues to exercise its influence on India's core interest in multilateralism even today. The pact committed India (and the other fourteen signatories) to outlaw war as an instrument of national policy and resolve disputes by peaceful means.[2]

The Treaty of Versailles also made India a founder member of the International Labour Organization (ILO). Following its structural reforms in 1922, the ILO's

Governing Body has included India as one of the ten 'States of chief industrial importance' whose governments are permanently represented among the twenty-eight governments in the fifty-six-member Governing Body. It is worth noting this fact when addressing issues of 'reformed multilateralism' today, as decisions in the ILO's Governing Body are by consensus, with a provision for majority voting in case there is no consensus. The ILO is the first tripartite—or 'multiple stakeholder'—multilateral organisation, consisting of governments, employers and workers.[3]

India was among the twenty-six countries invited to participate in the January 1942 Washington Conference of Allied Nations by then US President Franklin Delano Roosevelt. The conference issued a 'Declaration by United Nations', which committed its signatories to the objective of creating the UN.[4]

The UN was conceptualised as a post-Second World War global governance structure, which would rest on three pillars—political, economic and human rights. The UN General Assembly (UNGA) would oversee the functioning of the UN, while its Charter gave to the UN Security Council (UNSC) the 'primary responsibility' for maintaining international peace and security. Implementing the UN's socio-economic vision, including upholding fundamental human rights and freedoms, was entrusted to the Economic and Social Council (ECOSOC).

The first multilateral structures to 'sustain' global peace were created in July 1944, when forty-five countries, including the original twenty-six from the Washington Conference of 1942, participated in the UN Financial and Monetary Conference held at Bretton Woods in the United States. The International Monetary Fund (IMF) and International Bank for Reconstruction and Development (World Bank) were established to coordinate a supportive role for global monetary and developmental policies. The victorious powers of the Second World War acquired a privileged influence in IMF's decisions through a weighted 'quota' system. India's place in the IMF 'quota' system in 1944 was placed just below the five major military powers—the United States, the United Kingdom, France, Soviet Union and Republic of China.[5] Two elements from the Bretton Woods Conference that are relevant for India's role in multilateral platforms today are: its permanent membership of the Board of Governors of these two structures since 1945 and the inclusion of 'development' issues in the mandate of the IMF and the World Bank.[6]

Between April and June 1945, India joined forty-nine other countries in negotiating and adopting the provisions of the San Francisco Treaty—known as the UN Charter. Invitations to the San Francisco Conference were issued jointly by four of the Second World War's victorious military powers—the Republic of China, the United Kingdom, the USSR and the United States. The veto privilege of these four powers (extended to France as the fifth self-selected 'permanent' member or 'P5' of the proposed UNSC) was made a non-negotiable condition in the invitation letter to the other participating countries. Attempts to reopen this condition at the conference were rejected by the P5. The result was the domination of the UN's activities by the P5 using the UNSC after the Charter was signed in June 1945.

India played a prominent role in chairing the conference's discussions on economic and social issues to 'sustain' peace. India is credited for three of the Charter's provisions—its reference to 'promoting and encouraging respect for human rights and for fundamental freedoms for all' in Article 1; the withdrawal of the right to vote by a member state, which is in arrears in Article 19; and the criteria for non-permanent elected members in the first paragraph of Article 23.[7]

India's Contributions to the UN[8]

India became the first country to be elected president of the ECOSOC in 1946 by the UNGA. Under India's presidency of the ECOSOC, several major initiatives were taken by the newly formed UN. These included the convening of an International Conference on Trade and Employment,[9] which laid the foundation of today's World Trade Organization (WTO), and the creation of the Economic and Social Commission for Asia and the Pacific (ESCAP). India was elected the first executive secretary of ESCAP from 1947 to 1956.

India presided over the ECOSOC's first decisions for upholding fundamental human rights and freedoms. Three of these stand out. The first was non-discrimination. In 1946, India successfully inscribed in the UNGA the need to abolish discriminatory policies based on colour against Indians in South Africa, a UN member state. This metamorphosed into the wider anti-apartheid movement, which culminated with the successful multiracial elections in South Africa in April 1994 and the election of President Nelson Mandela, who led South Africa's delegation to the UNGA in September 1994.

The second was the outlawing of mass atrocity crimes. India joined Cuba and Panama to co-sponsor the 1946 UNGA resolution, mandating the negotiation of the UN Genocide Convention in 1948—the first global legal commitment on preventing genocide.

The third was gender equality. In 1948, India's delegate, Hansa Mehta—who became the first vice chancellor of MS University in Baroda—successfully replaced the words 'all men' to 'all human beings' to expand the scope of the first UN document on human rights—Universal Declaration on Human Rights (UDHR). Article 1 of the UDHR reads: 'All human beings are born free and equal in dignity and rights.'

Since 1950, India has voluntarily contributed troops to maintain international peace and security at the request of the UNSC. So far, over 240,000 Indian troops have served in fifty UN peacekeeping missions across the world, providing the UNSC with the resources to create conditions to pursue the peaceful resolution of disputes on its agenda. This is the single largest contribution by any member state for UN peacekeeping operations. However, the effectiveness of UN peacekeeping has been increasingly constrained by the growing ineffectiveness of the UNSC to use these resources on the ground. This is one of the reasons for seeking a reform of the UNSC, which is addressed later in this essay.

The principle of democratic decision-making in international relations, enshrined in the provision of 'one country, one vote' of Article 18 of the UN Charter, came to life following the independence of India in August 1947. Along with leaders of other newly independent countries, in December 1960, India spearheaded the unanimous adoption of the historic Decolonization Resolution in the UNGA, opening the doors for scores of newly independent countries to join the UNGA.

This resulted in a prominent Indian role in two platforms within the UNGA. The first was the political grouping of twenty-four member states that created the Non-Aligned Movement (NAM) in September 1961. The objective of NAM was to enable UN member states who were not part of the two ideological 'blocs' during the Cold War to address issues based on their declared national interest. The second was the creation of the Group of 77 (G77) developing countries in 1964, which turned the UN's focus to accelerated development priorities. In 1965, the UNGA responded to the aspirations of most of its developing country members for accelerated development by creating the United Nations

Development Programme (UNDP), which is today active in over 170 UN member states. India became the first Chair of the G77 in 1970. Today, even three decades after the end of the Cold War, the NAM has 122 member states in the UNGA. The G77 currently has 134 out of the 193 member states in the UNGA. Both these platforms will play a pivotal role in shaping the post-Covid-19 world.

The emergence of an agenda for accelerated development in the UN became a catalyst for concerns among several developed countries regarding the adverse impact that accelerated development would have on the environment. This led the UN to hold its first Conference on the Human Environment in Stockholm in 1972. Speaking on behalf of India, then Prime Minister Indira Gandhi emphasised on the link between eradication of poverty and sustainable development, when she said, 'poverty is the biggest polluter'.

The concept of 'sustainable development' converged the apparent contradiction between development and environmental protection in the UN's Brundtland Commission Report tabled in 1987. The report played a major role in the outcome of the 1992 Rio Summit—popularly called the Earth Summit—which adopted the UN Framework Convention on Climate Change (UNFCCC). The 2015 Paris Agreement is the most recent outcome of this process for climate action.

In parallel, the 1992 Earth Summit also created a framework for sustainable development. This twenty-year effort culminated in the mandate given to the UNGA by the 2012 Rio+20 Summit to negotiate the sustainable development goals (SDGs). Between March 2013 and September 2015, the UNGA identified and negotiated the targets of the seventeen SDGs which form the core of the ambitious UN Agenda 2030 for sustainable development. In a vindication of the position taken by India in 1972, the first and overarching SDG of Agenda 2030 is the eradication of poverty.[10]

Integrating Peace, Security and Development

Agenda 2030 is the dominant framework of the UN's activities today. The Preamble to Agenda 2030 specifically emphasises the interlinkage between peace, security and development. Implementing this framework on the ground is the objective of 'reformed multilateralism'.

In his three major addresses to the UN on its seventy-fifth anniversary in

2020, Prime Minister Narendra Modi placed the implementation of Agenda 2030 at the heart of the call for 'reformed multilateralism', saying that, 'We cannot fight today's challenges with outdated structures. Without comprehensive reforms, the UN faces a crisis of confidence. In today's interconnected world, we need a reformed multilateralism—that reflects today's realities, gives voice to all stakeholders, addresses contemporary challenges and focuses on human welfare.'

He said that, 'India is home to one-sixth of humanity. We are mindful of our weight and responsibility. We know that if India succeeds in achieving its development objectives, it will go a long way in achievement of the global goals.' India's transformation is dependent on implementing its national development objectives, which have been fully aligned with Agenda 2030 through India's NITI Aayog.[11] The most important external requirement for India to succeed in this task is to ensure a supportive international environment of peace and security.

Calls for 'reformed multilateralism'[12] at the UN's seventy-fifth anniversary session in September 2020 stressed two overriding priorities. First, the need for equal participation by member states in UN decision-making, which consolidates the 'surge to democracy' that has characterised international relations since the UN Charter was signed in 1945. Second, the imperative for an inclusive human-centric approach to sustainable development through the participation of multiple stakeholders in implementing multilateral policies. An inclusive approach provides the UN the much-needed financial, human and technological resources through partnerships to meet the major challenges in all its three 'pillars'—political, human rights and socio-economic development. Three global challenges to the UN's activities are the spread of international terrorism, the increasing number of natural and man-made disasters and the rapid and unregulated proliferation of new technologies.

India has been an advocate for UNSC reform since 1979[13] to make it more democratic, representative and equitable, so that the elected UNSC members can participate on an equal basis in its decisions.[14] World leaders gave a unanimous mandate more than fifteen years ago for an 'early reform' of the UNSC 'to make it more broadly representative, efficient and transparent, and thus to further enhance its effectiveness and the legitimacy and implementation of its decisions'.[15] This rationale for UNSC reform is even more valid in 2021, as the P5 continue to use their veto privilege conceptualised in 1945 to prevent the UNSC from responding to major crises confronting the world. The inadequacy of the UNSC's response to support an integrated global response to the Covid-19 pandemic in 2020—which has already claimed about two million lives worldwide in less than a year—illustrates the problem starkly.

In December 1963, the UNGA had amended the UN Charter to expand the UNSC through a resolution adopted by a two-thirds majority vote, which was implemented despite opposition by four of the P5 members of the UNSC. Reforming the UNSC will require a similar act by the UNGA now. During 2014-15, the Chair of the Intergovernmental Negotiations (IGN) under the UNGA succeeded in getting 120 member states in the UNGA—including France and the UK, but not the United States, Russia and China—to contribute to a working document for text-based negotiations on a resolution for UNSC reform.[16] The document, which includes the five areas [17] identified by the UNGA for UNSC reform, including the 'question of the veto', was proposed by the African President of the General Assembly (PGA) and adopted by consensus on 14 September 2015.[18]

Subsequent attempts at text-based negotiations in the IGN have been systematically opposed by China, backed by a group of twelve countries called 'Uniting for Consensus'.[19] Since 2016, successive PGAs have been persuaded to fragment the integrity of the IGN.[20]

To reform the UNSC, India must continue to be actively engaged with pro-reform member states, implementing both the sixtieth anniversary UN Summit mandate as well as the Agenda 2030's commitment under SDG 16.8, which calls for 'broadening and strengthening the participation of developing countries in the institutions of global governance'.[21] The UNGA needs to adopt a resolution to amend the UN Charter with a two-thirds majority vote, and not be diverted by obstructionist and untenable preconditions of 'widest political consensus'.[22] India must involve its strategic partners among the P5 in this campaign, including the United States that has publicly declared its interest in reforming the UNSC to include India as a permanent member.[23]

The second thrust of 'reformed multilateralism' is to implement Agenda 2030 effectively in a post-Covid-19 world for global welfare. This requires leadership in the UN system to keep the focus on the twin priorities of Agenda 2030—climate change and socio-economic progress. In parallel with reforming the UNSC and UN specialised agencies[24] to provide such leadership through the UN system, a holistic reform of the three multilateral institutions—IMF, the World Bank and WTO—that have sustained peace together with the UN after the Second World War must become a priority for India.

The UN needs to be ahead of the curve in responding to traditional and new challenges. This is especially true of the digital domain, which has been thrust into the UN's mainstream activities by the Covid-19 pandemic. A road map for a human-centric, multiple-stakeholder approach to securing and applying digital technologies drawn up by the UN Secretary-General must be integrated as a priority into the UNGA's agenda to bridge 'digital divides'.[25]

To achieve the structural and substantive requirements of 'reformed multilateralism', UN member states must identify and adopt a coherent and sustainable way ahead. This can be done by deciding to convene a UN General Conference to review the provisions of the 1945 UN Charter. The drafters of the UN Charter had anticipated this need in Article 109, which allows a UN General Conference to be held by 'a majority vote of the members of the General Assembly and by a vote of any seven members of the Security Council'.[26]

Two sets of issues suggest themselves for inclusion in any agenda of such a General Conference. One set of issues were agreed to or discussed by the UNGA earlier, such as deleting parts of the UN Charter overtaken by history. This includes references to 'enemy State' in articles 53, 77 and 107; deleting Chapter XIII of the UN Charter on the Trusteeship Council which had completed its work, along with any other references to the Trusteeship Council; reflecting the political changes in the membership of the UNSC, including substituting the 'People's Republic of China' for the 'Republic of China' and the 'Russian Federation' for the 'Union of Soviet Socialist Republics' in Article 23.1; and a review of the 'Military Staff Committee' in articles 45, 46 and 47 of the Charter.

A second set of issues flows out of the UN's experience over the past seven decades in responding to the new realities in international relations. The UN has created new structures and platforms for global governance to respond to these challenges which were not envisaged by the UN Charter. These include the UN Human Rights Council; UN Women; Peace Building Commission; climate change structures; and UN-led platforms for countering terrorism, sustainable development and digital cooperation. To integrate a human-centric vision into the UN Charter, the General Conference should consider streamlining these new structures into the UN Charter. This would include interlinking the new provisions of the UN Charter with the mutually cooperative arrangements between the UN and its specialised agencies, funds and programmes in the appropriate areas. The current concerns regarding the WHO's response to Covid-19, for example, would benefit from such an integrated framework.

A multiple stakeholder UN General Conference, organised along the lines of the UNGA process adopted for Agenda 2030, must become a priority for India and the UN to reform multilateralism and make the UN relevant for the twenty-first century.

Endnotes

1. Mukerji, Asoke Kumar. 'The Centenary of India's Membership of the League of Nations', *Indian Foreign Affairs Journal*, no. 2, vol.14 (April-June 2019): 149-64. Accessed 16 February 2021, http://www.associationdiplomats.org/Publications/ifaj/Vol14/14.2/Article%206.pdf
2. US Department of State, Office of the Historian, 'The Kellogg-Briand Pact, 1928'. Accessed 16 February 2021, https://history.state.gov/milestones/1921-1936/kellogg
3. International Labour Organization, 'How the ILO works'. Accessed 16 February 2021, https://ilo.org/global/about-the-ilo/how-the-ilo-works/lang--en/index.htm
4. US Department of State, Office of the Historian, 'The Formation of the United Nations, 1945'. Accessed 16 February 2021, https://history.state.gov/milestones/1937-1945/un
5. International Monetary Fund. 'Articles of Agreement of the International Monetary Fund,' March 2020'. Schedule A: Quotas. Accessed 17 February 2021, https://www.imf.org/external/pubs/ft/aa/index.htm. Today, India is at 13th place out of 24 in the IMF's quota holdings according to India's Ministry of Finance (see https://dea.gov.in/sites/default/files/India_IMF_0.pdf)
6. Rajadhyaksha, Niranjan. 'How India made its mark at the Bretton Woods Conference', *Mint*, 11 June 2019. Accessed 16 February 2021, https://www.livemint.com/opinion/columns/opinion-the-bretton-woods-conference-the-indian-story-1560254374554.html
7. Abdenur, Adriana Erthal. 'Emerging powers and the creation of the UN: three ships of Theseus', *Third World Quarterly* 7, vol. 37 (July 2016): 1171-86.
8. Mukerji, Asoke Kumar. 'The Impact of Multilateralism on India', *Indian Foreign Affairs Journal*, no. 4, vol. 13 (October-December 2018): 335-44. Accessed 16 February 2021, http://www.associationdiplomats.org/Publications/ifaj/Vol%2013/13.4/IFAJ-13.4-ARTICLE%202-F.pdf
9. Neumann, Peter. 'The Relationship between GATT and the United Nations',' *Cornell International Law Journal*, no. 1, vol. 3, Article 5 (1970). Accessed 16 February 2021, https://core.ac.uk/download/pdf/216740933.pdf
10. United Nations, 'Transforming our world: the 2030 Agenda for Sustainable Development', Accessed 16 February 2021, https://sdgs.un.org/2030agenda
11. NITI Aayog, Government of India, 'United Nations High-Level Political Forum on Sustainable Development, 2020'. Accessed 17 February 2021, https://niti.gov.in/un-high-level-political-forum
12. Ministry of External Affairs, India, 'Call for Reformed Multilateralism at the UN' by Asoke Kumar Mukerji, *India Perspectives*, no. 5 (2020). Accessed 16 February 2021, https://www.indiaperspectives.gov.in/en_US/call-for-reformed-multilateralism-at-the-un/

13. Mukerji, Asoke Kumar. 'The Impact of Multilateralism on India', *Indian Foreign Affairs Journal*, no. 4, vol. 13 (October-December 2018): 335-44, note 17. Accessed 16 February 2021, http://www.associationdiplomats.org/Publications/ifaj/Vol%2013/13.4/IFAJ-13.4-ARTICLE%202-F.pdf
14. Ministry of External Affairs, India. 'English translation of Prime Minister's address at 75th United Nations General Assembly', 26 September 2020. Accessed 16 February 2021, https://mea.gov.in/Speeches-Statements.htm?dtl/33064/English_translation_of_Prime_Ministers_address_at_75th_United_Nations_General_Assembly
15. United Nations, UNGA Resolution A/RES/60/1 (paragraph 153), 16 September 2005. Accessed 16 February 2021, https://www.un.org/en/development/desa/population/migration/generalassembly/docs/globalcompact/A_RES_60_1.pdf
16. Manohar Parrikar Institute for Defence Studies and Analyses, New Delhi. 'A Security Council for the 21st Century: Challenges and Prospects' by E. Courtenay Rattray, 20 July 2016. Accessed 16 February 2021, https://idsa.in/issuebrief/a-security-council-for-the-21st-century_ecrattray_200716
17. UN General Assembly Decision 62/557, p. 106, 15 September 2008. Accessed 16 February 2021, http://undocs.org/en/a/62/49(Vol.III)
18. United Nations, UN General Assembly, President of the 69th Session. Letter on 'Intergovernmental Negotiation on Security Council Reform' and Annexes, 31 July 2015. Accessed 16 February 2021, https://www.un.org/pga/wp-content/uploads/sites/3/2013/11/Security-Council-reform-IGN-31-July-2015.pdf
19. United Nations, '"Uniting for Consensus" Group of States introduces text on Security Council reform to the General Assembly', GA/10371, 26 July 2005. Accessed 16 February 2021, https://www.un.org/press/en/2005/ga10371.doc.htm
20. United Nations General Assembly, President of the 71st Session, Letter on 'Security Council Reform plenary and Co-Chairs appointment', 26 October 2016. Accessed 16 February 2021, https://www.un.org/pga/71/wp-content/uploads/sites/40/2015/08/Security-Council-Reform-plenary-and-Co-Chairs-Appointment-26-October-2016.pdf
21. See note 10 above. SDG 16.8.
22. Xinhua Net, 'China supports reasonable reform of the UN Security Council: envoy', 26 November 2019. Accessed 16 February 2021, http://www.xinhuanet.com/english/2019-11/26/c_138583219.htm
23. The White House, 'Remarks by the President to the Joint Session of the Indian Parliament in New Delhi, India', 8 November 2010. Accessed 16 February 2021, https://obamawhitehouse.archives.gov/the-press-office/2010/11/08/remarks-president-joint-session-indian-parliament-new-delhi-india
24. For a listing of UN specialized agencies, see https://www.un.org/en/sections/about-un/funds-programmes-specialized-agencies-and-others/. Accessed 17 February 2021.
25. United Nations, 'Secretary-General's Roadmap for Digital Cooperation', June 2020. Accessed 16 February 2021, https://www.un.org/en/content/digital-cooperation-roadmap/
26. UN Charter, Article 109 paragraph 3. Accessed 17 February 2021, https://www.un.org/en/charter-united-nations/

CHAPTER 24

INDIA AND THE GLOBAL CLIMATE CHANGE DISCOURSE IN THE POST-COVID-19 WORLD

DILIP SINHA

The global climate change discourse started in the mid-1980s when the scientific community noticed signs of global warming, which it attributed to the increased concentration in the atmosphere of greenhouse gases (GHGs) generated by human activity. The United Nations General Assembly (UNGA) set the ball rolling with a resolution in December 1988, declaring climate change to be a 'common concern of mankind'. International negotiations started in earnest in 1991, and world leaders demonstrated their seriousness by holding the Earth Summit in Rio de Janeiro the following year. The UN Framework Convention on Climate Change (UNFCCC) was one of the agreements adopted at the conference.

The UNFCCC entered into force in 1995, and, since then, has conducted climate change negotiations at a frenetic pace, albeit with limited progress. The participation of the scientific community and climate change activists has added zest and zeal to its meetings. Civil society has maintained sustained pressure on governments for climate action, but the intergovernmental negotiations have been viciously confrontational and divisive.

Finger-pointing became the name of the game in the negotiations. The tone was set by articles like a study in 1990 by the Washington-based World

Resources Institute, which attributed 45 per cent of global warming to developing countries. It declared India to be a major culprit because of its high methane emissions from rice cultivation.[1]

Developed countries wanted global warming to be declared a 'common responsibility', requiring 'mitigation'—action to reduce emissions—by all countries, regardless of their level of development. Developing countries charged that the accumulation of GHGs in the atmosphere was due to the historical emissions of developed countries. They bore the 'main responsibility' for global warming and should reduce their emissions. A compromise was coined—'common but differentiated responsibility'. Developing countries also demanded financial and technological assistance for the 'adaptation' measures to be taken by them to deal with the impact of climate change.

As negotiations gathered steam, both developed and developing countries split into smaller groups and the traditional north–south divide turned into a cacophony of shifting alliances. Some West European countries were willing to accept the target of stabilising emissions at 1990 levels by as early as 2000. But, the United States was adamantly against imposing emission reduction targets on countries and a framework that differentiated between developed and developing countries. It supported Japan's voluntary 'pledge-and-review' proposal and demanded that China and India be included in it. Small islands and other vulnerable developing countries called for strong mitigation action by all large emitters. Oil-producing countries opposed curbs on the production and consumption of fossil fuels. Large, emerging economies, like China, India and Brazil, were anxious to safeguard their economic growth and opposed the mitigation being imposed on them.

India made equity the centrepiece of its stand. It demanded that developed countries reduce their emissions and vacate atmospheric carbon space for developing countries. It also pressed for technical and financial assistance. India asserted this as early as 1989 at a conference in the Netherlands and the following year at a conference of developing countries in New Delhi. At a preparatory meeting for the Rio conference in Washington, an Indian delegate stated what would become the country's stand for over two decades: 'Those responsible for environmental degradation should also be responsible for taking corrective measures.'[2]

Despite these polemics, the UNFCCC produced its first agreement within two years. The Kyoto Protocol, as it was called, broadly identified six GHGs[3] in which developed countries agreed to take mitigation action through a 'cap-and-trade' system. The cuts cumulatively amounted to 5.2 per cent in five years over the 1990 level.[4] The scheme permitted trading in carbon—a market mechanism for the sale and purchase of carbon credits by companies to enable them to meet their emission targets through subrogation. India was sceptical about this scheme, but did not block it. The protocol also provided for an adaptation fund to finance projects in developing countries.

India demonstrated its commitment to climate action by hosting the UNFCCC conference in New Delhi in 2002. But the Kyoto Protocol was fatally wounded by the refusal of the United States to join it. It struggled to get to the required ratifications and took eight years to come into force. More trouble was in store for it. In 2008, when its five-year commitment period started, a financial crisis sent the global economy into recession, hitting developed countries the most. Rising unemployment sharply reduced their enthusiasm for climate action. In 2010, the European Union (EU) recorded a 2.4 per cent increase in its emissions—the biggest since 1990.

The rise of China also had a profound effect on climate negotiations. In 2006, it overtook the United States to become the world's largest emitter of GHGs. China had become the manufacturing hub of the world, but it still claimed a developing country status. Its emissions had trebled—rising from 10 per cent of global emissions in 1990 to 21 per cent in 2006. India's emissions doubled during the same period but its global share was still very low—4.2 per cent, up from 2.8 per cent.[5]

The United States seized the opportunity at the thirteenth Conference of the Parties of UNFCCC in Bali in 2007 to get members to work on a new climate agreement that would come into effect when the commitment period of the Kyoto Protocol ended in 2012. Developing countries were promised financial assistance if they voluntarily took mitigation action, which was termed 'nationally appropriate mitigation actions'.

India continued to hold tenaciously to the principle of equity. It proposed emission allowances on per capita basis. But, it realised that it would have to take some action on mitigation to deflect the mounting pressure and demonstrate its commitment to climate action. It announced a reduction of 20 to 25 per cent in the intensity of its emissions per unit of its gross domestic product (GDP) by 2020 over the 2005 level. It also announced that its per capita emissions would not exceed the average per capita emissions of developed countries.

Despite diminished enthusiasm, most developed countries were able to meet their modest Kyoto Protocol targets, thanks to their economic recession and the relocation of polluting industries to China and other developing countries. But not all countries met their targets. Canada's emissions went up by 19 per cent and Australia's by 30 per cent. These countries joined the US in opposing the Kyoto Protocol. Canada walked out of it, and Russia, Japan, Australia and New Zealand refused to take further commitments. Since no new agreement had been reached, it was decided to extend the Kyoto Protocol to a second phase after 2012, even though there were few takers for it.

At the UNFCCC conference in Copenhagen in 2009, the United States came close to getting the principles of a new agreement adopted. But it remained undeterred by its failure there and continued to press for a voluntary agreement, applicable equally to all countries. It was keen on such an agreement because it would not require ratification by its senate and would be politically more acceptable.

Brazil, South Africa, India and China formed a group—called BASIC—to deal with the combined pressure of the United States and small island developing states (SIDS). However, while India continued to doggedly adhere to the principle of 'common but differentiated responsibility', China, which had further increased its emissions, negotiated a side deal with the United States. It consented to a new agreement to replace the Kyoto Protocol, provided it came into effect after 2020. In the agreement, announced in November 2014, China declared that its emissions would peak 'around 2030' and it would reduce its emission-intensity per unit of GDP by 60 to 65 per cent over the 2005 level. The US agreed to reduce its emissions by 26 to 28 per cent by 2025 over the 2005 level.

The US–China deal set the stage for a new climate treaty to be adopted at the twenty first Conference of the Parties of the UNFCCC in Paris in December 2015. The Paris Agreement adopted the goal of keeping the rise in the mean global temperature to 'well below 2 degree Celsius'. To assuage the climate lobby, it added that members would 'pursue efforts' to keep it at 1.5 degree Celsius. The agreement required all countries to submit their action plans—called nationally determined contributions (NDCs). Every country would have to submit a compliance report on its action plan every two years. Developed countries agreed to give technical assistance to developing countries and a Green Climate Fund was set up with the ambitious target of raising US$ 100 billion by 2020 to finance adaptation projects.

The NDCs were submitted rapidly by countries. The EU promised to reduce its emission by 40 per cent by 2030 over the 1990 level. The US and China submitted the pledges they had made in their bilateral agreement. India submitted a fairly ambitious NDC to be achieved by 2030:

- Reducing emission intensity per unit of GDP by 33 to 35 per cent over the 2005 level.
- Forty per cent of installed electricity generation capacity to be from non-fossil fuels.
- Creating carbon sink of 2.5-3 billion tonnes of CO_2 equivalent through afforestation.
- Better adaptation in agriculture, healthcare, water resources, the Himalayan region, coastal regions and disaster management.

But, the NDCs of all countries, when aggregated, were found to be woefully inadequate. Experts assessed that even if all pledges were fulfilled, the mean global temperature would rise by at least 3 degree Celsius. The Green Climate Fund also remained empty. As of June 2021, it had received only US$ 10.3 billion in pledges.[6]

Meanwhile, global warming continues. The mean surface temperature is estimated to have already risen by 1.2 degree Celsius.[7] There is a possibility that it may 'temporarily' exceed 1.5 degree Celsius as early as 2024.[8] It is estimated that the 1.5 degree Celsius target may be attainable only if emissions fall by half by 2030 and are reduced to net zero by 2050. A 25 per cent reduction by 2030 and net-zero emission by 2070 may keep the temperature rise to 2 degree Celsius.[9]

The global economic recession caused by the Covid-19 pandemic has introduced a new and unpredictable element in climate negotiations. Since the pandemic is not over yet, it is too early to assess its long-term impact. The stimulus packages announced by governments to revive their economies add up to over US$ 12 trillion. Many of these packages support emission-intensive and environment-damaging industries. About 54 per cent of the stimulus of the

G20 countries in the energy sector is to fossil fuels.[10] Creating employment has once again become the top priority for governments.

But the immediate environmental relief due to the lockdowns gave some encouragement amidst gloomy economic and climate forecasts. Initial estimates of the UN Environment Programme (UNEP) had predicted a decline in global emissions by an unprecedented 7 per cent in 2020.[11] However, with the revival of economic activity, emissions have started rising and the world could soon be back to its old ways. Preliminary data compiled by the World Meteorological Organization finds that despite the Covid-19 setbacks, global emissions went up in 2020.[12]

Fortuitously, whether due to the pandemic or other factors, there is a noticeable revival of enthusiasm for climate action in the world. Several countries have announced more ambitious goals. Over 120 countries have announced targets for reaching carbon neutrality or net-zero emissions, implying that they will absorb at least as much carbon as they emit. The EU, the United Kingdom, Japan, South Korea and South Africa have announced that they intend to do so by 2050. Even China has promised to do it—by 2060. These developments have coincided with a change in the United States to a climate-friendly and multilateralist leadership.

What does this bode for India? The return of the United States to the Paris Agreement and President Joe Biden's ambitious climate action plan will reinvigorate the global climate action and lead to more ambitious outcomes in UNFCCC negotiations. Biden has issued an executive order, stating that 'climate considerations shall be an essential element of United States foreign policy and national security' and that he will work with other countries and partners to put the world on a sustainable climate pathway.[13] The two targets already accepted by several major countries—declaring the peak year for emissions and the target year for net-zero emissions—will now become the benchmarks for evaluating climate action. While the United States has not formally announced its net-zero year, Biden's plan includes cutting emissions from the power sector to net zero by 2035. The US president's special envoy on climate change, John Kerry, has called upon all big emitters to 'get on a path toward net-zero emissions by 2050'.[14]

The first salvo has been fired by the UN secretary-general. António Guterres has noted that the countries that have declared targets for net-zero emissions account for 65 per cent of global emissions. He has called upon India, Brazil,

South Africa, Saudi Arabia and Russia to join this coalition so that it covers 90 per cent.[15]

India's outspokenness in climate negotiations had earned it the reputation of a naysayer and made it a target for climate activists. This was aggravated by its alliance with China in BASIC. But, while China took advantage of the time gained and invested heavily in its infrastructure and power generation, India was more judicious. China's emissions have escalated to a whopping 28 per cent of global emissions. It has declared its peak and net-zero years comfortably in the distant future and can now sit back in the negotiations. India, however, still needs enormous investments in its infrastructure, which will cause a spike in its emissions at a time when the effects of climate change are becoming all too apparent.

This adverse turn of events is ironic for India, since its performance in climate action has been anything but sloppy. It rose to the top ten in 2019 in the global Climate Change Performance Index from the thirty-first position five years ago. This index has been developed by Germanwatch and NewClimate Institute of Germany, together with the Climate Action Network-International (CAN).[16] According to a report by the NewClimate Institute, 'Among the G20 countries, India has the most ambitious NDC compared to its fair share of the global emissions budget in scenarios to limit warming to 1.5 degree Celsius.'[17] India is also the only country among the G20 nations that is close 1.5 degree Celsius temperature rise pathway and is deemed to be '2 degree Celsius compatible'.[18] The US, Russia, Turkey, Saudi Arabia and Argentina are rated 'critically insufficient' while China is 'highly insufficient', along with Japan, South Korea and South Africa. All the others fall in the 'insufficient' category.

India is also well on track to achieve its NDC targets. It has already reduced its emissions intensity by 21 per cent.[19] The share of renewables has reached 24 per cent. It has now announced that it will scale up renewables from 90 GW at present to 175 GW by 2022. But, there is potential and need for stronger action. India's power generation is still skewed in favour of fossil fuels. The share of coal, India's sole significant fuel source, is falling but the National Electricity Plan 2018 (NEP 2018) envisages adding an additional 46 GW capacity from coal by 2022. India's subsidy on fossil fuels in 2019 was US$ 13.4 billion, below only Mexico and China in the G20.[20] India is also falling behind in its goal of additional forest cover to absorb 2.5 to 3 billion tonnes of CO_2.

India's unwillingness to specify its target years has already exposed it to criticism. It will have to be prepared for relentless international pressure in the build-up to the twenty-sixth UNFCCC conference in Glasgow later this year. With BASIC weakened, it will have to largely depend on its own diplomatic skills. This calls for a more nuanced and restrained strategy. It will be unwise of India to revert to its vocal espousal of the rights of developing countries and the responsibilities of developed ones. Announcing one or both target years, even in the distant future, will greatly ease the situation for it. Even if this is not considered feasible at present, it should join others in championing green growth enthusiastically and concentrate on emphasising its own commitment and achievements instead of obstructing and getting isolated.

Endnotes

1. Michaelowa, Katharina and Axel. 'India in the international climate negotiations: From traditional nay-sayer to dynamic broker', University of Zurich: CIS Working Paper (No. 70, 2011) p. 6.
2. Dasgupta, C. 'The Climate Change Negotiations' in *Negotiating Climate Change: The Inside Story of the Rio Convention*, Stockholm Environment Institute (1994) p. 133.
3. The gases are carbon dioxide, methane, nitrous oxide, hydrofluorocarbons, perfluorocarbons and sulphur hexafluoride.
4. These were thirty-seven countries listed in Annexure I of the Protocol. Not all targets were for reduction. Some were permitted an increase.
5. Our World in Data is a research body based in Oxford University. www.ourworldindata.org
6. As on 4 September 2021 on the Green Climate Fund website. www.greenclimate.fund
7. World Meteorological Organization, 'The State of the Global Climate, 2020'. www.public.wmo.int.
8. World Meteorological Organization, Press Release No. 02122020, 2 December 2020.
9. IPCC Special Report, 'Global Warming of 1.5° C' (Chapter 2), October 2018.
10. Climate Transparency, Global Transparency Report, 2020, 'Climate Transparency is a global consortium based in Germany to study the climate action of G20 countries', p. 15. www.climate-transparency.org
11. UN Environment Programme, 'Emissions Gap Report 2020', 9 December 2020. www.unep.org
12. World Meteorological Organization, 'The State of the Global Climate 2020'. www.public.wmo.int
13. Biden, Joe. 'Executive Order on Tackling the Climate Crisis at Home and Abroad', The White House, 27 January 2021.
14. Kerry, John. *The Times of India*, New Delhi, 21 January 2021.
15. 'António Guterres on the United Nations in a fractured world'. Interview to Gideon Rachman, *Financial Times*, 27 January 2021.
16. 'India in top 10 performers on climate change index', *The Times of India*, New Delhi, 8 December 2020.
17. NewClimate Institute, Germany, 'Brown to Green Report 2019', p. 20.
18. Climate Transparency, 'Brown to Green Report 2019', p. 20.
19. Statement by Prakash Javadekar, Minister for Environment and Forests, "*India not responsible for climate change, contributes on 6.8% of global emissions – Javadekar*", The Print, 12 December 2020.
20. Climate Transparency, Global Transparency Report, 2020, p. 69.

CHAPTER 25

INDIA AND THE INTERNATIONAL FINANCIAL INSTITUTIONS IN THE POST-COVID-19 WORLD

AJIT KUMAR

At present, it seems difficult to visualise the post-Covid-19 world with the resurgence of the pandemic in several parts of the world, including India. However, increasing number of vaccines being produced by India and other countries gives hope for the future. Like most countries, the pandemic has led to a severe setback in all aspects of India's development and economy. The effect of Covid-19 has had devastating impact on the Indian economy, as it saw the largest contraction of the gross domestic product (GDP) in the first quarter of 2020-21 since the early 1990s. Before the pandemic, the economy was already decelerating. This is where the cooperation with international financial institutions (IFIs) is crucial for India, as it would be a strong catalyst for development and economic resurgence in the post-Covid-19 world. The IFIs have assisted India in the past and are continuing to play their roles according to their mandates and our requirements.

BACKGROUND

Like the founder member of the United Nations (UN) in 1945, colonial India was also an original member in 1944 at the UN Monetary and Financial Conference (also known as the Bretton Woods Conference) of the Bretton Woods

Institutions (BWIs)—the World Bank Group and the International Monetary Fund (IMF). The purpose of the BWIs was to rebuild the world's economic system in the aftermath of the Second World War. The key decisions leading to the establishment of the BWIs were taken largely by USA, and to a lesser extent by the UK. The BWIs' focus and programmes have evolved over the years.

The BWIs have been seen as an instrument of US-led Western countries, and their role has been continually debated. The rise of China and then the emerging markets, like India, has shifted the fulcrum of global economic growth, which can be seen as a challenge to the Western stranglehold over the BWIs. The 2008 financial crisis, in particular, led to the IMF focusing on the world economy in order to avoid its recurrence. The Bank also changed itself dramatically as the knowledge bank having development expertise. Its current aim is to eliminate poverty by 2030 and boost shared prosperity. It provides loans to development projects and direct budget support to governments as well as financial support to the private sector. Over the past seventy years, the BWIs have become the largest source of financial assistance to the developing countries, including India.

The Role of World Bank in India

It is necessary to examine the past and present work of the Bank and IMF, as well as other regional banks in India to understand their relevance in the post-Covid-19 world. India is a member of four of the five constituents of the World Bank Group—International Bank for Reconstruction and Development (IBRD), International Development Association (IDA), International Finance Corporation (IFC) and Multilateral Investment Guarantee Agency (MIGA). India is not a member of International Centre for Settlement of Investment Disputes (ICSID). India has been accessing funds from the World Bank—mainly through IBRD and IDA—for various development projects.

Over the last seventy years, India has been the largest recipient of World Bank loans—US$ 103 billion (US$ 53 billion, IBRD, and US$ 50 billion, IDA).

The Bank's assistance programmes are guided by the Country Partnership Framework (CPF), which sets out how the Bank proposed to build a growing partnership with the Government of India (GoI). India is the Bank's largest client and one of its oldest partners.

Given the complex nature of the biggest challenges facing India, the Bank's CPF for 2018-22 adopted a multisectoral approach. The CPF has noted that half of India's population is under the age of twenty-five with twelve million young people entering the workforce every year. It has made building human capital as the core pillar of the new strategy. It has adopted a life-cycle approach, building the health, nutrition, education and skills of India's vast pool of young people to provide workforce for an emerging middle-income nation.

It may be noted that in many of the Bank's programmes on several projects, it is the GoI which is the main financer. The Bank supplements the crucial remaining finances. One of the recent successes of the Bank's assistance in this regard has been for the Golden Quadrilateral highway programme. It also provided technical assistance to complete the project. In the field of education, the Bank has provided more than US$ 1,000 million to support and finance the Sarva Shiksha Abhiyaan. Similarly, in infrastructure, it has invested US$ 1.8 billion which has converted 35,000 kms of rural roads to the benefit of eight million people.

To cite some other examples of the Bank's assistance to India in the healthcare sector, it has provided US$ 125 million to the Uttarakhand Health Systems Development Project, where the local government funded the remaining US$ 25 million. The project, to be completed in September 2023, has been moderately satisfactory so far. Also, the Bank assisted in Tamil Nadu Health Systems Project with the funding of US$ 210 million, resulting in highly satisfactory healthcare outcome, patient satisfaction and financial protection.

The Bank has realised the importance of the Indian states and has worked with them to address their development priorities. This is necessary, as the finances of some of the states are in a precarious situation. Today, the Bank is supporting India's development programmes with the funding of US$ 27 billion spread over more than 100 projects, together with a large volume of analytical and advisory services. Over the next CPF period, ending in 2022, the Bank expects to deliver US$ 25-30 billion financing to India.

India has appreciated the support of the World Bank for the many significant achievements India had made in its development process, including infrastructure, such as electric power, transport, communication, irrigation projects and the steel industry.

The Bank's Assistance for Covid-19

By end of June 2020, the Bank approved US$ 2.75 billion in emergency lending to support India's response to the Covid-19 crisis. The Bank responded by closely supporting the GoI strategy of tackling the pandemic in three phases. In the first phase, the Bank partnered with the GoI to support its immediate healthcare needs. The second phase saw a programme to help the poor and vulnerable communities deeply affected by the pandemic. The third phase was about economic stabilisation and included a Bank-supported project for micro, small and medium enterprises (MSMEs).

International Finance Corporation (IFC)

The IFC country head in India had stated that the Indian economy had evolved to a level where private sector could be counted on to close large developmental gaps. Over the past few years, the IFC has augmented its portfolio in India, improving profitability and investing in high-impact projects. India represents IFC's single largest country exposure and it has committed US$ 3.6 billion in India. The IFC has scaled up its presence in low-income states and north-eastern states by investing US$ 450 million in the past two and half financial years. It has also scaled up its portfolio in infrastructure by 30 to 40 per cent which now accounts for US$ 1.1 billion of its current committed portfolio of about US$ 3.6 billion in India. This is important, as deficit in infrastructure is one of the key factors impeding India's economy and development.

World Bank Reforms

There is a need to reform the Bank to support India's economic growth. It would be better for the Bank to change its lending strategy, from one of condition-based aid to that of development partnership. These conditions have attracted criticism of the Bank. The Bank also has influence over donors—they did not support India's proposal to borrow from the BWIs because of its nuclear tests in 1998 and the Gujarat riots of 2002. As a result, India stopped accepting assistance from several countries in 2002. The need is for the developing countries to have a greater say over the use of aid, within the framework of democratic ownership. India had also opposed conditions sought by the Bank for lending because it could end up increasing the cost of doing business with the Bank.

The dominance by the developed countries and the US remains in place. The developed countries would continue to dominate the BWIs because, by convention, the appointment of the Bank and IMF heads are from the US and Europe while Japan appoints the head of the Asian Development Bank (ADB). Though the developing countries represent over 80 per cent of the world's population and the Bank's membership where almost all of its loans are disbursed, the developed countries continue to hold the majority of voting power. India had indicated in the past that it was ready to take on a larger share of the World Bank governance based on its growing economy and population and supported developing countries' role in governance of the Bank. India had demanded a fundamental reform of voting structure, which was necessary for the credibility and legitimacy of the Bank.

Finally, in April 2010, the World Bank had approved the general capital increase and selective capital increase for the IBRD after which the voting power of the developing countries in IBRD would increase by 3.13 per cent to reach 47.19 per cent of the total voting power at the IBRD. India's voting power increased to 2.91 per cent from 2.77 per cent and it would become the seventh largest shareholder in IBRD from the present—eleventh largest shareholder. It is still not over 3 per cent.

International Monetary Fund (IMF)

The IMF keeps track of the economy globally and lends to countries with balance of payments difficulties and provides practical help to members. Countries have to join the IMF to be eligible to join the Bank. The IMF works to foster global monetary cooperation, secure financial stability, facilitate international trade, promote high employment and sustainable economic growth and reduce poverty around the world. But the basic purpose of the IMF is to ensure the stability of the international monetary system—the system of exchange rates and international payments that enables the countries to transact with each other. Both the Bank and IMF have 190 members. Therefore, the IMF provides short-term financial assistance to developing countries, while the World Bank provides long-term development goals.

While the purposes of the IMF remain unchanged, its operations—surveillance, financial assistance and technical assistance—have developed with the changing needs of its member countries in an evolving world economy, especially after being affected by the global economic crisis of 2008, which it failed to anticipate.

The Board of Governors is the highest decision-making body of the IMF, consisting of one governor and one alternate governor for each member country. The governor is appointed by the member country and is usually the minister of finance or the governor of the central bank. All powers of the IMF are vested in the Board of Governors. The Board of Governors may delegate to the executive board all, except certain, reserved powers. The day-to-day management of the IMF is carried out by the managing director. The Board of Executive Directors, consisting of twenty-four directors appointed/elected by member countries/group of countries, is the executive body of the IMF, of which the managing director is the chairman.

India and the IMF

India's current quota in the IMF of the Special Drawing Rights (SDRs) is 13,114 which is 2.76 per cent of the total and the voting percentage is 2.63.

India had accepted the obligations of Article VIII of the IMF Articles of Agreement on current account convertibility on 20 August 1994. India has subscribed to the IMF's special data dissemination standard.

Unlike the World Bank, India has not been a frequent user of IMF resources. In 1981-84, India had borrowed SDR 3.9 billion to respond to its Balance of Payment problems on two occasions. Again, during 1991-93, it borrowed an amount of SDR 3.56 billion—SDR 2.2 billion under two standby arrangements, and in 1991, it borrowed SDR 1.4 billion under the compensatory financing facility.

India repaid all the loans taken from the IMF on 31 May 2000. In fact, it is now a contributor to the IMF.

Under Article IV of the IMF's Articles of Agreement, the IMF holds bilateral discussions with members, usually every year, to review the economic status of the member countries. The Article IV consultations are generally held in two phases. With India, the IMF mission holds discussions with the Reserve Bank of India (RBI) and various relevant ministries/departments of the central government. The last round of the annual Article IV consultation with the IMF was held on 23 December 2019. These consultations are useful for India, as IMF experts carry out analytical work on the Indian economy.

In recent years, the Fund has provided India with technical assistance in a number of areas, including the development of the government securities market, foreign exchange market reforms, public expenditure management, tax and customs administration, and strengthening statistical systems in connection with special data dissemination standard. Since 1981, the IMF Institute has provided training to Indian officials in national accounts, tax administration, balance of payment compilation, monetary policy and other areas. In 2004, the GoI approved IMF's proposal for setting up a joint training programme at the National Institute of Bank Management, Pune. The first training programme was held in July 2006 under the coordination of the RBI. The institute caters to participants from regional countries, especially those from the South Asian Association for Regional Cooperation (SAARC) countries.

Criticisms

The IMF has been criticised for its governance structure, particularly the reallocation of quotas (and thus votes) as well as the composition of the chairs at the IMF executive board. Although four developing countries, including India, have been placed among the top ten IMF shareholders, the current formula to determine the relative position of an economy in the world is flawed and over-represents several developed nations despite their declining share in the world's GDP, especially after the global financial crisis of 2008.

The present distribution of seats in the Executive Board in favour of Europe may have reflected their economic weight in early years of the IMF, but today, there is a clear economic shift from Europe to the emerging market economies like India and China. In fact, till some years back, Belgium had more votes than China. Also, enhancing developing countries' voice in the IMF decision-making would translate into better-suited IMF loan conditionality.

Devised in a post-war colonial era, the BWIs' governance structure has not adequately adapted to the new norms of democracy, transparency and accountability. The BWIs' criticism is basically of democratic governance—structural under-representation of the South, undermining democratic ownership, inconsistent and biased decision-making and weak ability to learn from past mistakes.

So, the global financial institutions, including the BWIs, should adapt their governance and decision-making structures and processes to reflect the growing influential role of developing countries in the global political and economic arena. The BWIs, as global economic governance institutions, have to change. Reform is essential not only for developing countries, but also for the continued legitimacy and global relevance of these institutions. The BWIs need to take a closer look at themselves—whether they continue to be relevant as development actors or not.

Asian Development Bank (ADB)

The ADB is one of the regional multilateral development banks. India is a founder member of ADB and is now the bank's fourth largest shareholder. India has been ADB's top borrower.

The ADB's country partnership strategy 2018-22 for India aims to accelerate the country's inclusive economic transformation by building industrial competitiveness, creating jobs, accelerating growth of low-income states and addressing environmental and climate change challenges.

Since the ADB began co-financing operations in 1987, sovereign co-financing commitments for India have amounted to US$ 4.09 billion for thirty-six investment projects and US$ 136.12 million for 126 technical assistance projects. Non-sovereign co-financing for India has amounted to US$ 2.97 billion for twenty-six investment projects and US$ 1 million for two technical assistance projects.

The ADB's country partnership strategy for India is closely aligned with government's development priorities and transformative programmes, as it works closely with the Department of Economic Affairs. The ADB would continue to focus on support for industrial corridor development; national road safety; micro, small and medium size enterprises; the Jal Jeevan Mission; and logistics efficiency and urban transport, including metro rail and rapid rail transit system. The ADB would also expand its support to social sectors, such as national education and healthcare programmes. It would also specifically seek to accelerate efforts for financial leveraging to attract private investments and promote local resource mobilisation.

The ADB's considerable autonomy has been more accommodative towards India. One was impressed with the commitment and focus towards India when one visited ADB in 2019 to meet some officials.

India has appreciated the assistance provided by the ADB in its fight against

Covid-19 and urged it to increase the quantum of lending and private sector operation with a view to ameliorate poverty and for employment generation. In 2021, the finance minister, in the last ADB meeting, had stated that India had the absorptive capacity to receive about US$ 4 billion a year from sovereign operation and about US$ 1.5 billion annually from the private sector financing window. She also thanked the ADB for its timely and valuable support to India for the Covid-19 fight and that its loan assisted in the budget support to GOI for the increased public spending in boosting healthcare infrastructure and contributing to social support measures.

The ADB had provided US$ 1.5 billion counter-cyclical facility and US$ 3.00 million from Asia-Pacific Disaster Relief Fund, besides the regional technical assistance for the healthcare sector to fight Covid-19. One of the core strengths of the ADB had been its political neutrality, and it has a proven record of consensus decision-making and a history of effective project implementation and successful outcome.

New Development Bank

A consequence of the BWIs not sufficiently reforming led to the creation of new regional banks, such as the New Development Bank (NDB), created by the BRICS—Brazil, Russia, India, China, South Africa—summit in 2014 in Brazil. The objective of the NDB is to mobilise resources for infrastructure and sustainable development projects in BRICS countries and other developing countries, in addition to the existing efforts of multilateral and regional financial institutions to support the global growth and development. Headquartered in China, the NDB was founded with an authorised capital of US$ 100 billion and initial subscribed capital of US$ 50 billion, with contributions equally distributed between the five founding members of BRICS.

Like with the World Bank, India has availed the largest amount of loans from the NDB. It is managed by a Board of Directors and a Board of Governors, both composed of five seats, each occupied by the founding countries. The presidency of the bank is rotating and is periodically occupied by a representative of one of the BRICS members. The first president of the NDB was KV Kamath of India. Since its foundation, it has signed memorandums of understanding (MOUs) and cooperation agreements with several multilateral and national development banks, besides national commercial banks. Therefore, the BRICS Bank could be seen more as a complement and not a substitute for the existing financial institutions in both public and private sectors. It has helped to strengthen the voice of developing and emerging economies in the development finance architecture.

In December 2020, the GoI and NDB signed a loan for lending US$ 1 billion for supporting India's economic recovery from Covid-19 by supporting India's economic expenditure on rural infrastructure related to natural resource management and rural employment generation under the GoI's Mahatma Gandhi National Rural Employment Generation Scheme (MGNREGS).

While the NDB is a useful value addition for the global South, the current tense relations between India and China do not augur well for the NDB. The two big economies of the BRICS—India and China—have to rise above their differences to make NDB more relevant for the developing world. Moreover, both India and China have their own aid programmes assisting the developing countries.

Conclusion

The IMF in July 2021 reduced India's GDP growth to 9.5 per cent for 2021-22 from its earlier estimate of 12.5 per cent, citing the impact of second Covid wave on the economy and the recovery process. The IMF also projected India's GDP growth at 8.5 per cent in 2022-23, which would make India retain the tag of the fastest growing major economy. However, with the possibility of the third Covid wave and as the pandemic has caused enormous damage to India's economy and development—also India's challenges are really complex—the BWIs could play a useful role in assisting India's economic development in the post-Covid-19 world. The BWIs could learn from India's own development strategy to assist developing countries. The basic principle in India's development partnership is respecting the development partners and be guided by their development priorities.

The BWIs remain among the significant influencers of the international development and financial landscape. The World Bank, ADB and NDB have given emergency loans of billions of dollars to India to fight the pandemic.

The fact that India is the largest democracy in the world, representing one-sixth of humanity, the third biggest economy based on purchasing parity, having the fourth largest foreign exchange reserves and a member of G20 and as a global player, it deserves more voting rights in the BWIs. At present, they do not reflect the contemporary reality. The BWIs need radical reforms to give the rightful place to India.

It is true that India continues to benefit from the harmonious relations with the World Bank, being its largest client and a net creditor to IMF—it should continue its beneficial relations with the IFIs, including ADB and NDB, in order to meet the enormous challenges to the Indian economy in the post-Covid-19 world.

References

1. World Bank in India—Country Partnership Framework, 2018-22.
2. South Centre, 'Reform of World Bank Governance Structures', – Analytical Note, September 2007.
3. Bhasin, Niti and Gupta, Surbhi. 'Reforms in International Monetary Fund (IMF): Challenges and the Road Ahead, *Management and Economics Research Journal*, vol. 4, 2018.
4. Sehrawat, Vivek. 'Reforming the World Bank to transform India', *Law Review*, October 2017.
5. Singh, Anoop. 'IMF Reforms Still Not Enough' Gateway House: Indian Council on Global Relations, March 2016.
6. Bretton Woods Project, 'What are the main criticisms of the World Bank and the IMF?', June 2019.
7. Kapur, Devesh and Subramanian, Arvind. 'Can the World Bank Redeem Itself?' *East African Business Week News*, March, 2021.
8. Kapur, Devesh. 'The World Bank is like a "Slow" Old Ship', October 2015.
9. Srinivas, V. *India's Relations with the International Monetary Fund*, (Vij Books, India), 2019.
10. FLP Goncalves, et. al, 'New Development Bank', BRICS Policy Center, January 2018.
11. Asian Development Bank, 'Asian Development Bank and India: Fact Sheet', October 2020.

CHAPTER 26

INDIA AND THE WORLD TRADE ORGANIZATION @ 26 AND BEYOND

ANJALI PRASAD

The World Trade Organization (WTO) is presently going through perhaps the most turbulent phase of its twenty-six-year existence. Its architecture, structure and principles have been under attack by the developed and some developing countries over almost the last decade.

The onset of the Covid-19 pandemic and its catastrophic effect on the global economy is bound to make the dynamics in the WTO more difficult. All countries and sectors have been negatively impacted to a greater or lesser degree. But more than the numbers, it has seriously impacted the psyche of nations. Every country is dealing in its own way with the insecurity of excessive interdependence caused by the spate of indiscriminate, unbridled globalisation in the recent past.

The pandemic has not directly impacted the state of play except that developing countries, led by South Africa and India, have sought a waiver to suspend provisions of the Agreement on Trade Related Intellectual Property Rights (TRIPS) that could hinder prevention, containment or treatment of Covid-19.[1] This is a genuine pandemic-related proposal. However, the developed countries, notably the United States of America (USA), the European Union (EU), Japan and Switzerland, have blocked progress on it. The deadlock continues. As a result, trade rules have hindered rather than facilitated access to life saving medicine and equipment for the least developed and many developing countries. On the other hand, developed countries can very much be expected to use trade rules to get themselves out of the crisis. The process has already begun, with developed countries using the pandemic as an excuse to push long-standing pre-Covid contentious issues as well as 'new issues' for rule-making in the WTO.

In order to understand the post-Covid situation, the current state of play in the WTO and India's overall role will need to be analysed.

India is a founder member of the WTO (1995) as it was of the General Agreement on Tariffs and Trade (GATT, 1947), underlining its strong stake in an equitable, rule-based multilateral trading system. India values and stands by the core principles established in the GATT and that continue to form the foundation of the WTO—non-discrimination (most favoured nation treatment; national treatment); equity (special and differential [S&D] treatment for developing and least-developed countries [LDCs]) and decision making by consensus. Consensus is at the heart of the WTO's functioning as it gives every member—small or big, rich or poor—equal weight and voice in the decision-making.

Current State of Play: Towards 'Neo-globalisation'?

It is the whole system and its core principles that have been under attack.

The 2007-2008 global downturn on the one hand and the relative resilience and rise of the so-called 'large' developing countries on the other, appear to have been the trigger. Among these was especially one that was perceived to have manipulated the WTO system to become the top manufacturing and trading nation of the world. In the very recent past, this perception has led to calls for 'reform of the unfair trading system'. 'We cannot have free and open trade if some countries exploit the system at the expense of others',[2] is the underlying narrative.

The 'Reform' Agenda

It is highly unlikely that this push for the 'reform' of the multilateral trading system based on the so-called 'large' or 'advanced developing country' narrative, will be given up or even mellowed down, with the regime change in the USA, as the narrative had in fact been initiated under the same regime in its previous term. It has now taken fairly concrete shape with positions on both sides, the opponents being other developing countries including India, Africa Group, Bolivia, Cuba[3] and on the issue of S&D treatment, China as well.[4] Under the garb of 'strengthening and modernising the WTO'[5]; 'strengthening the deliberative function of the WTO'[6]; creating 'an undifferentiated WTO'[7]; and others, the attempt is to weaken or even dismantle the fundamental principles of consensus, the special and differential treatment for developing countries and the dispute settlement architecture. The latter is seen by some powerful developed members as going against them in more cases than they can reasonably accept.

The tenth Ministerial Conference (MC 10) at Nairobi (December 2015) proved to be a watershed in the developed countries' attempt to open up crucial fundamental rules of the WTO. Their attempt failed at Geneva (November 2015) in the run-up to the Nairobi conference as there was strong pushback from the Africa Group, China, India and other developing countries. However, in the Ministerial at Nairobi (December 2015), they managed to insert in the Ministerial Declaration language that gave them an opening to 'identify and discuss other issues for negotiation', 'explore new architectures' and state their belief that 'new approaches are necessary to achieve meaningful outcomes in multilateral negotiations'.[8] At the behest of developing countries, the fact that there are differences among the membership on each of these issues was underlined.

Also, consensus was reaffirmed as the bedrock principle for launching multilateral negotiations on 'other issues'.

This meant that there could be two tracks in the WTO. One in line with the rule book, dealing with existing issues and routine functions; the other involving the discussion, exploration and even pushing in new subjects, new architecture and new modes of negotiation. Given the reluctance of many developing countries on the so-called 'other/new' issues, the attempt by the proponents quite clearly is to bypass the requirement of consensus, and bring in rules and commitments through the backdoor by stretching the interpretation of existing rules if necessary.

MC 11 (Buenos Aires, December 2017), gave concrete shape to these attempts through the Joint Ministerial Statements by groups of members on the sidelines of the conference.

New Issues

These statements pertain to e-commerce,[9] investment facilitation,[10] MSMEs[11] and services domestic regulation.[12] There was also a Joint Declaration on Trade and Women's Economic Empowerment.[13] All the joint statements, using varying terminology, provide for 'exploratory'/'structured discussions' towards future WTO negotiations. The Declaration on Women, presently, seems confined to information sharing on participation of women in public procurement markets.

The US, notably, was formally party only to the joint statement on e-commerce at MC 11. Recently, they have become party to what is now called the Joint Initiative on Services, Domestic Regulation and are seeking conclusion of negotiations by MC 12 (Twelfth Ministerial Conference, Geneva, December 2021). India and South Africa are among the major developing countries not party to any of these.

Needless to say, the WTO is a rule-making and enforcing organisation. That discussions within the WTO can be of a development promotion, information sharing or exploratory nature, is far from the reality. Quite predictably, therefore, these joint statements, now Joint Statement Initiatives (JSI), are currently proceeding as plurilaterals,[14] as there is still no consensus for multilateral negotiations on these issues. In services, there is an attempt to harvest and multilateralise the outcome through a pragmatic interpretation of existing rules.

These so-called new initiatives have, in a way, changed the complexion and penetration of the trading system. Hitherto trade rules were, by and large, confined to border measures. But these 'new initiatives' are far more intrusive in a country's economic policy space, and have implications far more serious than border measures. For instance, on MSMEs, the rules will go down to the sub-national entity level whereas multilateral trade rules generally were conceived to operate between nations. India opposed a draft Ministerial Declaration on MSMEs in the General Council meetings in October, November and December 2015 in the run-up to MC 10.[15] It also blocked investment facilitation in the General Council meeting on 10 May 2017.[16] As a result, there could be no multilateral consensus on these issues at that stage.

Subsequent developments, though, make it seem that every activity, even women's empowerment, is so directly trade related that it could fall within the remit of WTO rule-making. This is increasingly the trend, probably because the WTO is one organisation which has teeth in the form of its dispute settlement system. Thus, it appears that, through the WTO, the developed world looks to control the markets and resource suppliers, that they so critically need to propel and sustain their own survival and growth. Uncomfortable and negative as it may sound, this is the 'new globalisation' that seems to be taking shape.

The Unfinished Doha Agenda

Besides the 'reform' agenda and the 'new issues', there are the pending issues already under negotiation (the Doha Development Agenda [DDA] issues) where the demandeur developing countries, including India, are seeking to level the playing field hitherto tilted in favour of the developed countries in the Uruguay Round. With the rules being more or less in their favour, the developed countries have no interest in taking the DDA negotiations forward. They are seeking instead to lock in rules in new areas, as detailed above, to further their development, while curtailing the policy space for developing countries before they are even able to enter it.

The Secretariat: Neutral or 'Surrogate Proponent'[17]

In this entire scenario, the role of the WTO Secretariat cannot be ignored. Over the past few years, particularly, the Secretariat has played a highly partisan, proactive role—bypassing rules, making processes difficult, especially for the less than powerful, thereby undermining the member-driven character of the organisation.

Hence, it has been called out on various occasions for deviating from mandated procedures to acting like proponents of new issues.

Existential Crisis

This is broadly the landscape in which India finds itself in the WTO today. India is not new to navigating multilateral trade negotiations with the vast range of issues and members with varied interests. But, currently, the situation is different as the very foundation of the system we have been used to working in since 1947 are under attack. It would not be an overstatement to say that the WTO, as it was constructed in 1995, is, for the first time in its twenty-six years, facing a serious existential crisis.

Under these circumstances, India will perhaps need a reset of strategy vis-a-vis its interlocutors, the Secretariat and its negotiating interests.

India in the WTO

Despite its small and relatively stagnant share in world merchandise trade (around 2 per cent 1948-2019)[18] and trade in commercial services (about 3 per cent in 2019),[19] India has been a major player in the multilateral trading system since its inception. This is perhaps mainly for two reasons.

Strong yet Vulnerable

The first reason is its large growing market. With over 1.37 billion people, 1 out of approximately every 6 persons in the world lives in India. According to a UN Report,[20] India is expected to become the most populous country by 2027 and remain the most populous with nearly 1.5 billion till the end of the century. To put it in perspective, it is currently the population size of about 4 USAs or 5 Indonesias or 6 Brazils. The middle class, a major driver of the market, is estimated to be about 200 million in itself, which is about eight times the total population of Australia.[21] Thus, no matter how small its share in world trade, the pull of its market potential makes India commercially very important in the WTO. And this position can be expected to continue despite the recent developments towards neo-globalisation.

The second reason is its historical credibility with many developing countries. India, like every other member, is needed for a consensus on any decision in the WTO. Many developing and small economies look up to members like India to safeguard the integrity of the rules-based system. This is not to say that India can claim to have a leadership role. Yet, it is perceived to have the strength to be able to gather a group of countries or even stand alone to obstruct a consensus. Hence, influential members and the Secretariat consider it prudent to take India along as far as possible. As such, India has almost always been at the high table (the Green Room) in all major negotiations.

However, socio-economic vulnerabilities put India in a unique and difficult position as far as negotiating interests are concerned. On the one hand, it is a large economy in terms of overall GDP, population and market size. On the other hand, its large-scale poverty, extreme income inequality, poor socio-economic parameters and volatile geopolitical environment make India quite vulnerable.

India's GDP per capita is US$ 2,104,[22] which is below the World Bank's lower middle-income category average of US$ 2,177 and the world average of US$ 11,429. About 139 million or 10.4 per cent Indians (close to Russia's total population of 140 million and more than Mexico's 120 million and Japan's 125 million) lived below the international poverty line of US$ 1.90 per day per capita in 2017.[23] India ranks 129th among 189 countries in the UNDP Human Development Index (2019), which tracks many life and death parameters other than just income.

Despite being so high on 'vulnerability scale', India is one of the targets of the 'advanced developing country' and 'graduation' narrative in the WTO. The implication being either case-by-case special and differential treatment or a complete graduation out of it. This is almost ridiculous when countries like Singapore, with a GDP per capita being as high as US$ 65,233 (higher than the USA's US$ 65,118),[24] call themselves 'developing'. Logically and objectively, India does not qualify for developed country status by any standard.

Negotiating Alliances

Negotiations of alliances in the WTO are not necessarily along 'developed–developing' lines but are a function of a complex set of factors. Developed and 'developed developing countries', like Singapore, generally are together. But for many developing countries and LDCs, factors like bilateral proximity to the proponents; dependence through preferential trading arrangements; historical relations; current geopolitical dynamics; and the leanings of the regime in power. Moreover, various sub-categories have been created among developing countries and LDCs, like small and vulnerable economies (SVEs); net food importing developing countries (NFIDCs) and others. In addition, there are issue-based as well as regional cross-cutting alliances. Hence, in this web of complex alliances, it is difficult for any one country to be a leader or pivot around which a large group gets together. Nevertheless, success in a negotiation is very much contingent upon numbers as it is on power. The developed countries led by the USA and EU definitely exert influence not only on the less powerful but also on the Secretariat, which, generally, manipulates in their favour.

India, because of its distinctive profile, often has equally distinctive and sometimes difficult negotiating interests. In such situations, it finds itself alone or with a small number of supporting developing countries and LDCs. South

Africa has generally articulated almost similar positions on most issues and so have some other countries in the Africa Group and Latin America.

However, backchannel bilateral political pressures have often weakened India's positions, especially in the run-up to and at the final stages of negotiations. Such climbdown has undoubtedly dented India's credibility, as India is generally the major player representing defensive developing country interests at the high table in the Ministerials.

Just as India is important for the WTO, so is the WTO important for India because of the stability and predictability that the rules provide, against the vagaries of distorted and manipulated markets. India, on its part, engages fully and constructively in all WTO processes. It is seen as more defensive than offensive in the positions it takes on most issues. However, given the vulnerabilities of its socio-economic structure, what is perceived as defensive from a global viewpoint is from India's viewpoint its offensive interest.

The Challenges and the Foreseeable Future

It is evident from the current state of play, that the WTO faces serious challenges, at least in the immediate future and the medium term.

The Covid-19 Impact

The developed country demand for liberalisation of developing country markets in health products and agriculture and the ban on export restrictions in agriculture would adversely affect their food and health security. The push for new digital trade rules would severely restrict if not close the policy space in the digital sector before developing countries have even entered it. Hence to pushback on this set of issues—not directly related to the pandemic—is the immediate challenge, for developing countries.

On the other side is the challenge of securing the directly pandemic related TRIPS waiver.

Additionally, developing countries are trying to take measures to strengthen their strategic sectors using security and general exceptions in the goods area, especially health products, and export restrictions for health and food security purposes. Developed countries are in any case using a variety of measures, including subsidies (otherwise prohibited), to strengthen their strategic and employment-generating sectors.[25] More and more such measures are likely to be seen in the foreseeable future.

'AatmaNirbhar Bharat' (self-dependent India) is India's response to the situation created by deindustrialising, dehumanising and inequitable globalisation. Unfortunately, however, it has taken a pandemic for this realisation not only in India but across the world. India also needs to take urgent measures to strengthen domestic production. Given the vulnerability of over 90 per cent of our very large population and the geopolitical situation around us, it would be most inadvisable to be dependent on global supply chains for food and health security and other strategic sectors. India, for instance, cannot be a pharmacy for itself let alone a 'pharmacy of the world' if we are import dependent to the extent of about 70 per cent for active pharmaceutical ingredients.

Given the current WTO landscape, our interests can only be secured if we build economic and strategic strength. India and other like-minded developing countries should use all the exceptions, ambiguities and flexibilities available in the WTO rules without hesitation or fear of retaliation as developed countries are doing so themselves. Resource-short developing countries can find taking such measures difficult, on their own. Working together and putting in place sustainable arrangements among themselves could be an option worth exploring.

The directly Covid-19 related TRIPS waiver is undoubtedly the most critical issue in the very immediate timeframe. But, the 'reform' narrative and 'new issues' remain centre stage. In fact, the Covid-19 impact is likely to strengthen developed country attempts to fast-track them. This is exactly what appears to be happening as 'substantial progress' is being reported by participating members on the JSI towards some sort of ministerial declarations/decisions in MC 12. On the other hand, deep differences continue to block the TRIPS waiver as developing countries struggle to deal with the pandemic.

While the push for further market opening in developing countries and restriction of their policy space in existing and new areas would be strengthened on the back of the pandemic, increasing protectionism will be seen in developed countries through the use of non-tariff barriers for goods and cross-border flow of services. The worst type of protectionism in the form of 'vaccine nationalism' can already be seen as developed countries hoard vaccines and other critical supplies through advance purchase agreements and export bans. In an interconnected world, no country is safe if the pandemic continues in another part of the world. Where will the developed countries get the markets and resources if the pandemic continues to decimate the very sources they plan to exploit is the question they need to ask themselves.

The role of the Secretariat in handling these challenges will be under the scanner. The existing trust deficit is bound to make their task difficult. However, given past experience, it is unlikely that the Secretariat can be as balanced and neutral as the rules mandate it to be.

The Fundamental Principles Challenge: An 'Undifferentiated WTO'?

India and other like-minded developing countries and LDCs face the serious challenge of safeguarding the fundamental principles on which the institution stands. Any negotiation involves compromises. The WTO was created with the developing countries ceding significant policy space in return for keeping the fundamental principles intact. If the compromises envisaged in future negotiations 'are blatantly asymmetrical to be almost devoid of logic, the process, fragile as it is, could suffer a breakdown'.[26]

A very strong alliance of developing countries and LDCs is the need of the hour. Currently, the attack is only on dispensations for developing countries. But, LDCs should also join this rearguard action as it will not be long before they are also targeted. It must be remembered that the developed countries are ultimately aiming at an 'undifferentiated WTO'. If they succeed, the developing countries and LDCs will lose the equitable protection of rules and an equal voice. It will become like any other organisation driven entirely by the powerful and for the powerful, but more potent because of the dispute settlement system.

Slowing Down 'Neo-globalisation'

The other major challenge is to slow down the neo-globalisation attempts—'new issues', 'new architecture', 'new ways of negotiation'—in the wake of increasing deindustrialisation at home; non-tariff barriers in developed countries; barriers to services trade from developing countries through pernicious trade and investment rules and hostile supply chains in the wake of territorial conflict or emergencies like a pandemic. What will also have to be done is to oppose rules that obstruct policy space in critical areas like food security, health security and other strategic sectors, and in fact counterpose rules that strengthen access to food and health security and other development imperatives.

A possible broad-brush counter could be a demand by developing countries and LDCs for an objective review of the extent to which the WTO has delivered on ensuring that 'developing countries, and especially the least developed among them, secure a share in the growth in international trade commensurate with the needs of their economic development".[27] In order to 'reform' any system there must be a performance appraisal at the outset. A 'reform' cannot be based just on the perception of a certain constituency, but rather on objective criteria. Developing countries and LDCs could ask for such a performance appraisal as a prerequisite to discussing any 'reform'. An appropriate proposal could be put forth preparatory to MC 12. This is also important to do before the ambit of the WTO is expanded to new and more intrusive areas. If inequities have persisted or grown further, which prima facie appears to be the case, there is hardly any justification to expand the WTO's ambit without first arriving at equitable outcomes in the core areas that are yet to be addressed, rather than cherry picking new areas of developed country interest.

All these are major challenges, which will require issue-based concerted push back from developing countries and LDCs, on the one hand, and proactive attempts to push a pro-developing country offensive agenda, on the other. India, South Africa and other like-minded countries will possibly have to take the lead.

Conclusion

The WTO is, presently, in a most difficult phase in its history. The membership and the Secretariat will have to balance developing country and LDC imperatives for development policy space, especially food and health security, vis-à-vis the developed country push for pure commercial gains. The choice between life and commercial gain is obvious. If developing countries fail to secure even their basic interests and perceive the Secretariat also as being party to their failure, the trust deficit will widen. The WTO will, unfortunately, be the weaker for it.

In her acceptance speech in February 2021, the incoming director general of the WTO said inter alia, that 'the WTO is about people ...'.[28] It must be understood that the WTO is not only about powerful people but also the less powerful and marginalised. The manner in which the interests of both are balanced will determine whether the WTO emerges stronger or weaker from the current crisis.

Being at the high table during the negotiations, India has a major role to play in securing developing country interests. But given the alliance dynamics in the WTO, India might often have to be the lone strong voice with a few small allies. Even so, we should not be seen as backtracking under so-called geopolitical backchannel pressures. A red line, based on national and common developing country interests, is a red line. We should not be shy of facing flak for standing firm on our red lines from interlocutors however powerful. The lights of the WTO have gone off (because of India, July 2014) and come back on in the past.[29] They will go off and come back on in the future as well. But if India backtracks from bread-and-butter and life-and-death issues, then it could cause irreparable damage not only to our developing and LDC constituency, but especially to our large vulnerable domestic constituency that reposes faith and sends its negotiators to raise their voice on its behalf. We should draw strength from the fact that, perhaps, the powerful need India more than India needs them.

ENDNOTES

1. IP/C/W/669, 2 October 2020: Waiver from certain provisions of the TRIPS Agreement...: India, South Africa, Kenya, Eswatini, Pakistan, Mozambique, Bolivia.
2. President Trump at the World Economic Forum, Davos, January 2018 as reported in the Washington Trade Daily, 29 January 2018.
3. JOB/GC/218/Rev. 2 etc., 26 July 2019: An Inclusive Approach to Transparency and Notification Requirements in the WTO: Africa Group, Cuba, India, Oman; WT/GC/W/778/Rev. 3, 4 December 2020: Strengthening the WTO to Promote Development and Inclusivity: Africa Group, Cuba, India.
4. WT/GC/202, 9 October 2019: Statement on Special and Differential Treatment to Promote Development: Africa Group, Bolivia, China, Cuba, India, Oman.
5. JOB/GC/201, 24 September 2018, Canada.
6. JOB/GC/211, 14 December 2018, Canada.
7. WT/GC/W/757/Rev1, 14 February 2019, USA.
8. WT/MIN (15)/DEC, 19 December 2015, Nairobi Ministerial Declaration.
9. WT/MIN (17)/60, 13 December 2017, Joint Statement on Electronic Commerce by 44/164 Members.
10. WT/MIN (17)/59, 13 December 2017, Joint Ministerial Statement on Investment Facilitation for Development by 42/164 Members.
11. WT/MIN (17)/58, 13 December 2017, Joint Ministerial Statement—Declaration on the Establishment of WTO Informal Work Programme for MSMEs by 57/164 Members.

12. WT/MIN (17)/61, 13 December 2017, Joint Ministerial Statement on Services Domestic Regulation by 32/164 Members.
13. 118 WTO members and observers supported it.
14. These plurilaterals are outside the legal framework as even plurilaterals within the agreement have to be approved by the membership by consensus.
15. WT/GC/M/160, 13 November and 7 December 2015, General Council.
16. WT/GC/M/167, 10 and 18 May 2017, General Council.
17. SUNS #8511, 27 July 2017, TNC Meeting, Uganda.
18. WTO: International Trade Statistics.
19. Ibid
20. United Nations, *World Population Prospects 2019*, New York.
21. Estimates based on World Bank population data.
22. 2019 World Bank, on current US$.
23. World Bank Poverty and Equity Brief: South Asia, October 2020.
24. World Bank 2019.
25. As compiled in the South Centre Policy Brief No. 77, May 2020, 'The EU Roadmap for Recovery' states inter alia, 'The Covid-19 pandemic has shown the pressing need to produce critical goods in Europe, to invest in strategic value chains and to reduce over-dependency on third countries in these areas.' The US has provided massive loans and grants to businesses. There is a whole government push on bringing production back to the USA through various measures, including tax breaks and 'reshoring subsidies'. Japan has launched a massive subsidy programme as part of the government's emergency stimulus package to encourage domestic manufacturers to transfer their overseas production bases to South East Asia. This was done as the Covid-19 pandemic has disrupted their supply chains heavily dependent on China (Kyodo news service).
26. SUNS #8060, 10 July 2015, Statement by India at the Heads of Delegation Meeting held on 8 July 2015.
27. Preamble to the Marrakesh Agreement Establishing the WTO.
28. JOB/GC/250, 16 February 2021, General Council—Statement of the DG Elect to the Special Session of the WTO General Council.
29. Office of the USTR, 'Statement by Ambassador Michael Punke at the WTO General Council', 25 July 2014: 'From far away Bali, we had flipped a switch that turned the lights back on at the WTO. Today, we are extremely discouraged that a small handful of members in this organization are ready to walk away from their commitments at Bali…to flip the lights in this building back to dark.' Context: In July 2014, India blocked the amendment protocol for the Trade Facilitation Agreement to get certainty in the language of the Bali Ministerial Decision on food security. By November 2014, the major opponent, the USA agreed to India's demand and the language was suitably amended.

CHAPTER 27

INDIA AND MEXICO: A CASE FOR A ROBUST STRATEGIC PARTNERSHIP

SUJAN R CHINOY

India–Mexico relations have always been characterised by mutual understanding and growing all-round cooperation. In 2020, the two countries celebrated the seventieth anniversary of the establishment of bilateral diplomatic relations. In fact, Mexico was the first country in Latin America to establish diplomatic relations with India on 1 August 1950.

Ties were elevated to a 'Privileged Partnership' during the Mexican president's state visit to India in 2007, which was followed the next year by a visit by then President Pratibha Patil. High-level meetings have given impetus to bilateral ties and deepened cooperation. Ties between the two countries have been close and cooperative, and the feelings of mutual respect and friendliness have prevailed regardless of the political parties in power on either side. Former Prime Minister Manmohan Singh visited Mexico in June 2012 to attend the G20 summit in Los Cabos. After Prime Minister Narendra Modi assumed office in 2014, the government of President Enrique Peña Nieto was keen on an early visit by Modi, but this could not work out due to scheduling issues. However, Prime Minister Narendra Modi subsequently visited Mexico in June 2016, and the visit was a major milestone, not the least because the Mexican president, in a special gesture, drove him to a Mexican restaurant for a vegetarian fare of which Mexican cuisine has a delightful variety. In fact, no Indian in Mexico fails to notice how similar the eating habits of the two countries are, especially the use of our hands to eat food and the ubiquitous consumption of beans and spices. What is more, the tortilla in Mexico is made in exactly the same way that the chapatti or the cornflour roti is made in India.

Despite the geographical distance between the two countries, there has been a steady flow of visitors both ways, even though one could say that there is scope for much more people-to-people and official engagement. There are regular meetings of bilateral interactive mechanisms, which include a Joint Commission and a Bilateral High Level Group (BHLG) on Trade, Investment and Economic Cooperation as well as consultations between the two foreign ministries.

An outstanding feature of the current engagement is the spurt in bilateral trade and investment in recent years. As emerging markets with a dazzling diversity, India and Mexico are both engaged in realising the similar goal of inclusive economic growth and development.

Ties Anchored in Historical Linkages

As two large and populous countries in Asia and Latin America, respectively, India and Mexico mirror one another in terms of their rich history, culture, plurality and the developmental challenges they face. The edifice of ties, and the profound goodwill between the two peoples, is founded on historical and civilisational contacts. These include contacts between the Mayans and southern India, which makes for intriguing similarity in our respective temple architecture. The howler monkey god, Hun-Ahan, of the Mayas resembles the revered monkey god, Hanuman, in Hinduism. The 'Feathered Serpent' god, Quetzalcóatl, resembles the Indian serpent god, Nagaraja. One is also reminded of the galleon trade in centuries past between the Philippines and Nueva España (as Mexico was known in the Age of Discovery), when trade and commerce flourished between Mexico and all the major countries of Asia, including India, China, Japan and Korea. This was the age in which Santa Catarina, the Catholic figure of Puebla, is reported to have come from Mughal India via Acapulco in the seventeenth century, bringing with her the typical Mexican women's dress of yore, the so-called La China Poblana. Of course, it had nothing to do with China as such, since 'La China' denoted the Orient as a whole, and China was just one of the many countries whose wares were carried across by the galleons from the Philippines, then a Spanish territory.

Some also say that the Mexican mole (pronounced mo-lay) sauce—salsa de mole—is linked to the Indian curry. The paliacate (pronounced pallia-catay) scarf of Mexico, with its motifs of mangoes and peacocks, definitely has its origins in the rich calico scarves of 'Pulicut' or Calicut of India—then the world's best centre for cotton cloth. The designs and motifs in Mexico, even today, are similar to Indian designs.

Looking at the Future: Logic of Closer Ties

India–Mexico relations and interactions have, in the past, been impeded by a lack of mutual awareness. The common people of Mexico do not know enough about contemporary India or its achievements. Among the elite sections of the society, Mexicans often have a romanticised notion about India. It is also quite ironic that the millions of Mexicans named Xavier do not know that the remains of their patron saint, St Francis Xavier, lie interred in a sarcophagus in the Basilica of Bom Jesus in Goa for the past five centuries. Mexico is a Catholic nation, and Mexicans are rather surprised to learn that Christianity has an even longer history in India dating back to St Thomas the Apostle in the first century AD.

Although there is a rich historical connect between the two countries, it is not enough to sustain relations in the age of globalisation. It is only in the recent decades that the two countries have made an effort to go beyond the ancient primer of civilisations—contacts and similarities—to search for new paradigms of engagement.

Today, India and Mexico face similar challenges of growth and development for their large populations. The global situation today is in a great flux. The challenge of the Covid-19 pandemic has only accelerated many existing geostrategic trends that the world was already facing, such as the unprecedented fracturing of political and economic power, US–China rift, weaponisation of trade and technology, trade protectionism, nationalistic hubris, ideological cleavage and retrenchment of multilateralism. Non-State actors, criminal groups and terrorists have also sought to exploit vulnerabilities. The greatest challenge is not just to revive economic growth and breathe new life into globalisation, but to also ensure that it is more equitable.

Multilateralism

In an age in which no single country is in a position to dominate in an interdependent world, India and Mexico need to work together and strengthen multipolarity and multilateralism. Both countries are members of the G20. Both are also non-permanent members of the United Nations Security Council (UNSC) for a two-year term that commenced on 1 January 2021. This presents an opportunity to build a better global consensus on climate change, sustainable development, renewable energy, terrorism and non-traditional threats.

Indo-Pacific

The term Indo-Pacific is gaining currency. It is a representative term that is inclusive and reflective of the contemporary age, just as the term Asia-Pacific represented the geo-economic impulses of the second half of the last century. The Indo-Pacific is also a throwback to the historical realities of the fusion of the Indian and Pacific oceans that was so well-recognised in the age of exploration. Even the colonial era that emerged had promoted seamless maritime contact between India and Nueva España via the Philippines and the robust galleon trade associated with Nao de China.

It is well-known that global economic growth engines have shifted in recent years to the Asia-Pacific region. China's growth story is well-documented, but there are other remarkable stories, too, across the vast Asian landmass that straddles the Pacific and Indian oceans, and is home to more than 60 per cent of the global population.

Today, economic growth and prosperity, once limited to Japan and China in East Asia and to the Asian Tigers—South Korea, Singapore, Hong Kong and Taiwan—have now spread to South East Asia and South Asia. In fact, before the pandemic struck, this growth story was spreading in India, and across Africa as well.

In the long run, once the pandemic is overcome, these trends will pick up again. They are irreversible. They are based on a youthful demographic profile, education, the universalisation of certain manufacturing technologies and supply chains and the opportunities of the information age. Both India and Mexico are part of this aspirational future.

Asia, Africa and Latin America will remain regions of high-growth potential. In Latin America, Mexico is the second largest economy, its largest trading nation and, given its geographical location on the North American continent, perhaps also its best docking point.

The historical backdrop, current realities and future trends all point in the direction of a renewal of links between Mexico and the Indo-Pacific region, mirroring the ancient connect of past centuries. It is obvious, therefore, that a reawakening of an older and proven order, albeit through the conduct of trade and investment ties on a more level-playing field in the twenty-first century, stands to benefit both Mexico and India.

Strengthening Economic Synergies

India is the world's seventh largest country, with the world's second largest population. It is also among the world's top seven economies. Half of India's population—of nearly 1.3 billion people—is below the age of twenty-five, making it the largest reservoir of youth anywhere in the world at a time when the rest of the world is rapidly ageing. The Indian economy is expected to bounce back to a high growth trajectory within 2022. Whether to diversify and create resilient supply chains as part of global risk-mitigation strategies or to chase labour cost arbitrage, investors from around the world will continue to place a long-term bet on India—a democracy that is destined to become one of the top three economies in the next three decades. On its part, the Government of India, under the leadership of Prime Minister Narendra Modi, has taken several new initiatives to tap the emerging potential. These include the focus on world-class infrastructure, Digital India programme, Skill Development training programme, Smart Cities Mission, industrial corridors, information highways and opening up the Indian economy to foreign direct investment (FDI) in railways, defence and insurance sectors, which can be a new magnet for Mexican companies.

Mexico is an upper middle-income, emerging economy, clearly more developed than developing in many ways due to its propinquity to USA. As an active member of the G20, it shares important responsibilities in shepherding and regulating the global economy. It is a large oil producer, and has the sixth largest reserves of shale oil. It is the largest trading nation in Latin America and is the first G77 country to have graduated to the ranks of the Organisation for Economic Co-operation and Development (OECD). It is the only Latin American country to be located on the North American continent, and the only one that was part of the former North American Free Trade Agreement (NAFTA)—known as the United States–Mexico–Canada Agreement (USMCA) in its renegotiated avatar. It is also the only one with active trading ports and routes through both the Pacific and Atlantic oceans, with several smaller countries of Central America and the Caribbean region. It is an important member of the World Trade Organization (WTO), the World Bank, International Monetary Fund (IMF), Asia-Pacific Economic Cooperation (APEC), Pacific Alliance and Comprehensive and Progressive Agreement for Trans-Pacific Partnership (CPTPP). At a strategic level, Mexico is also part of the key Nuclear Suppliers Group (NSG) that India hopes to join.

The Logic of Trade and Investment

Mexico has emerged as the largest trade partner of India in Latin America and the Caribbean region and the second in all of the Americas, after the US. India–Mexico bilateral trade has also surpassed India's bilateral trade with Brazil. India is Mexico's ninth biggest global trade partner. Interestingly, India happens to be the third largest buyer of Mexico's crude oil.

The fifth meeting of the India–Mexico BHLG was held on 9 October 2020, through a video conference, with the participation of the commerce secretary of India and the vice minister for foreign trade of the Government of Mexico as co-chairs. Bilateral trade in goods increased from US$ 1.75 billion in 2010 to US$ 9.33 billion in 2019, and had crossed the US$ 10 billion mark in 2018. Mutual investments have also grown well in this period, with Mexico being the main Latin American destination for Indian investments and also the largest investor from Latin America in India.

Indian companies are very competitive globally. They are looking for better investment opportunities. Many of them see Mexico as a major investment destination with access to the United States–Mexico–Canada market, Europe and Latin America.

In order to facilitate bilateral trade, an India–Mexico Business Chamber (IMBC) was launched in May 2019, based on an idea that the author explored and recommended as India's ambassador to Mexico between 2012 and 2015. It is premised on the simple logic that the business community must be made direct stakeholder in efforts to promote commercial relations.

Mexico's experience can be invaluable to India in the creation of smart cities and in promoting tourism—both domestic and inbound. There is much that India can imbibe from Mexico's experience with its Programa Pueblos Mágicos (Magical Towns Programme)—an initiative spearheaded by Mexico's Secretariat of Tourism with support from other federal agencies, aimed at promoting a series of towns around the country showcasing their natural beauty, culture, traditions, folklore, local history, arts, crafts and cuisine. The 'Pueblo Mágico' is a certification that helps increase tourism around the country, especially to smaller towns in rural areas. A similar scheme would be of great benefit to India.

India and Mexico must strengthen cooperation in the three sectors in which India is doing well in Mexico—pharmaceuticals, automotive and information technology. India exported 870,000 doses of AstraZeneca's Covid-19 vaccine—domestically developed by the Serum Institute of India—to Mexico. The shipment from India made up about 42 per cent of the two million doses of AstraZeneca's vaccine. On this, India's External Affairs Minister S Jaishankar tweeted, 'Expressing our Amistad. Mexico receives Made in India vaccines.' The word 'amistad' captures the sentiment well—of being close friends.

In the automotive and processed foods sectors, both countries are living up to their reputations as large domestic markets and global hubs, and recognise the advantage of expanding their reach by leveraging the favourable conditions in the other, in a win–win outcome for both. It is not unusual to see Bajaj and TVS two- and three-wheeler products in Mexico, especially in the southern states.

Whereas India has a clear advantage in the information technology sector, with the presence of virtually every major Indian IT company in Mexico, the latter has its own advantages in the entertainment sector, where its standards match those of the US. Cinépolis, which is Mexico's biggest movie theatre company, owns hundreds of screens around the world and has plans to set up 500 screens in multiplexes throughout India.

Forecasting Natural Disasters and Food Security Collaboration

As global warming and unpredictable weather patterns take their toll, Mexico could also become an important partner in India's endeavours in earthquake forecasting and formulating disaster-mitigation strategies as well as food security. The International Maize and Wheat Improvement Center (CIMMYT), based in Mexico, has played and can, once again, play an important role in conservation agriculture, increasing wheat and maize production and research and development (R&D). After all, in the 1960s, Mexico had contributed to India's agricultural revolution through its high-yielding Sonora variety of wheat.

Energy and Chemicals Sector

Hydrocarbons will continue to be relevant in India's economic growth. Mexico is estimated to have reserves equivalent to about 450 billion barrels of oil. This is comparable to the resource base of Saudi Arabia. Mexico also has large shale oil and gas reserves. According to the US Energy Information Administration (EIA) agency, Mexico possesses the world's fourth largest shale oil reserves. Moreover, Mexico's offshore fields in the Gulf of Mexico are among the world's most accessible fields. Since India is one of the world's largest consumers of oil, and one of the world's fastest growing economies, there is potential to buy more oil from Mexico in the future in order to meet the energy requirements of our economic growth. At present, India buys crude oil from Mexico, but sells refined petroleum products back to Mexico, backed by India's large refining capacity.

India needs to examine the potential for making long-term investments in the energy sector in Mexico. It could look at participation in the power sector, fertiliser plants, pipeline infrastructure projects and information technology platforms for PEMEX's—Mexico's State-owned petroleum company—energy sector operations across the spectrum. There is also greater scope for India–Mexico cooperation in the renewable energy sector. Like India, Mexico plans to scale up investments in this sector, particularly solar energy. This would match well with India's drive to enhance solar energy capacities. Mexico's interest is visible from the fact that it is a member of the International Solar Alliance (ISA), initiated by India and France in 2015.

Mexico has a robust chemicals and petrochemicals industry of its own, but is also a major importer. It is among the largest importers of essential oils and aroma chemicals used in making perfumes. It also has a sizable market for agrochemicals. Additionally, the Mexican market offers good potential for setting up manufacturing facilities, especially taking into account easy access to the US market under the United States–Mexico–Canada Agreement.

Mining Sector

For India, there is much potential for investment in Mexico in the mining sector, particularly to meet India's growing need for raw materials and minerals. For Mexican investments in India, there are promising opportunities awaiting in infrastructure, housing and food processing, in particular. India requires a large investment to upgrade its infrastructure and will spend US$ 1 trillion in the next few years in this sector alone. Mexican companies have ample opportunities to look into the opportunities in India in different infrastructure sub-sectors. The large-scale development of the housing sector, especially vertical development in urban areas, also offers opportunities to Mexican companies to promote their technologies and products.

Textiles Sector

There is considerable scope for garments and textiles. Indian fabrics, designs and garments are gaining in popularity in the Mexican market, and major stores have been sourcing supplies from India, but the potential still remains far from being optimally exploited.

Banking Sector

Mexico's banking sector is considerably liberalised and lucrative, and is, therefore, dominated by foreign and multinational banks. The presence of Indian banks in Mexico suggests good business opportunities, besides facilitating and promoting rapidly growing bilateral trade, business and investments.

Cooperation in Regional Fora/Third Countries

India must focus on deepening trade ties with Mexico in the Community of Latin American and Caribbean States (CELAC) and the Pacific Alliance (PA). The PA—whose membership includes Mexico, Chile, Colombia and Peru—offers a platform for closer trade arrangements between these countries and India, particularly with India having acquired observer status. At some point in time, one can expect the PA to act as a bloc in trade negotiations with Asian countries such as India. Mexico, the PA's largest economy, will play the role of the natural leader in such an exercise. The Association of Caribbean States (ASC) is another regional forum where India has observer status and Mexico plays an important role.

Both India and Mexico have an interest in Africa. Hence, they should explore the possibility of joint projects in selected countries, bilaterally or in tandem with third countries like Japan, with whom both India and Mexico have good relations. Japan is the biggest investor from Asia in Mexico. It is also the biggest single-country investor in India, not counting multisource 'window' economies like Singapore and Mauritius. India and Japan have a Special Strategic and Global Partnership that provides for cooperation in capacity-building projects in Africa. Trilateral cooperation in Africa could provide Mexico an opportunity to promote its role and potential in the Indo-Pacific region, and to rediscover a historical legacy connection.

Mexico is already well-connected with East Asia and the Asia-Pacific region through bilateral trade and investment ties, and its membership of Asia-Pacific Economic Cooperation and dialogue with Association of Southeast Asian Nations (ASEAN). Mexico's membership to MIKTA—group of Mexico, Indonesia, the Republic of Korea, Turkey, Australia—further strengthens its ties with South Korea, Indonesia and Australia, all important countries in the Indo-Pacific region.

Some areas of interest in the Indo-Pacific for Mexico are infrastructure, food processing, digital innovation and healthcare. The Blue Dot Network—which establishes standards for infrastructure and connectivity projects—could be of interest to Mexico. As maritime nations, we should also look at cooperation in the Blue Economy, including in third countries, especially small island nations.

Education Beyond the Pandemic

With the world having gone to new ways of learning, teaching and interacting in the aftermath of the pandemic, there is great scope to expand online university education cooperation between India and Mexico. In this context, the Mexico–India University Presidents' Forum—announced during the visit of Mexico's Vice Foreign Minister Julian Ventura in September 2019—should convene at the earliest to chalk out concrete ideas.

The bilateral dialogue at the level of think tanks is, however, not satisfactory. Our exchanges have been few, if any. This could be amped up.

Defence Collaboration

A new area of interest is the defence sector in India, which is open to 100 per cent foreign direct investment. Mexico has well-known strengths in aerospace and defence manufacturing which are of interest to India. The author recalls helping to expand the defence wing in the Mexican embassy in New Delhi in 2015. In May 2020, the Government of India had raised the limit through the automatic route to 74 per cent and even higher through the government approval route. Recently, the Government of India has announced a self-reliance programme, known as AatmaNirbhar Bharat Abhiyaan, to encourage 'Make in India' in defence manufacturing. One hundred and one items have been identified which will no longer be imported, but progressively made in India. This opens up vast opportunities for fresh investments by Mexican companies for joint ventures and partnerships in defence manufacturing in India. A bilateral dialogue between industry representatives, including the Confederation of Indian Industry (CII) and Federation of Indian Chambers of Commerce and Industry (FICCI), and their counterparts in Mexico should be held soon to identify opportunities at the earliest.

Naval cooperation could be boosted, too. Unfortunately, it has been fairly dormant so far. Both countries resumed bilateral naval visits in 2017 after almost a decade, to celebrate 100 years of the Mexican Constitution. Exchanges between defence training institutions such as the National Defence College (NDC) in New Delhi and the Defence Services Staff College (DSSC) in Tamil Nadu and their counterparts in Mexico could be explored.

India and Mexico could also establish regular dialogue on interdiction of drugs smuggling and border surveillance techniques against illegal crossings. Both countries have unique experience in this regard.

These suggestions can raise the India–Mexico Privileged Partnership to a strategic level in the future.

Conclusion

Alongside all this, at a more fundamental level, people-to-people ties between Mexico and India are growing. There is a growing mutual fascination among high-end tourists in both countries. Indians want to visit the beautiful resorts of Los Cabos, Cancún and the Maya Riviera and even Acapulco, the famous destination of the 1970s, often for weddings and events. Today, there is a need to introduce the hinterlands to one another. Mexico's cultural treasures lie in Chichén Itzá, Uxmal, Tulum, Palenque and many such wondrous destinations. Indians are gradually awakening to their beauty, and are as struck by the majesty of the Aztec ruins in Teotihuacán as are Mexicans by the stunning art of the Taj Mahal, Khajuraho or the beautiful temples of Madurai.

In a country frequently wracked by cartel violence, Mexicans have adopted Mahatma Gandhi as their own, for the universal values of peace and non-violence that he espoused. These values resonate well with the nation's Catholicism.

Octavio Paz, the poet-author-scholar-diplomat who was Mexico's ambassador to India from 1962 to 1968, wrote many books on India. His most famous work, *In Light of India*, brought about a much deeper understanding of India among Mexicans of his generation. Others, like the late Graciela de la Lama, who was also ambassador to India, brought the two countries closer through her deep scholarship on Indian history, including India's classical literature. Generally speaking, Mexican diplomats have tended to be former politicians, like the first ambassador, former President Emilio Portes Gil, or scholars from the field of culture. India, on the other hand, has generally sent professional diplomats to represent the country, except for Vijaya Lakshmi Pandit, Jawaharlal Nehru's sister, who was India's first (non-resident) ambassador to Mexico. Regardless of their background, they have all played a key role over the years in bringing the two countries closer together.

With joint efforts and a 'whole of government' approach, both sides can do much to strengthen bilateral ties in the twenty-first century. They will be supported in this by the two peoples, who are united by their mutual admiration.

CHAPTER 28

STRATEGIC SYMBOLISM AND SOFT POWER DIPLOMACY: A STUDY OF INDIA'S RELATIONSHIP WITH THE LATIN AMERICA AND CARIBBEAN REGION

Amarendra Khatua

Any policy paper or analytical study on India's relationship with the Latin America and the Caribbean (LAC) region—which incorporates thirty-three Latin American and Caribbean island nations—will highlight that the region and India have transcended a huge geographical distance assiduously to increase trade cooperation substantially; soft power diplomacy in a profound manner; south–south cooperation occasionally; and multilateral positions-togetherness symbolically. However, both regions still have a long way to go to exploit similar strategies and global philosophy of state policies to forge political linkage and consultation systems matching existing potential and open up a large gamut of cooperation framework in other areas. This article is basically a limited approach study, but a diverse presentation of current ground realities of India's relationship with the region and possible growth in the post-Covid-19 era.

Brief History of the Beginning of Contact and Cooperation

The LAC nations, as former colonies of European powers, always nurtured the popular and political presence of India in the sphere of soft power, migration and suffering under the colonial yoke and symbiotic possibilities of reaching out.

The presence of a large Indian diaspora in Caribbean countries—as *imported* and bonded labour and gradually emerging as a distinct social and political group—added to the emotional undercurrent of attachment of these counties, culturally, to India. Huge migrants from Italy, Spain, Portugal and other countries of Europe, having colonial tales of plunder and blunders from India, spread the spiritual, cultural, mythical and exotic image of India among the settlers in Latin American nations. As it is said, many of the Latin American countries, including Argentina, Uruguay, Chile, etc, after annihilation of local tribes and aboriginal population, are like 'Europeans suffering in Latin America', and in then distant Latin settlements, Indian image stayed and given in their minds.

At present, India has sixteen missions—two are being opened in Dominican Republic and Paraguay—in the area covering the thirty-three LAC countries. The LAC region is represented by twenty-two embassies of these countries in New Delhi. Historically, it must be known that before Independence, India had set up a trade commission in Argentina as early as 1943.

Regional Interests at Variance and Political Relationship with the Region

Notwithstanding geographical distance, politics of underdevelopment, social-welfarism politics by post-dictatorial regimes in Latin America and Nehruvian international policy of established 'popular linkage'—even if a substantive relationship takes time in terms of trade and institutionalisation of political consultation process—there has been increasing proximity between India and the region in fora including NAM, G77, Commonwealth Heads of Government Meeting (CHOGM) and UN body system (later extended to Brazil, Russia, India, China, and South Africa [BRICS], G20 and Indian participation in regional leadership meets). While India's political consultations and interaction with countries like Cuba, Brazil, Caribbean nations and Venezuela stayed at a visible level in the early years, other Latin American countries under dictators only highlighted India's soft power strength and leadership in the third world bodies as well as UN bodies.

Finally, with the flavour of socialism and democracy entering into the body politics of the region in the eighties, growing political engagement with the region commenced with the motto of struggle against new colonialism, combating underdevelopment issues, supporting each other in multilateral fora to enjoy benefits of global 'aid, assistance and grants' politics and identification of global causes seeking political support (eg African statehood and war issues, conflict and wars in South East Asia and Middle East).

India's seeking leadership voice inside the Non-Aligned Movement (NAM) found symbolic support among the nations in the region. Three issues where India nurtured its political presence in the region included support for India on Jammu & Kashmir dispute against Pakistan, limited support for India's ambition for a permanent membership of United Nations Security Council (UNSC) and seeking India's support in various multilateral and UN fora for individual struggle of nations in the region against colonialism, attacks and sanction by the European powers and USA and for individual global ambition of countries like Brazil, Argentina, Mexico and Cuba at various stages for positions in global, multilateral and UN bodies.

Politically, despite so many commonalities, relationship between India, a country with unity in diversity, and LAC countries with 'diversity in unity in their Weltanschauung', has only 'growing engagement'. The reasons for absence of substantive and strategic political relationship, as explained above, flows from visible difference in regional political priorities and Latin obsession on intensified political continuity and interaction within the region (especially with immediate neighbours through wars and assimilation. Since the 1960s, the region has seen sixty-two wars and skirmishes and civil wars within and fighting off 'love and war' political contacts with Europe and USA.

Since 2009-10, Indian political dialogue to increase relationship from symbolic to regular and strategic level has commenced with the region. Growing trade, cultural relationship and people-to-people contact have added the momentum. But what has contributed to solidifying the process now is that in place of sporadic, small delegation level or occasional symbolic high-level visits, a large number of planned visits at working level, VIP level and VVIP level are taking place on continuing basis. Regular political consultations and follow-ups have helped in concretising agreements over a large number of spheres. Prime Minister Narendra Modi, in the recent past, has visited Argentina, Brazil and Mexico four times, the president of India has visited four countries in two years (Bolivia and Chile in 2019 and Cuba and Suriname in 2018) and the vice president has visited Costa Rica, Paraguay, Peru, Guatemala and Panama over a period of two years. Twenty-seven ministerial visits have taken place from India over a period of five years since 2016. Eleven such visits from the region, including that of presidents of Brazil and Argentina, have taken place in India.

Adding to this, meeting of Indian external affairs minister (EAM) with the annual India–CARICOM (Caribbean Community and Common Market) foreign ministers meeting and the quartet ministerial meeting of the Community of Latin American and Caribbean States (CELAC) on the sidelines of the United Nations General Assembly (UNGA) have been institutionalised and have helped in regular exchange of views on India's national foreign policy priorities and Latin American and Caribbean issues of political priorities. Besides, the prime minister's regular meeting with the LAC leaders on the sidelines of G20, BRICS, CHOGM and UNGA and during the first ever head of states/head of government level India–CARICOM leaders meeting held on the sidelines of UNGA helped in increasing the level, scope and range of political exchanges that used to lack the following-up process in the past. In fact, all fifteen CARICOM countries were represented in the meeting with the prime minister. To prioritise its long-term ambition to establish effective political exchange of views and interaction, India has started ministerial level visits to each of the thirty-three LAC countries under the Abhinav Pahal Yojana for the last five years.

India's political messages, including support of Argentina's claim to Malvinas Islands against British colonialism; non-intervention by USA and other powers in the internal political conflicts in countries like Venezuela, Bolivia, Cuba (and in Central American countries' fight against dictatorship in the past); support to LAC permanent membership in the UNGC; and protection and promotion of indigenous people's rights and claims under the existing laws of the governing countries, have been appreciated by the leadership of the concerned countries at the highest level and by the regional bodies in their summit meetings.

India's Covid-19 support politics has found popular support in Latin America, including the Brazilian president's '*Hanuman carrying Sanjivani*' message of immense significance. India has supplied medical assistance to twenty-seven LAC countries and is preparing grounds for long-term supply, export and grant of vaccines to these countries. Commitment of a donation of 5,70,000 doses of vaccines to CARICOM countries and supply to other LAC countries, including Argentina, Mexico and Brazil, has been a political success, flowing from Indian

EAM's discussion on cooperation issues to tackle the pandemic with twenty-four LAC foreign ministers.

India's relations with Argentina were cemented to the level of strategic partnership during Former President Mauricio Macri's visit to India in February 2019. Foreign office consultations mechanism has been institutionalised with regularity, and pre-finalised agenda-based discussions on India's strategic partnership with Brazil were intensified bilaterally during a visit of prime minister of India (2019) and the visit of President Jair Bolsonaro in 2020. Multilateral exchanges at multilateral and plurilateral fora, including G20, IBSA (India, Brazil, South Africa), G4, BASIC (Brazil, South Africa, India and China), BRICS, International Solar Alliance (ISA), BP and in UN bodies, are now contributing teeth to the strategic alliance between India and Brazil. Mexico, which had seen establishment of diplomatic relations with India in 1950, has now strengthened its political consultation process with India, both bilaterally through visits at highest level between the two countries (this includes Prime Minister Modi's July 2017 meeting on the sidelines of G20 meeting at Hamburg and a state visit to Mexico in June 2016) and working closely together in G77, G15, G20 and in multilateral and UN bodies and by upgrading bilateral relations to 'privileged partnership' in 2007 (and committed to upgrade same to strategic partnership in near future).

Growing Trade and Economic Cooperation: Moving Ahead

Trade and economic cooperation with the LAC region grew substantially over a span of ten to twelve years, starting from the early '90s; and with tremendous scope for future growth, it will add substantially to the process of overall strategic linking-up. Despite a global slowdown and impact of the Covid-19 pandemic, India's bilateral trade with the LAC region constituted almost 3.44 per cent of its global trade. During 2019-20 (April-March), our imports stood at 3.60 per cent of the global share and exports at 3.21 per cent of our trade turnover with the region; during 2018-19, it was US$ 30,287 million (imports of US$ 20,547.11 million and exports of US$ 9,740.72 million); and during 2019-2020 was for US$ 27,134 million (consisting of imports of US$ 17,075 million and exports of US$ 10,059 million). Though imports decreased by about 37.07 per cent and exports by 8.26 per cent due to the Covid-19 pandemic and slowdown, based on the growth chart, India's trade turnover is estimated to touch US$ 50,000 million by 2025.

The top ten trending partners of India are Brazil, Venezuela, Argentina, Peru, Chile, Colombia, Bolivia, Ecuador, Dominican Republic and Panama, accounting 92.71 per cent of India's trade with the region. Almost 18 per cent of our energy requirements is met by the region. India's top ten imports are of crude oil, gold, vegetable oils, bulk minerals and ores, timber and timber products, sugar, coal, iron and steel, petroleum products and inorganic chemicals, and the top ten exports include petroleum products, agro-chemicals, pharmaceuticals, motor vehicles, yarns and fabrics, auto parts, two/three wheelers, drug intermediates, iron and steel products and dyes and intermediates.

Strategically, and with trade planning and market development, Latin America could substantially meet India's energy needs through supply of crude, shale oil and gas; become important source for India's food security in supplying edible oils (soybean oil, sunflower oil and olive oil), pulses and lentils, animal feed, oil seeds, food grains (for South Asia and third country exports via India); and major suppliers of important mineral resources, including copper, zinc, rare earth minerals and lithium (so vital for solar energy policy). Substantial scope for future growth in trade volumes exists as northern regions are highly complementary in the natural resources, services, pharmaceuticals, energy, auto and other sectors.

Towards improving the facilitating framework for increasing trade, in addition to the existing India–Chile preferential trading arrangement (PTA) and India–Mercosur (Southern Common Market) PTA (with Argentina, Brazil, Uruguay and Paraguay), India is negotiating a PTA with Peru, a comprehensive trade agreement (CTA) with Ecuador and studying possible expansion of the PTA with Mercosur by adding individual agreements with each Mercosur country. Bedsides, a joint feasibility study for a partial scope agreement (PSA) with Colombia has commenced.

Indian investments, which were almost non-existent till 2010, are now touching US$ 13 billion. Lack of active government-level promotional efforts, language issues and lack of single-window facilities are some of the reasons for the slow investment movement from India to Latin America. Indian firms, including Godrej, United Phosphorus Limited, Hero, Renuka Sugars, ONGC,

Aditya Birla Group, Tata Group, Reliance, BPCL, Videocon, Infosys, etc. either have direct project investments and production and service facilities in Latin America or have investment operations related to trading and third country operations there.

At sub-regional levels, besides Mercosur, trade, economic, investment, development partnership and region and country-specific trade arrangements with the Central American Integration System (SICA), Pacific Alliance, CARICOM and CELAC have been expanded. An integrated programme, 'FOCUS LAC', which was launched in 1997 with an objective to deepen India's trade relations with the region was extended till March 2021 in line with the foreign trade policy (FTP) and grants incentives to exporters and directly involving export promotion councils, EXIM Bank, Export Credit Guarantee Corporation of India (ECGC), commodity boards and chambers of commerce and industry. Institutional mechanism, including the India–Brazil Trade Monitoring Mechanism (TMM), India–Argentina Joint Trade Committee (JTC), India–Ecuador Joint Trade and Economic Committee (JETCO) and India–Colombia Joint Committee of Business Development Cooperation (JCBDC) now directly help in trade promotion and market penetration efforts.

In the CARICOM region, through the development partnership initiative, Indian contributions over the recent years include linkage projects and ocean ferry in Guyana (US$ 10 million), major infrastructure development projects in Grenada, supply of medical equipment and medicines to Jamaica and contribution of US$ 1 million as aid to CARICOM Development Fund. India has, over the period of 2014-19, extended development assistance in the form of lines of credit worth US$ 580 million and grants at US$ 12 million to the region. Information technology (IT) centres of excellence have been set up in fourteen countries in the region and two are being set up in Uruguay and Argentina.

Soft Power Diplomacy and People-to-People Connect

The presence of India's soft power in the popular conception of Latin mind is huge. This encompasses music, dance and performing arts of all kinds, yoga, Ayurveda, spiritualism and all forms of tourism related to 'India, the land of mystery, happiness and meaning'. Today, there are almost 2,100 performing arts training centres, mostly run by local artists, either trained in India or by invited artists from India; forty-one universities and institutions giving degrees and diplomas in yoga and Ayurveda; seventeen universities having courses in Hindi, Indian languages and philosophy; 1,800 yoga training institutes and organisations; fifty-nine India-centric friendship and provisional societies; and more than 800 spiritual centres, temples and religion-related promotional entities in the region. Presence of almost 1.1 million Indian diaspora in Caribbean makes the cultural attachment and root-seeking alignment of the local populace emotionally significant. Among the Caribbean nations, Suriname has 30 per cent Indian diaspora population; Trinidad and Tobago, almost 42 per cent; and Guyana, 43 per cent. Non-interventionism aspects of the Indian foreign policy has kept its possible dominant presence in the Caribbean limited to cultural, tourism and development partnership related spheres.

The existing ongoing cultural exchange programmes with individual countries, increasing number of Caribbean students coming to India for higher education under Indian Technical and Economic Cooperation programme (ITEC) and other cooperation programmes, and the functioning of Indian cultural centres are success stories. Tourism from the LAC region has grown immensely, and from a meagre 60,000 per year till the late 1990s, tourism traffic has increased to almost 9.8 per cent of the total annual tourist turnover figures, reaching almost 5.7 lakh in 2019-20. Learning of Sanskrit and Indian languages as well as providing Indian studies in various universities are also helping increase the exchange and study visits by students, youth, interns and academicians.

Cooperation in the Areas of Science and Technology, Defence, Space Research and Other Areas

India has a number of bilateral agreements for cooperation in the field of science and technology with Argentina, Brazil, Mexico, Chile, Colombia and others. With a number of countries, besides the umbrella agreement, agreements on sectoral and sub-sectoral research and cooperation have been identified and signed. The umbrella agreement signed with Mexico in 1975 works out framework programmes and project-based listings on three-yearly basis, and these projects cover areas including solar energy, seismology, nanotechnology, biotechnology, material sciences, atmosphere sciences, etc. Continuing workshop method with counterpart identified bodies has been introduced for harvesting outcomes. The agreement for science and technology cooperation with Brazil (this was expanded during the 2020 visit of President Bolsonaro to add a programme of scientific and technological cooperation, the POC S&T) undertakes projects, workshops and joint research in areas of low-carbon technologies, ocean sciences, biofuel mixing and genetic research on cattle, animal husbandry, etc. The areas covered under Indo-Argentine scientific and technological cooperation include biotechnology, high-yielding variety seeds, renewable energy, nanotechnology, space research, etc.

While cooperation with the region in the defence sector is still at a nascent stage, potential to import small arms from Latin America; supply helicopters, fighter planes and arms to Latin America; conduct joint exercises for sharing experiences; and coordinate on White Shipping information through data sharing agreement exist. Joint venture talks to produce small arms in India by Brazilian firms are under way.

A number of agreements have been signed in the recent past with Argentina, Brazil, Mexico, Chile and few other countries on security cooperation matters, including the Mutual Legal Assistance Treaty in Criminal Matters, the Extradition Treaty, and in the area of cybersecurity.

Framework agreement for inter-institutional cooperation with the space agencies of Brazil and Argentina have been signed. Besides future satellite launching facilitation required by the countries, the areas of cooperation include programmes on nano-satellite building, data sharing and satellite tracking, training of astronauts and exchange of research and resources data.

Cooperation in the Global Multilateral Bodies, UN and Other International Fora

As it has been mentioned before, political priorities of India and the LAC regions are vastly different, contiguous area-centric and linked to global superpower differences in a vertical manner. While within NAM, G20, G77 and CHOGM, cooperation on broader issues is based on goodwill and mutual understanding, convergence on issues of India obtaining support for its permanent membership of UNSC, peaceful use of nuclear energy and disarmament, Law of the Sea, and UN reforms are yet to be achieved. Constant policy and interest-based integration of the region with USA and European powers also add to the divergence.

Future Growth Possibilities and Medium- and Long-term Projection: Post-Covid-19 Era

A recent policy paper presented to an Uruguay-based think tank body of senior and retired officials of the LAC region, identified areas which could substantially invigorate relations between the region and India and will help in converting the existing potential into strategic form of vibrant relationship included following broadly:

- Geographical distance, high freight rates, absence of regular and large-scale transportation movement, language and consular regulations are some of the problem areas confronting growth in trade relations which offer short- and medium-term growth of immense value and diversified basket of goods. Immediate identification of sources to support India's food security needs in the edible oil sector, pulses and lentils sector, food grains sector and third country trading with the Middle East, Africa and South Asia with the help of India in food grains, fruits and vegetables. Imports per year will go up from the existing US$ 17,075 million to US$ 30,000 over a period of ten years (overall trade turnover from US$ 27,134 million to US$ 50,000 million).
- Indian investment in a planned (government and leading chamber-supported and identified trade and industry-led) and monitored manner in petroleum and shale gas sector, lithium mining, ferrous and non-ferrous mineral sectors, agricultural and plantation sector in farming on export and trading basis.
- Establishment of joint cooperation talks, target reviewing and implementation monitoring mechanism in various economic ministries in India, with reviews being done on monthly basis with the help of diplomatic missions of the region and India.
- Setting up of summit-level meetings with Central America and Mexico, Caribbean countries and Latin America (divided into three due to economic, regional, geographical diversities and political and geostrategic priorities) once in two to three years. Pre-fixed agenda issues of political and economic importance can be prepared by the foreign ministers, preferably during the UNGA sessions (on the margin) prior to the summit meeting.
- Strengthening technical cooperation and developmental partnership

agreements with the LAC region through specified activities, including establishing IT centres of excellence, English-speaking education facilities, renewable energy projects, participation in infrastructure development projects and encouraging student exchange programmes.

- Expanding consultation mechanism with CELAC, CARICOM and other LAC regional bodies through active participation by a high-powered group of regional ambassadors (with mandated brief approval by the EAM) or by the EAM. Besides providing preparatory insight, this will help in setting up action bodies during visits and special occasions with individual countries for furthering political and other relations.
- Cooperation in the sectors of science and technology, space research, nuclear energy, agricultural sciences, ocean sciences, defence supply and research and solar energy provide immense long-term possibilities. Time has come to prepare joint studies for medium- and long-term implementation goals and schedules.
- Cultivating diaspora as well as increasing number of Indians settling down in Latin America for setting up active friendship, lobbying and bilateral bodies of influence, contact, information sharing and futuristic projections. Organisational linkage related to 'Routes to Roots' infusion and 'Pravasi Bharatiya' will help.
- Soft power diplomacy of India is working as a potent fermenting agent. But, most of it is not planned. Time has come to set up Indian cultural centres (especially to promote yoga, Ayurveda, Sanskrit, Indian performing arts and translation of Indian texts into Spanish) in most of the countries, build up a directory of institutes and organisations which promote Indian arts, performing arts and culture; link up and facilitate institutional linkage with universities and bodies having Indian studies and Oriental studies facilities; and working out a short- and medium-term work programme.
- Review by the government to establish more air and sea link with the region, encourage third countries to enhance and provide such linkage and support regional governments for promoting such linkage on commercial basis. Such long-term measures will match the outgo by way of revenues earned from increased tourism, cargo earnings and resultant growth in all connected sectors.

- Government, based on all the above, must set up permanent review committees inside the nodal ministries with support from Indian embassies, institutionalise visit by the ministers of commerce and industry and external affairs at regular intervals, institutionalise think tank dialogues on annual or biannual basis, support diaspora interaction through active encouragement and enhancing the strategic partnership agreements with implementation monitoring mechanism.
- India–Mercosur Preferential Trade Agreement includes India's offer of margin of preference (MoP) on 450 tariff lines and Mercosur's offer of MoP on 452 tariff lines. Due to the existing potential and complementarities, on the one hand India must expand the scope and range of PTA and also think in terms of signing individual PTAs with Mercosur countries covering few vital commodities and products of its interest, while on the other, it must protect Indian-sensitive agricultural and plantation products from unhealthy competition. Future medium-term strategy must also include second expansion of the India–Chile PTA and finalisation of India–Peru, India–Colombia and India–Ecuador JETCO agreements.
- Chinese economic presence is huge in the LAC region, and China is the biggest trading partner to each of the LAC countries. Chinese investment covers vital areas of economic interest to the native countries, including mines, forests, agricultural lands, ports, infrastructure etc. and, today, is valued at US$ 300 billion. Indebtedness, Chinese approach to trading activities and Chinese presence dominating local policymaking areas, along with large Chinese migration, are gradually creating anti-Chinese popular and political sentiments. India must explore trilateral cooperation foray with USA and European powers, like Spain, France, UK and Germany, to create alternative investment and economic support-providing axis over the long term. Think tanks of countries like Brazil, Bolivia, Argentina, Central American region and Caribbean have prepared alternative policy papers seeking replacement of Chinese economic presence in the region. Opening of EXIM Bank offices in major economies in Latin America and initiating viable credit and financial support measures could be our medium-term approach.

Conclusion

India and the LAC share folkloric history-making super structural mutual linkages—with the presence of Rabindranath Tagore as a grand poetic legend, of Gabriel García Márquez and Pablo Neruda being translated to seventeen Indian languages, in the movie *Guide* being a celluloid legend in all Caribbean countries—with a strong influence of Indian spiritual mysticism in the minds of the restless post-colonial youth of Latin America and immense goodwill. The post-Covid-19 platform should be to sustain and transform this goodwill into short-term magical jump in trade and people-to-people contact sphere, building up of political consultancy, lobbying and exchange of support base (bilaterally, regionally and in the multilateral fora) over medium term and strategic partnership covering areas of scientific and technical cooperation, economic development partnership and multi-pronged workable and achievable project areas in agricultural, biotechnology, Antarctica research, ocean studies, solar energy, etc. from now over the long term.

CHAPTER 29

A LOOK AT INDIA–BRAZIL RELATIONS

Sunil Lal

India and Brazil are world leaders in cattle wealth—the earliest traces of Indian cattle in Brazil date to the late nineteenth and early twentieth centuries, when Portugal was the link between the two. The story of Cid, the rancher from the Rio de Janeiro area, is worth recounting. Cid came to India in 1959 and came across a newspaper item on a prize-winning bull. The bull belonged to the Raja (King) of Bhavnagar and Cid beseeched the Raja to sell it to him. The Raja was hesitant, as he opposed breeding livestock for consumption. Cid assured the Raja that there would be no slaughter for ten generations and clinched the deal with a contract that included placing a representative in Brazil to monitor compliance. Today, more than 80 per cent of Brazil's cattle have an Indian DNA and are known by the generic name Zebu. Brazilian cross-bred cows have demonstrated an astounding output of 45 to 60 litres a day. As India and Brazil are signatories to the Biodiversity Convention, results of the research ought to have been shared by Brazil with India, the source country. This hasn't happened, even though the two sides have agreements on cattle genomics and milk production. The influential cattle ranchers' lobby in Brazil that finances research on the cross-breeding programme has been reluctant to part with its trade secrets. Brazilian researchers, however, require bovine embryos from India to validate their findings; herein lies the opportunity to find a via media to benefit both sides. The two governments have been negotiating a work plan covering embryo transfer technology, along with the setting up of a

Brazil-aided Animal Husbandry Centre for Excellence in India, but this initiative is languishing. Perhaps it is time for India to buy prize bulls like Jabriel from Brazil with the potential of raising over half a million offspring! Jabriel's price in 2018 was said to be around US$ 1 million.

Brazil is over two-and-a-half times the size of India and has one-sixth its population. One of the most significant assets of Brazil is the Amazon river basin, which contains more water than the next six biggest rivers of the world combined. As an ecosystem, the Amazon is one of the most biodiverse regions on the planet. Over three million species live in the rainforest, and over 2,500 tree species, or one-third of all tropical trees that exist on earth, can be found here. India has supported Brazil with satellite imagery in the Amazon and Indian Space Research Organisation (ISRO) launched Brazil's Amazonia-1 satellite on 28 February 2021. Massive deforestation in recent years, coupled with mining activity and unregulated expansion of agribusiness, has led to heightened environmental risk.

The BASIC (Brazil, South Africa, India and China) grouping had worked closely to align environmental policies with developing country interests on the principle of 'common but differentiated responsibilities'. This provided leeway for developing countries like India and Brazil to implement voluntary measures; the devastating effects of climate change have come as a wake-up call and there is a clamour to arrest the slide. The UN Climate Change Conference (COP26), to be held in November 2021 in Glasgow under UK's chairmanship, is expected to see concerted efforts by the US and its European allies, to bring climate change to the centre stage as they push for universal commitments and pitch for clean technologies. India is on track to reduce emissions intensity for its gross domestic product (GDP) to 33 to 35 per cent, and is playing a constructive role in climate change negotiations. Brazil, under President Jair Bolsonaro, has followed former US President Donald Trump's lead in repudiating the science behind climate change. Persuading Brazil to join the consensus on climate change will require tact and incentives. External pressures and threats to derail the European Union–Mercosur free trade agreement (FTA) or to block Brazil's entry in the Organisation for Economic Co-operation and Development (OECD) are likely to be counterproductive. Influential Brazilian agribusiness and industrial lobbies are better placed to persuade Bolsonaro, as environmental groups have been given short shrift by him. An asset like the

Amazon gives Brazil immense leverage; the government is able to drum up popular support against foreign interference in its internal affairs.

Brazil gave up its nuclear option in 1998 when it signed the Non-Proliferation Treaty (NPT). Its constitution abjures nuclear weapons, though Brazil refused to sign the additional protocol and has even resisted International Atomic Energy Agency (IAEA) inspections. Signing the NPT and having a US nuclear umbrella has been advantageous to Brazil in terms of membership of nuclear control regimes and attendant benefits. But, doubts have lingered on lack of nuclear weapon power status undermining Brazil's stature. This realisation may have dawned when Brazil and Turkey, as non-permanent members of the UN Security Council, brokered a nuclear deal with Iran in 2010. This turned out to be a pyrrhic victory, as the US refused to endorse it. India has been opposed to an inequitable non-proliferation regime, and in the absence of steps towards universal disarmament, decided to become a nuclear weapon state in 1998. Brazil was amongst a small group of countries that raised concerns relating to India's non-membership of NPT, the need to follow a criteria-based approach in deciding Nuclear Suppliers Group (NSG) membership of non-NPT countries, and for India to assume additional responsibilities in return for acceptance as a member. India, in response, assured all NSG members that its aim in joining the group is to strengthen NSG's non-proliferation objectives and have a predictable basis to develop nuclear power to meet its burgeoning energy needs. This is proposed through civil nuclear cooperation with NSG members. The US has staunchly supported India's case on merits but consensus hasn't been possible without China's acquiescence. Brazil has an understanding with India on 'respecting each other's aspirations' which suggests that Brazil will not be a hurdle to India's NSG membership if consensus is possible. India–Brazil trade was insignificant in the early 2000s, reached a high of over US$ 12 billion in 2012-13, but plateaued to around US$ 7 billion in 2019-2020. This was mainly on account of an ongoing global economic downturn since 2014-15 and, more recently, as a fallout of the Covid-19 pandemic. Major Indian exports to Brazil include processed petroleum products, agrochemicals, chemicals, pharmaceuticals, textured filament yarn and unwrought aluminium. Brazilian exports to India include crude oil, soya oil, gold, cane sugar, cotton, gum, turpentine oils and iron ore concentrates. Indian investments in Brazil have been to the order of US$ 6 billion whereas Brazil's investment in India is around US$ 1 billion. An Investment Cooperation and Facilitation Treaty and a Social Security Agreement have paved the way for enhanced investments. The India–Mercosur Preferential Trade Agreement, signed in 2004, has had marginal impact on trade, as only around 6 per cent of its basket of 450 items have actually been traded. Efforts to expand the list have not materialised and for all practical purposes, this agreement is a dead letter that needs to be replaced with an FTA, albeit with some exceptions. Lip service continues to be paid to the virtues of the PTA agreement without serious intent of expanding its ambit. Domestic lobbies in both countries oppose entry of additional items that compete with their products, and the two sides have been at their wits' end to provide mutually acceptable lists. In Brazil's case, there is the added challenge of getting other Mercosur members on board. The India–Brazil Trade Monitoring Mechanism has been less than effective, as it has met sporadically and with little continuity in interaction amongst key interlocutors who have kept changing.

India's largest upstream investment in South America is in Brazil. ONGC Videsh Limited (OVL) and Bharat PetroResources Limited (BPRL) have together invested over US$ 3.2 billion in exploratory and production assets in Brazil. Inclusion in the annual work plans of the Brazilian Petroleum Ministry with Petrobras as the lead implementing player has been a prerequisite for the monetisation of foreign oil and gas assets in Brazil. In this context, Indian oil and gas majors have been waiting for investments to bear fruit. This situation is likely to improve going forward when the Sergipe–Alagoas basin, where India has stakes, is cleared for implementation to service the needs of Brazil's north-eastern region. In 2018-19, India imported 3.4 million metric tonnes of crude worth US$ 1.6 billion from Brazil. Brazil's crude oil reserves of 13.4 billion barrels are second only to Venezuela in South America, and its oil production has been rising for decades from 1.2 million b/d (barrels per day) in 2000 to 3 million b/d in 2020, according to Platts Analytics, which forecasts this to rise to 4 million b/d by 2040. Cooperation in biofuels offers great potential for Brazilian investments in India, particularly in ethanol blending, for which Brazil is the world leader. The present level of blending in Brazil is at 27 per cent, where flexible-fuel engines have long become the norm. India is looking to achieve a blending target of 10 per cent. Brazil has also signed the International Solar Alliance Agreement, a joint initiative of India and France for efficient consumption of solar energy to reduce dependence on fossil fuels. With 121 countries, this alliance, headquartered in Gurugram, has become the second largest grouping of states worldwide after the United Nations (UN).

Former Brazilian Presidents Fernando Henrique Cardoso and Luiz Inácio Lula da Silva had invested heavily in the bilateral relationship with India, and this was reciprocated by the Indian leadership. The economic downturn after 2014 and the internal upheaval in Brazil following corruption scandals saw President Dilma Rousseff being impeached in 2016 and derailed Brazil considerably. Bolsonaro, on assuming office in January 2019, has wanted to change Brazil's foreign policy orientation to align with the US and Western democratic governments and reduce economic dependence on China. The Chinese deftly used their leverage to put ties back on track after Bolsonaro's visit to China in October 2019. The Brazilian president has developed a good rapport with Prime Minister Narendra Modi after three face-to-face meetings, and was the chief guest at India's Republic Day celebrations in 2020. During this State visit, it was agreed to strengthen and revitalise the strategic partnership that began in 2006, through a joint action plan. Agriculture and food processing, biofuels, space, defence, trade, and investment have been identified as priority areas.

Brazil and India are members of BRICS (Brazil, Russia, India, China and South Africa), a prestigious bloc that has added heft to India and Brazil as emerging global powers. IBSA (India, Brazil and South Africa) is perceived as a dormant grouping for South–South cooperation and critics contend it is subsumed under BRICS; nevertheless, it is seen by participants as a useful platform that could be utilised better. BASIC is an environment initiative to promote developing country interests. The two countries see their role in the G20 as an endeavour to make the international financial system more equitable. Both countries have led developing country efforts in the World Trade Organization (WTO) and its predecessor, General Agreement on Tariffs and Trade (GATT), with mixed success; Brazil's Roberto Acevedo was elected WTO's director general from 2013 to 2020. India and Brazil see benefit in a liberal, rule-based, democratic international order in the shape of the UN, but want it to be more representative and efficacious, in sync with contemporary reality. This entails an expanded UN Security Council (UNSC) with the inclusion of the G4 countries—Brazil, Germany, India and Japan. The G4 face opposition from the current permanent membership of the UNSC or the P5, who are unwilling to share or dilute their powers. The 'Coffee Club' countries are opposed to adding new members, as they feel this will merely create another privileged group at their expense. India has enhanced its reputation as one of the largest contributors to UN peacekeeping; Brazil's participation in this sphere has also been significant. Hosting of prestigious events like the Soccer World Cup in 2014 and the Rio Olympics in 2016 have been part of Brazil's endeavour to demonstrate capabilities at par with the best. India has made similar efforts in hosting cricket world cups and Commonwealth Games; hosting a summer Olympics is clearly on its agenda in the future.

BRICS, with two of the five permanent members of the UNSC—China and Russia—and three emerging nations that are democracies—Brazil, India and South Africa—is often dismissed as an ineffectual and disparate group. But the reality is quite different. BRICS has shown cohesion and consistency in its deliberations on global governance structures and has provided alternative narratives on key areas, such as developmental assistance without stringent World Bank/International Monetary Fund conditionality; Internet governance and international payment systems. The New Development Bank and Contingent Reserve Arrangement have been able to finance renewable energy and infrastructure development projects in developing countries. BRICS has been able to set aside ideological differences and rivalries to focus on issue-based cooperation in the broader context of making the international order more inclusive. The approach of BRICS countries is not anti-West, but one that seeks to supplement the efforts of Western institutions to make them more responsive. There has been significant convergence amongst BRICS nations on tackling the scourge of terrorism. Its proactive role to help poorer countries in dealing with the Covid-19 pandemic has been noteworthy. India and Russia have jointly worked on the Sputnik vaccine even as India has cooperated with the UK, US and a host of other countries in developing alternatives. India made available Covid-19 vaccine doses to Brazil at short notice after the Brazilian president made a personal request.

While dialogue between India and Brazil at the highest political level on global issues has been frequent due to annual BRICS summits and G4 meetings on the fringes of UN General Assembly in New York, there has been less focus on strengthening bilateral ties. This is reflected in the fact that despite the large number of mechanisms, such as the joint commission at the level of foreign minister for a holistic approach to the broad spectrum of ties; strategic dialogue at the level of national security advisor; foreign office consultations at the level of secretary, Ministry of External Affairs; trade monitoring mechanism at the level of commerce secretary; economic and financial dialogue at the level of finance secretary; joint defence committee at the level of additional secretary ministry of defence; joint committee on science and technology at level of director general; and a group on cyber security at functional level; bilateral outcomes have not been noteworthy. The Business Leaders Forum, a key business facilitator, has been dormant for a few years now. The State Bank of India (SBI) has opened an office in Sao Paulo, the business capital of Latin America, but its performance has been lacklustre. The frequency of exchanges for the mechanisms mentioned has been sporadic except in the case of defence ties. The joint commission at foreign minister level, for instance, is scheduled to meet every year alternately in the two capitals, but these meetings have often occurred after gaps of two or three years. Science and technology cooperation was intense for a number of years, but slowed down after the economic downturn of 2014-15; both sides need to ensure that funding for this endeavour is maintained at the required levels so that the immense depth in scientific know-how that both sides possess is utilised for mutual benefit.

Increasing stakes through mega projects that act as enablers is, perhaps, the best way to consolidate economic ties. Brazil can be an important contributor to India's energy and food security and India has the potential of becoming a major partner in Brazil's economic development. India's democracy and reputation as a non-aggressive, peace-loving country stands it in good stead. It is not a coincidence that Mahatma Gandhi remains popular in Brazil and doubts about the intentions of both the US and China have persisted. Getting Brazilian aeronautics major Embraer to Make in India or Indian shipyards to construct coastal vessels for Brazil, could be game changing. If the Ministry of AYUSH could open Ayurveda centres across Brazil, along with programmes to promote yoga, then the connect with Brazilian society and its polity can be transformational. The two countries have an agreement on traditional medicine and the Amazon has all the herbs required for Ayurvedic cures. But multinational corporations have been able to act as spoilers to protect their turf.

Language and distance constraints are not insurmountable and can be bridged with enhanced business ties, tourism exchanges and deeper people-to-people contacts. The number of non-resident Indians in Brazil is less than

5,000 while there are only a few hundred Brazilians in India—these numbers are woefully inadequate for countries who call themselves strategic partners. The case for direct air links and shipping channels is axiomatic. It takes twenty-two hours to travel from India to Brazil by air and there are no direct flights; container cargo ships take, on average, fifty to fifty-five days. Unless trade consistently crosses the 15 to 20 billion mark annually, the potential of the partnership will remain largely unfulfilled.

India and Brazil are aware that the twenty-first century will be dominated by the knowledge economy, and those in control of 5G networks, cyberspace, artificial intelligence, robotics and other cutting-edge technologies will be at an advantage. The rise of China and its increasing global influence through trade and economic linkages has created the possibility of an emerging bipolar world divided between the US and China. China's Belt and Road Initiative (BRI) seeks to integrate an expanded version of the old Silk Road through the Eurasian landmass, giving it a driver's seat in the global economy. China's recent behaviour in the South China Sea, on its borders with India and its aggressive countering of its Covid-19 culpability narrative (Bolsonaro's son was also assailed for blaming China) suggest that its President Xi Jinping might be prepared to play for bigger stakes. China and Russia have drawn closer to each other, so much so that the BRI, which has the potential of increasing Chinese influence in Central Asia at Russia's expense, has been backed by Moscow. Russia, China and Iran are on the same side in West Asia; the US, Israel, Saudi Arabia and the UAE are on the other. Russia has leaned towards China, but this appears to be on account of US overreach in Ukraine. The US–Saudi-led move for regime change in Syria put the Middle East region in turmoil; a stalemate has resulted due to Russia's staunch backing of Syrian President Bashar Assad. Irritants in such key relationships tend to spill over to countries like India and Brazil who do not wish to choose sides. India's long-standing ties with Russia and Iran fall in this category. Brazil has a substantial population of Middle Eastern descent that wields considerable influence. Brazil is currently facing a 5G dilemma with President Bolsonaro hinting at keeping Huawei out of the bidding process to favour a US-led Western consortium, while Vice President General Hamilton Mourao has put out contrary signals. Huawei, meanwhile, has hired former Brazilian President Michel Temer as consultant to canvass its case. India will make its 5G choice aware that its core interests are at stake.

The global landscape going forward looks fraught with uncertainty in what may become a bruising tussle between current hyperpower, the US, and its closest competitor, China. The US has led the liberal, rule-based international order and continues to have the economic, military and technological edge over its rivals. China is catching up on the economic front, and the next two decades may see them increase their leverage in global affairs through economic integration and various forms of dependence. Climate change and the Covid-19 pandemic have brought home to all the need for united actions to confront global challenges. Cooperation and competition are expected to go hand in hand for the major powers. Rapid ageing and automation are two critical factors that may soon impact the world and could work in favour of the US and its industrialised partners. China, whose safety net is tenuous, may feel the pinch within a decade and be under pressure to make the best of its current window of opportunity; Brazil may have till 2035 and India till 2040 to leverage their demographic dividends. Covid-19 has taken a heavy toll on global economic activity in 2020-21 and its ill-effects are being felt in India and Brazil. India's hopes of becoming a US$ 5 trillion economy in real terms by 2025 have been dashed and may only be realised after 2030. Brazil would take longer to reach this milestone and could face a reversal of the poverty alleviation gains made a decade earlier. India isn't immune to this predicament either and could falter without social cohesion.

India and Brazil share the strategic vision of a multipolar world where each has an important say in matters affecting national and regional interests, and a voice that is heard globally. Consensus-building has been the forte of both countries, and this should prove useful in the period ahead. But, for either country to carve a niche for itself, sustained economic growth with peace and stability over the next two decades will be essential. Both sides need to step up domestically, foster closer bilateral and regional ties and act as catalysts for a rule-based and equitable international order. Economic development that keeps pace with twenty-first century competition will require serious heavy lifting. India and Brazil have large markets, broad industrial bases and material as well as manpower resources to maintain their places in the world's premier economies in decades ahead. The self-deprecating Brazilian joke that 'Brazil is the country of the future, and will always be' could well apply to India if we do not get our act together.

CHAPTER 30

INDIAN FOREIGN POLICY AND THE NORTH EAST IN THE POST-COVID-19 WORLD

TSEWANG TOPDEN

North East India comprises eight states, of which Assam is the most populous and Arunachal Pradesh the largest. The other states are Meghalaya, Tripura, Nagaland, Manipur, Mizoram and Sikkim. The region is strategically located, bordering five countries—China (after its occupation of Tibet), Nepal, Bhutan, Bangladesh and Myanmar. It is linked to the rest of mainland India by the narrow Siliguri corridor, often referred to as the 'Chicken's Neck'. Darjeeling and Kalimpong districts in West Bengal blend with the North East Region (NER) here and should be included in the North East Council (NEC) in the future for development purposes to secure this strategic region of India that rubs up against an aggressive and hostile People's Republic of China (PRC) in the Himalayas.

Strengthening connectivity and developing the economy of the vulnerable and isolated, but resource rich, NER are compelling strategic objectives of India's foreign and domestic policies that are aimed to secure the region and promote the development needs of the people of the area, as PRC forges ahead with its 'national restoration project', pushing its agenda in the Himalayas, Indian Ocean, South China Sea and the Indo-Pacific region in a bid for 'superpower' status.

The Look East Policy (LEP), now called the Act East Policy (AEP) since 2014, and Neighbourhood First Policy are the two fundamental pillars of India's foreign policy linked with the NER which are to serve as India's gateway to the economically dynamic and politically significant South East and East Asia.

The scope of this article is confined to India's foreign policy and how it can help in the development of the NER in the post-Covid-19 world. To appreciate this, it would be necessary to put in context India's Neighbourhood First Policy and the LEP/AEP, and then see how these policies contribute to the development of the NER.

The LEP was launched in 1992 by Prime Minister PV Narasimha Rao. It came at a time when things were falling apart for India. At the end of the Cold War and the collapse of the Soviet Union, India found itself marginalised from the global mainstream and was on the verge of financial and economic collapse. The LEP was a strategic shift in India's vision of the world and its place in the evolving global economy. Significantly, it was aimed at reaching out to India's eastern neighbours with whom it has deep historical, civilisational and cultural links from time immemorial. The LEP was oriented to the tiger economies of the Association of Southeast Asian Nations (ASEAN); and for over two decades, India has done well to integrate with the broader open international global economy. Trade between India and ASEAN was around US$ 86.9 billion for 2019-20, with trade in favour of ASEAN. Two-way foreign direct investment (FDI) from 2000 to 2018 was over US$ 107 billion, with higher FDI flows from ASEAN into India.

India–ASEAN relations are central to India's LEP/AEP. India became a sectoral dialogue partner of ASEAN in 1992 and a full dialogue partner in 1996. The relationship was further elevated in 2002 to the Summit level. India became a founding member of the East Asia Summit (EAS) in 2005 along with China, Japan, Republic of Korea, Australia, New Zealand and ten members of the ASEAN. The ASEAN–India Free Trade Agreement (FTA) in goods was signed in August 2009 and for services in November 2014.

ASEAN has all along clearly indicated that it wants India as an active player in the region. ASEAN sees India as a major power that is democratic, plural and benign, and provides a regional balance to China. Even after India's decision not to join the Regional Comprehensive Economic Partnership (RCEP) in

November 2020—after years of deliberations—members of the region and Japan kept the door open for India. However, it created a doubt about India's commitment to AEP.

The three pillars of India's cooperation with ASEAN are: economic cooperation; security cooperation; socio-cultural, science and technology and related cooperation. In 2012, a strategic partnership was enunciated and, in 2018, substantive discussions on maritime security were put in place. In 2014, the LEP was upgraded to Act East Policy (AEP) by Prime Minister Narendra Modi at the ASEAN–India Summit in Myanmar. Under the AEP, India devoted considerable diplomatic energy in strengthening relations with key East and South East Asian partners, Japan and countries in the Indo-Pacific region. Former National Security Advisor Shivshankar Menon says India must work with other powers to ensure that the region stays multipolar and China behaves responsibly.

The other complementary subregional groupings linked to the NER are the Bay of Bengal Initiative for Multi-Sectoral Technical and Economic Cooperation (BIMSTEC), the Mekong–Ganga Cooperation (MGC) and the BBIN countries—Bangladesh, Bhutan, India and Nepal—which serve as building blocks in India's thrust for regional cooperation. However, these should be strengthened, as, in the past, commitment and implementation of projects lagged behind the rhetoric and hype.

Equally important is a peaceful periphery to sustain India's growth and development. And, India's Neighbourhood First Policy is vital in this respect. India's relations with Nepal, Bangladesh, Bhutan and Myanmar and how well we can promote and create stakes for them in India, and the bigger challenge of how well we can manage relations with China, will be key for the country and the NER.

Since our independence in 1947, the NER has been a restive region in most parts. All the states, except Sikkim, have seen insurgency either for independence or for some other cause. The Armed Forces Special Powers Act (AFSPA) and Disturbed Area Act have, for years, created an atmosphere of mistrust and bitterness and resulted in economic uncertainty and deterred investors. On top of this, the region has been afflicted by transborder illegal migrations from Bangladesh, leading to all sorts of social and political tensions that are to be addressed diplomatically.

In the pre-Independence period, the NER was one of the fastest growing and well-connected integrated economic regions of India, with transborder connections with all its neighbours. These were disrupted with the Partition of India in 1947 at the time of Independence, virtual closure of Burma and the Chinese occupation of Tibet. The flourishing trade with the plains of East Bengal, Tibet and Burma came to a halt, making the NER the most regulated, sensitive and exposed border region, says Dr Thongkholal Haokip.

According to Dr Haokip, after Independence, the Government of India adopted several different policy approaches towards the NER. These were: (i) the 'Nehruvian policy framework' of quick administrative expansion, with protectionist approach towards tribal development and ethnic tribal identity; (ii) security considerations after the sudden Chinese aggression in 1962 and rising insurgent movements; (iii) the conception in the 1970s that the region required political representation, and new states were formed; and (iv) the development paradigm in the 1980s, with various development packages announced by successive prime ministers.

Broadly, the development policy approach has been comprehensive. The NER is protected and promoted by some of the most unique and progressive constitutional, financial, institutional and governance provisions, including provisions under Article 371 and the Sixth Schedule of the Indian Constitution. The special category states status from 1969 to 2014, setting up of the North Eastern Council (1971), Ministry of Development of North East Region (2001) and a range of regional and sector-specific institutions have triggered far reaching impact on the region.

According to Professor Mahendra Lama, focused development strategies to promote industrial and other service sector ventures, setting aside 10 per cent of the development budget of most ministries in Government of India as Non-Lapsable Central Pool of Resources scheme, inducting multiple development partners/private sector players/civil society organisations and opening several sectors for both investment and cross-border trade are aimed towards promoting a fast development trajectory for the NER.

The vision for the NER is captured in the 3 Cs—Connectivity, Commerce and Cultural commonalities. To realise this vision, India's foreign policy is in full drive at the bilateral, plurilateral (BIMSTEC, MGC and BBIN) and multilateral levels through its Neighbourhood First Policy and AEP.

India's warm and friendly ties with Bangladesh, Bhutan and Myanmar have resulted in closing down of major insurgent safe havens and taking up of connectivity projects of bilateral and regional significance, contributing to the security and stability of the region.

To begin with, the NER is a region well-endowed with natural resources, such as hydrocarbons, coal, limestone, uranium and other minerals. It is rich in cultural diversity, with cross-border cultural and civilisational linkages to its neighbours. It was the seat of four kingdoms and several small principalities in the past, and has a wide diversity of people, including over 200 different indigenous tribes. The region is blessed with more than forty-one rivers that flow from the Himalayas and the Tibetan plateau, of which the largest is the Brahmaputra. The other big rivers are Barak and the Teesta. Most of these rivers disgorge into the Bay of Bengal in Bangladesh. Four rivers—Imphal River, Manipur River, Tiau Lui and Kaladan (Chhimtuipui) flow into Myanmar across the Patkai Range. The network of rivers reflects the immense potential of the region for hydropower and inland waterways that could transform and reduce its isolation.

A web of roads, rail, waterways, air and digital connectivity projects are being implemented in the NER that are of India's domestic and foreign policy priorities. Some of these are linked with Bangladesh and others with Myanmar; still others under the BBIN with Nepal and Bhutan. Under the AEP and Neighbourhood First Policy, capital-intensive projects of development partnership through credits and grants are being executed in these countries. The connectivity corridors are expected to act as force multipliers in economic development; generate investment, trade and employment opportunities; and facilitate greater people-to-people contact in the region.

According to Foreign Secretary Harsh Vardhan Shringla, India has revived five rail links that used to be operational between India and Bangladesh (then East Pakistan) before 1965. The prime ministers of India and Bangladesh jointly inaugurated the rail link between Haldibari in West Bengal and Chilahati in Bangladesh during a virtual summit held in December 2020. Work is ongoing on two more connections. Other connections between Karimganj in Assam and Sylhet in Bangladesh and between Akhaura in Bangladesh to Agartala are under construction, to be ready in 2022. Passenger trains such as Maitree Express and Bandhan Express link India and Bangladesh.

Also, on the riverine front, goods from West Bengal can now reach Tripura through waterways up to Ashuganj port in Bangladesh and then by road to Agartala under the India–Bangladesh agreement on the use of the Chittagong and Mongla ports. For the first time, Tripura was connected to Bangladesh through the inland waterways route. These new initiatives provide alternative and shorter routes for transporting goods between the NER and the rest of India through Bangladesh. There are other planned projects on the Brahmaputra–Barak River system that would transform the entire region, says Foreign Secretary Shringla.

Land customs stations and integrated check posts have been set up on the road transport links between Shillong–Dhaka and Agartala–Kolkata via Dhaka. Along these connectivity corridors, economic synergies have also started developing. Liquefied petroleum gas (LPG) now reaches Tripura through Bangladesh, cutting transportation costs.

Bangladesh is importing power—generated in Bhutan—through adjoining states in India. Surplus hydropower potential of the NER could be sold to Bangladesh and Myanmar.

Air connectivity between Guwahati and Bangkok and between Guwahati and Dhaka is in place, which is to be resumed once the Covid-19 pandemic abates.

The recent leasing of 10 Gbps bandwidth from Bangladesh to the NER is a welcome development that should help speed up Internet connectivity, which is vital for economic activity, services and security.

With Myanmar, the two flagship projects are the Trilateral Highway project connecting the NER with Myanmar and South East Asia and the Kaladan Multi-Modal Transit Transport project. These are vital for making the NER a bridgehead to ASEAN.

The Trilateral Highway will provide land connectivity between the NER and South East Asia. The India–Myanmar Friendship road from Moreh (Manipur)/Tamu (Myanmar) to Kalemya and Kalewa was inaugurated in 2001. India undertook the construction of seventy-one bailey bridges on this road in Myanmar that connects the NER to Mandalay. Bus and trucks should be able to cover the distance in twelve to fourteen hours. Two international entry/exit points have been operationalised at Moreh/Tamu and Zowkhawthar (Mizoram)/Rhi (Myanmar). India is also part of the Asian Highway project.

Plans are also being made to link the NER with the rest of South East Asia by road and rail via Myanmar, Thailand, Laos, Cambodia and Vietnam. The recent historic ASEAN–India car rally opened up the route taken by ancient Buddhist emissaries of Emperor Ashoka to spread Buddhism from India to South East Asia.

According to former Ambassador VS Seshadri, the Kaladan Multi-Modal Transit Transport project will give the NER access to sea through the Sittwe port in Myanmar. Vessels from Indian ports to Sittwe will transport cargo by barges on the Kaladan River to Paletwa and then by road to Zorinpui on the India–Myanmar border and then onwards to Lawngtlai, Lunglei and Aizwal in Mizoram.

There are several other projects planned that should enable greater trade and economic activity and make the NER the logistic linchpin between India and ASEAN. Studies by Indian think tanks show possibilities for a wide range of items, from handicrafts and textile to pharmaceuticals, which can be manufactured in the NER. Multi-product special economic zones (SEZs) in Manipur, trade support centres, commodity exchanges, logistic servicing, warehousing facilities and transportation support hubs can come up on the Indian side of the border. Hydropower potential from Sikkim and Arunachal Pradesh to the region and across to the neighbours is immense. However, these should be taken up on a sustainable development basis, and not on a massive scale as the region is in a seismic zone. Also, cultural sensitivities should be respected and dam sites avoided in holy places.

On the Myanmar side, there are good prospects for Indian companies to set up copper-based industries, locomotive factories in Sagaing region and coach factories in Mandalay, and revamping existing textile mills, garment units, timber-based industries, agro industries, dairy farming and rice and oil mills.

States in the NER close to the Kaladan project—Mizoram, Tripura and lower Assam—could find added markets in the Rakhine and Chin states of Myanmar. The Sittwe port could be a good outlet for exports from the NER to ASEAN. However, these prospects will depend on peace and stability in the Rakhine region that is disturbed presently.

With Bhutan, India has agreed to open four new trade routes for its trade and transit—Nagrakata (land customs station), Agartala, Jigighopa and Pandu (two riverine ports in Assam on India's national waterways along the Brahmaputra).

The Agartala route will enable Bhutan's trade with Bangladesh. In October 2020, the Ahllay–Jaigaon axis was opened to decongest the existing Phuentsholing–Jaigaon route. With the new developments, Bhutan will be able to export boulders and riverbed materials along with traditional exports of oranges, ginger and cardamom to India and other countries.

With Nepal, India opened integrated check posts in Birgunj and Biratnagar, with two more to be opened—one in Nepalgunj and the other in Bhairahawa. The BBIN subregional initiative is envisioned to improve economic cooperation and connectivity among the four South Asian countries. This initiative is expected to help the landlocked neighbours of the region to integrate more effectively with India, amongst themselves and with the global economy. The BBIN Motor Vehicles Agreement (BBIN MVA), signed in June 2015, should make cross-border trade and transport in and through the NER to these countries more efficient. The agreement will allow vehicles to enter each other's territory and eliminate the need for costly and time-consuming transhipment. This would be strategically advantageous to all the members of the region. While India, Nepal and Bangladesh have gone ahead with the agreement, Bhutan is yet to join, pending completion of its internal procedures for ratification.

To energise these initiatives of connectivity in the NER, following areas of focus are recommended. First, fast and reliable Internet connectivity will be a critical factor for the economic development of the NER. At present, the NER suffers from poor and patchy Internet connectivity in most parts. All business verticals in the future will require a horizontal digital platform, and, with faster and broader bandwidth, the NER should be able to connect smoothly with mainland India and the rest of the world. The recent leasing of 10 Gbps bandwidth from Bangladesh is a move in the right direction. However, a majority of the NER states are yet to access this bandwidth. High-speed broadband connectivity drawn from alternate sources, in addition to the limited existing connection, will facilitate e-commerce, entrepreneurship development, start-ups, skills-development, micro, small, and medium enterprises (MSMEs), innovation hubs, IT centres, technology incubators, digital payment and services and education and also enhance security. It will result in higher productivity, speed up the ease of doing business and generate employment in the NER.

Second, the NER is blessed with a talented young population with a high literacy rate. Once the corridors of economic connectivity open up fully with mainland India to the west and ASEAN and adjoining regions to the east, capacity building and skills development should be ramped up to international standards. Besides, the ongoing support from the Ministry of Skill Development and Entrepreneurship to the NER and linkages and exchanges with foreign partners, such as Japan, Singapore, Korea and Germany, should be reinforced and encouraged. The NER has, for a long time now, been isolated under the Inner Line permits, security considerations and hard borders. These need to be eased further. Planned outreach programmes of the Ministry of External Affairs (MEA) with the NER and interlocutors in neighbouring countries and South East Asia are positive steps. The government of Assam has set up a designated department for AEP matters, and others have identified their planning department to interface with the MEA.

Third, the NER could be an education destination for students from neighbouring countries and ASEAN. Those from CLMV countries—Cambodia, Laos, Myanmar and Vietnam—can avail the Indian Technical and Economic Cooperation (ITEC) programme of the MEA. The numerous public schools, engineering and medical colleges and universities in the NER should have greater representation from these countries with good connectivity.

The NER could also be a medical destination for our neighbours, with state-of-the-art hospitals coming up in Assam, Meghalaya and Sikkim. Hospitals in Manipur attract patients from Myanmar; and some from Nepal and Bhutan visit hospitals in Sikkim and the Jamyang Kongtrul Eye Centre in Kalimpong that abuts Gangtok.

Fourth, tourism and culture are areas where the NER has a natural advantage, with its rich diversity of culture, ethnicity and shared commonality with its neighbours and ASEAN. Expanded connectivity should give boost to the hospitality industry. And, for those seeking tranquil surroundings to rejuvenate themselves in the post-Covid-19 world, the NER will be an ideal destination, with its snow-capped mountains, immense biodiversity and friendly people.

Buddhist pilgrims arriving from South East Asia to Bodh Gaya and Nalanda University will find the holy sites of Vajrayana Buddhism in Sikkim and Arunachal Pradesh enlightening. Many of these tourists visit Bhutan and could travel to the NER if they are made aware of these destinations.

For studying ethnic similarities and culture, those from ASEAN and the Far East will find the NER interesting. For instance, Japanese tourists have been visiting Lepcha reserves in north Sikkim. Studying languages and similarities is another field that could bring the regions closer to each other. To promote tourism, reputed journalists, anthropologists, linguists and high-profile personalities should be sponsored by the Government of India to visit the region and write for maximum publicity abroad. Travel agents in the NER should link up with their counterparts in ASEAN and the Far East. These linkages are limited at the moment.

Recent visa relaxation has seen an increased flow of tourists from Bangladesh to Gangtok, some other parts of the NER, Darjeeling, Kalimpong and Kolkata.

Various types of tourism, such as traditional herbal therapy, river cruises, sports—golf (Meghalaya, Mizoram and Assam) and polo (Manipur)—music festivals, art museum (Tripura), war memorials (Nagaland), ethnic food, tea, Buddhist circuit (Sikkim and Arunachal Pradesh), wildlife, mountain to sea adventure and paragliding have much scope in the NER. Film shooting, as done in Switzerland, is another model that should be followed by the NER. All this is good, provided stakeholders do not insist on inner line restrictions, which is counterproductive for tourism.

Fifth, organic farming will be a major industry in the future for the NER. Already, Sikkim has taken a lead in this. The global organic food and beverage market is expected to reach over US$ 320 billion in 2025. The six agroclimatic zones of the NER are conducive for a large variety of fruits, vegetables and spices that are grown in abundance here. Many of these spices are good for medicinal purposes and have geographical indication tags. These can be cultivated on economies of scale in the NER. According to Professor Mahendra Lama, the objective is to make organic farming consumer-driven and farmer-powered, and a major constituent of the functional food that would ultimately trigger transformation in the rural economies by interconnecting the production clusters that remain largely segregated and disconnected today. This is another area where the North East should leverage AEP for investments, design and knowhow, transport, logistics and markets.

The NER has a good base in floriculture, especially in Sikkim which has many exotic varieties of orchids. With good air connectivity to mainland India, ASEAN and the Far East, this is a segment of business that should power the NER.

Sixth, industry is critical for the NER to turn from a net importing region to a productive region, capable of driving an Act East Policy by adding value to natural resources and primary products, generating employment and absorbing surplus labour from farms and contributing to trade and exports. Several state-centric flagship projects in food processing, sericulture, orchid centres, textile promotion, bamboo and cane, fashion technology and design need to be scientifically integrated. These, along with its massive tea industry, should help transform the NER.

Finally, we need to develop smart, liveable cities in the NER that are designed organically, with recreational sports facilities and parks for leisure and tourism and better roads with guard rails for safety, to make life comfortable and pleasant for all. As former Ambassador Gautam Mukhopadhaya says, 'South East and East Asia provide good examples of liveable and smart cities that could be tapped to improve North East cities.'

India's foreign policy priority is to transform the NER and make it India's gateway to ASEAN. The NER has the potential to become that linchpin and prosper.

Bibliography

1. *India's Look East Policy and North East India*—Thongkholal Haokip
2. Draft Vision Statement for NER 2035—Professor Mahendra Lama
3. Impact of Neighbourhood First and Act East Policies on the North East (speech)—Foreign Secretary Harsh Vardhan Shringla
4. Moving Trade and Development Relations Forward (DPG Policy Brief)—Dr VS Seshadri
5. North East, Act East (presentation)—Gautam Mukhopadhaya
6. India's Foreign Affairs Strategy—Shivshankar Menon
7. *The India Way*—S Jaishankar
8. *Strangers No More*—Sanjoy Hazarika
9. *Shadow States*—India and China and the Himalayas 1910-1962—B Guyot Richard
10. *Tibet and the British Raj*—Alex McKay
11. *Tibet, Past and Present*—Charles Bell
12. *Ten Lessons for a Post-Pandemic World*—Fareed Zakaria

CHAPTER 31

INDIA'S SOFT POWER DIPLOMACY PREDATES JOSEPH NYE

SURENDRA KUMAR

The spirit of 'soft power', if not the letters, existed in India more than 3,000 years before Joseph Nye wrote his much talked-about book, *Bound to Lead: The Changing Nature of America's Power*. When the Shanti mantras were written in the Vedic period, especially in the *Brihadaranyaka*, the invocation of Shanti—'*Om dyauh shantir antariksham shantih*'—conveyed a message that wasn't confined to India alone. The mantra prays for peace on earth, peace in the forest, peace in the ocean, peace in the skies, peace for all the beings in the universe. This soaring invocation for world peace by the seers of India might, arguably, be the earliest of its kind in the world. And decades before the communication revolution and the explosion of social networks, it had impacted great minds thousands of miles away. The US-born British poet and Nobel laureate, TS Elliot was greatly influenced by the Bhagavad Gita and Upanishads, which can be seen in his famous poem, *The Waste Land*. In the final Chapter, he says, 'What the thunder said, mentions three cardinal Vedic virtues Damyata (Restraint), Datta (Charity) and Dayadhvan (Compassion)'. He ends the poem with 'Shantih, Shantih, Shantih'. Wasn't this the quintessential Indian soft power in action without state sponsorship and without hyped sloganeering by self-appointed custodians of India's culture?

Lord Buddha (563 BCE-483 BCE) gave the clarion call for non-violence—'*Ahimsa paramo dharma*'. Emperor Ashoka (268 BCE-232 BCE) sent his own son and daughter, Mahinda and Sanghamitta, to spread the gospel of non-violence and tenets of Buddhism to Sri Lanka. In later periods, Buddhism spread to various countries in Asia and South East Asia. Its footprints are visible today in South Korea, Japan, China, Thailand and Myanmar. Afghanistan had some of the world's tallest Buddha statues in Bamiyan before these were destroyed by the Taliban. The Angkor Wat in Cambodia and Borobudur in Indonesia are living examples of the influence of Hinduism, Buddhism, spiritualism and centuries old Indian cultural traditions.

It's a known secret that the Ramayana has been staged, for decades, with great enthusiasm by Muslim actors and actresses in Indonesia, which has the largest Muslim population in the world. Interestingly, political leaders of this Muslim country, from Sukarno to Suharto to Suryaputri, have had more Sanskritised names than most Hindus in India. This religious, cultural and intellectual interaction and co-option took place not on account of military conquests, like in the case of Alexander the Great, or marauding, predatory invasions, like that of Genghis Khan or Ahmad Shah Abdali, but through the voyages of Indian traders, businessmen, scholars, priests and artists. This was the transmission and impact of India's soft power sans forceful imposition.

Nearly 1,000 years before Oxford University and the Cambridge University in the United Kingdom (UK) and Harvard University, Massachusetts Institute of Technology, Princeton University and Columbia University in the USA were founded, the Nalanda, Vikramshila and Taxila universities of India were the largest campuses of their kind and attracted students from numerous foreign countries. The accounts of the Chinese scholars Fa-Hien and Huen Tsang provide evidence of the extent of dissemination of India's soft power.

Nearly 500 years ago, Emperor Akbar and his great-grandson Dara Shikoh had the Ramayana, Mahabharata and Upanishads translated from Sanskrit to Persian. The *dohe* (couplets) written by one of Akbar's Navaratnas, Abdur Rahim Khan-i-Khanan, figure in the prescribed Hindi textbooks in northern India. Both Fatehpur Sikri and Taj Mahal are examples of a fascinating synthesis of Persian, Turkish and Indian architectural traditions and motifs. It was as much a tribute to the Mughal rulers, unmatched skills and ability of the architects and masons as the abiding appeal of great Indian epics and scriptures.

Neither Vasco da Gama nor any of the other Portuguese, British, French and Dutch navigators headed towards India on perilous sea voyages to impart lessons in democracy. They were all lured by the stories of India's riches. Thus, it is no wonder that, at the peak of its colonial might, when the sun never set in the British Empire, India was called 'the jewel in the British crown'.

Thanks to the impact of various invasions, the reign of the rulers who came from outside; subsequent advent of the British colonial rule, and above all, her own rich cultural heritage going back three millennia, today, India is a multi-racial, multi-religious, multi-ethnic, multilingual, pluralistic society of bewildering diversity, woven through an invisible unifying thread of unity. Those who are aghast by the occasional instances of communal riots should bear in mind that the tiny Jewish community of 150 (Jews came to India from Babylonia in 600 BCE following their persecution) doesn't feel threatened amidst 1.35 billion Indians and the Parsi community of less than 100,000, which migrated from Iran to escape persecution (800 ACE) has produced some of the most successful business tycoons, legal luminaries, decorated generals and philanthropists.

Indian Council for Cultural Relations (ICCR) was founded in 1950 by India's first Education Minister Maulana Abul Kalam Azad to participate in the formulation and implementation of policies and programmes pertaining to India's external cultural relations and foster and strengthen cultural relations and mutual understanding between India and other countries. It's done through cultural exchanges with other countries and people: visits of performing artists (dancers, singers and instrumentalists), writers, poets and painters and gifts of busts or statues of Mahatma Gandhi, which have been installed in over 150 countries. It administers the prestigious Jawaharlal Nehru Award for International Understanding, which was initiated in 1965 and, since then, has been bestowed upon Nelson Mandela, Wangari Mathaai (both Nobel Peace Prize laureates), Kenneth Kaunda, Julius Nyerere, Yasser Arafat, Hosni Mubarak and Angela Merkel among others. The award conveys a subtle political message through soft power diplomacy.

The ICCR also awards ITECH scholarships under which hundreds of students from Asia, Central Asian Republics (CAR), South East Asia, Africa and Latin America have availed of educational facilities in India. The Professional Course for Foreign Diplomats conducted by the Foreign Service Institute (FSI) of the Ministry of External Affairs is a highly sought after outreach programme of India. The FSI has organised specially tailored courses at the request of friendly countries/groups of countries. It is heartening to come across individuals in Asia, Africa, Latin America and CAR who have availed the scholarship of the ICCR or attended the professional course of the FSI. This soft power diplomacy has generated considerable goodwill for India.

Shashi Tharoor is right in claiming that, presently, most of the soft power instruments: Bollywood, films, music, dance, yoga, Ayurveda and cricket happen independent of the government's support and sponsorship. But one shouldn't lose sight of the fact that most iconic personalities in the world of music and dance from India, like Pt Ravi Shankar, Pt Jasraj, Pt Shiv Kumar Sharma, Ustad Amjad Ali Khan, Ustad Zakir Hussain, Pt Birju Maharaj, Indrani Rehman, Sonal Mansingh and Malavika Sarukkai, have gone on performing tours abroad arranged by the ICCR, especially at the initial stage in their illustrious careers. However, once they became successful and famous celebrities, their concerts were mostly organised through the initiative of rich and influential people of Indian origin or organisations in different countries at the most prestigious venues like Carnegie Hall, the Chicago Symphony Orchestra Hall, Royal Albert Hall, the Sydney Opera House and others.

Much before Joseph Nye's book was released, India and the UK had jointly organised a very ambitious, carefully curated multi-art form event called Festival of India in March 1982, presenting fascinating glimpses of India's rich cultural heritage in London. It was attended by Indian PM Indira Gandhi, the British PM Margaret Thatcher and the Crown Prince Charles; at its inauguration sang the legendary MS Subbulakshmi. The Ministry of External Affairs, Ministry of Culture, National Museum, ICCR, Indian High Commission, British government and British museums and art galleries played a huge role in putting together such a mega display. It left the British public awestruck by the sheer depth and diversity of India's culture. Encouraged by its tremendous success, similar festivals were held in Paris at the base of Eiffel Tower and in Washington DC at the Kennedy Centre in 1985, showcasing the best of India's rich and diverse culture. The festivals in France and the US moved to different cities offering a fascinating glimpse into the cultural panorama of India.

The above instances vindicate beyond any doubt that India's soft power has been harnessed and imaginatively used for creating better understanding and appreciation of India as a country, building bridges of friendship and cooperation and enhancing and expanding productive relations.

Nye touches upon three dimensions of power: *coercion*: threatening the use of force, i.e., military power; financial and monetary inducement, i.e., economic power and co-option of others or soft power. According to him, co-optive power (soft power) means, 'the ability of a nation to structure a situation so that other nations develop preferences or define their interests consistent with one's nation'. Thus, soft power is the power of example, which is used through intangible means, to create your positive image in others' eyes that could generate interest in you and persuades them to accept your preferences or come closer to them.

In his *Arthashastra* (300 BCE), Kautilya refers to four forms of power that were used by the rulers in the Vedic period. Interestingly, the use of soft power was the first option:

Sam Niti: Resolving differences and conflicts through dialogue, discussion and exchange of ideas and arriving at mutual understanding.

Dam Niti: Rewarding people to get things done; offering financial and monetary incentives. Today, this would be termed as economic diplomacy.

Dand Niti: Using the rod, i.e., punishment. When persuasion and rewards don't produce the desired result, using force was the next option for the ruler to achieve one's objective.

Bhed Niti: The divide and rule policy; weaken your enemy's camp by fostering divisions and desertions and strengthen one's own position by taking advantage of these divisions. The East India Company and then the British Raj used Bhed Niti extensively with tremendous success and ruled over India for nearly 250 years.

Some myths about the impact of soft power ought to be cleared. As soft power works through intangible cultural elements—history, philosophy, religion, political system, music, dance, various arts forms, literature, films, games and sports, tourist attractions, cuisines, dresses, ways of life, flora and fauna, it appeals to people at large and generates people-to-people understanding, friendship, bonhomie and goodwill. Many a times, in spite of shared values like democracy, rule of law, human rights, multi-racial, multi-ethnic, multi-lingual, multi-religious and pluralistic societies, two nations may not be the best of friends on account of different political national interests. This is especially true in the case of India and the US. Notwithstanding all the shared values, during the Cold War, the US suspected India of being close to the Soviet Union. Similarly, India wasn't happy about America's pro-Pakistan tilt and concerned about its CIA's activities. So, the two countries had a rather strained relationship.

In 1971, when the Pakistani army, under instructions from President General Yahya Khan was committing genocide in East Pakistan, killing over 93,000 East Pakistanis, raping thousands of women and throwing their bodies in marshy land, the government of the oldest democracy, the US (President Richard Nixon and Secretary of State Dr Henry Kissinger), instead of standing by the largest democracy, India, chose to support the military rulers of Pakistan and sent their Seventh Fleet to the Bay of Bengal to intimidate India. Thus, shared values were set aside to serve American interests as seen by the government of the day. Yet, millions of Americans empathised with India. Senator Edward Kennedy even visited refugee camps for Bangladeshis in Calcutta.

No wonder that President Clinton was the first US president to visit India in twenty-two years in March 2000. However, over the last twenty years, this relationship has been transformed beyond recognition. We are now strategic partners.

Assertions of die-hard soft power votaries that it is more effective than hard power are cut off from realpolitik. Similarly, advocates of soul power (Gandhian values and principles of justice and righteousness) mostly exaggerate its impact. While soft power and soul power do create a certain degree of positivity and comfort level, help break the ice at times, solves stalemates, no leader is willing to budge an inch to protect them when vital national interests are at stake. In April 2017, President Trump invited Chinese President Xi Jinping to his Mar-a-Lago Golf Resort, received him warmly and made his granddaughter serenade for Xi. The Chinese president returned the hospitality, unfolding the longest red carpet to welcome Trump when he visited China (November 2017) and hosting a state banquet at the Forbidden City, an honour not shown to any other American president. However, these gestures didn't prevent the two countries from getting drawn into a debilitating trade war.

PM Modi attended an informal summit with President Xi in Wuhan in 2018 and hosted him at an informal summit at Mamallapuram in 2019. But these informal summits couldn't prevent PLA's incursion and attack on 15 June 2020 that left twenty Indian soldiers dead. Though twelve rounds of commander-level talks and two face-to-face meetings between the Indian EAM

Dr Jaishankar and his Chinese counterpart Wang Yi in Moscow in September 2020 and Dushanbe in July 2021 on the sidelines of the meeting of the foreign ministers of the Shanghai Cooperation Organisation (SCO) have led to the disengagement of two countries' troops at Pangong Tso lake and Gogra post, complete de-escalation will still take a long time.

There are millions of fans of Pakistani singers in India and Indian singers in Pakistan. We have tried cricket diplomacy and gifts of mangoes and sweets with Pakistan, but the relations are presently in limbo. Barely a week after PM Modi stopped over in Lahore to wish PM Nawaz Sharif a happy birthday on 25 December 2015, Pakistani terrorists attacked the Indian Air Force base in Pathankot on 2 January 2016, killing not only security personnel but also the very spirit of Modi's gracious and unprecedented friendly gesture. Thus, soft power is really soft when dealing with insincere and dishonest persons/nations and rogue elements.

It is generally assumed that stressing the convergences and commonalities will deepen understanding and bring you closer to your interlocutor. But this is not necessarily true in every instance. Late SK Singh, who served as the high commissioner of India in Islamabad and later as the foreign secretary and capped his career as a governor, used to say that the worst faux pas an Indian diplomat could commit in Pakistan was to tell his/her interlocutor how similar Pakistani people were to Indian people. Pakistani leaders strive hard to underline their different identity.

The bottom line is that soft power works by impacting and influencing opinion makers. Therefore, the kind of soft power and the manner of its use depends a lot on the form of the government and the political ideology a country follows and the freedom of press and expression it allows.

In 1893, at the World Parliament of Religions in Chicago, Swami Vivekananda's speech made a huge impact. In 1930s, much before India became independent, Pt Uday Shankar, an iconic dancer, lived in Paris and was admired internationally. Films of Satyajit Ray, the only Indian film director to receive a lifetime Oscar, were always a big draw in Paris and were often screened at the George Pompidou Centre.

Sitar maestro, Pt Ravi Shankar, whom the Beatles adored, was a pioneer who introduced Indian classical music to Western audiences. Late Ustad Ali Akbar, Ustad Amjad Ali Khan, Ustad Zakir Hussain, Pt Hari Prasad Chaurasia and Pt Shiv Kumar Sharma have performed world over. Jagjit Singh, the ghazal singer, had millions of fans.

Raj Kapoor was the biggest international film star India has ever produced. Long before the communication, television and social network explosion and the advent of colour films, his black-and-white movie *Awaara* was immensely popular in the Soviet Union, Central Asian Republics, Eastern Europe, China, Greece, Middle East, South and South East Asia and Turkey. It's title song is still hummed by millions. When he and Nargis went to Moscow for its premier (1956), their car was lifted on shoulders by Muscovites. *Awaara* remains the only film that was seen by Chinese helmsman Mao Zedong and Soviet leaders Nikita Khrushchev and Mikhail Gorbachev! Today, thanks to the rich and influential Indian diaspora, live stage shows by Indian film stars, Indian international film festivals in foreign capitals and 24x7 access to social media, actors like Amitabh Bachchan, Shahrukh Khan, Salman Khan have large fan following abroad. Madame Tussauds has acknowledged their popularity by displaying their wax figures in its museums. Aamir Khan's *Dangal*, whose *Lagaan* was nominated for an Oscar, did business in China worth over Rs 1,000 crore. For a decade, Aishwarya Rai Bachchan was treated like a queen at the Cannes film festival. Priyanka Chopra Jonas has made it big in the USA on her own. She was invited to the White House by President Obama. Her television series, *Quantico*, has made her a recognisable face in 200 countries. Shashi Kapoor, Om Puri, Naseeruddin Shah, Irfan Khan, Anil Kapoor and Anupam Kher have been featured in Hollywood films and appreciated. *Salaam Bombay*, *Slumdog Millionaire*, *The Namesake*, *Monsoon Wedding* and *Lagaan* have deepened Western interest in Indian films. Surprisingly, Indian films were reportedly liked even by *mujahideens* in Afghanistan and ISI fighters in Iraq!

While interacting with the media and people from different walks of life, i.e., opinion makers, from functioning democracies in the western world is alright, but such endeavours in totalitarian regimes and many Islamic countries can invite strong adverse reactions. Therefore, practitioners of soft power must respect local conventions, practices and ethos.

In cricket-playing countries, Sunil Gavaskar, Kapil Dev, Sachin Tendulkar and Virat Kohli are unofficial brand ambassadors of India. The winner of the gold medal at Tokyo Olympics, Neeraj Chopra, the winner of a silver medal at Rio Olympics, PV Sindhu, winner of multiple Grand Slams, Sania Mirza and

Leander Paes and chess grandmaster, Vishwanathan Anand are applauded for their achievements.

Though we haven't won a Nobel Prize for literature after Tagore, Indian English writers have won many literary awards. Renowned economists such as Amartya Sen, Abhijit Banerjee (both Nobel Prize laureates), Raghuram Rajan, Dipak Jain and Lord Meghnad Desai, and CEOs of American giants like Satya Nadella, Sundar Pichai and Indra Nooyi have raised India's profile.

A country needs both soft power and hard power, they aren't exclusive of each other. Getting 21 June declared as International Day of Yoga, holding virtual summits with SAARC leaders in the face of Covid-19, dispatching medicines to over 150 countries and sending nurses and doctors to some Gulf countries was Modi's soft power diplomacy at its best.

CHAPTER 32

THE INDIAN DIASPORA ENTERS THE GOLDEN ERA

SURENDRA KUMAR

The phrase, 'Indian diaspora', has been used extensively in the last two decades. The word 'diaspora' is derived from the ancient Greek word *diaspeiro*, which meant 'to scatter abroad'. Diaspora was, thus, used to refer to the dispersion of people. There are biblical references to the Jewish diaspora expelled from Israel by the Babylonians in the sixth century BC.

In recent times, people of any particular country with common origin and culture living outside their own country for various reasons are referred to as diaspora of that country. Taking a more liberal view, some scholars believe that the antiquity of Indian diaspora can be traced back to the Indus Valley civilisation, when small merchant communities might have traded with ancient Mesopotamia and Egypt. There are references to maritime voyages from India during the reigns of Emperor Ashoka and Samudragupta and the Chola rulers. Romani gypsies are believed to have migrated from India to Europe around eleventh century AD.

Dutch merchants are believed to have sold Indians as slaves in the then Dutch Cape colony of South Africa as early as 1653. A century later, thousands of Indians were brought from Bihar, eastern UP, Tamil Nadu and Andhra Pradesh and forced to work as indentured labourers; some Gujarati traders followed them as 'free passengers'. They were made to live in inhuman conditions. Some of them also worked in coal mines, dockyards, railway depots and municipal services and as domestic helps. Over the years, in South Africa, a section of the Indian community attained success in trade and business, which attracted the ire of the government that enacted discriminatory laws and the white Afrikaners who insulted and humiliated them routinely. It goes to the credit of Mohandas Karamchand Gandhi, who arrived in South Africa in 1893 to lead a long struggle of labourers, industrial workers and traders against racial discrimination and injustice. His movement for equality and dignity led to the establishment of the Natal Indian Congress (1894) and later to the Transvaal Natal Congress. In commemoration of Gandhi's return to India with his wife, Kasturba, on 9 January 1915, the Government of India has been organising the Pravasi Bharatiya Divas since 2003.

Large-scale migration of Indians to different parts of the world took place in the nineteenth century, mostly against their will, and it didn't follow any uniform pattern. Most of it was triggered by a huge demand for labourers in the British and French colonies after slavery was abolished in Britain in 1833-34. While the French took them to Mauritius—the Indian diaspora accounts for 70 per cent of the population—and Reunion Island—30 per cent of the population is composed of the Indian diaspora—the British transported them to Trinidad and Tobago, Guyana and Fiji and the Dutch took them to Suriname to work as indentured labourers. Today, they constitute a sizeable percentage of the population of these countries. The British colonial rulers also brought a large number of Indians, largely from Punjab, to build the railway line from Mombasa (Kenya) to Kampala (Uganda); many were attacked and eaten up by wild animals while working on this project.

On 4 April 1914, a Japanese ship, *Komagata Maru*, carrying 376 Indians aboard, mostly Sikhs from Punjab, was refused permission to dock at British Columbia, Canada; all of them were sent back to Calcutta (now Kolkata), except twenty-four people, who were allowed to disembark. Upon return, most of them were detained by the British as agitators and incarcerated; twenty of them were shot dead by the police. In May 2016, Canadian Prime Minister Justin Trudeau tendered an apology in the Parliament for this historic injustice saying, 'No words can erase the pain and suffering they experienced.'

Presently, while the Indian diaspora is spread over 200 countries, they are found in the US, UAE, Saudi Arabia, UK, South Africa, Australia, Canada, Kenya and Uganda in large numbers. The Gulf region alone accounts for over nine million Indians, many of whom were brought in the 1970s to work in oil fields when the Arab world was witnessing the oil boom. While 70 per cent of the Indian diaspora in the Gulf region comprises white-collar, skilled and semi-skilled workers, the remaining 30 per cent includes traders, bankers, engineers, doctors, teachers, hotel managers and other service providers.

Successive Indian governments have undertaken the herculean task of evacuating thousands of Indians and people of Indian origin, even some foreigners, when an unforeseen upheaval would develop in countries like Iraq, Kuwait, Libya and Yemen. It will be worthwhile to draw an evacuation strategy along with other interested countries in the region where large number of Indians happen to be working.

In the 1960s, Indian doctors, engineers, information technology (IT) experts and academics migrated to the USA and UK in large numbers in search of better economic prospects. During the Vietnam War, when thousands of injured American soldiers were being repatriated, there was a huge demand for Indian doctors. Today, in America, Indian-origin doctors—numbering over 45,000—which include some of the most respected specialists, are well-organised and their association, American Association of Physicians of Indian Origin (AAPI) is one of the most influential organisations of the Indian diaspora.

In 2000, the threat of the Y2K virus, a software bug, also called the Millennium Bug, especially targeting the banking, transportation and power sectors, led to an influx of Indian IT experts, mostly from Indian Institute of Technology, to the US. Indian IT engineers contributed significantly to the establishment of Silicon Valley in USA. Individuals like Vinod Khosla, Vinod Dham, Sabeer Bhatia and Vinod Gupta became the poster boys of the IT revolution and joined the Billionaires' Club; roughly 40 per cent of tech companies in Silicon Valley are owned by Indian-Americans. No wonder, iconic American multinational companies (MNCs), like Microsoft and Google, are headed by two Indian-Americans—Satya Nadella and Sundar Pichai, respectively.

In the late 1960s, average Americans perceived India as a country of snake charmers, ash-smirched mendicants and poverty-stricken boys and girls with begging bowls; the supply of dark, chipped wheat under the PL-480 programme saved millions of lives in India. However, phenomenal success of excellence-driven Indian IT engineers in Silicon Valley transformed the perception of India and the Indian diaspora. While President Donald Trump tried to restrict the entry of Indian techies by putting a cap on the H-1B visa and raising the visa fee in the name of 'America First', American MNCs, such as Apple, Microsoft, Google, Facebook, WhatsApp, etc. voiced their opposition to this decision by pointing out that their business will suffer without them. President Joe Biden's decision to reverse Trump's executive order in this regard has been widely welcomed.

Though Indian-Americans account for just 1 per cent of the total of 17,000-strong workforce of the National Aeronautics and Space Administration (NASA), several of them have earned high praise and appreciation for their professional services.

The list of 'Fabulous Five'—Kalpana Chawla, first Indian-American to go on space shuttle Columbia STS-87 and who perished on the second voyage in 2003; Sunita Williams, two flights to the International Space Station (ISS), twenty-nine hours of spacewalk and 129 days in space; Dr Anita Sengupta, aerospace engineer, project manager and mission manager for an ISS fundamental physics lab; Dr Madhulika Guhathakurta, NASA astrophysicist; and Sharmila Bhattacharya, head of NASA's bimodal performance and behaviour lab—has now been joined by an Indian-American, Dr Swati Mohan, who spearheaded the development of attitude control and the landing system for NASA's Perseverance rover which touched down on the surface of Mars on 25 February 2021. Indian-Americans have become an essential part of NASA's success story today.

Since 1955, when Dalip Singh Saund became a member of the US Congress—he was re-elected twice—the Indian-American community, now numbering around 4.1 million and accounting for just 1.1 per cent of eligible voters, has attained such financial resources and clout that in the last presidential election, both the Democratic and Republican candidates were vigorously seeking their support. Ro Khanna, Raja Krishnamoorthi, Ami Bera and Pramila Jayapal are four Democratic members of the Congress. With Senator Kamala Harris, now the vice president, they formed the Samosa Caucus that aspires to reflect the growing voice of Indian-American politicians. While Vice President Kamala Harris may run for presidency in 2024 on the Democratic ticket, Nikki Haley, originally from Punjab, who served as the US ambassador to the UN under President Trump, might be the Republican candidate.

In the first sixty days of his presidency, Joe Biden had nominated more than fifty bright Indian-Americans to serve in key administrative positions, nearly half of them women. Some of the prominent nominations are Vivek Murthy (US Surgeon General), Vinay Reddy (Director of Speechwriting); Vanita Gupta (Associate Attorney General); Uzra Zeya (Under Secretary of State for Civilian Security, Democracy and Human Rights); Sonia Aggarwal (Senior Adviser for Climate Policy and Innovation), Sumona Guha (Senior Director for South Asia) and Tarun Chhabra (Senior Director for Technology and Security). Evidently, the second generation of Indian-Americans is going to play a crucial role in America's political life in the years to come.

Besides their talent, motivation, determination, perseverance, hard work and Indian values, which have contributed considerably to the success of Indian-Americans, a huge credit goes to the ecosystem and the enabling atmosphere which the US offers; it encourages them to give their best and make their dreams come true. That's what President Biden stressed, 'One of the reasons why we are such an incredible country is [that] we are such a diverse country. We bring the best of out of every single solitary culture in the world here in the USA and we give people an opportunity to let their dreams run forward.'

On 4 March 2021, during a virtual interaction with NASA scientists, President Biden quipped in jest: 'Indian-Americans are taking over US' and told Dr Swati Mohan, 'Thank you. You guys are incredible.' That underlines the realisation of the salience of the Indian-American community at the highest echelon of the US leadership.

Indian-origin academics have done India proud. The legacy of Dr S Chandrasekhar and Dr Har Gobind Khorana, both Nobel laureates, is being carried forward by the likes of Abhijit Banerjee, Nobel laureate and professor of economics at the Massachusetts Institute of Technology (MIT), and Raghuram Rajan, professor of economics at the University of Chicago and former governor of the Reserve Bank of India (RBI). Twenty years back, Professor Dipak Jain became the first person of Indian origin to be the dean of the Kellogg School of Management. In 2016, Professor Sunil Kumar became the first person of Indian origin to ever serve as the provost of the prestigious Johns Hopkins University. Today, over a dozen Indian-Americans head American business schools, including the Harvard Business School which is headed by

Nitin Nohria. Late Professor CK Prahalad's book, *The Fortune at the Bottom of the Pyramid*, remains a seminal study of mobilising resources.

The average annual income of Indian-Americans, estimated to be US$ 120,000, is higher than the national average, and this community can boast of more graduates and postgraduates than any other community in USA.

Thousands of Indians migrated to various European countries when the British, French and Portuguese colonies attained independence in Africa. For example, many Indians from Mozambique and Angola migrated to Portugal when Portuguese colonial rule ended in these countries. A virtual exodus of Indians took place from Uganda in August 1972 when its dictator, Idi Amin, ordered their expulsion; most of them arrived in the UK where, in the following decades, they formed a successful business community.

According to the UN report, 'International Migration 2019', the Indian diaspora, comprising nearly twenty million people (non-resident Indians and overseas citizens of India), is the largest such emigrant community followed by Mexico and China. The Indian diaspora is present in 200 countries in small numbers, in thirty countries, its number runs in thousands, and around a dozen countries have the diaspora population of one million or more. In developed countries, members of the Indian diaspora are actively engaged in diverse professions—engineers, doctors, academics, lawyers and bankers. Many are running their own businesses—manufacturing plants, IT companies, department stores, hotels, motels, chains of restaurants, insurance companies, travel and tourism facilities, farming, etc.

It's a matter of pride that in countries such as Mauritius, Suriname, Trinidad and Tobago and Guyana, its members have served as the president and prime minister several times. Even developed countries, like Portugal, Ireland and Singapore, have seen political leaders of Indian origin rising to the top posts. In Canada, quite a few cabinet posts, including that of the defence minister, are held by the Canadian Sikhs.

The British Raj prevailed over India in the most oppressive and exploitative manner for over 200 years. But, in the last two decades, the UK has witnessed the most significant rise of the Indian diaspora in politics. Rishi Sunak, son-in-law of Infosys co-founder NR Narayana Murthy, and Priti Patel, respectively the chancellor of the exchequer and the home secretary, hold two of the most important posts in Boris Johnson's cabinet. And there are around twenty members of the Indian diaspora, including Lord Meghnad Desai, in the House of Lords.

Many members of the Indian diaspora have earned international name, fame and recognition for their artistic and literary talent. Both late Ustad Ali Akbar and Pandit Ravi Shankar had established their academies/foundations in the US decades back. Ustad Zakir Hussain has been living in USA for many years. Zubin Mehta is the most famous orchestra conductor whose roots are traced back to Mumbai.

Salman Rushdie, VS Naipaul, Ved Prakash Mehta and Jhumpa Lahiri are some of the prominent names of the writers of the Indian diaspora.

Deepa Mehta (from Canada; known for *Fire, Earth, Water, Midnight's Children*), Gurinder Chadha (*Bend it Like Beckham, Bhaji on the Beach, Beecham House*) and Mira Nair (*Salaam Bombay!, Monsoon Wedding, The Namesake, Kama Sutra, A Suitable Boy*) are film directors who have done India proud. The face of Priyanka Chopra, who has won the most popular TV serial artist award in the USA twice, is recognised in over 200 countries.

Sir Anish Kapoor, originally from Mumbai, is one of most celebrated British Indian sculptor. Who can say that the Indian diaspora hasn't come of age?

But, their migration to different parts of the world in the beginning, in most cases, involved inhuman suffering and exploitation for long, dark years. The resilience, survival instincts and struggle of the generations of Indian diaspora to their rise to the present prominent status makes a fascinating and inspiring story.

The perception of the NRI, over the years, in the eyes of an average Indian, has undergone a sea change. From derisively called Not-required Indian (NRI) causing 'brain drain' to today's respectable status of Overseas Citizens of India (OCI) credited with 'brain gain' and willing to pay back, has been an incremental transformation, which can be attributed to the success of the people of Indian origin abroad and efforts of successive Indian governments in the three decades to identify the Indian diaspora, recognise their importance, undertake a vigorous outreach campaign, dismantle many rules and regulations which discouraged them from visiting India and revisiting their ancestral connections and introduce a series of measures which will make the Indian diaspora feel welcome in India and encourage them to be a part of India's success story.

While the first prime minister (PM), Jawaharlal Nehru, might have advised the Indian diaspora to assimilate and become a part of the country of their adoption, PM Rajiv Gandhi, recognising their potential, invited the Indian diaspora to participate in India's economic development. The High Power Committee, constituted by Prime Minister AB Vajpayee and headed by Dr LM Singhvi, included Ambassador JC Sharma as member secretary. It did pioneering work in collecting reliable data about the Indian diaspora all over the world. The creation of a separate Ministry of Overseas Indians Abroad by the Vajpayee government was a far-sighted step. While the United Progressive Alliance (UPA) government retained this ministry, it was made a part of the Ministry of External Affairs (MEA) by the Narendra Modi government in 2014. Various policy decisions of the present government have contributed significantly towards bringing the Indian diaspora closer to India. There have been concerted efforts to offer hassle-free and timely passport and visa services by all Indian missions/posts abroad.

A strict watch on the procedures and practices of exporters of Indian labourers, verification and vetting of the credentials of the employers, attestation of work contracts, visit by consular officers to work sites to assess the working and living conditions, retention of their passports by workers and urgent intervention with the local government concerned in the case of contractual non-compliance/adherence to local laws have ameliorated considerably the conditions of the Indian diaspora in the Gulf region.

Since 2015, the Ministry of External Affairs has launched the eMigrate system that requires all foreign employers to register Indian employees in the database. And, in 2016, the present government launched a scheme called the Know India Program (KIP) for the diaspora's engagement, which helps the Indian-origin youth (eighteen to thirty years) to familiarise themselves with their Indian roots and contemporary India. Similarly, the Visiting Advanced Joint Research (VAJRA) faculty scheme, which envisages a rotation programme for top NRI scientists, engineers, doctors, managers and professionals to serve in Indian public sector organisations for a brief period to explain and share their expertise, is an imaginative initiative to benefit from the success stories of the Indian diaspora.

Holding the annual Pravasi Bharatiya Divas and honouring diaspora achievers with Pravasi Bharatiya Samman have been thoughtful policy initiatives to connect with and generate goodwill with the Indian diaspora. Organising a separate queue at the airport for the incoming OCI card holders has been widely welcomed.

The Indian diaspora remits around US$ 70-80 billion every year, which is supposedly the second highest after the remittances of the Chinese overseas community. While some members of the diaspora, like Lakshmi Mittal and the Hinduja brothers, both from the UK, have sizeable investments in India, many successful members of the diaspora pay back to their states or alma maters. Some of them were instrumental in the setting up of Indian Business School in Hyderabad. Game-changing projects of the government, such as Swachh Bharat Mission, National Mission for Clean Ganga, Make in India, Digital India and Skill India, might interest the Indian diaspora if presented intelligently. Besides trade, business and investment, they can also help in information and communications technology, education, healthcare and research.

Many of them are exemplary brand ambassadors of India, retaining, nurturing and promoting the rich cultural heritage and traditions of India and celebrating Indian festivals with great enthusiasm. Thousands of dance and music schools and yoga teaching centres are manifestation of this phenomenon. Their religious, cultural, emotional and spiritual links and Indian values spur them to organise donations and relief material whenever there is a natural calamity in India. They also campaign and press the governments of their countries to adopt a pro-Indian stance, as did many Indian-Americans for lifting of sanctions imposed on India after it carried out nuclear tests in 1998 and for the signing of the Civil Nuclear Agreement between the two countries in 2005.

On the Khalistan issue, some radical Sikhs of Indian origin based in Canada and UK have regrettably played a hostile role by funding and supporting Sikh extremists. Even in the ongoing farmers' protests, some Canadian Sikhs have allegedly been trying to foment violence. Sadly, the Canadian government has been reluctant to rein them in adequately on account of their political clout.

Narendra Modi is arguably the most popular Indian prime minister among the Indian diaspora. His inimitable oratorical skills, enviable ability to connect and forceful projection of India's glorious past and an inspiring vision for its future and his fulsome praise of the achievements of the diaspora have catapulted him as a cult figure. Irrespective of the venue—Wembley Stadium in London; Madison Square Garden in New York; NRG Stadium in Houston,

Texas; Allphones Arena, Sydney—he is greeted with a rock star-like rousing welcome. At the 'Howdy Modi' event in Houston, Texas, in September 2019, the then US President Donald Trump saw with his own eyes how ecstatic were Indian-Americans to see and hear Modi.

This mutual admiration serves both sides. Taking note of their emotional connect with Modi, the government of the concerned country takes the Indian diaspora more seriously. Didn't we see Trump displaying his pictures with Modi to woo Indian-Americans to vote for him in the last presidential election? And, by demonstrating his hold on the psyche of the Indian diaspora, Modi leverages his influence to be accorded much higher prominence. It was the British PM David Cameron who introduced him in the Wembley Stadium and thirty to forty congressmen and senators were present at the Madison Square Garden in New York at the Indian diaspora's reception for him. Above all, it enhances his larger-than-life persona back home in India.

At the first People of Indian Origin Parliamentary Conference on 9 January 2018, Vice President M Venkaiah Naidu said, 'The presence of such a large number of elected representatives of Indian origin in legislatures of such a large number of countries from across the world goes beyond the symbolism of the expanding horizons of the influence of India in the global scheme of things. In my considered view, it is a clear reflection of the strength of the Indian values of inclusivity and assimilation, nurtured and consolidated over the centuries since ancient times.'

The day is not far when someone from the Indian diaspora rises to head the governments in the US and the UK.

INDEX

V

CONTRIBUTORS

Shyam Saran is a former Foreign Secretary of India and has served as Prime Minister's Special Envoy For Nuclear Affairs and Climate Change. After leaving government service in 2010, he has headed the Research and Information System for Developing Countries, a prestigious think tank focusing on economic issues (2011-2017) and was Chairman of the National Security Advisory Board under the National Security Council (2013-15). He is currently Life Trustee of India International Centre, Member of the Governing Board of the Centre for Policy Research and of the Institute of Chinese Studies, a Trustee at the World Wildlife Fund (India) and Member of the International Advisory Council of the Confederation of Indian Industry (CII). Saran also serves as a member of the Governing Board of Welham Girls' School. He has recently published a book, *How India Sees the World.*

Shyam Saran was awarded the Padma Bhushan, the third highest civilian award, in 2011 for his contributions to civil service. In May 2019, he was conferred the Spring Order Gold and Silver Star by the Emperor of Japan for promoting India–Japan relations.

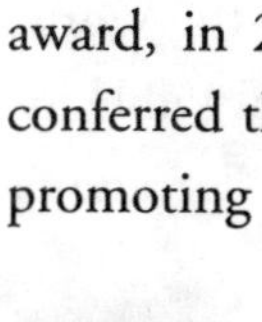

Ambassador Shivshankar Menon is currently a Visiting Professor at Ashoka University, India; Chairman, Advisory Board, Institute of Chinese Studies, New Delhi; Distinguished Fellow of the Centre for Social and Economic Progress, India; Distinguished Visiting Research Fellow at the National University of Singapore; Member, Board of Trustees, International Crisis Group; and, a Distinguished Fellow, Asia Society Policy Institute, New York.

He was previously National Security Advisor to the Prime Minister of India, January 2010-May 2014; Foreign Secretary of India, October 2006-July 2009; and has served as the Indian Ambassador or High Commissioner to China, Pakistan, Sri Lanka and Israel.

In 2016, he published *Choices: Inside the Making of Indian Foreign Policy*. His book on *India in Asian Geopolitics: The Past, Present* is forthcoming in 2021.

He has been a Fisher Family Fellow at the Kennedy School, Harvard University, and Richard Wilhelm Fellow at MIT in 2015. He was chosen one of the "Top 100 Global Thinkers" by *Foreign Policy* magazine in 2010.

Rahul Chhabra took over the post of Secretary (Economic Relations), Ministry of External Affairs on 8 June 2020. Prior to that, he was High Commissioner to Kenya, Ambassador to Somalia and Permanent Representative to the United Nations Environment Programme (UNEP) and the United Nations Human Settlements Programme (UN-HABITAT), based in Nairobi from November 2018 to June 2020. He was Ambassador to Hungary and Bosnia & Herzegovina from August 2015 to October 2018.

At Headquarters, he worked as Joint Secretary (Central Europe). He conceived and organised the first two editions of the India–Central Europe Business Forum, which has now become a regular feature in the Indian business calendar.

While earlier serving in New Delhi, he worked to promote foreign investment flows into India, having been part of India's delegation to the World Economic Forum at Davos. Later, he served as Director for External Publicity at the Ministry of External Affairs and Director in the Foreign Secretary's Office.

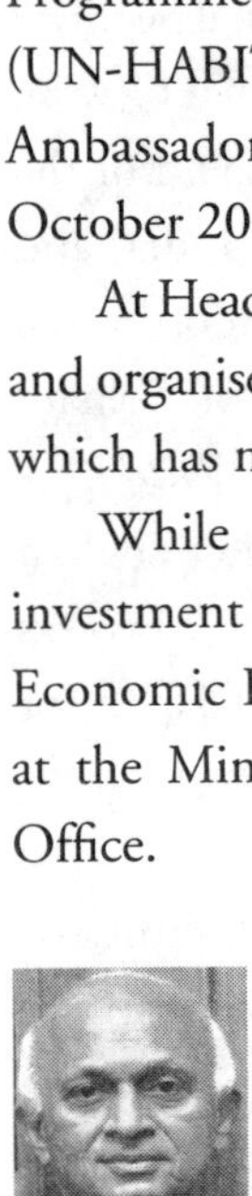

Ranjan Mathai joined the Indian Foreign Service in 1974, and held diplomatic assignments in Vienna, Colombo and Washington (1976-85). He then worked in the Ministry of External Affairs as Deputy Secretary in the BSM Division, responsible for India's relations with Bangladesh, Sri Lanka, Myanmar and the Maldives in 1985 and 1986. He served as Counsellor in the Indian Embassy in Tehran and was the

Deputy Chief of India's Mission to the European Union in Brussels (1988-94). He returned to the MEA as Joint Secretary (BSM) from 1995 to 1998.

Mathai was Ambassador of India in Israel from 1998 to 2001 and in Qatar (2001-05). He served as India's Ambassador in France from 2007 to 2011 and, while in Paris, he was concurrently appointed as the first Indian Ambassador to Monaco.

He was the Foreign Secretary of India for two years from August 2011 to July 2013. After his retirement, Mathai was appointed High Commissioner of India to the United Kingdom (December 2013-December 2015).

Jayant Prasad was Director General, Institute for Defence Studies and Analyses, New Delhi. He had earlier served as India's Ambassador to Afghanistan, Algeria, Nepal and the UN Conference on Disarmament, Geneva. He was lecturer in history at St Stephen's College, University of Delhi, before his thirty-seven-year long public service career in the Indian Foreign Service.

TCA Raghavan retired from the Indian Foreign Service in December 2015 while Indian High Commissioner to Pakistan (2013-15). He had earlier served as Deputy High Commissioner in Pakistan (2003-07) and High Commissioner to Singapore from 2009 to 2013. He has also served in Kuwait, the United Kingdom and Bhutan.

He was awarded a PhD by the Jawaharlal Nehru University in 1992 for his dissertation relating to the economic history of India. His current interests are historical research, strategic analysis and the diplomatic and intellectual history of modern India. He writes, lectures and participates in discussions on issues relating to Indian and South Asian diplomatic history, Pakistan, Iran, Afghanistan and South East Asia. He is the author of *Attendant Lords: Bairam Khan and Abdur Rahim, Courtiers and Poets in Mughal India*—awarded the Mohammad Habib Memorial Prize by the Indian History Congress in December 2017—and *The People Next Door: The Curious History of India's Relations with Pakistan* (2017). His latest book is entitled *History Men: Jadunath Sarkar, GS Sardesai, Raghubir Sinh and Their Quest for India's Past* (2019). He was Director General of the Indian Council of World Affairs during July 2018–July 2021.

KC Singh is the former Spokesman of Ministry of External Affairs, Ambassador to UAE and later Iran. He was Secretary (Economic Relations) at Headquarters before retirement.

Deb Mukharji was a member of the Indian Foreign Service from 1964 to 2001.

His foreign assignments included Switzerland (1965-1968), Pakistan (1968-1971), Germany (1971-1974) and Dhaka (1977-1980). He has served as Consul General, San Francisco (1983-1986), High Commissioner to Nigeria, with concurrent accreditation to Chad, Benin and Cameroon (1986-1989), High Commissioner to Bangladesh (1995-2000) and Ambassador to Nepal (2000-2001).

At Headquarters, he served as Deputy Secretary (Pak), Director (External Publicity), Director/OSD (Americas), OSD/Joint Secretary (BSM) and Addl. Secretary (Policy Planning), besides Joint Secretary DEA in Ministry of Finance.

Deb Mukharji is the author of *Magic of Nepal, Kailash* and *Manasarovar: Visions of the Infinite, A Quest Beyond the Himalaya* and *Perspectives on Nepal.*

Ranjit Rae is a diplomat with over thirty-five years of experience in the Indian Foreign Service. He has served as Ambassador to Nepal, Vietnam and Hungary with concurrent accreditation to Slovenia and Bosnia and Herzegovina. At Headquarters, he has worked in various capacities, including as Press Secretary to the President of India and the Head of the Northern Division dealing with Nepal and Bhutan. His first book, *Kathmandu Dilemma: Resetting India–Nepal Ties* is expected to be published shortly.

VP Haran was in the Indian Foreign Service from 1980 to 2014. After postings in Moscow, Kabul, Colombo and Brussels, he was appointed as Deputy Permanent Representative to the World Trade Organization (WTO) (2000-03) and later as Deputy Chief of Mission, Kathmandu (2003-06). He was Ambassador to Syria (2009-12) and Ambassador to Bhutan (2013-14). He retired from service in July 2014.

Post retirement, he contributes articles for journals of think tanks, participates in seminars and gives lectures at universities on foreign policy, regional cooperation in South Asia, neighbourhood diplomacy and the situation in and relations with countries such as Syria and Bhutan.

Neelam D Sabharwal served as a member of the Indian Foreign Service from 1974 to 2008. She was Ambassador of India to The Netherlands and Permanent Representative to the Organization for Prohibition of Chemical Weapons (OPCW), The Hague; High Commissioner of India to Republic of Cyprus; Ambassador and Permanent Representative of India to UNESCO, Paris.

During her diplomatic career, she gained expertise in handling assignments in both bilateral and multilateral areas. After doing a tenure as Commercial and Political officer in Washington, she was India's Deputy Permanent Representative to UN offices at Geneva. As a Chinese language and domain specialist, she was posted in Hong Kong and served two terms in Beijing, the second time as India's Deputy Chief of Mission. At Headquarters, she served on China, Pakistan, East Europe Desks and at the FSTI.

After retirement, she joined the University of Maastricht as Associate Professor from 2010 to 2016, and Advisor to the University's EU Project on International Mobility and Migration from 2014 to 18.

She has edited a book, *India and The Netherlands: Changing Images, Lasting Visions*.

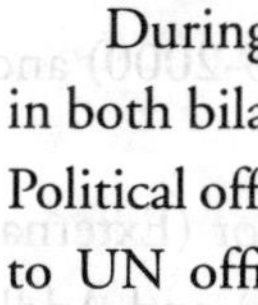

Gurjit Singh was an Indian diplomat for thirty-seven years. He has been the Ambassador of India to Germany, Indonesia, Timor-Leste and ASEAN and Ethiopia, Djibouti and the African Union besides having been in Japan, Sri Lanka, Kenya and Italy on assignments.

As ambassador to Indonesia and ASEAN, he leveraged several ideas to enhance the AEP. His book *Masala Bumbu* brought forth Indian and Indonesian thought leaders to contribute ideas. His comic book in Bahasa on the history of India and Indonesia was well received.

He is an Honorary Professor of Humanities at the Indian Institute of Technology (IIT), Indore. He chairs the CII Business Task Force on Trilateral

Cooperation in Africa. He also comments on current events on TV and in journals. He is associated with the social impact investment movement and is working on expanding it in Africa, along with other trilateral initiatives for B2B engagement. His new book on India and Africa is under publication.

Deepa Gopalan Wadhwa has been a career diplomat who joined the Indian Foreign Service in 1979 and retired in December 2015.

She has served as Ambassador of India to Japan (2012–15), Qatar (2009–12) and Sweden (2005–09). She was concurrently accredited as Ambassador to Latvia (from Stockholm) and Republic of the Marshall Islands (from Tokyo). She has also held other significant assignments in Geneva, Hong Kong, China, the Netherlands, the International Labour Organization (ILO) and the Ministry of External Affairs.

In the course of her career spanning over thirty-six years, she has handled a wide swathe of issues and subjects related to India's relations with key countries, such as Pakistan, China and Japan; participated in international conferences and negotiations related to climate change, sustainable development, disarmament and human rights; and was instrumental in the active promotion of India's economic interests in areas of trade, technology, investments and energy security during postings in Europe, the Gulf Cooperation Council (GCC) and Japan. Wadhwa is currently Chairperson of the India–Japan Friendship Forum and is on the governing council of the Asian Confluence based in Shillong. She also serves as independent director and adviser on a few boards of companies.

Vishnu Prakash, a law graduate (gold medallist) and a career diplomat (IFS, 1981), retired as India's High Commissioner to Canada in 2016. Hitherto, he was the Ambassador to South Korea, Official Spokesperson of Ministry of External Affairs and Consul General to Shanghai. He also held various positions in Indian Missions/Posts at Tokyo, New York, Moscow, Islamabad, Vladivostok and Cairo.

Prakash did a sabbatical with the Asia Pacific Center for Security Studies in Hawaii in 1996. In 2013, he was conferred an honorary doctoral degree in business administration by Tongmyong University, Busan, and recognised as Ambassador of the Year, 2014 by the Asia Society, Korea Center.

Presently, he is a foreign affairs specialist, speaker, columnist, educationist and mentor. His focus is on the Indo-Pacific region, especially north-east Asia (China, Japan and Koreas), ASEAN and South Asia, the US, Canada and Israel.

Arun K Singh was India's Ambassador to the United States (2015–16), France (2013–15) and Israel (2005–08). He was also involved for nearly a decade in the formulation and implementation of India's policies related to Afghanistan, Pakistan and Iran, including in the period following the 9/11 attacks. His other tours of duty have included Moscow, Tokyo, Addis Ababa and Indian Mission to the UN in New York.

Currently, he is a member of India's National Security Advisory Board, Visiting Professor at Ashoka University (India), a Halle Institute Distinguished Fellow at Emory University (Atlanta, Georgia, US), and a Distinguished Non-Resident Senior Fellow in the Asia Program at the Washington, DC-based German Marshall Fund of the US. In the spring of 2017, he taught courses on US Foreign Policy in South Asia and Current Global Trends and Challenges at both American University and the School of Advanced International Studies at Johns Hopkins University in Washington, DC. He was also a Distinguished Visiting Professor at Center for Advanced Study of India at the University of Pennsylvania.

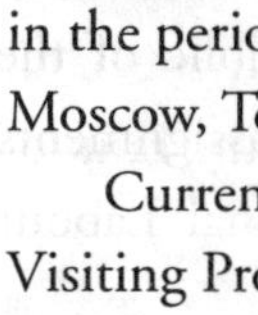

PS Raghavan was a career diplomat from 1979 to 2016. He was Ambassador of India to Russia, Czech Republic and Ireland. He held other diplomatic positions in the USSR, the UK, Poland, South Africa and Vietnam.

He was Joint Secretary in the Prime Minister's Office (2000-04), dealing with foreign affairs, nuclear energy, space and national security. As Secretary (2013-14) in Ministry of External Affairs, he was in charge of India's external economic relations and the administration, security and e-governance departments. He headed (2012-13) the Development Partnership Administration, which coordinates India's economic partnership with developing countries.

He served two terms (2016-20) as Chairman of the National Security Advisory Board, advising India's National Security Council on strategic and security issues.

Vinod Kumar joined the Indian Foreign Service in 1983 after briefly working in State Bank of India. He served as Ambassador of India to Uzbekistan (2015-19), the Permanent Representative of India to SCO RATS and Ambassador to Fiji and four other Pacific Island countries (2010-14). In his other diplomatic assignments, he served in the Soviet Union, Russia, Thailand, Bhutan and Australia. At Headquarters, he worked in the East Europe and Central Asia (1992-93) Divisions among others. He was Joint Secretary (Public Diplomacy) and Joint Secretary (Multilateral Economic Relations) in 2009-10. He served as Additional Secretary (International Organisations) in 2014-15 and dealt with the UN, counterterrorism and cybersecurity. He superannuated in 2019 in the rank of Secretary.

Anil Wadhwa has served as Secretary (East) in the Ministry of External Affairs, and was the Indian Ambassador to Poland, Oman, Thailand and Italy.

As a career diplomat, **Ambassador Anil Trigunayat** has served in the Indian Missions in Cote d' Ivoire, Bangladesh, Mongolia, USA, Russia, Sweden and Nigeria. He served in Moscow as Deputy Chief of Mission in the rank of Ambassador. He was also India's Ambassador to Libya, Jordan and High Commissioner to Malta. He superannuated in 2016.

He is associated with several think tanks in India and abroad and is a regular commentator and contributor on foreign policy issues. He is heading the West Asia Experts' Group at the Vivekananda International Foundation and serves on the Governing Council of Raisina House and Usanas Foundation. He is also on the Board of Advisers of BRICS Chamber of Commerce and Asia Africa Chamber of Commerce as well as Honorary Member International Trade council, Brussels.

As a peace ambassador, he is closely associated with the interfaith dialogue, peace and harmony efforts in the society especially through the Unity Dialogue and World Congress of Religions, Kazakhstan.

Ambassador Ruchi Ghanashyam was a member of the Indian Foreign Service for thirty-eight years (1982-2020). During her career, she served as High Commissioner of India to Ghana and later to South Africa. She concurrently served as Ambassador of India to Burkina Faso, Togo and Sierra Leone from her post in Ghana and as High Commissioner to the Kingdom of Lesotho from South Africa. She retired as High Commissioner of India to the United Kingdom, Envoy to the Commonwealth and Representative to the IMO. She was also Secretary (West) in the Ministry of External Affairs. She is currently a writer and a columnist and tweets @RuchiGhanashyam.

Manjeev Singh Puri joined the Indian Foreign Service in 1982 and has served as ambassador of India to the EU, Belgium, Luxembourg and Nepal. Earlier, he had served as Ambassador/ Deputy Permanent Representative of India to the UN during the time that India was on the Security Council. He retired on 31 December 2019 in the rank of Secretary, Government of India.

Puri has also headed the division in the Ministry of External Affairs dealing with UN issues on the social and economic side and was involved as a lead member of the Indian delegation at numerous global negotiations on climate change, sustainable development, migration, human rights and UN reforms. In addition, he has served twice in Germany (in Bonn and Berlin), in Cape Town, Muscat, Bangkok and Caracas.

Yashvardhan Kumar Sinha was sworn in as Chief Information Commissioner, Central Information Commission, by the President of India in November 2020. He was earlier appointed an Information Commissioner in January 2019. He is a seasoned diplomat and during a career in diplomacy spanning over thirty-seven years, he handled several important assignments at the Ministry of External Affairs, New Delhi and in Indian diplomatic Missions in South Asia, the Middle East, Europe, South America and the Permanent Mission of India at the United Nations in New York. Among the senior positions held by him as a diplomat were High Commissioner of India to the United Kingdom, High Commissioner of India to Sri Lanka, Additional Secretary/Joint Secretary, heading the important Pakistan–Afghanistan–Iran Division at the Ministry of External Affairs, New Delhi, Ambassador of India to Venezuela and Consul General of India in Dubai. He superannuated from the Indian Foreign Service in October 2018.

Asoke Kumar Mukerji served for over thirty-seven years in the Indian Foreign Service, retiring as India's Ambassador and Permanent Representative to the United Nations in New York in December 2015. He led India's negotiation of Agenda 2030 on Sustainable Development adopted in September 2015 by world leaders at the UN Special Summit, and spearheaded the successful implementation of Prime Minister Narendra Modi's proposal for the UN to declare 21 June as International Yoga Day, with 177 cosponsoring countries of a UN resolution adopted in a record time of seventy-five days.

His earlier diplomatic assignments include Washington DC, London, Moscow, Geneva, Dubai, Almaty, Tashkent and Belgrade.

In 2017, he chaired the Multiple Stakeholder Group in India's National Security Council Secretariat to recommend cyber norms for India.

Since 2019, he is on the faculty of the Geneva-based Diplo Foundation. He is also a member of the International Institute of Strategic Studies (IISS), London.

Among his seven published books is *India and the United Nations 1945-2015: A Photo Journey*, the first copy of which was presented by Prime Minister Narendra Modi to the former UN Secretary-General Ban Ki-moon in September 2015.

Dilip Sinha is a former diplomat. In his capacity as Additional Secretary (International Organisations and Environment Diplomacy), he participated in the UNFCCC Conference of the Parties in Cancun in 2010 and Durban in 2011. He was India's Permanent Representative to the UN in Geneva from 2012 to 2014. Earlier, he was head of the Pakistan–Afghanistan–Iran Division in the Ministry of External Affairs and Ambassador to Greece. He has served in India's missions in Germany, Egypt, Pakistan, Brazil and Bangladesh. He is the author of *Legitimacy of Power: The Permanence of Five in the Security Council.*

Ajit Kumar, a postgraduate from St Stephen's College, Delhi, has served as the Ambassador and Permanent Representative of India to United Nations offices and other international organisations in Geneva, Ambassador to Zimbabwe and Consul General in Durban, Frankfurt and Atlanta.

Joining the Indian Foreign Service in 1979, he has held posts in Damascus, Mexico City, Islamabad and New Delhi. He was also the deputy leader of the Indian delegation to the Conference on Disarmament in Geneva, and has participated in multilateral negotiations on the Comprehensive Nuclear Test Ban Treaty (CTBT).

Kumar had served as Director and Joint Secretary in the Disarmament and International Security Affairs (D&ISA) Division in the Ministry of External Affairs (MEA) and became Secretary in 2014. He has attended several sessions of the United Nations Disarmament Commission and the UN First Committee on Disarmament and International Security Affairs issues in New York and several international conferences.

Anjali Prasad, an Indian Administrative Service (IAS) officer of the 1983 batch, has a Masters in Economics from the Delhi School of Economics, with specialisation in international trade. She has served in the states of Uttar Pradesh and Uttarakhand in a variety of field and Secretariat assignments. She has also served in the Government of India, primarily in assignments relating to trade and investment policy and negotiations spanning over a decade, including as India's Ambassador to the World Trade Organization, Geneva 2014-2017. Parts of her article are based on her personal knowledge and experience.

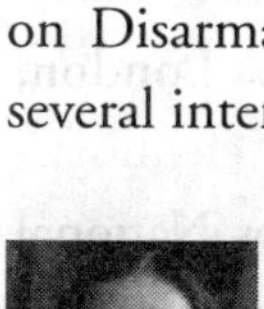

Sujan R Chinoy is the Director General of the Manohar Parrikar Institute for Defence Studies and Analyses, New Delhi. A career diplomat from 1981 to 2018, he was India's Ambassador to Japan and Mexico, and High Commissioner of India to Belize and the Republic of the Marshall Islands. A specialist on China, he headed the Indian expert group dealing with the boundary dispute and confidence-building measures. During his foreign service career, he was also the Deputy Chief of Mission in Saudi Arabia and Consul General of India in Shanghai and Sydney, besides serving in Hong Kong and Beijing. He was India's representative to the First Committee at the UN from 1992 to 1995, dealing with disarmament and international security. On deputation to India's National Security Council Secretariat, he anchored policy issues and strategic dialogues with counterpart organisations around the world. He has a rich experience in dealing with security challenges in India's extended neighbourhood, terrorism and extremism, maritime security, defence reforms and modernisation, infrastructure and connectivity. He also had the distinction of serving in all the Quad countries. Ambassador Chinoy contributes extensively to newspapers and journals, besides lecturing in India and overseas.

Amarendra Khatua, a retired Secretary, Ministry of External Affairs, is a former Ambassador and India's WTO Trade Negotiator. He is the Founder Director of Millennial Chamber of Commerce, Industry and Agriculture; Chairman of International Culture and Economic Cooperation (ICEC); and is associated with a number of chambers, trade bodies and NGOs. A major contemporary Indian poet with more than forty published volumes in English, Odia, Hindi and Spanish, he lives in Delhi.

Ambassador Sunil Lal has been India's Ambassador to Brazil (2014-17) and Spain (2011-2014). He joined the Indian Foreign Service in 1982 and has done stints in various capacities at Indian Embassies in Havana, Berlin, Ankara, and Washington DC. He spent one year at Georgetown University, Washington as an Associate and taught a course on the politics of South Asia in the year 2000. He attended the 44th Defence Staff College Course at Wellington in 1988-89 and joined the Northern Division of MEA (Ministry of External Affairs) at the end of 1989, where he handled matters relating to Nepal and His Holiness the Dalai Lama. He was appointed Director, External Publicity or Deputy Spokesman of MEA in 1996, a post he held till 1999. He worked in the National Security Council Secretariat at the level of Director General in 2005-2006. He was the first head of MEA's Public Diplomacy division in 2006. From the beginning of 2007 till August 2011, he held the post of Chief of Protocol.

Tsewang Topden has served in India's neighbourhood as Ambassador in Laos, Counsellor (Political) in Nepal and Second Secretary in Myanmar (then Burma) in his career in the Indian Foreign Service. In 1988, while posted in Washington DC, he was sent by the MEA on a special assignment to Yangon during the military crackdown on the democracy movement in Myanmar. He has also served in Prague (Czech Republic) just after the Velvet Revolution, Frankfurt (Germany) as Consul General, High Commissioner in Namibia and Ambassador in Greece.